STUDIES IN THE
NATIONAL INCOME AND EXPENDITURE OF
THE UNITED KINGDOM

a series published under the joint auspices of the
NATIONAL INSTITUTE OF ECONOMIC AND SOCIAL RESEARCH, LONDON
and
DEPARTMENT OF APPLIED ECONOMICS
UNIVERSITY OF CAMBRIDGE

GENERAL EDITOR
RICHARD STONE
P. D. LEAKE PROFESSOR OF FINANCE AND ACCOUNTING
AND FELLOW OF KING'S COLLEGE, CAMBRIDGE

2

THE
MEASUREMENT OF CONSUMERS'
EXPENDITURE AND BEHAVIOUR
IN THE UNITED KINGDOM
1920-1938

VOLUME II

STUDIES IN THE
NATIONAL INCOME AND EXPENDITURE
OF THE UNITED KINGDOM

The scope of the series is the measurement and analysis of the size, trend and interrelationships of the components of the British national income, output, expenditure, saving and asset formation. The investigations published in these *Studies* are confined to those undertaken at the National Institute of Economic and Social Research or at the Cambridge University Department of Applied Economics by members of their respective staffs and others working in direct collaboration with them. The production of a jointly sponsored series under a single editorship is being carried out in order that the intellectual unity underlying the many segments of research should be emphasized and made plain.

The National Institute of Economic and Social Research and the Department of Applied Economics assume no responsibility for the views expressed in these *Studies*.

The titles in this series are:

THE
MEASUREMENT OF CONSUMERS' EXPENDITURE AND BEHAVIOUR IN THE UNITED KINGDOM
1920-1938

VOLUME II

BY

RICHARD STONE
P. D. LEAKE PROFESSOR OF FINANCE AND ACCOUNTING
AND FELLOW OF KING'S COLLEGE, CAMBRIDGE

AND

D. A. ROWE
NATIONAL INSTITUTE OF ECONOMIC AND SOCIAL RESEARCH

CAMBRIDGE
AT THE UNIVERSITY PRESS
1966

PUBLISHED BY
THE SYNDICS OF THE CAMBRIDGE UNIVERSITY PRESS
Bentley House, 200 Euston Road, London N.W. 1
American Branch: 32 East 57th Street, New York, N.Y. 10022

©

CAMBRIDGE UNIVERSITY PRESS
1966

Printed in Great Britain at the University Printing House, Cambridge
(Brooke Crutchley, University Printer)

LIBRARY OF CONGRESS CATALOGUE
CARD NUMBER: 54-2815

CONTENTS

LIST OF TABLES

LIST OF FIGURES

PREFACE

In this volume we conclude our work on consumers' expenditure in the years 1920–38 by giving estimates for all those commodity groups which were not covered in the first volume, published in 1954. These detailed estimates form the subject-matter of the first ten chapters of the book. Chapter XI gives a summary of total consumers' expenditure during the inter-war period, knitting together the two volumes and making it possible to compare our results with those of other studies in the same field. And chapter XII surveys the course of consumers' expenditure from 1900 to 1955, linking our figures at one end with those given by Prest in another volume in this series, *Consumers' Expenditure in the United Kingdom, 1900–1919*, and at the other end with the official estimates given in the *Statistical Digest of the War* and in the Blue Books on *National Income and Expenditure*.

In contrast with volume I, this time we have contented ourselves with just presenting the figures; we have not added a separate section on the analysis of market demand. Our principal reason for this omission is that since the first volume was published we have changed our approach to the subject. In volume I we combined budgets with time series to carry out a static analysis for each individual commodity; in recent years we have tried to evolve a dynamic analysis of the whole complex of goods and services, in which adjustment rates and cross-elasticities are estimated simultaneously in a consistent manner. Preliminary trials suggest that this new method is very promising. But much more work is needed to bring it to completion. As the main purpose of this series is to fill some of the worst gaps in our quantitative knowledge of past economic events, and as this particular volume was already much overdue, we did not think it right to delay its publication still further for the sake of rounding off our treatment of demand analysis. This book is therefore simply a collection of statistics.

We should like to express our gratitude to Mrs Muriel Hill for making innumerable calculations, as well as checking and rechecking the tables; to Mrs Alison Rowlatt for her part in the preparation of the manuscript; and to Miss Jane Harington for her help with the proof-reading.

Cambridge
London
February 1966

RICHARD STONE
D. A. ROWE

CHAPTER I

CLOTHING AND OTHER PERSONAL EFFECTS

1 GENERAL REMARKS

Expenditure on clothing and footwear in 1938 amounted to £438 m., or just under 10% of total consumers' expenditure. In earlier years the proportion had tended to be slightly higher, and in 1920, an exceptional year, it was more than 15%. In 1938, expenditure on footwear represented 15% and purchased apparel 80% of the total. A further 5% was accounted for by dress materials bought in the piece for making up at home. These proportions were fairly constant throughout the period. Although there had been a steady decline in the proportion spent on materials for home dressmaking, this was only a small part of the total. More significant was the relative increase in expenditure on women's and girls' wear at the expense of men's and boys' wear. The change took place largely in the second half of the period, expenditure on women's and girls' wear rising from 55% of total apparel in 1930 to 63% in 1938.

Expenditure on other personal effects, which include stationery, jewellery, toilet requisites, and similar goods, amounted to £130 m. in 1938, or 3% of total personal expenditure. This proportion had been growing slowly through the period, and expenditure on these goods had increased at almost twice the rate of expenditure on clothing. It is to be expected from the nature of the goods in this group, which are almost wholly luxuries, that expenditure on them should increase more than proportionately with the rise in income.

Expenditure on clothing at constant prices shows a rising trend through the period. In part this was due to the growth of population, but there was also a net increase in expenditure per head of just over one-half of one per cent per year. This upward movement was interrupted by a marked slump in 1921 and by a much slighter dip in the early 'thirties. Between 1920 and 1921 the volume of clothing purchased fell by nearly 20%. More than the ordinary forces must have been at work to produce a change of this order. The level of purchases in 1919 and 1920 was, in all probability, abnormally high as a result of restocking after the shortages of the war period, so that there would in any case have been some falling off in demand in 1921; this was

further accentuated by the effect of lower incomes. The decline after 1929 was much slighter; the largest decrease, between 1931 and 1932, was only of the order of 4%. In the last two years of the period the volume of purchases fell back slightly from the high point reached in 1936.

Since clothing is a durable good, it may be considered more appropriate to define consumption in terms of the current use obtained from the garments owned, rather than the amount purchased. On this basis, consumption is a weighted average of current and past purchases and, consequently, a much smoother series than purchases. The difference between purchases and consumption in any year constitutes net investment in clothing by consumers. A simple form of reducing balance depreciation, where consumption is defined as a constant proportion of the depreciated stock, may be applied, using a uniform depreciation rate representative of the average experience of all consumers. The depreciation rate for clothing must be fairly high, between two-thirds and four-fifths of the stock probably being consumed in a year. Even so, there is quite a marked difference in the movement of purchases and consumption. In the opening years of the period, the violent fluctuations in purchases during the years 1920–2 produce only a slight fall in the level of consumption. This is followed by a smooth rise until 1930, a gradual decline to 1933, and a subsequent rise to the peak level for the period in 1937.

The smooth development in consumption appears more systematic than the fluctuations in purchases. Much of the variation in purchases, however, may be explained in terms of stock movements, as consumers attempt to adjust their consumption to the desired level. An essentially dynamic form of demand function is involved, which gives rise to both long- and short-term elasticities in respect of income and price changes. From an econometric analysis of these data,[1] it has been found that the elasticity of purchases with respect to income was 1·9 in the short period and 1·5 in the long period. The comparable figures for price are −0·5 and −0·4,

---

[1] See [89a] Richard Stone and D. A. Rowe, 'The market demand for durable goods', *Econometrica*, xxv, no. 3 (July 1957), p. 423.

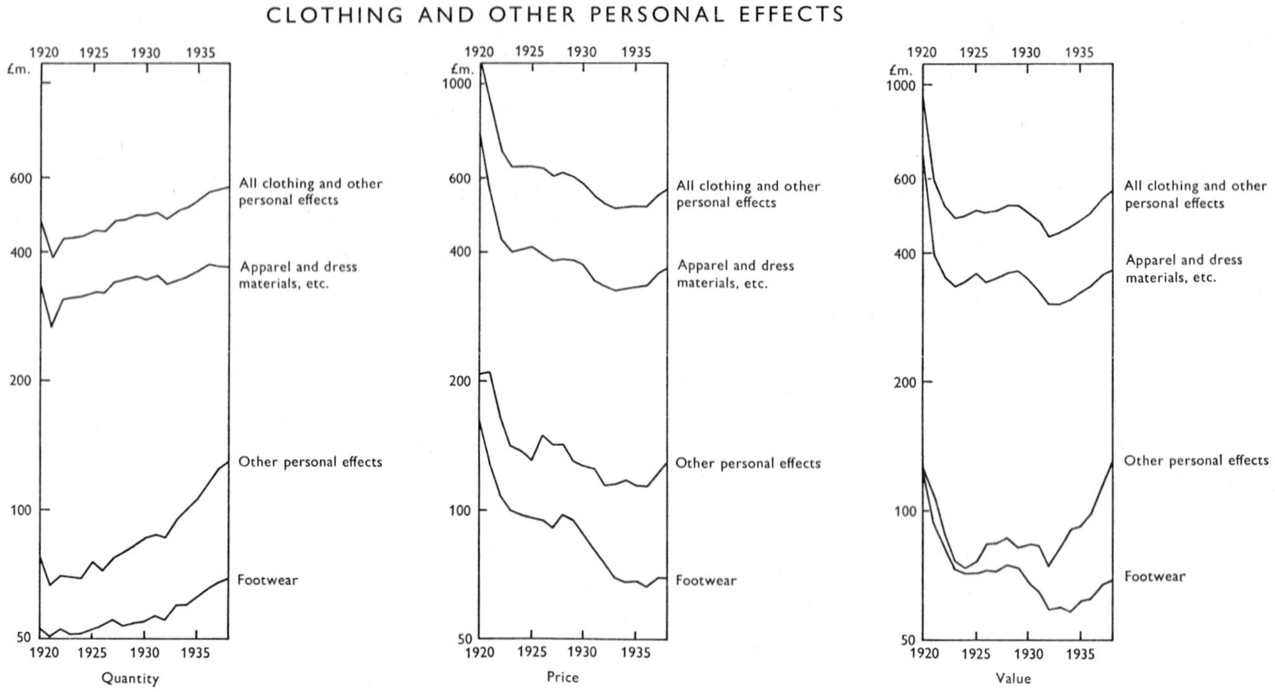

CLOTHING AND OTHER PERSONAL EFFECTS

Fig. 1. The variations in the quantities purchased, average prices and expenditure on clothing and other personal effects for final consumption in the United Kingdom, 1920–38.

respectively. These results indicate the great importance of income in determining the fluctuations of clothing purchases. While the short-term elasticity is of more significance for estimating immediate repercussions, the long-term value is a measure of the ultimate underlying response and may be compared with the value of the income elasticity obtained, for instance, from family budget studies. The family budget surveys of 1937–8 indicate an income elasticity of 1·4 for clothing, which agrees closely with the value obtained from the time series.

The quantity movements for footwear during this period are smoother than those for clothing. The number of pairs bought per head of the total population increased from an annual average of $2\frac{3}{4}$ pairs to $3\frac{3}{4}$ pairs. At the same time the proportion represented by rubber footwear more than doubled, rising from less than one-tenth to be one-fifth. The increase in the volume of purchases was more marked in the second half of the period. These figures, however, make no allowance for any quality changes. It is possible that an improvement in the quality of shoes bought would result in fewer being sold over a particular period. On the other hand, a greater degree of conformity to rapidly changing fashions would stimulate the demand for a more decorative and less durable form of footwear.

The consumption of other personal effects, as shown by annual expenditures at constant prices, is characterized during this period by a marked upward trend.

The level of purchases had almost doubled by 1938, compared with what it was in the early 'twenties. Some of the details of this change can be seen from Table 3 on p. 8 below, which shows the expenditure on different commodity groups for each of the years 1924, 1930 and 1935. While there were only moderate increases in the purchases of such items as jewellery and plate or leather goods, there was a rapid growth in the demand for perfumery, cosmetics and toilet requisites, and, to a less extent, for stationery and photographic goods also.

2 METHODS OF ESTIMATION

Scope of the estimates. The estimates discussed in the first four sections below relate to expenditure on all forms of clothing and footwear, including the value of dress materials bought in the piece and the cost of making up, but excluding all expenditure on alterations and repairs.[1] By definition, only purchases for final consumption should be included in the estimates, but it is probable that they also include some items of clothing, rubber boots for example, worn by workers in special occupations and more usually regarded as equivalent to working tools or similar equipment. Uniforms, however, are wholly excluded. Other clothing, even when worn mainly for working purposes, is considered to provide some consumer satisfaction and treated as an item of final consumption.

---

[1] See Chapter III, §(*f*), below, for these excluded items.

In the final section the estimates for a group of miscellaneous goods are discussed. These are mostly items of a purely personal character and fall almost entirely within the category of luxuries, as commonly understood; in addition to fancy goods and toilet wares, various items of personal equipment—stationery, clocks, cameras and smokers' requisites—are also included. Apart from stationery, problems of consumer allocation are of little importance for this group, almost all business purchases being only of the indirect kind made through expense accounts.

It is necessary, finally, to exclude purchases by tourists and other non-residents and to include expenditure abroad by United Kingdom residents. These adjustments are probably negligible for clothing but may be quite considerable for miscellaneous fancy goods. With the data available, however, it has not been possible to construct reliable estimates of these expenditures analysed according to the different items purchased. It has only been possible to set out (in Chapter X) estimates of the total amount spent annually on these accounts.

General procedure. For purposes of estimation, expenditure on clothing other than footwear is divided into two main groups. The first comprises all forms of apparel purchased as such, whether bespoke or ready-made. The second group consists of materials purchased directly by the housewife, either for making up at home or by a dressmaker. The cost of making up done outside the home is also included.

Direct estimates of expenditure on the separate items of apparel can be made only for the years of the period for which Census of Production returns are available. The data for the three years 1924, 1930 and 1935, in which complete returns were made, are accordingly given in more detail in the following sections; both because they form the basis for subsequent interpolation and because of the intrinsic interest of the components of such a large and varied group of expenditures. For other years of the period it was only possible to make estimates of total expenditure by interpolation and extrapolation of the census values. Employment figures could be used for this purpose and also, from 1930 onwards, indices of retail sales.

Dress materials purchased in the piece represent only a small part of the total output of piece-goods and are not separately distinguished as such in the Census of Production returns. Both the estimates for census years and the methods of interpolation used are necessarily much cruder and subject to a wider margin of error.

Complete records of the output of footwear are similarly available only for the census years. Output in other years was estimated on the basis of employment figures. Use was also made of the output returns for a large sample of firms in the industry. The output of rubber boots and shoes was separately calculated.

The price series for both clothing and leather footwear are based upon components calculated for the cost-of-living index. Series for rubber boots and shoes were derived from the average values of exports and imports.

Estimates for the final group of other personal effects were made in a similar way to those for clothing. The basic data were derived from the census returns and varied for other years of the period on the basis of employment figures, the series being checked against an index of retail sales. A price index was derived from average export values.

Methods employed. The methods of estimation used are discussed below in the following order:

(a) Apparel.
(b) Dress materials.
(c) Leather footwear.
(d) Rubber footwear.
(e) Other personal effects.

(A) APPAREL

The items in this group include expenditure on all forms of outergarments, bespoke and ready-made; shirts, fancy hosiery, underwear and nightwear; corsets and brassières; stockings and socks; hats, caps and millinery; ties, scarves, gloves and braces, etc.; and miscellaneous items such as handkerchiefs, baby clothes, umbrellas and walking-sticks.

From 1930 onwards, indices of retail sales are available for the two categories of men's and boys' wear and women's, girls' and children's wear. The actual value of sales in the two groups was estimated for the three years 1924, 1930 and 1935. As only a part of the census data is thus distinguished, it was necessary to make a rough division of many of the items recorded. The proportion for all items taken together is probably substantially correct, and the errors in the components will cancel out when the two categories are combined.

For pricing purposes, it is also necessary to divide the output of both men's and women's outergarments between the three categories of wholesale tailoring, bespoke wholesale tailoring and bespoke retail tailoring. The wholesale tailoring section of the trade is engaged in the manufacture of ready-made garments, principally for sale by independent outfitters. Wholesale bespoke tailoring is the bespoke trade undertaken by the large multiple shop firms; orders taken by the local shop are sent to a central workshop to be made up. The retail bespoke trade is carried on by the independent tailor with a shop and a workroom, probably employing less than thirty workers. In the census returns the value of output in the first category is recorded at factory cost, but the value of wholesale bespoke tailoring includes a proportion of wholesale costs and the value recorded for retail bespoke tailoring represents the price paid by the final consumer. The recorded output of large firms in 1935 is divided between the three categories for 1935, but for 1930 only the value of wholesale tailoring is shown separately and for 1924 no separate figures are given. Estimates were made for the two earlier years in the following way.

The proportion of expenditure on men's outergarments represented by bespoke wholesale tailoring during this period may be estimated from a knowledge of the development of large-scale multiple shop retailing, since it was these firms who were almost entirely responsible for the bespoke wholesale trade. It has been estimated that this trade increased by more than 260 % between 1920 and 1935.[1] In 1935 the proportion of total retail expenditure on men's outergarments represented by wholesale bespoke tailoring was 22 %. The proportions of wholesale and retail bespoke tailoring were 59 and 19 % respectively. At the estimated rate of increase the proportion of the total represented by wholesale bespoke in 1920 would be only 7 %. It may be assumed that this branch of tailoring developed equally at the expense of both the trade in ready-made garments produced by the wholesale manufacturer and the bespoke trade of the independent tailor. Therefore the proportions allotted to those two categories in 1920 were 67 and 26 % respectively. The percentages in 1920 and 1935 were linearly interpolated to obtain estimates for 1924 and 1930. The figures were then adjusted for distribution costs to obtain the equivalent proportions in terms of census values. The recorded value for wholesale tailoring in 1930 serves as a partial check on this procedure.

The adjustment necessary for women's wear is much simpler. In this case more than four-fifths of expenditure was accounted for by wholesale tailoring and, of the two forms of bespoke tailoring, wholesale bespoke was the less important. Nor was there any development comparable with the growth of large multiple shop firms offering a bespoke service which characterized the trade in men's wear. In these circumstances it seems probable that little error will be introduced if the proportions shown for 1935 are applied for the whole period.

The output of small firms with less than ten employees was recorded by the Census for 1924 only, when it amounted to one-quarter of the total for the main tailoring and dressmaking trade. It is important, therefore, not to omit the output of these firms in 1930 and 1935. Gross output per head was varied in the same proportion as gross output per head in large firms and multiplied by the estimated total number of persons employed. The value of total output was then divided between the different items in the same ratio as in 1924.

More than two-thirds of the output of small firms consists of outergarments and there is little doubt that these would be made mainly for the retail bespoke trade. For, while the largest establishments are likely to be found among firms engaging in the wholesale bespoke trade with their numerous retail branches and their evident desire to take advantage of the economies of large-scale operation, the small establishments are most likely to be engaged in the retail bespoke side of the trade, doing high-quality work with close attention to customers' individual requirements. Undoubtedly, some small firms were engaged in making up and specialist work for large wholesale firms and some may have produced ready-made garments direct for the wholesale trade. It is reasonable, however, to assume that by far the greater part of the output of small firms was for the retail bespoke trade. Accordingly 80 % of their output was allocated to retail bespoke and the remaining 20 % to wholesale tailoring.

Tables 1 and 2 set out the estimates of retail expenditure on the different items of men's and women's wear in each of the three census years 1924, 1930 and 1935. To derive these figures the value of output recorded by the Census was first adjusted for imports and exports.[2] In making this adjustment the recorded value of exports was reduced by 10 % to exclude the cost of carriage between the factory and the port. The factory value of supplies available for home consumption was then raised to retail value by the addition of the appropriate margin to cover the costs of distribution.[3] No allowance was made for any time-lag between output and sales or for changes in the level of distributed stocks.

The specific assumptions adopted in making these estimates and the sources of the basic data are given in the notes to Tables 1 and 2.[4]

Estimates for other years were obtained by interpolation and extrapolation of the census figures. The estimates of output at factory value, before adjusting for exports and imports, were converted to a quantity basis by dividing through by the retail price index. A comparison of these 'quantities' with the numbers employed in the clothing trades[5] in each of these years suggests that

[1] See [74] James B. Jefferys, *Retail Trading in Britain, 1850–1950*, National Institute of Economic and Social Research, Economic and Social Studies, XIII (Cambridge University Press, 1954), pp. 304–6.

[2] See [8] *Annual Statement of the Trade of the United Kingdom*, vol. I, 1920–1938.

[3] See [73] James B. Jefferys, *The Distribution of Consumer Goods*, N.I.E.S.R. Economic and Social Studies, IX (Cambridge University Press, 1950), pp. 307–37.

[4] See pp. 5–6 below.

[5] See [69] Agatha L. Chapman, *Wages and Salaries in the United Kingdom, 1920–1938*, Studies in the National Income and Expenditure of the United Kingdom, 5 (Cambridge University Press, 1953), table 44, pp. 99–100; the numbers of wage-earners employed in the hosiery and clothing trades were combined for this purpose.

TABLE 1. ESTIMATED CONSUMERS' EXPENDITURE ON MEN'S AND BOYS' APPAREL IN THE UNITED KINGDOM IN 1924, 1930 AND 1935 (£ M.)

	1924	1930	1935
Outergarments:			
Bespoke retail	17·2	15·0	11·5
Bespoke wholesale	7·7	13·0	14·0
Ready-made	51·5	53·0	48·3
Shirts, collars, etc.	13·5	13·8	12·5
Fancy hosiery	3·3	2·9	2·8
Underwear and pyjamas	14·5	16·5	15·4
Socks and stockings	12·5	10·9	8·2
Hats and caps	12·3	10·5	6·3
Ties and scarves	5·5	3·4	3·3
Braces and suspenders	2·2	2·5	2·5
Gloves	2·7	2·5	2·7
Handkerchiefs	1·1	1·0	1·2
Umbrellas and sticks	0·9	0·7	0·5
All items	144·9	145·7	129·2

TABLE 2. ESTIMATED CONSUMERS' EXPENDITURE ON WOMEN'S, GIRLS' AND CHILDREN'S APPAREL IN THE UNITED KINGDOM IN 1924, 1930 AND 1935 (£ M.)

	1924	1930	1935
Outergarments:			
Bespoke retail	9·7	9·1	8·2
Bespoke wholesale	4·9	5·2	6·3
Ready-made	58·5	62·3	63·8
Furs and fur garments	11·4	9·9	10·9
Fancy hosiery	16·3	14·6	13·9
Corsets and brassières	6·4	7·1	8·0
Underwear and nightwear	14·5	16·5	15·4
Stockings and socks	18·8	21·1	20·5
Hats and millinery	22·9	23·5	17·9
Scarves, embroidery, baby clothes, etc.	2·6	1·8	2·2
Gloves	5·4	5·0	5·4
Handkerchiefs	1·1	1·0	1·2
Umbrellas	1·9	1·5	1·0
All items	174·4	178·6	174·7

The composition of the various clothing groups in Tables 1 and 2 is described in the following notes. The sources of the different items in the census data and the foreign trade statistics are noted and the assumptions made in allocating the proportions for men's and women's wear are also given.

Outergarments: in addition to all items of bespoke and ready-made clothing, both retail and wholesale, this group includes the following items, also taken from the output of the *tailoring, dressmaking, etc., trade*—mackintoshes of various kinds, overcoats, aprons and overalls, etc., leather clothing, and legal and ecclesiastical robes, etc. An estimate of the total output of small firms was obtained as described in the text.

Exports and imports are classified in the trade statistics in a substantially similar way. Most items of outerwear are recorded separately as men's or women's. The exceptions are: mackintoshes, etc., of unclassified materials, which were allocated in approximately the same proportion as those of specified materials; and legal and ecclesiastical garments, etc., of which two-thirds was allotted to men's wear and one-third to women's. Apart from garments of woven fabrics, imports and exports are not distinguished as between men's and women's wear. The values involved are relatively small and approximately the same proportions as for home output were taken.

Shirts, collars, etc.: the whole of the output by large firms in the *tailoring, dressmaking, etc., trade* recorded under this heading was allotted to men's wear. Imports and exports are recorded separately in the trade statistics.

Furs and fur garments: the output of wearing apparel recorded by the *fur trade* was allotted wholly to women's wear. An estimate of the output of small firms was added. Exports and imports were taken from the trade statistics.

Fancy hosiery: this item comprises jumpers, cardigans and similar garments of knitted wear produced by the *hosiery trade*. The data for the inter-war census years do not distinguish between men's and women's wear. In the returns for the 1948 Census, however, the items are recorded in much greater detail. From this enumeration it appears that men's wear represents only one-sixth of the total. Although clothes rationing was in force during this year, these figures are probably satisfactory as a broad indication of the proportionate division during the earlier period. Exports and imports, as recorded in the trade statistics, were divided in the same proportions.

Corsets and brassières: the output of these items recorded by large firms in the *tailoring, dressmaking, etc., trade* was allotted wholly to women's wear. Exports and imports were taken from the trade statistics.

Underwear and nightwear: includes items of various materials recorded under this heading in the output of the *tailoring, dressmaking, etc., and hosiery trades*. An estimate of the output by small firms in these trades was included and imports and exports were taken from the trade statistics. For none of the items of knitted and woven wear included in this group is a distinction made between men's and women's wear. The total value has simply been divided equally between the two categories. This procedure is supported by the returns for the 1948 Census, where a large part of the output is classified in much greater detail.

Socks and stockings: the total production of these items is included in the output of the *hosiery trade* and is classified according to the materials used, i.e. cotton, wool, silk and other materials (mainly artificial silk). The exports and imports recorded in the trade statistics are classified in the same way. It was assumed that the proportion of men's wear included would be one-quarter of cotton socks in all years and two-thirds of woollen socks in 1924 and three-quarters subsequently. Exports and imports were allocated in the same way.

Hats, caps and millinery: the output of these wares is recorded by the Census under both the *hat, cap, etc., trade* and the *tailoring, dressmaking, etc., trade*. It is evident that in part the output of millinery recorded by the latter trade represents material purchased from hat manufacturers. The degree of double-counting involved cannot be more than roughly assessed. It has been estimated to be of the order of £2 m., and this amount was deducted in each year. The output of hatters' wares, in so far as they are separately recorded, was wholly excluded from the reckoning. An estimate of small firms' output was added; exports and imports were taken from the trade statistics. These data classify hats and caps only according to the material of which they are made. It was assumed that men's hats represented half the total value in 1924 and one-third in 1935. These proportions were interpolated for the intervening years. For imports and exports, which are quite small, it was assumed that 30 % of the total was men's hats in all years.

Ties, scarves, etc.: this is a comprehensive item including products of both woven and knitted material from the *tailoring* and *hosiery trades*. An estimate of the output by small firms in the latter trade was added. It seems probable that the greater part consists of ties and other items of men's wear. Accordingly only one-quarter of the total in each year was allotted to women's wear. The same proportions of exports and imports were taken.

Also included in this item, and allotted wholly to women's wear, are the various articles of embroidery and baby clothes, so far as they are separately recorded in the output of the *tailoring trade*.

Braces and suspenders: includes the output of these articles by the *leather* and *tailoring trades*, *plus* an estimate of the output of small firms in the former trade. Imports and exports are separately recorded in the trade statistics.

Gloves: includes both gloves of leather and fabric produced by the *glove trade* and those of knitted wear produced by the *hosiery trade*. A small quantity of rubber gloves used for household purposes is also included. An estimate of the output of small firms in the *glove trade* was added. After adjustment for exports and imports, it was assumed that one-third of the total would be men's gloves.

Handkerchiefs: the output of linen handkerchiefs, made exclusively by linen manufacturers in Northern Ireland, is recorded for all census years, and imports and exports are also recorded separately for the whole period. Complete returns of cotton handkerchiefs and other kinds produced by firms in the *tailoring* and *cotton weaving trades* are given for 1935 only. In the trade statistics for years before 1934, exports and imports of cotton handkerchiefs are included in an item comprising 'flags, handkerchiefs and shawls, wholly of cotton, not in the piece'; for later years they are recorded separately. From an examination of these data, it seems probable that in the years after 1930 there was in fact a marked substitution of cotton for linen handkerchiefs and that the census figures involve no serious omissions. It may also be assumed that, for the years up to 1930 at least, exports and imports of cotton handkerchiefs were small. The total value available was divided equally between men's and women's wear.

Umbrellas, etc.: the recorded output of finished goods by the *umbrella and walking-stick trade* was adjusted for exports and imports and one-third of the total was allocated to men's wear.

output per head varied little during this period. Output in other years could therefore be calculated directly from the employment series. Money values were obtained by multiplying through by the price index. The value of output was adjusted for imports and exports in each year and raised by the appropriate margin to cover distribution costs in order to obtain the retail value of sales. The average margin for all items of apparel had varied only slightly between the three census years and it seemed reasonable to adopt a figure of 67 % for all other years of the period.

This method of interpolation, admittedly, is not very refined and makes no allowance for variations in stocks, but it does not otherwise appear to be subject to any particular bias. Alternative estimates can be made for the second half of the period by using the indices of retail sales for men's and women's wear compiled by the Bank of England, which represent the monthly movement of the value of sales for a sample of retail shops from 1930 onwards. At this period the returns were heavily overweighted by department stores and for this reason the series are likely to show some bias compared with total sales for all kinds of shop. In order to correct this bias the trend of each series was adjusted to the estimated retail sales for the two census years 1930 and 1935. This was done simply by raising the index to the average level of the census values, linearly interpolating the proportionate adjustment between the census years, and extrapolating at the same annual rate for 1936–8. It appears from these figures that the sample series for men's clothing had a pronounced upward bias during these years, while that for women's clothing was more closely representative of the trade as a whole, with only a very small downward bias. These conclusions are confirmed by what is known of the development of retail trading

during this period and the relative importance of department stores in the total trade.[1]

The sum of the two expenditure series for men's and women's wear, calculated in this way, shows the same general movement as the total series estimated on the basis of the employment figures, but differs in detail for particular years. Part of the discrepancy must be due to stock movements. A part must also be the consequence of the difference in coverage between the two series, since the sample figures may be expected not only to be biased in their trend but also to show an amplitude of variation unrepresentative of the trade as a whole. Finally, there must of course be some random error arising from the methods used. In only one year, however, is the discrepancy larger than 2 % of the total. On balance, it is probable that the estimates derived from the sample series, which are directly representative of sales rather than output, will be the more reliable. These figures, therefore, were taken for the years from 1930 onwards and the estimates based on employment for the earlier half of the period.

The proportionate division of total expenditure between men's and women's wear changed only very slightly in the period from 1924 to 1930. In subsequent years the proportion of women's wear tended to rise. Accordingly, for the years before 1930, for which no retail sales series are available, the proportionate division has been simply interpolated back to 1924 and kept constant at that level for the earlier years.

Separate price indices were then calculated for men's and women's clothing. For this purpose individual price series for the principal types of clothing, compiled on a sample basis, were combined with the appropriate weights for each category.[2] Errors of weighting are not of much importance here, since the different series follow fairly closely a common pattern. The figures are directly representative of the most important items of clothing and may be considered roughly indicative of the general movement of prices for the other more miscellaneous items.

(B) DRESS MATERIALS

It has not been possible to do more than establish an order of magnitude for this item since the small proportion of dress piece-goods and other materials sold directly to the final consumer cannot be distinguished at all precisely from the great bulk of supplies going to the wholesale clothiers. The information to be derived from the 1935 Census of Production has been supplemented by some rough estimates of deliveries and utilization

---

[1] See [74] Jefferys, *Retail Trading in Britain, 1850–1950,* pp. 312–15 and 347–9.
[2] The individual price series used here were supplied confidentially for the purpose of this inquiry.

made by those in the trade. For other years of the period it was assumed that the purchases of apparel would provide an approximate index of the movement of sales from year to year. It seems reasonable, however, that these fluctuations should be combined with a downward trend, since it is generally acknowledged that the extent of home dressmaking diminished during this period. The details of the method are as follows.

Examination of the 'output' and 'materials used' tables for the textile trades in the 1935 Census of Production suggests that the value of materials bought for home dressmaking was roughly of the order of £17 m. in that year. A comparable figure of £20 m. may be taken for 1924 and it is thought that by 1938 the figure would have fallen to £15 m. To these figures it is necessary to add the costs of making up, which probably amount to one-third of the cost of the materials, or one-quarter of the cost of the garment. This total cost includes not only the value of textile piece-goods but also purchases of knitting wool and miscellaneous haberdashery such as sewing cottons, buttons, needles, etc. For other years of the period the total cost of materials and making up was simply varied as a proportion of expenditure on apparel. This proportion, of course, shows a downward trend during the period, falling from over 8% in 1924 to less than 6% in 1938. As a proportion of expenditure on women's clothing the downward trend is slightly steeper.

An index of price movements for this item was compiled by combining separate series for cotton material and the costs of making up, with weights of 3 and 1 respectively.

(c) LEATHER FOOTWEAR

This item includes expenditure on boots and shoes made wholly or mainly of leather and of other materials except rubber. Slippers, houseshoes and sandals are also included. Boots and shoes of rubber, including plimsolls and the like, are discussed in the following section.

The home production of leather footwear is recorded for the five census years, 1924, 1930 and 1933–5.[1] Output in other years of the period was estimated on the basis of the numbers employed in the industry. For this purpose, the output per head in each of the census years was linearly interpolated and extrapolated. Total output in each year was then derived by multiplying by the number of wage-earners employed in each year.[2]

The reliability of these figures could be checked against a series of annual returns of output collected from a sample of firms producing approximately 40% of the total output of the industry.[3] The number of firms in the sample varied from year to year and showed a particularly marked decline in the first four years of the period.

It is likely that these variations were not in all cases typical of the industry as a whole and that average output per head, or per firm, would be better than total output as a basis for comparison. The numbers employed by the firms in the sample are not known. However, between 1924 and 1935 the number of firms in the sample represented a steadily increasing proportion of the total number of firms recorded by the Census,[4] and average output per firm in the three years 1924, 1930 and 1935 varied in the same way for the sample as for the industry as a whole. The ratios of the number of firms in the sample to the total in each of the three census years were interpolated and extrapolated to provide approximate estimates of the total number of firms in other years. The number of firms calculated in this way was multiplied in each year by the average output per firm varied proportionately with the average output of the sample firms. Comparison with the previous estimates shows substantial agreement in their annual movements for most of the period, the greatest discrepancies appearing at the beginning and end of the period when the number of firms in the sample moved somewhat differently to the trend in employment.

The estimates of output were adjusted for exports and imports in each year to derive home consumption.[5]

A general price series for boots and shoes sold retail was available in index form. This index, which is probably not representative of the whole range of leather footwear, shows an upward bias compared with the average factory value of footwear in the census years. The factory values were first converted to retail prices by the addition of 57·5% to cover distribution costs[6] and were then compared with the prices obtained by adjusting the index to the same value for 1930. The discrepancy between the two series appeared to be very largely a difference in trend. The prices for other years of the period were calculated from the index, making due allowance for this trend.

(d) RUBBER FOOTWEAR

Included in this item are all boots and shoes made wholly or mainly of rubber, such as goloshes, bathing shoes, rubber sandals, plimsolls and the like.

The output of rubber boots and shoes in the United Kingdom is recorded for the six years 1924, 1930, 1933–5

[1] See [32] *Fifth Census of Production (1935)*, part I, table V B, p. 445.

[2] See [69] Chapman, *Wages and Salaries in the United Kingdom, 1920–1938*, table 44, p. 100.

[3] This information was supplied by the Incorporated Federated Association of Boot and Shoe Manufacturers of Great Britain and Ireland.

[4] No comparison can be made for 1933 or 1934 since the number of firms making returns for the purpose of the Import Duties Act Inquiries is not known.

[5] See [8] *Annual Statement of the Trade of the United Kingdom*, vol. I, 1920–38.

[6] See [73] Jefferys, *The Distribution of Consumer Goods*, p. 304.

and 1937.[1] The quantities exported and imported in each year of the period are also known.[2] Between 1924 and 1930 the consumption of rubber footwear almost doubled. The whole of this expansion was due to the increase in imports, since home output fell slightly between the two years. To estimate consumption in other years before 1930, the home output in the two census years was linearly interpolated and extrapolated, exports were deducted and imports added. After 1930, consumption appears to have increased at a slightly slower rate and to have involved a fairly rapid substitution of home output for imported supplies. Thus while imports represented two-thirds of total supplies in 1930, in 1935 they were only one-fifth. By 1938, however, imports were double what they had been in 1935 and it is evident that this increase was partly at the expense of home output. Accordingly, between 1930 and 1933 home output was simply interpolated; similarly between 1935 and 1937, the slight increase shown being extrapolated to 1938. Exports were deducted and imports added to derive home consumption.

The average factory value of home-produced boots and shoes of rubber is known for the five census years. For other years it was assumed that the average factory value varied roughly in the same way as the average value of exports. To obtain retail prices, 68% was added to cover the costs of distribution.[3] Similarly, 68% was added to the landed value of imports, including duty paid under the Import Duties Act, 1932.[4] Finally, the values for home-produced and imported supplies were summed for each year.

(E) OTHER PERSONAL EFFECTS

Under this heading is included a variety of different goods, mainly personal, which can be conveniently considered together: stationery, jewellery and plate, watches and clocks, fancy goods of leather and plastic, photographic materials, toilet requisites, and chemists' wares other than drugs and medicines. Estimates of the home output of these commodities for the years 1924, 1930 and 1935 were obtained from the Census of Production. The particular items included are shown in the notes to Table 3. So far as possible, purchases for other than final consumption have been excluded. For many of the items involved the whole output may be allocated to final consumption with little discrepancy, but there are also items such as stationery which are bought equally for personal and other use. No precise information is available and the proportions allotted to the different uses must be largely guesswork. It is even less plausible to allow for any variation of these proportions over the period, apart from a few exceptional cases. The actual proportions adopted are given in the notes to Table 3.

The estimates of home output were adjusted for exports and imports and raised by the appropriate percentage margin to cover distribution costs. Retail expenditures on the different groups in the three census years are given in Table 3.

TABLE 3. ESTIMATED CONSUMERS' EXPENDITURE ON OTHER PERSONAL EFFECTS IN THE UNITED KINGDOM IN 1924, 1930 AND 1935 (£ M.)

	1924	1930	1935
Pens and pencils, etc.	5·2	5·5	6·3
Stationery	12·4	14·6	15·8
Jewellery and plate	18·1	16·0	18·1
Fancy leather goods, etc.	5·2	6·5	6·1
Plastic goods, etc.	9·4	8·9	6·3
Smokers' requisites	1·8	1·3	1·4
Clocks and watches	5·7	8·7	8·9
Perfumery and cosmetics	6·8	11·4	16·2
Other toilet requisites	3·6	4·7	6·1
Photographic goods	1·6	2·0	2·5
Other goods	3·7	4·5	5·0
All goods	73·5	84·1	92·7

The composition of the different groups of other personal effects shown in Table 3 is described in the following notes. The sources of the different items in the census data and the trade statistics are noted and the proportions of output allocated to final consumption are also given.

Pens and pencils, etc. (including artists' materials): this item includes all non-paper stationery items—pens, fountain pens, pencils and all artists' materials (paints and colours, cabinet work, etc.) from the *pens, pencils and artists' materials trade*; artists' brushes from the *brush trade*; writing ink and ink powders, gum and paste, etc. and sealing wax from the *ink, gum, etc., trade*. An addition was made for the estimated output of all small firms in each year. Imports and exports of stationery, other than paper, artists' brushes and other materials, so far as separately specified, were taken from the trade statistics.

Stationery: only a part of some stationery items are purchased for final consumption and the proportions taken are shown in brackets after the particular item. The following items were taken from the *manufactured stationery trade:* notepaper and envelopes (half), boxed stationery, postcards, playing cards, Christmas cards and calendars, luggage labels, paper patterns and transfers, dish papers, etc., paper novelties, bonbons and crackers, picture and photo mounts, other and unclassified manufactures of paper and cardboard (half), and other stationers' goods. From the *printing, bookbinding, etc., trade* were taken: manuscript books (one-quarter) and albums and diaries (three-quarters); and from the *paper trade*, blotting paper (one-quarter). Estimates of the output of these goods by small firms were added. Imports and exports of stationery were taken from the trade statistics.

Jewellery and plate: includes all goods made by the *plate and jewellery trade* with the exception of knives, spoons and forks (included with hardware and hollow-ware, see Chapter II, § (e)) and rough stampings for the trade; and cases for jewellery and cutlery from the *fancy goods trade*. The estimated output of all small firms in each year was added. Imports and exports are recorded for all years in the trade statistics.

[1] See [32] *Fifth Census of Production (1935)*, part III, Rubber Trade, p. 467, table V C, and [35] *Final Report on the Census of Production for 1948*, vol. II, trade A, Rubber, p. 12.
[2] [8] *Annual Statement of the Trade of the United Kingdom*, vol. I, 1920–38.
[3] See [73] Jefferys, *The Distribution of Consumer Goods*, p. 306.
[4] See [8] *Annual Statement of the Trade of the United Kingdom*, vol. II, 1932–8.

Fancy leather goods: includes handbags, purses, pocketbooks and other fancy goods of leather and of materials resembling leather made by the *leather goods trade.* An estimate of the output by small firms was added. Imports and exports were taken from the trade statistics.

Plastic goods and miscellaneous fancy articles: includes hair combs, fancy goods not elsewhere specified, picture frames and mouldings therefor from the *plastic goods and fancy articles trade.* This group includes numerous toilet requisites, haberdashery articles and accessories made of plastic materials and out of ivory, bone, amber, mother-of-pearl, etc. The estimated output of all small firms was added. The value of imports and exports of fancy goods is recorded in the trade statistics for all years of the period.

Smokers' requisites: includes tobacco pipes, holders for cigars and cigarettes, and parts sold separately from the *plastic goods and fancy articles trade;* clay pipes, so far as separately recorded, from the *china and earthenware trade;* and mechanical lighters, complete, from the *hardware, hollow-ware, etc., trade.* Other smokers' requisites, such as cases, pouches and ash-trays, etc., are already included in other items—jewellery, fancy leather goods or plastic goods—according to the material of which they are made. The estimated total output of tobacco pipes by small firms was added. Imports and exports of pipes, including parts, and lighters, excluding parts, were taken from the trade statistics.

Clocks and watches: a considerable proportion of the recorded output and imports of watches and clocks consists of parts sold separately, that is, cases or movements only. To a large extent these parts are assembled by distributors and consequently the finished output is not recorded by the Census. The degree of duplication in the census output itself appears to be quite small. Accordingly the total output of goods made by the *watch and clock trade* is included here (*plus* an estimate of the output by small firms, i.e. 10% of large firms' output), and the total value of watches, clocks and parts imported was added, and exports deducted, from the trade statistics. It is probable that something more should be added to cover the cost of assembling by distributors. On the other hand some deduction is probably necessary to exclude purchases not for final consumption. It has been assumed that these adjustments are of the same order of magnitude and would therefore largely cancel each other out.

Perfumery and cosmetics: includes perfumed spirits, perfumery, cosmetics and toilet preparations from the *soap, candle and perfumery trade.* In addition to perfumes and cosmetics this group includes tooth-paste, shampoos and bath salts. An estimate of the output by small firms was added. Imports and exports of perfumery, cosmetics, etc., are recorded by the trade statistics for all years of the period. Some articles for further manufacture appear to be also included but it seems reasonable to assume that any discrepancy involved will be small.

Other toilet requisites and accessories: includes toilet brushes of all kinds (tooth-brushes, shaving brushes, etc.) from the *brush trade.* The small additional output of toilet brushes by small firms was estimated. Also included are safety razors, complete, and blades sold as such, other razors, and nail polishers, clippers, cleaners, etc., from the *cutlery trade;* hair pins (including curlers and wavers) from the *needle, pin and metal smallwares trade;* the output of these goods by small firms is negligible. The trade statistics record the imports and exports of toilet brushes separately for all years of the period. Of the other goods included here only razors are separately recorded for all years; these figures include small quantities of component parts other than blades. From 1934 onwards other toilet requisites are also recorded separately. It is possible that in earlier years some part of these items was included under the heading of fancy goods. A proportion (two-thirds) of imported sponges was also included.

Photographic goods: the output of these goods is recorded with other items of the *scientific instruments trade* under general headings which do not distinguish between goods for commercial and personal use. The items most likely to be purchased by final consumers are: cameras, other than cinematograph cameras, complete, and plates, films and spools (half). It may be assumed that the purchases for commercial use included here will be largely offset by those other goods for final consumption, for example magic lanterns and materials bought for home developing, which have been omitted. At any rate the discrepancy involved will be negligible. The very small output by small firms can be ignored. Imports and exports of these goods are recorded for all years of the period in the trade statistics.

Other goods: the output of hot-water bottles by large firms in the *rubber trade* is recorded separately in the Census from 1933 onwards. For earlier years a similar proportion of the output of all hot-water and air goods was taken. The output of small firms is negligible. Imports and exports are recorded separately in the trade statistics from 1935 only. However, the quantities involved are small and may be ignored for earlier years. The output of toilet paper by the *manufactured stationery trade* is recorded separately for 1935 only; rough estimates were made for other years. The total output of sanitary towels is recorded under the *cotton weaving trade,* appropriate proportions of more general headings being taken for 1930 and 1924. No adjustments for small firms, exports or imports were made for either of these last two items. Finally, £500,000 was added in each year for contraceptives, which are not recorded separately by the Census or the trade statistics.

A price index for the group as a whole was constructed by using export average values derived from the trade statistics. The series included represented just over half of the total output of goods in the group; for the rest, exports were recorded by value only or not at all. The value of output in the Census was used to weight the series, combining them in a simple aggregative index. As a check on the reliability of these figures a more comprehensive index was compiled for the three census years from the census data themselves. All items were included for which estimates of output at 1935 prices were given or could be derived. Approximately 85% of the total was covered by these figures. The trend of the index based on export prices was corrected by adjusting the figures to the census index in the three years, linearly interpolating and extrapolating the discrepancy for other years of the period. This adjustment was probably adequate to correct the series for any bias due to the unrepresentativeness of the export series and the arbitrary selection of components imposed by the data.

Employment data were used as a basis for extending the estimates of output in census years to cover the whole period. Separate series of the numbers employed over the period 1924–38 were obtained from the national insurance returns[1] for the following industries: stationery and typewriting requisites (not paper); paper and paper board; cardboard boxes, paper bags and stationery; leather goods; watches, clocks, plate, jewellery, etc.; chemicals; and scientific and photographic instruments and apparatus. The total number of insured workers in each industry is recorded for July of each year 1923–38. For the years 1923–7 the figures relate to workers aged 16 and over. From 1928 onwards only workers aged 16–64 were covered. Since there are published estimates of the numbers aged 16–64 at July 1927 a rough proportional adjustment could be made for the earlier years. The average number insured in each calendar year was calculated by combining the figures for the preceding, current and succeeding July with relative weights of 1, 6 and 1, respectively, in this way assuming a linear change in the number insured between successive Julys. The number of insured workers unemployed is recorded monthly throughout the period. The average for each calendar year was deducted from the estimated number insured to derive the number of insured employed. A proportionate adjustment to exclude those aged 65 and over before 1928 was applied in the same way as for

---

[1] See [20] *Statistical Abstract for the United Kingdom.*

the number insured. A change in the method of counting the unemployed made in September 1937 necessitated a similar small adjustment to the published figures for 1937–8.

It is evident that a large part of the workers included in these estimates would not be engaged in the production of goods included here. It seems reasonable, therefore, to weight the component series when combining them in a single index. So far as they were available, the numbers of employees recorded for census trades or subdivisions of trades were used for this purpose; in other cases the weights were based on the value of output.

To carry the figures back to 1920 the estimates of the numbers of wage-earners in a group of miscellaneous manufacturing industries were used.[1] The ratio of the two series varied little more than 5% over the whole period and it was assumed that the ratio would be the same in the years 1920–3 as in 1924.

When output at constant prices in the three census years was compared with the movement of the employment series, it was found that the ratio of the two series showed a fairly uniform rise over the eleven-year period. Accordingly, the ratios for 1924 and 1930 were interpolated for the intervening years and carried back at the same rate to 1920. Similarly, the trend in the ratio between 1930 and 1935 was extended forward to 1938. In this way estimates of factory output were obtained for all years of the period and figures at current values could be calculated by applying the price index. Retail expenditures were derived by adjusting for exports and imports, including duty charges, and adding the appropriate margins to cover distribution costs.

3 THE RELIABILITY OF THE ESTIMATES

The reliability of the estimates for apparel may be considered in terms of the three stages involved in their compilation: that is, the adjustment and collation of the census data; the division between men's and women's wear and the allocation of retail margins; and the methods of interpolation and extrapolation used to derive estimates for other years of the period.

The output of clothing is recorded in the census returns under a number of different trades and it is possible that in combining these data some double-counting will have been involved. But it is unlikely to be large, since an attempt was made to correct this duplication in the more important instances. On the other hand, it is possible that some items of clothing were omitted because they were not separately enumerated in the census tables or were included with the output of mainly unfinished products.

A more important source of error in the estimates for census years is the calculation of output by small firms. The discrepancy in this case is due mainly to the assumption that the value of gross output per head for small tailoring and dressmaking firms, engaged mainly in the bespoke trade, would change at the same rate over the period as for large firms. However, the change in gross output per head for large firms between 1930 and 1935 is very similar for both the wholesale and bespoke tailoring sections of the trade. Moreover, in 1924 output per head was almost the same for large and small firms, although it may be noted that small firms employed proportionately twice as many outworkers, the value of whose output is included although the numbers employed are not. There is, of course, a further source of error, common to all the estimates of small firm output made in this study, in the assumption that the average output of small firms that made no returns would be the same as for those that did.

It may be assumed that the error due to these estimates of small firm output is negligible in 1924 but increases for 1930 and 1935. The only indication of the division of the total output of small firms between the different items of clothing is provided by the recorded figures for 1924, but it is unlikely that the proportionate distribution would have changed sufficiently to invalidate estimates made on the basis of these figures.

The division of output between men's and women's wear has been made, for the most part, on a fairly arbitrary basis. In the case of those items for which the results of the 1948 Census are available the figures may be assumed to be more firmly based. Any allowance for variations in the proportionate division between the two categories during the period was introduced in only a few cases. Taking into account the possibility of the cancellation of errors, it may be expected that the percentage margin of error attaching to the total figures will be smaller than for most of the component items.

The appropriate percentage margins to cover distribution costs were added separately for each of the commodity groups shown in Tables 1 and 2. In fact the margins vary little between the different items, and, although there were changes in the composition of the total, the average margin remains the same for the three census years. The costs of distribution account for more than half the value of retail expenditure on clothing but the proportionate error due to the estimation of this component will be small, probably not more than 2 or 3%. It is possible that a certain amount of systematic error will have been introduced by assuming the same

---

[1] See [69] Chapman, *Wages and Salaries in the United Kingdom, 1920–1938*, table 44, p. 100. The insurance trades covered by this group are: rubber, oilcloth, linoleum, etc.; brushes and brooms; toys, games and sports requisites; stationery and typewriting requisites (not paper).

margin for the whole period. However, what evidence there is on this point would suggest that any changes in the average margin during the period could have been only slight.

Finally, it is necessary to consider the additional errors which occur in non-census years as a result of the methods of interpolation adopted. These concern not so much the absolute level of the estimates as the year-to-year variations. Alternative estimates are available for the second half of the period and it has been noted that the substantial agreement between the two series suggests that the variation displayed is certainly not random in character. The margin of error is probably of the order of 5%. It would appear that even in a period when stock adjustments might be expected to be more pronounced they were not important compared with the movements in the actual level of demand. Accordingly a higher degree of reliability may be attached to the estimates for the earlier part of the period than would otherwise have seemed likely. It is also probable, however, that the employment figures taken as the basis for interpolation are less reliable for these earlier years of the period, particularly for the years before 1924. In any case it may be assumed that the trend of the figures is reliable for this period.

It may be noted that the price series used in these calculations is a base-weighted index representative mainly of clothing materials rather than of finished garments. Although this price series was used to deflate both the factory value of output and the value of retail sales, no discrepancy is introduced if the margin for distribution costs remained constant during the period. It has been indicated that this assumption is reasonable. The procedure adopted, moreover, ensures the consistency of the final price and quantity series.

It is clear that the estimates of the value of dress materials purchased and the costs of making can be little more than an indication of the order of magnitude involved. The trend of the series is merely an indication of the most probable course of development. The price series was independently estimated and any error in the trend will appear also in the quantity movements.

It has already been shown, by the comparison with the sample figures, that the estimated quantity movements of leather footwear are probably a reliable indication of the actual variations in output for most of the period. The margin of error is almost certainly not more than 10%. It is reasonable to assume that the prices obtained by adjusting the base-weighted index to the trend of average values in the three census years reflect the movement of average values, uncorrected for quality changes, throughout the period. In its original form the index would not be appropriate to value a quantity series based simply on the number of pairs bought.

The quantity series for rubber footwear was constructed piecemeal for different sections of the period. Nevertheless, the figures should have a fair degree of reliability. In the first half of the period, imports, which are known accurately from the trade statistics, represented on average more than 60% of total supplies. This proportion decreased in later years, but the changes in home output can then be more reliably estimated from the more frequent census data. The price series is probably established at the right level and should provide a reliable indication of the general trend.

The methods employed to estimate expenditure on other personal effects are very similar to those used for clothing and are subject to the same sources of error. The magnitude of the error, however, may be expected to be appreciably larger for a number of reasons. Certain items in the group, such as stationery, clocks, and photographic goods, are bought by business and consumers, but it is not possible to make more than a very rough allocation of the total output between the alternative uses. The employment series used to extend the census estimates to other years is a much cruder indicator than in the case of clothing; the coverage is approximate and the weighting is uncertain. There is little direct evidence about price movements and it has been necessary to rely on an index of average export values for a selection of goods which may be far from representative of the whole group. While the trend of the series, based on the census data, is likely to be reasonably reliable, there is scope for a considerable margin of error in the figures for individual years. A total error of up to 20% might well be expected. A large part of this error, however, is likely to represent systematic bias rather than purely random deviation.

4 THE MAIN TABLES

The annual estimates obtained by the methods described in the earlier sections of this chapter are given in the following tables. Quantity series are shown in Table 4. An absolute quantity measure is available for footwear only; for the composite groups of other clothing and personal effects no more than an indicator of relative quantity movements can be given. The corresponding price series are shown in Table 5, actual expenditures in Table 6. Finally, in Table 7, quantity and price series for all the main groups are provided in a comparable index number form. The quantity series are base-weighted aggregate index numbers and the price series current-weighted aggregates. Their product is thus a simple index of expenditure. Each index has been multiplied through by actual expenditure in 1938 and is shown in this form in the diagrams of §1.

TABLE 4. ESTIMATED QUANTITIES OF CLOTHING AND OTHER PERSONAL EFFECTS PURCHASED FOR FINAL CONSUMPTION IN THE UNITED KINGDOM, 1920–38

	1920	1921	1922	1923	1924	1925	1926	1927	1928	1929	1930	1931	1932	1933	1934	1935	1936	1937	1938
Apparel (1929 = 100·0)																			
Men's and boys' wear	93·4	73·5	86·0	88·9	90·8	92·9	91·6	96·1	98·3	100·0	97·8	96·6	91·1	93·0	93·0	96·9	96·5	92·5	85·8
Women's, girls' and children's wear	91·5	76·5	87·3	87·7	88·8	90·3	91·0	97·2	97·9	100·0	99·5	103·7	100·5	103·8	105·9	109·4	116·5	118·1	124·1
Dress materials, etc. (1929 = 100·0)	120·9	88·3	91·3	91·3	92·2	93·9	94·8	101·3	98·3	100·0	99·1	100·0	93·9	97·0	99·6	100·4	97·8	93·5	87·0
Footwear (million pairs)																			
Leather footwear	113·0	107·9	112·9	109·9	110·1	112·2	114·3	118·2	113·1	114·3	114·0	116·2	113·4	123·1	122·9	129·0	134·2	139·4	142·0
Rubber footwear	13·8	11·8	11·7	11·1	11·4	12·2	14·2	13·4	17·0	19·2	22·4	25·9	27·3	28·9	29·4	30·1	33·5	34·8	36·2
Other personal effects (1929 = 100·0)	94·4	80·6	84·8	84·4	83·9	91·4	87·0	93·3	96·2	100·0	104·7	105·5	103·9	113·6	121·5	127·8	138·1	150·2	156·4

TABLE 5. ESTIMATED AVERAGE PRICES OF CLOTHING AND OTHER PERSONAL EFFECTS PURCHASED FOR FINAL CONSUMPTION IN THE UNITED KINGDOM, 1920–38

	1920	1921	1922	1923	1924	1925	1926	1927	1928	1929	1930	1931	1932	1933	1934	1935	1936	1937	1938
Apparel (1929 = 100·0)																			
Men's and boys' wear	197·5	147·0	112·9	104·0	105·0	106·9	103·5	100·5	100·0	100·0	98·0	92·1	88·6	86·6	87·6	87·6	88·6	95·5	99·0
Women's, girls' and children's wear	198·3	138·9	109·4	103·8	105·6	108·1	103·0	98·7	100·4	100·0	96·6	88·5	85·9	83·8	84·6	85·9	86·3	92·3	94·9
Dress materials, etc. (1929 = 100·0)	164·7	130·7	112·4	106·6	107·6	109·0	102·1	96·8	101·3	100·0	95·6	88·3	86·3	83·1	81·6	83·9	83·1	84·7	85·4
Footwear (s. per pair)																			
Leather footwear	21·15	16·65	14·03	12·96	12·62	12·37	12·12	11·78	12·59	12·30	11·34	10·44	9·70	9·06	8·87	8·95	8·62	8·95	9·03
Rubber footwear	5·02	4·63	3·94	3·62	4·02	4·50	4·73	4·28	4·72	4·05	3·70	3·44	2·95	2·93	2·82	2·82	2·90	3·31	3·11
Other personal effects (1929 = 100·0)	160·4	162·3	127·1	108·9	106·2	100·5	116·7	109·6	109·5	100·0	97·4	95·7	87·4	88·4	90·5	87·6	87·2	93·9	100·3

TABLE 6. ESTIMATED EXPENDITURE ON CLOTHING AND OTHER PERSONAL EFFECTS PURCHASED FOR FINAL CONSUMPTION IN THE UNITED KINGDOM, 1920–38 (£M.)

	1920	1921	1922	1923	1924	1925	1926	1927	1928	1929	1930	1931	1932	1933	1934	1935	1936	1937	1938
Apparel																			
Men's and boys' wear	280·5	164·3	147·7	140·7	144·9	151·0	144·2	146·9	150·2	152·1	145·7	135·4	122·8	122·4	124·0	129·2	130·1	134·3	129·1
Women's, girls' and children's wear	337·4	197·5	177·6	169·2	174·4	181·5	174·1	178·2	182·8	185·9	178·6	170·6	160·4	161·7	166·5	174·7	186·9	202·6	218·9
Dress materials, etc.	53·6	31·1	27·7	26·2	26·7	27·5	26·1	26·4	26·8	26·9	25·5	23·8	21·8	21·7	21·9	22·7	21·9	21·3	20·0
Footwear																			
Leather footwear	119·5	89·8	79·2	71·2	69·5	69·4	69·3	69·6	71·2	70·3	64·6	60·7	55·0	55·8	54·5	57·7	57·8	62·4	64·1
Rubber footwear	3·5	2·7	2·3	2·0	2·3	2·7	3·4	2·9	4·0	3·9	4·1	4·5	4·0	4·2	4·1	4·2	4·9	5·8	5·6
Other personal effects	125·1	108·2	89·1	76·0	73·5	76·0	84·0	84·5	87·1	82·7	84·1	83·5	75·0	83·0	91·0	92·7	99·6	116·5	129·7
All clothing, etc.	919·6	593·6	523·6	485·3	491·3	508·1	501·1	508·5	522·1	521·8	502·6	478·5	439·0	448·8	462·0	481·2	501·2	542·9	567·4

TABLE 7. INDEX NUMBERS OF QUANTITY AND AVERAGE PRICE FOR CLOTHING AND OTHER PERSONAL EFFECTS PURCHASED FOR FINAL CONSUMPTION IN THE UNITED KINGDOM, 1920–38

(Expenditure in 1938 is taken as the base for each series)

	1920	1921	1922	1923	1924	1925	1926	1927	1928	1929	1930	1931	1932	1933	1934	1935	1936	1937	1938
Apparel and dress materials, etc.																			
Quantity index	329·8	265·9	304·5	309·6	314·6	320·7	320·2	339·3	343·4	350·0	345·5	351·6	336·0	345·4	349·9	362·1	373·4	368·9	368·0
Price index	749·3	543·8	426·6	399·5	404·7	413·1	395·8	381·2	385·6	383·7	372·6	345·2	334·0	325·8	328·6	331·9	334·0	357·3	368·0
Footwear																			
Quantity index	53·1	50·5	52·8	51·3	51·5	52·6	53·8	55·5	53·7	54·6	55·0	56·5	55·4	60·1	60·0	62·9	65·8	68·3	69·7
Price index	161·5	127·7	107·6	99·5	97·2	95·5	94·2	91·0	97·6	94·7	87·1	80·4	74·2	69·6	68·0	68·6	66·4	69·6	69·7
Other personal effects																			
Quantity index	78·2	66·9	70·3	70·0	69·4	75·8	72·2	77·3	79·7	82·9	86·6	87·6	86·1	94·2	100·9	106·1	114·5	124·5	129·7
Price index	207·5	209·8	164·4	140·8	137·4	130·0	150·9	141·8	141·7	129·4	126·0	123·6	113·0	114·3	117·0	113·3	112·8	121·4	129·7
All clothing, etc.																			
Quantity index	461·1	383·3	427·6	430·9	435·5	449·1	446·2	472·1	476·8	487·5	487·1	495·7	477·5	499·7	510·9	531·1	553·7	561·7	567·4
Price index	1,131·6	878·7	694·8	639·0	640·1	642·0	637·2	611·1	621·3	607·3	585·4	547·7	521·7	509·6	513·1	514·1	513·6	548·4	567·4

CHAPTER II

FURNITURE, FURNISHINGS AND HOUSEHOLD EQUIPMENT

1 GENERAL REMARKS

Expenditure on household furnishings and equipment, which constitute the greater part of consumers' durable goods, amounted to £263·7 m. in 1938, or just under 6% of total consumers' expenditure in the year. Almost the same percentage was spent on these goods in 1920, but the proportion had fallen to just over 5% by 1925; it rose steadily to 6¼% in 1935 and again fell off slightly in the final years of the period.

Expenditure on furniture and furnishings alone accounted for 60% of the whole in 1938. This proportion had been rising throughout the period from a figure of 42% in 1920. Further details for this subgroup are shown in Table 8 on p. 17 below. Furniture of wood, metal and wicker accounted for 45%, soft furnishings for something over 10% and carpets and linoleum for approximately 25%. Expenditure on radios and gramophones increased almost fourfold between 1924 and 1935, while expenditure on musical instruments, principally pianos, fell by 50%.

In addition to soft furnishings and household linen purchased ready-made, a certain amount has always been bought in the piece and made up by the housewife at home. It is not possible to make very precise estimates of these sales and little more than an order of magnitude may be hazarded. It appears that expenditure on household textiles and piece-goods represented a little over 10% of all furniture and furnishings, but the proportion had been falling throughout the period.

The other major category in this group is expenditure on hardware and hollow-ware. Some details are given in Table 9 on p. 21 below. Expenditure on hardware and hollow-ware represented on average 25% of the total for the whole group. The proportion varied little throughout the period and showed no significant trend. The year 1920, however, was exceptional, with a proportion of over 40%. This was undoubtedly due to restocking after the wartime stringencies. Domestic hollow-ware accounted for approximately one-quarter of the whole; domestic machinery of all kinds, including per-

ambulators, for a further 15%. A marked increase in expenditure during the period is shown for electrical appliances, lamps and lighting accessories; together, these goods represented 18% of the total in 1924 and 37% in 1935.

The two further categories of household durables separately distinguished in the estimates are china and glassware. Expenditure on both has fallen relatively, compared with other categories in the group. From nearly 10% in the earlier years of the period the proportion spent on china and pottery had fallen to less than 5% in 1938. Expenditure on glassware amounted to about one-third of this in most years.

Expenditure on furniture and furnishings at constant prices during the period is dominated by a persistent upward trend. After a slight initial setback in 1921, purchases rose uninterruptedly at an average rate of 5% per annum until 1936; the volume of purchases more than doubled during this period. It is significant that this rapid rate of growth was only slightly relaxed during the depression of the early 'thirties. In the final two years of the period, however, there was a fall of over 10% in the volume of purchases. A similar trend movement is shown by the series for hardware at constant prices, but in this case the year-to-year variations are more marked. In particular, there was a fall of some 40% in purchases between 1920 and 1921. The effect of the depression is also more evident and purchases were falling, though only slightly, between 1929 and 1932. A more marked fall, of the same order of magnitude as that for furniture, is again apparent in the final years of the period. It may be conjectured that this decline was associated with a temporary saturation of demand for household durables at the current level of income. This aspect can be discussed more usefully if an attempt is made to distinguish between consumption and net investment in consumer durables. Some analytic results are given later for the whole group of household durables taken together.

Purchases of china and pottery are alone remarkable in that they show a downward trend during this period. There was a marked fall of more than 20% between 1920

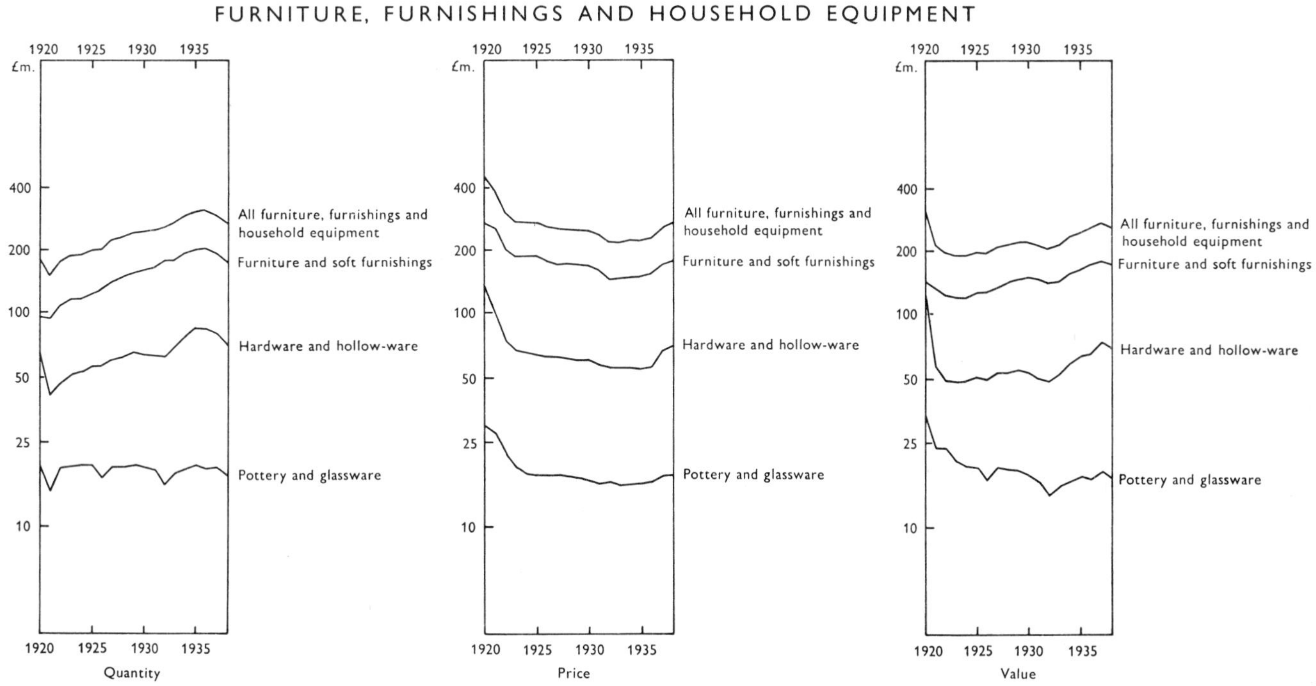

FURNITURE, FURNISHINGS AND HOUSEHOLD EQUIPMENT

Fig. 2. The variations in the quantities purchased, average prices and expenditure on furniture, furnishings and household equipment for final consumption in the United Kingdom, 1920–38.

and 1921 and another smaller fall in 1926. In each case the recovery was immediate and almost complete. The depression of the 'thirties was characterized by a steady decline from 1929 to 1932 followed by a gradual recovery until 1935, when the downward trend was resumed. Throughout the period as a whole the average trend represented an annual fall of just over 1 % cumulative, despite an annual increase in population of almost one-half of one per cent. It only seems possible to account for this persistent downward trend in terms of some long-run change in tastes and habits. For glassware the trend of purchases was upwards, as for other household durables. In 1932, however, this movement was broken by a drop of some 30 %. The upward trend was resumed in subsequent years, but at a lower level. This fall was due to the imposition of a heavy duty on imported glassware, which had accounted for approximately four-fifths of total supplies. In later years imports continued at less than two-thirds of their former level.

Since the commodities in this group are for the most part highly durable in use, it is of interest to divide the volume of purchases between consumption and investment demand. These magnitudes cannot be observed directly, but may be derived from purchases if the rate of depreciation is assumed to be known. The same assumptions are adopted here as were applied to clothing in the preceding chapter. Depreciation, or consumption, is assumed to be a constant proportion of the depreciated stock. With a given depreciation rate, the level of con-

sumption in any year can then be obtained as a weighted average of past purchases. By definition, the difference between purchases and consumption represents net investment, and is equal to the net change in the level of the stock between the beginning and end of the year. Estimates have been made in this way of consumption, net investment and stocks for household durable goods as a whole. The assumed rate of depreciation can be no more than a broad average for this quite heterogeneous group of commodities. A figure of one-quarter was taken, and some support for this value was obtained from the analysis itself. This rate of depreciation implies that a good is written down to one-tenth of its original value in just under eight years. The series for consumption is consequently much smoother than that for purchases, and shows only slight deviations from an upward trend. This movement is halted, however, in 1938 when consumption remains at the same level as in 1937, and for the first time in the period there is net disinvestment. For the greater part of the period net investment varied about an average level of £25 m. at 1938 prices. Exceptional years were 1920, when net investment stood at twice the average level, followed by a fall to only £13 m. in 1921, and 1937, when it again fell to the same low level. In most years net investment in household durables represented between 10 and 15 % of current purchases. This implies a rapid rate of accumulation and, in fact, the level of stocks more than doubled during this period. This growth of stocks is a factor of some importance in assessing the standard of living, and one which is not brought out by a consideration of purchases alone.

An econometric analysis of this material has also yielded results of some interest.[1] The formulation of the demand equation allowed for a lag in response to income and price changes and both short- and long-term elasticities could be calculated. The short-term elasticities are a measure of the immediate adjustment effected within the unit time period (a year in the present analysis), while the long-term values represent the ultimate adjustment made or, alternatively, the shift in the equilibrium level of purchases. As might be expected from the nature of the goods, the income elasticities are high. The short-term elasticity is found to be 2·83 and higher than the long-term elasticity of 2·42. This latter figure may be compared with the equivalent long-term value of 2·35 obtained from family budget data for 1937–8. The price effect is less markedly elastic. The short-term price (sub-stitution) elasticity is −1·15 and the long-term elasti-city, −0·97. It may also be noted that the demand equation obtained from this analysis not only accounts for the greater part of the variations in purchases during the inter-war period, but that a comparable analysis for the post-war years gives closely similar results. This is some confirmation of the structural significance of the responses evaluated. It is also of considerable interest that these basic responses should persist unchanged de-spite the great disruption of normal consumption patterns during the war.

2   METHODS OF ESTIMATION

Scope of the estimates. The estimates discussed in this chapter relate to all goods of a durable nature purchased for household purposes. These are commodities that pro-vide a utility common to the family as a whole without being appropriated to the exclusive use of any individual. In addition to purchases by households, the estimates also include the consumption of non-profit-making bodies and the comparable element involved in the com-posite service provided by restaurants and hotels. An attempt has been made to exclude all purchases, such as office furniture and furnishings, for purely business use.

A large part of the goods dealt with in this chapter are durable goods with an extensive life and might more satisfactorily be treated as forms of personal asset forma-tion rather than consumption. The principal objection to this procedure is the inadequacy of the statistical data, since it requires a knowledge of not only annual pur-chases but also the size of the current stock and the average life of the commodity. In the treatment adopted in this study, only purchases of land and houses are regarded as asset formation by persons. But even this simplification raises special problems of definition, some of which are discussed in §(*e*) below.

Finally, it is not possible to make detailed adjustments to exclude purchases by tourists and other non-residents. Similarly, expenditure abroad by United Kingdom resi-dents is not included. Estimates of the net balance for all items on these accounts are given in Chapter X.

General procedure. The principal sources of information for most of the household goods treated in this chapter are the enumerations of output provided by the Census of Production. These are available for certain years only and various methods of interpolation had to be adopted to derive comparable estimates for other years of the period. Employment data and indices of retail sales were used for this purpose. The amount of detail given in the annual series is strictly limited by the data available. Where possible, however, a more de-tailed breakdown of the larger groups has been given for certain census years. Price series were compiled from many sources. They are mainly given in index form since it is not possible to obtain average values in terms of a common unit for the many different commodities included in the groups.

Methods employed. The methods of estimation used for the different items of household furnishings and equip-ment are discussed below in the following order:

(*a*) Furniture and furnishings.
(*b*) Household textiles.
(*c*) China and pottery.
(*d*) Glassware.
(*e*) Hardware and hollow-ware.

(A) FURNITURE AND FURNISHINGS

The range of goods covered in this item includes domestic furniture and upholstery of all kinds, soft furnishings and lace curtains, carpets, linoleum and oilcloth, wireless sets, gramophones, musical instruments and sheet music. All household textiles bought in the piece and made-up articles such as towels, table cloths, blankets and fancy linens are excluded.

These are goods which are bought almost entirely for final consumption, including in that category expendi-ture by hotels and by various non-profit-making bodies, of which the most important are probably voluntary hospitals. A small proportion of expenditure on floor coverings was deducted to exclude purchases for business premises. The basic data are taken from the Census of Production and the principal difficulties are due to in-sufficient detail in the classification rather than any special problems of consumer allocation such as arise,

---

[1] See [**89a**] Stone and Rowe, 'The market demand for durable goods', *Econometrica*, xxv, no. 3 (July 1957), p. 423.

for instance, in connexion with certain items of hardware and hollow-ware. In the notes following Table 8 below are given the list of goods covered and an account of the adjustments necessary to obtain figures on a comparable basis for the three census years. The estimates of retail expenditure on the main subgroups of furniture and furnishings are shown for each of the years 1924, 1930 and 1935 in Table 8. These figures were derived from the census data by adjusting for imports and exports and adding the appropriate margins to cover distribution costs. Estimates for other years of the period were built up with the help of employment data and an index of retail sales for the years 1930–8. An index of prices and and index of the number employed had to be constructed for this purpose.

TABLE 8. ESTIMATED CONSUMERS' EXPENDITURE ON FURNITURE AND FURNISHINGS IN THE UNITED KINGDOM IN 1924, 1930 AND 1935 (£M.)

	1924	1930	1935
Furniture of wood	38·9	55·4	61·6
Metal furniture	2·7	2·9	2·7
Wicker furniture, etc.	1·7	1·9	2·1
Soft furnishings	11·1	13·7	14·6
Lace curtains	5·7	4·8	3·2
Carpets	22·3	24·6	24·8
Linoleum, etc.	9·8	8·6	9·2
Radios and gramophones, etc.	7·1	18·3	27·1
Musical instruments	9·3	6·0	4·6
All items	108·6	136·2	149·9

The composition of the various subgroups of furniture and furnishings shown in Table 8 are described in the following notes. The sources of the different items in the census data and the trade statistics are noted and the proportions of output allocated to final consumption are also given.

For the main furniture trades returns were made for the Census of Production in 1924, 1930 and 1935, but not for the Import Duties Act Inquiries of 1933, 1934 and 1937. Accordingly the data for all items in this group have been extracted for the three census years only.

Furniture and cabinet-ware of wood: includes all finished goods recorded under this heading in the output of the *furniture and upholstery trade.* Component parts of furniture are recorded separately and these are excluded. A deduction must also be made for wireless cabinets and gramophone cases which are included but not separately enumerated. For this purpose £500,000 was deducted in 1935, £400,000 in 1930 and £250,000 in 1924. An estimate of the output of small firms was added. Imports and exports of furniture and cabinet-ware, including some parts, are recorded separately in the trade statistics.

Metal furniture: includes metal bedsteads, other metal furniture for domestic use and wire mattresses from the *hardware, hollow-ware, etc., trade, less* one-third of wire mattresses to exclude sales to the trade. Imports and exports of bedsteads are recorded separately in the trade statistics. It was assumed that other metallic furniture imported and exported was for non-domestic use only.

Wicker furniture, basketware, etc.: includes furniture of basketware and of imitation basketware, fitted baskets and one-third of other baskets and basketware (the same proportion of all baskets being taken for earlier years as found for 1935) from the *cane and wicker furniture, etc., trade, plus* an estimate of the output of small firms. Furniture of basketware is

separately recorded in the trade statistics. One-third of the exports and imports of other basketware was taken. To these figures £250,000 was added to include the output by philanthropic institutions.

Soft furnishings, etc.: includes the various items of soft furnishings classified to the *furniture and upholstery trade* in census returns; that is, curtains and blinds (including venetian blinds), cushions, quilts, counterpanes, etc., of other materials than cotton and linen; also mattress overlays, divans, and lampshades of silk, paper, etc. An estimate of the output of small firms was added. Exports and imports of beds, cushions, quilts, etc., were taken from the trade statistics. The census reports also record the value received by retail stores for making up or altering carpets, curtains and draperies, etc. This is clearly a part of the cost to the final consumer (*less* a small proportion for business expenditure), but must be added at the final stage to the estimated retail value of the goods.

Lace curtains, etc.: includes the finished output by the *lace trade* of the following goods—cotton lace curtains and other cotton lace made on curtain machines, muslin curtains, artificial silk net and artificial silk curtains.[1] The total finished output of these items by both lace manufacturers and lace warehouses is only recorded for 1935. For earlier years only the value of the output by manufacturers at the unfinished stage is recorded in detail. An examination of the 1935 figures suggests that 15% should be added to cover the cost of finishing *less* the amount sold for finishing outside the trade. An estimate of the output by small firms was added; that is, cotton lace curtains, etc., made on curtain machines and one-third of lace and lace goods finished. Imports and exports of cotton lace curtains and (half) of artificial silk lace, whole and mixed (from 1925 onwards) were taken from the trade statistics.

Carpets (including rugs and mats): includes carpets and rugs, felts not elsewhere specified, and cloth and rag rugs and mats from the *woollen and worsted trade;* jute carpets and carpeting from the *jute trade;* coir mats and matting from the *coir fibre, etc.,* trade, raised by 25% to include the output of philanthropic institutions; skin rugs and mats from the *fell-mongery trade;* and mats and rugs of fur from the *fur trade.* An estimate of the output of small firms was added for those items for which this was not negligible. Imports and exports of carpets of wool, hair, jute, coir and cotton (taking the same proportion of household goods before 1935) and straw mats and matting were taken from the trade statistics.

Linoleum and other floor coverings: includes linoleum, inlaid and other, cork carpet, felt-base floor coverings and oilcloth for floor coverings from the *linoleum and oilcloth trade.* The output of small firms in this trade is negligible. Imports and exports of these items, taking one-third of oilcloth exports for other uses than upholstery before 1934, are recorded for all years in the trade statistics.

Radios and gramophones, etc.: includes wireless receiving sets and radio-gramophones from the *electrical engineering trade;* gramophones and gramophone records from the *musical instruments trade;* and gramophone needles from the *needle, pin, etc.,* trade. The output of small firms with respect to these items is mainly repair work and is not included here. Imports and exports of gramophones and records are given in the trade statistics for all years of the period. Wireless sets are recorded separately only from 1931 onwards and appropriate proportions of the composite items were taken for the earlier years.

Musical instruments, etc.: includes pianos, complete, stringed instruments and parts, wind and other musical instruments, not elsewhere specified, complete, from the *musical instruments trade, plus* an estimate of the output of small firms; sheet music is also included here and for this purpose the census value for music printing recorded in the output of the *printing, bookbinding, etc.,* trade was doubled to include the publishers' costs. Imports and exports of these items are recorded for all years in the trade statistics.

In the absence of more satisfactory information, the price index for furniture and furnishings had to be derived largely from export figures. The items chosen for this purpose were those for which both quantity and value figures are given in the trade statistics for the whole period.[2] These are: metal furniture, lace net, woollen carpets, linoleum, oil cloth, gramophone records

---

[1] See the chapter on 'The Lace Industry' by F. A. Wells in **[89]** *Studies in Industrial Organization,* ed. H. A. Silverman (London, 1946), in particular pp. 61–8.

[2] **[8]** *Annual Statement of Trade,* vol. 1, 1920–38.

and pianos. The average export values of these commodities were combined, using the expenditures in census years as weights. The index could hardly be representative unless a component for furniture and cabinet-ware were also included. Accordingly the export price series was combined with an index of furniture prices derived from quotations in the daily press, again using expenditure weights. Finally the trend was corrected to that shown by a comparable price index calculated (from the census data) for 1924, 1930 and 1935; this included all items in the furnishing group for which there was a price series given in the Census or for which such a series could be derived from the published figures. It was assumed that the change in the ratio of the two indices was linear between the Censuses, and that the rate of change from 1920 to 1924 was the same as from 1924 to 1930 and that from 1935 to 1938 the same as from 1930 to 1935. In this way the export price index was raised to the level of the Census of Production index.

In order to construct the index of numbers employed, separate series were obtained for the following trades: furniture and upholstery, cane and wicker furniture and basketware, lace, carpets, musical instruments, and wireless apparatus. Published estimates of the numbers of wage-earners in the first two trades are available for all years of the period.[1] For the other trades the numbers of insured workers are known for the period 1924–38[2] and rough estimates were made for the earlier years.[3] The numbers engaged in the production of wireless apparatus were roughly estimated by taking appropriate percentages of the estimated total number of wage-earners employed in electrical engineering.[4] The percentages, derived from census data, increased only slightly between 1924 and 1930 but almost doubled between 1930 and 1935. Between the census years the figures were simply interpolated and the percentage was varied at the same rate before and after 1924. For the years after 1935 the same percentage as in that year was taken, since this seemed the most reasonable procedure from an inspection of the recorded wireless output between 1935 and and 1937.[5] The estimated numbers employed in the various trades were summed for each year of the period. Although some of the components of this index are necessarily far from exact and the weights involved are only approximate, it seemed more important that every trade should be represented than that each component be equally reliable.

The value of home output at constant prices in the three census years was obtained by dividing through by the index of prices calculated above. The resulting figures were compared with the index of numbers employed in the three years. The logarithms of the ratios for the three years showed the same average rate of

increase for the two periods 1924–30 and 1930–5. It was assumed that the rate of increase was uniform throughout the inter-war period and the figures were interpolated and extrapolated logarithmically for all years. Multiplying through by the employment series and the price index, estimates of home output at current prices were obtained for each year of the period.

The factory value of home output was adjusted for exports and imports,[6] including duty,[7] and raised by the appropriate percentage margin to cover wholesalers' and retailers' selling costs.[8] These margins were added to the component items of furniture and furnishings in census years so far as information was available. The changes in the composition of the total cause a slight variation in the average margins for the three years and the figures were linearly interpolated and extrapolated for other years of the period.

Alternative estimates of expenditure from 1930 to 1938 could be obtained from an index of retail sales compiled from information supplied by department stores and a number of multiple shop firms. The index was converted to money values by taking the sum of expenditures in 1930 and 1935 as a base. The agreement is close for these two years and was made exact by distributing the small discrepancy linearly over the intervening years. In comparison with the estimates of expenditure derived from the employment figures, this series shows a much smaller amplitude of variation but the two series are closely correlated and the average expenditure for the nine years is very nearly the same. Although independent retailers are not adequately represented in the sales index, the small dealer is probably less important than in the hardware trade, for instance, and it seems reasonable to assume that the estimates derived from the sales index are likely to be the better indication of actual expenditures. A simple linear regression equation was fitted to the two series for the years 1930–8 and this was used to obtain adjusted estimates of expenditure for the earlier part of the period.

The estimates of retail expenditure for each year of the period were divided by the price index to derive an index of quantity changes during the period.

[1] See [69] Chapman, *Wages and Salaries in the United Kingdom, 1920–1938*, table 44, p. 100.

[2] [62] *Ministry of Labour Gazette, passim.*

[3] The figures given by Chapman, [69] *Wages and Salaries in the United Kingdom, 1920–1938*, for composite groups of trades were used for this purpose, extrapolating the ratios found for later years.

[4] [69] Ibid. p. 98.

[5] [35] *Census of Production, 1948*, vol. IV, trade M, table 8, p. 6.

[6] [8] *Annual Statement of Trade*, vol. I, 1920–38: 10% was deducted from the declared value of exports to exclude transport costs, etc.

[7] Ibid. vol. II, 1920–38.

[8] [73] Jefferys, *The Distribution of Consumer Goods*, pp. 269–78 and 300.

(B) HOUSEHOLD TEXTILES

No more than an order of magnitude can be given for this item of household equipment. The goods represented are principally towels, sheets, pillow-cases and blankets, etc., and a small amount of furnishing materials excluded from the 'soft furnishings' of the preceding section. These goods were bought largely in the piece by the housewife and the final finishing done at home. As a consequence the various items are very rarely distinguished in the output statistics, apart from the general heading of textile piece-goods. For the present purpose, a rough estimate of the level of expenditure has been varied simply as a proportion of total expenditure on furniture and furnishings.

From an examination of the census returns it may be roughly estimated that the value of household textiles purchased for final consumption in 1935 was of the order of £17 m. A comparable figure for 1924 would appear to be slightly lower, that is £14 m. For other years of the period these figures were simply interpolated and extrapolated as a proportion of expenditure on furniture and furnishings.

Since these figures can claim to be no more than a very rough estimate, it was thought adequate to assume that prices would move directly with the series calculated for other furnishings.[1]

(C) CHINA AND POTTERY

In this item is included all china and pottery for domestic use, whether purchased by private households, non-profit-making bodies, or hotels and other catering establishments. The inclusion of this last category accords with the procedure, adopted throughout this study, of estimating expenditure in hotels and restaurants under its several heads of food, rent, fuel, etc.

The value of the home production of domestic china and earthenware is recorded for the six census years 1924, 1930, 1933–5 and 1937.[2] For other years of the period output was estimated on the basis of an employment series. It was first necessary to correct the census values for price changes and an index of the retail prices of pottery was used for this purpose. An index of actual factory values would have been more appropriate but it is unlikely that the use of the retail series introduces any significant discrepancy; imports form only a small part of total supplies and it is probable that there were only slight changes in the average costs of distribution during the period. The estimates of output at constant prices were then compared with the numbers of wage-earners employed in the manufacture of china and earthenware in each year.[3] It was found that the ratio of output to the number employed decreased at an almost uniform rate

between 1924 and 1937. Accordingly the ratios for census years were simply interpolated and extrapolated to cover all years of the period, and multiplied throughout by the number employed to obtain estimates of output. These figures were converted to money values by applying the index of retail prices.

Home production was then adjusted for exports and imports.[4] For this purpose 10 % was deducted from the declared value of exports in order to exclude the costs incurred between the factory and the port. The small amount of duty charged on imported china and pottery from 1932 onwards is negligible for the present purpose.

Retail values were obtained by adding 90 % in each year to cover the costs of distribution.[5] An estimate of expenditure at constant prices was obtained by dividing through by the price index.

(D) GLASSWARE

Included in this item are all forms of domestic and fancy glassware. For most of these products the home output is known for census years and can be estimated for other years on the basis of an employment series. The output of glass mirrors, also included in this item, is not separately recorded except for 1933–5, and then by value only. The value of final expenditure on this commodity could only be roughly estimated for other years of the period.

For the greater part of domestic and fancy glassware, other than glass mirrors, output is recorded by both quantity and value for the six census years 1924, 1930, 1933–5 and 1937.[6] It was assumed that the small amounts which were recorded by value only could be taken to have the same average value as the rest, and the total quantity produced in each of the census years could therefore be estimated. These quantities were divided by the number of wage-earners employed in the glass trade[7] in each year, and the figures of average output per head were interpolated and extrapolated over the other years of the period and multiplied by the numbers employed to estimate output in these years. Although only a small part of those employed in the glass trade would be engaged on the production of domestic and fancy glass-

---

[1] See p. 17 above.

[2] See [31] *Census of Production, 1930 (Fourth)*, part IV, pp. 126–7; [34] *Import Duties Act Inquiry, 1934*, part II, pp. 266–7; [35] *Census of Production, 1948*, vol. I, trade G, pp. 7–8. An estimate was made of the output of small firms in the years other than 1924.

[3] See [69] Chapman, *Wages and Salaries in the United Kingdom, 1920–1938*, table 44, p. 98.

[4] [8] *Annual Statement of Trade of the United Kingdom*, vol. I, 1920–38.

[5] See [73] Jefferys, *The Distribution of Consumer Goods*, p. 282.

[6] See [31] *Census of Production, 1930 (Fourth)*, part IV, p. 141; [34] *Import Duties Act Inquiry, 1934*, part II, p. 275; [35] *Census of Production, 1948*, vol. I, trade I, pp. 6–7. An estimate was made of the small output by firms with not more than 10 employees for the years after 1924.

[7] [69] Chapman, *Wages and Salaries in the United Kingdom, 1920–1938*, table 44, p. 98.

ware, it seems more reasonable to vary output in this way than to interpolate linearly between census years.

Before adjusting for exports and imports it was necessary to estimate the current value of this output in all years. It was found that the average value of home output in census years varied closely with the average value of exports, although the export figure was more than twice the other. Assuming that this relation would hold for all years of the period, the factory price of home output in each year could be derived.

From these estimates of home output exports were deducted and imports were then added;[1] 10 % was deducted from the declared value of exports in order to exclude the costs incurred between factory and port. The duty charged on imported glassware from 1932 onwards[2] was added to the declared value of imports. Finally, to obtain retail values 90 % was added to the value retained in each year to cover the costs of distribution.[3] Retail prices were derived by dividing values by the quantity sold in each year.

(E) HARDWARE AND HOLLOW-WARE

This item includes all forms of hardware and domestic hollow-ware except china and glassware; that is to say, most forms of kitchen equipment, gas cooking-stoves and portable fires, and electrical appliances, accessories and fittings.

The basic data were taken from the returns of the Census of Production and Import Duties Act Inquiries for the six years 1924, 1930, 1933–5 and 1937. Home output in other years of the period was estimated on the basis of an employment series, and figures of home consumption were derived by deducting exports and adding imports.

These goods are recorded on the schedules for many different trades in the census returns and, in most cases, formed only a part of the total output of each trade. The employment figures, however, are only available for each trade as a whole. It is necessary, therefore, to relate output to the total number employed in those trades producing a large part of hardware and hollow-ware.

The selection of items from the census data involved numerous problems of consumer allocation. In some cases these problems arise only because the classification of the census returns, or the trade statistics, is not sufficiently fine for the purpose in hand. In other cases there is a real difficulty in deciding how much of a particular good used for both industrial and domestic purposes should be allocated to each category. A detailed account of the adjustments to the census data and the proportions of particular items taken for personal consumption is set out in the notes to Table 9. These proportions are only indications of the probable order

of magnitude and are the result of more or less informed guesses. It may be hoped, however, that the errors in particular estimates will to some extent cancel out and that the total will more closely approximate to the true figure than if items had been simply included or excluded as they were judged to be mostly for domestic or industrial use.

The problem is twofold. It is necessary to exclude not only goods used by industry, for example electrical fittings in factories and offices, but also those goods which are clearly bought by private households but are classified as asset formation, not consumption. In the treatment adopted throughout this study private asset formation is confined to the acquisition of houses; other durable consumer goods, such as clothing and motor-cars, are treated as items of consumption. The principle is clearly significant and useful, but the exact delimitation of the concepts is to a certain extent arbitrary. Not only the purchase of the house itself but also the money spent on the maintenance of the fabric must be counted as capital expenditure. This would indicate that external decorations and repairs, which preserve as well as adorn the outer fabric, are capital expenditure in this sense, but that most internal decoration and fittings should be consumption expenditure. It seems necessary, however, to draw a further distinction between movable furniture and furnishings, which are clearly part of consumption in the same sense as clothing, and interior decoration in the form of wallpaper and paint, which is usually undertaken by the landlord and may be classed as capital expenditure. The clearest distinction it is possible to make seems to be on the basis of what people moving house tend to take with them, as opposed to what they tend to regard as part of the permanent fabric. On this test capital expenditure would include the purchase of heating and cooking equipment of the cast iron type—boilers, radiators and kitchen ranges—and electrical fittings and accessories in the form of meters, switches, lamp-holders and ceiling rosettes, etc. Consumption, on the other hand, should include gas and electric cookers and portable fires and heaters as well as lampstands, globes and shades and other electrical fittings of this kind. It is on these lines that the selection of items and the various consumer allocations have been made.

It will also be noted that where the output of parts is recorded together with the finished article, the value of parts has not been included. Some of these parts will, of course, go into the making of the finished article and must be excluded in order to avoid double-counting. The rest

---

[1] See [8] *Annual Statement of the Trade of the United Kingdom*, vol. I, 1920–38.

[2] Ibid. vol. II, 1932–8.

[3] See [73] Jefferys, *The Distribution of Consumer Goods*, p. 282.

will be used for replacement and repairs and are excluded here since the gross value of repair work has been included in the estimates elsewhere.[1]

Estimates of retail expenditure on the subgroups of hardware and hollow-ware in the three census years 1924, 1930 and 1935 are shown in Table 9. These figures were obtained from the census data by deducting exports and adding imports, including duty, and raising the figures to the retail level by the appropriate percentage distribution costs.[2] Distribution margins were assumed constant throughout the period for the individual items and were calculated for a slightly more detailed grouping than that shown in the table.

TABLE 9. ESTIMATED CONSUMERS' EXPENDITURE ON HARDWARE AND HOLLOW-WARE IN THE UNITED KINGDOM IN 1924, 1930 AND 1935 (£ M.)

	1924	1930	1935
Cutlery	5·4	4·3	4·1
Brooms and brushes	3·8	4·0	3·5
Hollow-ware, etc.	14·2	14·2	15·3
Brass goods	1·6	2·5	2·4
Nails, etc.	1·5	1·5	1·9
Cord and net	1·2	1·0	0·9
Woodware	2·3	3·3	3·6
Tools and implements	1·2	1·1	1·3
Domestic machinery	5·6	5·3	5·2
Perambulators, etc.	3·6	2·5	2·6
Electrical appliances	2·1	3·7	11·3
Lamps and lighting accessories	6·9	11·1	13·0
All items	49·4	54·5	65·1

The composition of the different groups of hardware and hollow-ware shown in Table 9 are described in the following notes. The sources of the different items in the census data and the trade statistics are noted and the proportions of output allocated to final consumption are recorded.

Cutlery: includes knives complete, knife sharpeners and canteens and cased cutlery from the *cutlery trade, plus* an estimate of small firm output. Spoons and forks and plated knives, complete, are taken from the *plate and jewellery trade.* Pocket knives as well as table knives are included but not surgical knives or machine knives. Trade statistics give figures for knives, including a small proportion of blanks and other parts, and plated spoons and forks.

Brooms and brushes: includes all household brooms and brushes, mops and feather brushes (estimated for 1937) from the *brush trade, plus* an estimate of small firm output. Imports and exports of household brooms and brushes are taken from the trade statistics.

Domestic hollow-ware, etc.: from the *hardware, hollow-ware, etc., trade* the following items were taken as wholly for personal consumption: (i) hollow-ware for domestic purposes, other than boxes and containers. This includes enamelled and galvanized ware such as dustbins, buckets, etc. (tanks and cisterns could only be excluded for 1937 but the value is small, £138,000) and aluminium ware, kettles, saucepans, etc.; (ii) cash and deed boxes, trunks and suitcases of metal (this is a small item and any deduction for industrial use would be negligible in the total); (iii) hearth furniture; (iv) domestic utensils and appliances not elsewhere specified.

For the other items in this trade only a part of the recorded total was allotted to personal consumption. These are: (i) locks, latches, etc. It seems probable that only padlocks would be sold directly to consumers; in 1948 they represented one-sixth of the total and the same proportion was taken for the inter-war years. (ii) Lamps and lanterns. In each year two-thirds of the total was taken for final consumption. (iii) Stoves for domestic heating and cooking. As stoves of cast iron are not included here, these are presumably appliances which would not be embedded in the fabric of the building, and are therefore treated as a part of consumption and not capital equipment. Before 1935 the figures include cooking and washing boilers, which must be mainly for non-domestic use. The same proportion was deducted as obtained in 1935. Parts have been excluded in the same way. In the 1948 Census Report a further £500,000 has been added to the 1935 figure and it is also stated that fish-frying equipment is included. The additional value has been transferred from the iron foundries trade and is stated to be 'stoves of sheet iron for domestic heating and cooking'. It can be assumed that these are stoves of the portable type to be included here and the revised figure was taken for this year but no deduction was made for industrial use. For earlier years estimates were made by taking the same proportion of the output of gas stoves classified to the *iron foundries trade* as in 1935. (iv) Enamelled signs, hearth-plates, etc., of which half was taken in each year.

Estimates of the output of these items by small firms were added. There are a number of other items which must be bought in part by consumers—bolts and hasps, fire extinguishers, etc.—but it may be expected that these omissions will be compensated for by over-estimates in other items.

Of the items of hardware and hollow-ware recorded in the trade statistics, stoves for cooking, etc., may be assumed to be wholly of cast iron and not relevant here. Cash and deed boxes, etc., and aluminium hollow-ware for domestic purposes are recorded separately. Hollow-ware of iron and steel is recorded under a single heading which distinguishes between materials but not between domestic and industrial use. From the classification adopted in early years it seems probable that mainly domestic hollow-ware is involved. Imports and exports of hollow-ware have been assumed to be wholly domestic. In the same way hardware is not distinguished by use, but in this case it seems more reasonable to assume that both exports and imports are non-domestic.

Brass goods: the only item recorded separately in the output of the *finished brass trade* which can clearly be allotted to final consumption is art metal work. There are also two residual items, other and unspecified finished brass goods, which are likely to contain articles of domestic consumption, although ships' propellers are apparently also included. In each year two-thirds of these items was taken for final consumption. It was assumed that the residual group recorded for 1924 was comparable with these groups. An estimate of the output by small firms was added. Since brass manufactures are for the most part not separately distinguished in the trade statistics, and domestic consumption forms only a small part of total output, it was assumed that any adjustment for imports and exports could be neglected.

Nails, bolts and screws: although the items included here are certainly bought by final consumers, these sales must represent only a small part of the total available for all purposes. In the absence of any precise information all that can be done is to calculate the total supplies of those goods purchased to any extent by final consumers and to take an appropriate proportion in each year. In this case it is thought that purchases for final consumption represented one-eighth of the total and this proportion was taken in all years. The particular items included are as follows. From the *chain, nail, screw, etc., trade* were taken nails (but not rivets or washers), screws, bolts and nuts of iron and steel and other metals. For the items not recorded separately the same proportion of the composite figure was taken as found for later years. An estimate of the output of small firms was added. The output of wire nails by the *wire trade* was also added in each year. From the trade statistics were taken the imports and exports of wire nails, nails and tacks (the same proportions as in 1926 being taken for earlier years when rivets and washers were also included), screws, and bolts and nuts of iron and steel.

Cordage: clearly the greater part of the output of these products will also be used for various industrial and commercial uses. It was assumed that one-tenth of the total available would represent purchases for final consumption in each year. The output of cordage, cables, ropes, twine,

---

[1] See below, Chapter III, §(*f*), p. 31.
[2] See [73] Jefferys, *The Distribution of Consumer Goods*, pp. 279–98.

nets and netting was taken from the *rope, twine and net trade* and an estimate of the output of small firms was added. Imports and exports were taken from the trade statistics.

Woodware: includes horticultural woodwork, domestic woodware and manufactures of cork other than stoppers (i.e. 70%) from the *timber trade*, *plus* 10% for the output of small firms. No information for 1933-4 or 1937 is available for this trade and rough estimates were made for these years. Imports and exports of domestic woodware were taken from the trade statistics.

Tools and implements: includes the following items from the *tool and implement trade* of which only the specified proportions were taken for final consumption: (i) saws, other than hack-saws, one-sixth; (ii) spades and shovels, half; (iii) forks, half; (iv) carpenters' and joiners' tools, not elsewhere specified, half; (v) all light steel implements (corkscrews, tin openers, etc.); and (vi) scissors and secateurs, half, from the *cutlery trade*. An estimate of the output of small firms was added. The figures were adjusted for imports and exports estimated from the trade statistics. The classification for earlier years was in most cases not sufficiently detailed but it was enough for the present purpose to take the same proportion of the combined group as found for later years.

Domestic machinery: includes, from the *mechanical engineering trade*: (i) lawn mowers, hand-driven, complete, adjusted for exports and imports; (ii) wringers and mangles for domestic use, complete; (iii) refrigerating machinery, including electric refrigerators, adjusted for exports and imports and one-fifth taken for final consumption. No information is given for 1924 for these two items and the value was assumed to be the same as in 1930; (iv) sewing machines, complete, *less* one-third for 1934 and earlier years to exclude boot- and shoe-making machinery, and adjusted for exports and imports; (v) garden rollers, so far as recorded separately.

Perambulators, etc.: includes perambulators and mail carts for children, steel folding baby cars, invalid carriages and bath chairs and other vehicles (including wheelbarrows) from the *carriage, cart and wagon trade*, *plus* an estimate of the output of small firms. Imports and exports were taken from the trade statistics. No information is given for 1933-4 and rough estimates were made for these years.

Electrical appliances: includes the following items from the *electrical engineering trade*: (i) vacuum cleaners, complete, adjusted for imports and exports; (ii) electrical heating apparatus for domestic use and electrical cooking apparatus. Imports and exports of both these last two items are only recorded from 1932 onwards. In earlier years one-tenth was deducted to allow for excess of exports over imports; (iii) electric irons, so far as recorded separately.

Electric lamps, fittings and accessories: includes the following items from the *electrical engineering trade*, the proportions specified being taken for final consumption: (i) all electric lamps (other than arc lamps, searchlights, etc.), adjusted for exports and imports; (ii) all bulbs over 20 volts (40% in 1924, falling to 30% in 1935 and subsequent years),[1] *plus* bulbs under 20 volts, other than those used for motor-cars; (iii) batteries, primary, complete, for hand flash lamps and half of other primary batteries, both adjusted for exports and imports; (iv) electric lighting accessories and fittings, adjusted for exports and imports, two-thirds. Also included are: (v) three-quarters of lamps, pendants, electroliers, etc.; (vi) switches, lamp-holders, etc., one-eighth, both from the *finished brass trade*; (vii) globes and shades from the *glass trade*, two-thirds, adjusted for exports and imports; (viii) mantles from the *incandescent mantles trade*, adjusted for exports and imports, half.

On the basis of the data for the six census years, estimates were derived for all other years of the period in the following way. The total figures of home output at factory values were deflated by an index of retail prices for domestic ironmongery and hardware to obtain output at constant prices. For other years of the period these figures were varied with the numbers employed in the principal trades concerned.[2] For this purpose the ratios of output at constant prices to the numbers employed in the census years were interpolated and extrapolated linearly to cover all years of the period. Multiplying by the numbers employed and by the price index gives the factory value of output for all years. Exports, less 10%

of the recorded figure to exclude distribution costs, were deducted and imports, including the duty charged from 1932 onwards, were added.[3] Retail expenditures were obtained by adding distribution costs. Although the same percentage margins were added for the different items throughout the period, the change in the composition of the group resulted in a fall in the average for the whole group from 92 to 89% between 1924 and 1937. Margins for the intervening years were obtained by interpolation.

These estimates, together with the figures for pottery and glassware calculated in the earlier sections, may be compared with an index of the retail sales of these goods for the years 1930-8. Although they are highly correlated and the average level is the same, the sales index shows a smaller amplitude of variation, falling less in 1932 and not rising so sharply in 1937. The reason for this may be the omission of any adjustment for stock changes from the estimates, which if included might be expected to smooth the series. On the other hand, the sample from which the sales index was derived is largely composed of department stores in the London area, multiple shop firms and co-operative stores, and cannot be considered as completely representative of the trade as a whole. It is probable that it does not adequately reflect the expenditure of the lower income groups; that is, those people who are most likely to make their purchases at the small independent local shop. For this reason the sales index would tend to have a bias towards stability. It is likely that this bias in the index is the principal cause of the discrepancy and that the estimated series would be the more reliable. It must be remembered, however, that the absence of any stock adjustment will contribute a systematic error to these figures.

An index of quantity movements for hardware and hollow-ware was derived by dividing through the series of retail expenditures by the index of prices.

3 THE RELIABILITY OF THE ESTIMATES

The methods of estimation for the series presented in this chapter are similar in character and a single discussion of the probable errors involved will be relevant to all of them. The estimates for furniture and furnishings are considered in detail and the other categories are then

---

[1] See [50] Monopolies and Restrictive Practices Commission, *Report on the Supply of Electric Lamps*, 1951, p. 42, footnote.

[2] See [69] Chapman, *Wages and Salaries in the United Kingdom, 1920-1938*, table 44, p. 99. The series used was the number of wage-earners in the 'other metal goods trades', which include the following census trades: tool and implement; cutlery; chain, nail, screw, etc.; wire; hardware and hollow-ware, etc.; and needle, pin, etc.

[3] [8] *Annual Statement of Trade*, vol. I, 1920-38; for duty payments, ibid. vol. II, 1932-8.

treated quite briefly. In each case, however, some indication will be given of the order of magnitude of the total error involved.

The principal sources of error may be divided between those likely to bias the absolute level of the series and those affecting the year-to-year variations; the particular methods of estimation employed make this distinction a useful one in the present instance.

Bias in the series is likely to arise chiefly from the adjustments and approximations involved in the use of the census data. In many cases the classification of products in the census records is not sufficiently detailed for it to be possible to select exactly the goods required by the definition of personal consumption. The error involved is likely to be larger for the earlier part of the period when the census records were less detailed in their classification. The proportions allocated to final consumption are often no more than reasonable guesses, and though crude, it is unlikely that the figures are subject to any persistent bias; the number of items involved will allow for a considerable degree of cancellation of errors in the total.

A further source of bias is to be found in the distribution margins applied to obtain retail values. These figures relate principally to 1938 but, for want of any further information, have been applied unchanged throughout the inter-war period. Any variation in the proportionate value of distribution costs is therefore limited to the small changes in the relative importance of different commodities in the total. It is unlikely that there were any pronounced changes in distribution costs during this period but there may have been a gradual trend movement associated with long-term changes in methods and channels of distribution. It is known that the development of furniture retailing during this period was dominated by the growth of multiple shop firms.[1] These firms gained economies in transport and in buying but incurred higher costs in providing elaborate showrooms and extensive credit facilities. Their success was due more to the attraction of the extra services provided than to any reduction of distributive costs. In view of this it seems not unlikely that the relative importance of distribution costs increased during this period, but the change must have been comparatively small.

It is possible to be more precise in specifying the sources of error affecting the annual variations rather than the absolute level of the series. The variations of expenditure from year to year are largely determined by the independently estimated output and price movements. Output changes are only indirectly known through the changes in employment. Although these two series will not be exactly correlated over time, to a great extent variations in productivity and associated factors will either be directly related to changes in employment or take the form of a regular trend movement. Interpolating between census years introduces a continuous readjustment, to some extent taking account of these other factors. The least reliable figures are likely to be those where it is necessary to extrapolate beyond the census years at the beginning and end of the period. This is especially so for the years before 1924, when the employment figures themselves are much less accurate and the normal relationships are likely to have been disturbed by the problems of the post-war readjustment. The price movements have been corrected in a similar way by adjusting the index derived from the export data and price quotations for furniture to the census average values.

Some direct confirmation of the reliability of the methods used is afforded by the comparison between the expenditure figures obtained from the estimates of output and average values and those derived from the index of retail sales for the years 1931–8. The two series are found to move closely together with some difference of amplitude. A discrepancy of this sort between output and sales is likely to arise when there are significant variations in traders' stocks. It was found that the relation between the two series could be adequately expressed by a simple linear equation, including a trend term, and a regression equation of this form was used to adjust the figures for earlier years to a sales basis. The volume of sales at constant prices was then estimated by dividing through by the price index.

Similar methods were employed for the estimates of the other items given in this chapter. The method used differed slightly, however, in the case of china and glassware, since no index of retail sales was available for these goods, and no check could be made on the price and quantity series obtained. In so far as imports are of much greater importance relative to home supplies, as is the case for glassware, the quantities available in each year are more precisely known. For the two principal groups, furniture and hardware, imports amount to less than 5% of the total supplies available.

It may be concluded that for furniture and furnishings the most serious sources of error relate to the absolute level of the estimates. It is not possible to specify the direction of this bias but an adjustment of up to 10% either way in the level of the expenditure figures would be within reason. The year-to-year variations of the series are more firmly established apart from some doubt as to the amplitude of the movements. The estimates for the years before 1924 are the least reliable.

[1] See [74] Jefferys, *Retail Trading in Britain, 1850–1950* (1954), pp. 420–9.

The two smaller items, pottery and glassware, are much more homogeneous. There is less difficulty in obtaining consistent figures of output from the census records, and the interpolation on the basis of employment figures for other years is evidently more satisfactory. Nothing is known of stock changes, however, and this may give rise to some discrepancy in the year-to-year variations of the series. The price series are similarly more reliable. The high proportion of imports in the total supplies of glassware also increases the reliability of the estimates. A random error of some 5 % would probably cover the greater part of the discrepancy inherent in these figures.

The final item, hardware and hollow-ware, is both large and heterogeneous, and the principal sources of error are very similar to those already enumerated for furniture and furnishings. In this case, however, the question of consumer allocation gives rise to greater difficulties. The census items to be included in personal consumption are less obvious and it is more difficult to distinguish goods as being wholly for final con-sumption or for industrial use. The absolute level of the series is therefore subject to a somewhat wider margin of error.

4 THE MAIN TABLES

The annual estimates derived by the methods described above are given in the following tables. The quantity series are shown in Table 10. For the composite groups of commodities which are dealt with here, no more than indicators of relative quantity movements can be given. The corresponding price series are shown in Table 11, and the actual expenditures in Table 12. Finally, in Table 13, quantity and price series for the principal combined groups are given in a comparable index number form. The quantity series are base-weighted aggregate index numbers and the price series current-weighted aggregates. Their product is thus a simple index of expenditure. Each series has been multiplied through by actual expenditure in 1938 and is shown in this form in the diagrams of §1.

TABLE 10. ESTIMATED QUANTITIES OF FURNITURE, FURNISHINGS AND HOUSEHOLD EQUIPMENT PURCHASED FOR FINAL CONSUMPTION IN THE UNITED KINGDOM, 1920–38

(Index numbers: 1929 = 100·0)

	1920	1921	1922	1923	1924	1925	1926	1927	1928	1929	1930	1931	1932	1933	1934	1935	1936	1937	1938
Furniture and furnishings	61·5	60·2	69·9	74·8	74·7	78·7	83·0	90·7	95·4	100·0	103·3	106·5	114·4	116·1	123·7	128·9	131·5	124·4	114·9
Household textiles	67·9	66·1	75·6	79·8	79·2	82·1	85·7	92·9	96·4	100·0	101·8	104·2	110·7	110·7	116·7	120·2	120·8	113·1	103·0
China and pottery	105·5	81·4	104·1	104·1	103·4	100·7	83·4	99·3	98·6	100·0	95·2	89·7	85·5	91·0	95·9	99·3	94·5	93·8	85·5
Glassware	91·5	63·8	76·6	83·0	91·5	95·7	97·9	97·9	100·0	100·0	106·4	110·6	63·8	91·5	91·5	97·9	97·9	106·4	102·1
Hardware and hollow-ware	102·6	62·7	72·2	79·7	82·1	87·6	87·0	93·4	95·3	100·0	97·6	96·5	95·7	105·8	117·9	128·1	128·0	123·2	108·3

TABLE 11. ESTIMATED AVERAGE PRICES OF FURNITURE, FURNISHINGS AND HOUSEHOLD EQUIPMENT PURCHASED FOR FINAL CONSUMPTION IN THE UNITED KINGDOM, 1920–38

(Index numbers: 1929 = 100·0)

	1920	1921	1922	1923	1924	1925	1926	1927	1928	1929	1930	1931	1932	1933	1934	1935	1936	1937	1938
Furniture and furnishings	157·9	147·8	118·3	108·7	109·0	109·1	104·1	100·5	100·8	100·0	99·0	94·6	85·2	85·4	87·1	87·2	90·5	99·1	103·3
Household textiles	157·9	147·8	118·3	108·7	109·0	109·1	104·1	100·5	100·8	100·0	99·0	94·6	85·2	85·4	87·1	87·2	90·5	99·1	103·3
China and pottery	179·4	162·3	134·8	116·7	108·4	106·5	105·8	106·3	103·2	100·0	97·9	95·3	94·3	92·7	91·9	92·2	95·3	102·1	105·3
Glassware	177·9	171·8	118·5	95·7	90·1	90·7	92·7	95·0	96·2	100·0	95·5	85·9	100·9	91·8	98·7	99·4	95·3	100·0	94·8
Hardware and hollow-ware	221·7	167·3	121·7	109·5	107·1	105·1	103·1	103·1	101·6	100·0	99·4	94·2	91·6	90·9	90·9	90·3	92·6	109·5	116·3

TABLE 12. ESTIMATED EXPENDITURE ON FURNITURE, FURNISHINGS AND HOUSEHOLD EQUIPMENT PURCHASED FOR FINAL CONSUMPTION IN THE UNITED KINGDOM, 1920–38 (£ M.)

	1920	1921	1922	1923	1924	1925	1926	1927	1928	1929	1930	1931	1932	1933	1934	1935	1936	1937	1938
Furniture and furnishings	129·3	118·7	110·3	108·4	108·6	114·6	115·2	121·7	128·3	133·3	136·2	134·4	130·0	132·3	143·6	149·9	158·8	164·4	158·4
Household textiles	17·4	15·8	14·5	14·1	14·0	14·6	14·5	15·2	15·8	16·2	16·4	16·0	15·3	15·4	16·5	17·0	17·8	18·2	17·3
China and pottery	26·1	18·2	19·3	16·8	15·4	14·8	12·2	14·5	14·0	13·8	12·8	11·8	11·1	11·6	12·1	12·6	12·4	13·2	12·4
Glassware	8·0	5·4	4·5	3·9	4·1	4·3	4·5	4·6	4·8	4·9	5·0	4·7	3·2	4·2	4·5	4·8	4·6	5·3	4·8
Hardware and hollow-ware	127·9	58·9	49·4	49·1	49·4	51·8	50·5	54·2	54·4	56·2	54·5	51·1	49·3	54·1	60·3	65·1	66·6	75·9	70·8
Total	308·7	217·0	198·0	192·3	191·5	200·1	196·9	210·2	217·3	224·4	224·9	218·0	208·9	217·6	237·0	249·4	260·2	277·0	263·7

TABLE 13. INDEX NUMBERS OF QUANTITY AND AVERAGE PRICE FOR FURNITURE, FURNISHINGS AND HOUSEHOLD EQUIPMENT PURCHASED FOR FINAL CONSUMPTION IN THE UNITED KINGDOM, 1920–38

(Expenditure in 1938 is taken as the base for each series)

	1920	1921	1922	1923	1924	1925	1926	1927	1928	1929	1930	1931	1932	1933	1934	1935	1936	1937	1938
Furniture and soft furnishings																			
Quantity index	96·1	94·1	109·0	116·5	116·3	122·3	128·8	140·6	147·6	154·6	159·5	164·3	176·2	178·6	190·0	197·8	201·5	190·4	175·7
Price index	268·2	251·1	201·2	184·7	185·2	185·6	176·9	171·1	171·5	169·9	168·1	160·8	144·9	145·3	148·0	148·3	154·0	168·5	175·7
Pottery and glassware																			
Quantity index	19·6	14·8	18·7	19·0	19·3	19·1	16·7	19·0	19·0	19·2	18·8	18·2	15·4	17·5	18·2	19·0	18·3	18·6	17·2
Price index	29·9	27·4	21·9	18·7	17·4	17·2	17·2	17·3	17·0	16·8	16·3	15·6	16·0	15·5	15·7	15·8	16·0	17·1	17·2
Hardware and hollow-ware																			
Quantity index	67·1	41·0	47·2	52·1	53·7	57·3	56·9	61·1	62·3	65·4	63·8	63·1	62·6	69·2	77·1	83·8	83·7	80·6	70·8
Price index	135·0	101·7	74·1	66·7	65·1	64·0	62·8	62·8	61·8	60·8	60·5	57·3	55·8	55·4	55·4	55·0	56·3	66·7	70·8
Total																			
Quantity index	182·8	149·9	174·9	187·6	189·3	198·7	202·4	220·7	228·9	239·2	242·1	245·6	254·2	265·3	285·3	300·6	303·5	289·6	263·7
Price index	445·3	381·7	298·5	270·3	266·8	265·5	256·5	251·1	250·3	247·4	245·0	234·1	216·7	216·3	219·1	218·8	226·1	252·2	263·7

CHAPTER III

HOUSEHOLD OPERATION

1 GENERAL REMARKS

The goods and services discussed in this chapter represent, for the most part, miscellaneous running expenses which are incurred by households in addition to the basic requirements of heat, light and shelter. Together they amount to some 7 % of total personal expenditure and in all years account for a larger outlay than the purchase of household durable goods. The largest single item, more than half of the total, is expenditure on domestic service. In 1938 this item accounted for £176 m. out of a total for the group of £311 m. Next in importance were laundry services, £33 m., and expenditure on soap, £30 m. The other items included are: polishes and similar cleaning materials, £14 m.; matches, £10 m.; and a group of miscellaneous services including repairs of all kinds, furniture storage and removals, £55 m.

Expenditure on domestic service was at its highest level for the period in 1920, when it amounted to £194·2 m. By 1923 it had fallen to £139·0 m. It continued a little above this level until 1934, when it began to rise again, reaching a level £175·9 m. by 1938. The numbers employed in domestic service, of whom 80 % were women, probably increased by a third during the period. As far as the evidence goes it would appear that there was no decline in the relative importance of domestic service as an item of personal consumption during the inter-war period. Since then the position has changed radically. By 1955 the volume of domestic service was less than one-third of the 1938 level, and the decline has persisted throughout the post-war years. It may be noted that the definition of domestic service adopted here is fairly wide, including outdoor workers such as gardeners and chauffeurs as well as all those employed within the house.

The results of the family budget inquiries for 1937–9 show that while less than 10 % of the working-class families were found to employ any domestic help, for which they paid on an average just over 2s. per week, more than half the middle-class families did so and paid on the average more than 6s. 6d. per week. In the richest of the middle-class income groups—households with an average expenditure of over £800 a year—more than 80 % employed domestic help and paid on the average

more than 12s. per week.[1] These figures do not include the value of payments in kind, for which an allowance is made in the estimates of expenditure given below, and it seems probable that the budget returns cover domestic service in the narrowest sense only.

Expenditure on laundry and dry cleaning services was rising in most years of the period; the total amount paid increased by over half between 1920 and 1938. The variation in the prices of these services during this period is not known but it seems likely that there was at least a comparable rise in the volume of services rendered. The use of laundry services was much more widely spread through all classes of the community than was the case with the employment of domestic help, as is evident from the results of the family budget inquiries.[2] It was found that a half of all working-class households in the sample recorded some payment for laundry services during the inquiry, while for middle-class households the proportion was three-quarters. Expenditure elasticities calculated from these data were found to be as high as 2·0 for the working class and just over unity for the middle class.

Expenditure on soap represented approximately one-tenth of this group of household expenses, the proportion tending to fall slightly during the period. Expenditure fell from £39·3 m. in 1920 to £27·9 m. in 1923, rose slightly in subsequent years but again declined during the depression of the 'thirties, to £25·3 m. in 1933. By the end of the period expenditure had again risen to £29·9 m. The quantity of soap purchased increased by more than one-third. Less than 10 % of the total quantity was toilet soap, the rest being various forms of household soap. Ordinary hard or washing soap accounted for two-thirds of the total quantity in the earlier years but by 1938 was less than half. On the other hand there had been a marked increase in the purchase of soap powders and flakes, which rose from 15 % of the total to almost 40 %.

---

[1] See **[86]** S. J. Prais and H. S. Houthakker, *The Analysis of Family Budgets*, University of Cambridge Department of Applied Economics, Monographs, 4 (Cambridge University Press, 1955), p. 348. For the present purpose the average expenditures have been calculated only for those families who recorded any expenditure on domestic service.
[2] See **[86]** Prais and Houthakker, *The Analysis of Family Budgets*, p. 347.

HOUSEHOLD OPERATION

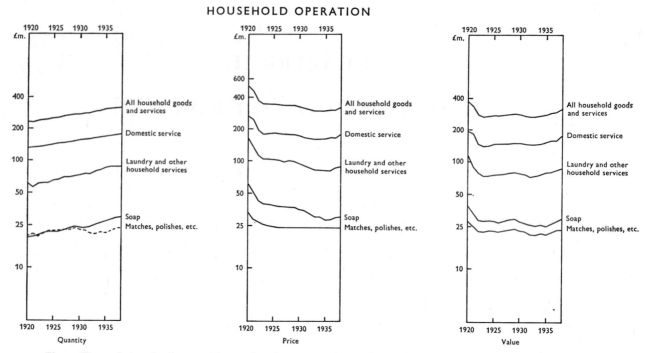

Fig. 3. The variations in the quantities purchased, average prices and expenditure on household goods and services for final consumption in the United Kingdom, 1920–38.

No details are available to make an independent estimate of expenditure on polishes and other cleaning materials during this period. However, it is apparent from the family budget data that this item amounted to approximately one-half of the household expenditure on soap.

The quantity of matches bought varied only slightly during the period and betrays no particular trend. The price shows only a slight downward trend, the fall being less than 10 % over the whole period. This all but constant price implies, however, a quite considerable rise in the relative price of matches compared with the average price level for all commodities. It must not be assumed, therefore, that the stable consumption of this period is an indication of demand at saturation level and inelastic in response to price and income changes. It may be that the price and income effects, working in opposite directions, have tended to cancel out. Consumers' expenditure on matches has remained close to an average level of £10 m. throughout the period.

The final group of miscellaneous services is of considerable importance, accounting for between 15 and 20 % of household expenses, but very little is known about any of the items individually. It is estimated that one-tenth of the total represents expenditure on furniture repairs, dealers' margins on second-hand purchases, the costs of storage and removals. A further fifth represents clothing alterations, second-hand purchases and repairs. The repair of boots and shoes is a much larger item and

accounts for nearly three-fifths of the total, an amount equivalent to more than 40 % of the value of purchases of new footwear. The remaining fraction accounts for repairs to hardware, jewellery, sports and travel goods, together with a group of minor household services.

2 METHODS OF ESTIMATION

Scope of the estimates. The estimates discussed in this chapter relate to goods and services which may be described as running costs incurred in the maintenance of households. Like household durable goods they may be said to provide a utility common to the family as a whole. This definition, however, has not been strictly adhered to. It is transgressed by the inclusion within the personal sector of the vicarious consumption of non-profit-making bodies and by the piecemeal treatment of the composite service provided by restaurants and hotels. In this connexion it may be noted that no part of the service element of hotels is included in the estimates of domestic service given in this chapter, which are concerned only with servants in private households.

For second-hand purchases only the dealers' gross margin is included in the estimates of expenditure given here. The remaining part of the cost must be set off against the receipts from sales by persons and so constitutes only a transfer within the personal sector.

It is not possible to make detailed adjustments to exclude purchases by tourists and other non-residents.

Similarly expenditure abroad by United Kingdom residents is not included. Estimates of the net balance for all items on these accounts are given in Chapter X.

General procedure. The Customs and Excise returns provide comprehensive information on the quantities of matches entered for home consumption and an index of price changes was available.

The basic material for the soap estimates was supplied by experts in the trade. Data on domestic consumption and retail prices of various kinds of soap for five base years were extended to cover all years by the use of estimates of total consumption and an index of soap prices. The figures of the different varieties were then combined to form estimates of the total value of the domestic consumption of soap.

For the service items, which were derived largely from figures of the numbers employed and average earnings, estimates of expenditure only are given.

Methods employed. The methods of estimation are discussed below in the following order:

(*a*) Domestic service.
(*b*) Matches.
(*c*) Soap.
(*d*) Polishes and other cleaning materials.
(*e*) Laundry, cleaning and dyeing services.
(*f*) Other household services.

(A) DOMESTIC SERVICE

Estimates of expenditure on domestic servants in private households have been made by Chapman.[1] Those estimates are simply reproduced here and reference should be made to the original source for full details of the methods employed.

The figures relate to 'indoor and outdoor domestic servants whether resident on their employers' premises or not, and a small proportion of persons in other occupational categories such as teachers (presumably governesses) and clerical workers' employed in private households. The numbers employed were estimated from Census of Population data for 1921 and 1931, assuming a straight-line trend throughout the period. The average earnings of salaried workers and of wage-earners were separately estimated, including an allowance for the value of income received in kind.

(B) MATCHES

Throughout the period under review matches were subject to customs and excise duty and both home output retained and imports entered for home consumption are recorded annually.[2] In 1927 the basis of taxation was altered from the match to the container and the returns distinguish between containers with not more than twenty matches and containers with more than twenty

matches. It was assumed that the average contents of the former was twenty matches, and of the latter fifty matches. Any difference between safety and other types of matches was ignored.

The average price of a single box of fifty matches over the whole of the period was 1*d.*, but there were some slight variations in the price per dozen boxes from 10½*d.* to 11*d.*[3] There were also a few makes of dearer matches. A representative index of the retail price of matches in this period indicates some small annual variations in the average price. It was assumed for the present purpose that the average price for the period as a whole was 1*d.* per box of fifty matches, and on this basis the yearly prices were calculated from the index.

A deduction of 10 % in each year was made to exclude business consumption.

(C) SOAP

This item includes domestic expenditure on soap and soap products of all kinds.

Estimates were available for the years 1924, 1930, 1934, 1935 and 1938 of total consumption, domestic consumption and retail prices in Great Britain and Northern Ireland of various types of soap and soap products, namely hard, soft and toilet soap, powders, flakes, scourers, and all other types including shaving soap.[4] In addition estimates were supplied of the total consumption of soap in the British Isles (including Eire) for the years 1922–38 with a rough estimate for 1921. On the basis of these figures, 1920 could also be roughly estimated.

From the two estimates of total consumption in the five base years, total consumption in Eire in these years was estimated. The figures for intervening years were obtained by linear interpolation, the rate of change between 1924 and 1930 being carried back to 1920. These estimates of consumption in Eire were deducted from those for the British Isles to give total consumption in Great Britain and Northern Ireland.

The figures for total and domestic consumption were used to obtain non-domestic consumption in the five years mentioned above. Proceeding as for Eire, non-domestic consumption was interpolated linearly to obtain estimates of the domestic consumption of soap in all the years 1920 to 1938. The quantities of domestic consumption of the different categories of soap for the five

[1] See [**69**] Chapman, *Wages and Salaries in the United Kingdom, 1920–1938*, pp. 215–18.
[2] See [**1**] *Trade and Navigation Accounts*; for example, January 1939, account v, p. 172 and account vii, p. 179. Before 1 April 1923 the consumption of home-produced matches in Northern Ireland was assumed to be 1·7 % of the Great Britain figure, the average proportion in 1924–6. No adjustment was made to the import figures.
[3] Information supplied by the trade.
[4] Information supplied by Lever Brothers and Unilever Ltd.

base years were found as percentages of total domestic consumption. These percentages were interpolated linearly for each variety of soap, carrying the 1924–30 rate of change back to 1920, to estimate the domestic consumption of the different varieties for each year of the period.

To interpolate the prices given for these five years an index of soap prices for the years 1920–38 was used for several of the varieties. This index only refers to hard soap. The interpolation was done in the following way.

Hard soap. For each of the periods 1924–30, 1930–4, and 1935–8 the ratio of the base year prices to the index mentioned above was interpolated linearly. For years before 1924 the price was varied in proportion to the index.

Soft soap. Since the price was 1*d.* per lb. higher than that of hard soap in each of the five base years, this relationship was assumed to hold throughout the period 1924–38. Before 1924 the price was varied in proportion to the index.

Toilet soap. Since the price estimates for 1934, 1935 and 1938 are the same, the price was assumed constant from 1934 to 1938. For earlier years the method described above for hard soap was used.

Powders. The method described for toilet soap was used.

Flakes. The slight rise in price between 1935 and 1938 was assumed to have taken place between 1936 and 1937 in view of the increase in the index then. For earlier years the method described for hard soap was followed.

Scourers. Since the price given in all five base years is the same, the price was assumed constant from 1924 at 4¾*d.* per lb. For years before 1924 it was assumed that the price was falling at the rate of ¼*d.* per year.

Other types including shaving soaps. The price being the same in all five base years, it was assumed constant at 5*s.* per lb. from 1924 to 1938 and was assumed to be falling at the rate of 3*d.* per year before 1924.

From the quantities and prices of the different varieties the total value of personal consumption of soap was calculated.

(D) POLISHES AND OTHER CLEANING MATERIALS

Apart from the soaps and scourers discussed in the preceding section, there are numerous other polishes and cleaning materials used by the housewife and all these are included here. For lack of data the estimate is no more than an indication of the order of magnitude with a rough statement of the trend through the period.

Their relative importance may be judged from the results of the family budget inquiries of 1937–9.[1] It was found that the average weekly expenditure on soap and on soda, polishes and cleaning materials varied as follows for families in different social classes:

	Soap	Soda, polishes and cleaning materials
Working class:		
Agricultural	7¾*d.*	3½*d.*
Industrial	9¼*d.*	4¼*d.*
Middle class	1*s.* 0½*d.*	5¾*d.*

If these figures are roughly weighted by the proportions of the population represented by each class,[2] the corresponding total annual expenditure on soap is found to be £27·8 m., while for soda, polishes and cleaning materials it is £12·9 m. In the preceding section of this chapter, total personal expenditure on soap in 1938 was estimated to be £29·9 m. Taking account of the approximate nature of the weighting, the agreement between the two figures is reasonably close. It may be assumed that the figure for soda, polishes and cleaning materials—a closely similar item of general, regular consumption—is at least as reliable. It also seems reasonable to assume that expenditure in other years would bear a similar relation to expenditure on soap. Accordingly this same proportion, 46 %, of estimated expenditure on soap has been taken for all years.

As a price series for this item, a representative index of soda prices was used.

(E) LAUNDRY, CLEANING AND DYEING SERVICES

This item includes all expenditure by private persons, non-profit-making bodies and hotels for laundry services, dry cleaning and dyeing, carpet beating, etc.

The output of establishments in the laundry, cleaning and dyeing trades was recorded by the Census of Production in 1924, but not in subsequent years.[3] It has been possible, however, to obtain a series of estimates of gross output per worker in the years 1926, 1929 and 1931–8 for a sample of laundries.[4] A comparable figure for 1924 can be calculated from the census data. Comparison of the figures for 1924 and 1926 suggests that the sample figures are obtained as a ratio of total gross output to the number of operatives, not to the total number of

[1] See [62] *Ministry of Labour Gazette*, December 1940 and February 1941, and [80] Massey, 'The expenditure of 1360 British middle-class households in 1938–39'. *J. R. Statist. Soc.* CV (1942), part III, p. 159.
[2] See Vol. I of this study, p. 168.
[3] [30] *Census of Production, 1924* (Third), 'Food, drink and tobacco trades etc.', pp. 339–48.
[4] This information was supplied by the trade for the purpose of this inquiry.

employees including salaried staff. Accordingly the level of gross output per head in other years of the period was roughly estimated on the basis of average annual earnings of wage-earners.[1] Total gross output was calculated by multiplying by the number of wage-earners employed in each year.[2]

A check on these figures could be obtained from the family budget data for 1937–9, which give the average weekly payments for laundry service (not dyeing or dry cleaning, which are included with clothing repairs) by agricultural, industrial working-class and middle-class families. Taking a weighted average of these figures, annual expenditure by all households is estimated to be approximately £23·4 m. In 1924, the only year for which details are available, the total output for large firms recorded by the Census was £21·1 m., of which £16·8 m. represented laundry work. It may be assumed that work done for clients other than households accounted for 10 % of the total, and that, apart from some carpet beating, this was entirely laundry work. On this assumption household laundry expenditure would be £14·8 m., or 70 % of the total. The figure calculated from the budgets represents 69 % of the estimated total expenditure in 1937–8. This indicates that at least the order of magnitude of the estimates is correct and suggests that, although total expenditure increased by 50 % during this period, there was little change in the ratio of laundry to cleaning and dyeing expenses.

It is not necessary to deduct the whole of non-household expenditure for the present purposes, since expenditure by hotels and various non-profit-making institutions, in particular voluntary hospitals, is included with personal expenditure. Accordingly the total figures were reduced by only 5 % throughout the period.

A price series for laundry services was constructed by combining the index of average earnings with series of coal and soap prices. The weights used (70:15:15) were based on the census returns.

(F) OTHER HOUSEHOLD SERVICES

This final section covers a miscellany of household services which can be conveniently grouped together. Only very rough estimates of expenditure can be made for each of the items involved, but it is hoped that the total will at least be of the right order of magnitude and represent the general trend throughout the period. The services included are: clothing alterations, second-hand purchases and repairs; footwear repairs; furniture repairs, second-hand purchases, removals and storage; miscellaneous repairs to hardware, jewellery, etc., sports and travel goods; and sundry other household services such as those of chimney sweeps, window cleaners, plumbers, etc.

The most important of these items is expenditure on boot and shoe repairs. No direct information is available about this item but an order of magnitude can be established from family budget data. In 1937–9 household expenditure on boot and shoe repairs amounted to 40–50 % of new purchases.[3] This is equivalent to a total expenditure of £30 m. in 1930. The most reasonable assumption for other years is that expenditure on repairs varied proportionally with the value of new purchases. Accordingly the 1938 figure has been varied throughout the period with the estimated expenditure on leather footwear.[4]

Expenditure on clothing repairs is a very much smaller item but an allowance for second-hand purchases is here of some importance. It may be guessed that the gross value of second-hand purchases would probably be some 10 % of apparel sales, or £35 m. say, in 1938. Of this total the dealers' gross margin would represent one-third,[5] that is £12 m. in 1938. For other years this figure was simply varied proportionally with expenditure on apparel.

A sample survey for 1948–9 indicates that at that period expenditure on furniture removals and storage amounted to approximately 2s. 6d. per person per year;[6] that is, a total expenditure of about £6¼ m. Further, the recorded sales of second-hand furniture dealers in 1950 were of the order of £5 m.; the gross margin being one-third of this figure.[7] It is known that sales of second-hand furniture increased very considerably during the war years but it seems probable that they would be falling off by 1950. These recorded sales, moreover, do not cover all second-hand furniture dealing. In view of this it seems reasonable to put the total value of furniture removals, repairs, and the margin on second-hand purchases at a figure of £5 m. in 1938. This same figure has also been taken for all other years of the period.

There are various other smaller items of repair work for which some estimate of expenditure must be included here. It is only possible to make a guess at the amounts involved relative to other expenditures. The figures adopted for 1938 are: £2 m. for repairs to jewellery and

---

[1] See [69] Chapman, *Wages and Salaries in the United Kingdom, 1920–1938*, table 83, p. 215.

[2] Ibid.

[3] Because of the evident bias in budget records of clothing expenditure the absolute value cannot be satisfactorily determined from this source. The ratio of repairs to new purchases is likely to be more reliable. In this connexion see [86] Prais and Houthakker, *The Analysis of Family Budgets* (1955), pp. 40–1.

[4] See p. 13 above. Expenditure on rubber footwear may be ignored for this purpose since the value of repairs to rubber boots and shoes must have been proportionately very small.

[5] See [36] *Census of Distribution* (1950), part II.

[6] [55] The Social Survey, *Expenditure on Repairs etc.*, n.s. 704/3 (1950).

[7] See [36] *Census of Distribution* (1950), part II.

other personal effects; £2 m. for repairs to hardware, gas and electrical appliances; and £1 m. for repairs to sports and travel goods. For other years of the period these figures were simply varied proportionately with total expenditure on new purchases in the corresponding groups.

Finally, there are the numerous other minor household services; for example, the services of chimney sweeps, window cleaners, plumbers, itinerant knife-grinders and others. It may be noted that the value of many household services, such as those of charwomen, gardeners, chauffeurs, etc., has already been included in the estimates for domestic service.[1] Again there is practically no information on which to base an estimate and it is only possible to suggest the appropriate order of magnitude with some indication of the probable trend. It has been assumed that expenditure in 1938 was of the order of £3 m., and for other years of the period this figure was varied proportionately with the level of expenditure on domestic service.

3 THE RELIABILITY OF THE ESTIMATES

It is evident that the broad level of expenditure on domestic service can be no more than approximately determined by the method employed here of combining the census figures of the numbers engaged and a series of estimated average earnings. Nor will any greater degree of accuracy obtain for the year-to-year variations, since it has been necessary to assume a simple trend through the period in the estimate of numbers employed; though it may be doubted whether this series would be likely to show any very marked short-term variation. It is probable that the resulting series involves a proportionate standard error of the order of 20 %.[2]

The estimates for the consumption of matches are derived from the tax statistics, figures that have a high degree of accuracy. But nothing precise is known of the allocation of purchases between business users and final consumers and the assumption of a constant proportion for all years will inevitably introduce some error into the estimates. The average level of prices is also open to some doubt. While the modal price remained at 1d. per box of fifty matches throughout the whole period, the mean price may well have been anywhere within 10 % of this figure. On both counts the error is likely to bias the estimates of expenditure through the period. It is unlikely, however, that this bias exceeds £1 m. in any year.

In the five years for which detailed information is available, the estimates of the total quantity of soap for domestic use are based on the total trade with a fairly steady and reliable allowance for Irish and non-domestic consumption; they are believed to be reasonably accurate. The breakdown into different types in intermediate years gives scope for more error, but the additional margin of error should not amount to more than 1 or 2 %. Any such errors will be reflected in the estimates of total value because of the wide range of prices for the different varieties of soap. In spite of this, the margin of error in total value, due to inaccuracies in the quantity estimates, which are random rather than systematic, may be placed at about 2–3 %. Since the price index used in interpolation is one for hard soap, the error involved in pricing hard soap, which is the most important type of soap, should not be great. The prices for soft soap and toilet soap should have about the same degree of accuracy. The prices for the remaining varieties may be less accurate. For the influence of prices on total value the margin of error may be as much as 5 %. These remarks relate to the additional error introduced by the manipulations described above and do not include an allowance for the margin of error in the basic material. Finally, it must be remembered that the errors involved in these estimates are likely to be the greater the further they are removed in time from one of the five base years. The errors before 1924, when estimates had to be obtained by extrapolation, are likely to be greater than those for the later years when interpolation was used.

The estimates for laundry and dry cleaning are derived largely from output data, though the average level of expenditure is broadly confirmed by information from family budgets. In spite of the broad agreement shown between the two sources of information, it is likely that a margin of error of at least 10 % must be attributed to the figures in most years. The figures are less reliable for the earlier years, when the sample data are not available and gross output has had to be estimated on the basis of average earnings.

Expenditures on the other two subgroups discussed in this chapter—polishes and other cleaning materials, and miscellaneous household services—have been no more than roughly estimated. The only claim that can be made for these figures is that to have omitted them would have introduced an evident downward bias into the estimates. They are based upon little information, some of it contradictory, and the degree of error is certain to be large. Nevertheless, these estimates will not contribute more than a relatively small component of random error to the estimate of total expenditure.

---

[1] See § (a) above.
[2] See [69] Chapman, *Wages and Salaries in the United Kingdom, 1920–1938*, p. 233.

4 THE MAIN TABLES

The annual estimates obtained by the methods described in the earlier sections of this chapter are given in the following tables. Quantity series are shown in Table 14. While an absolute quantity measure is available for some items, for other composite groups only an indicator of relative quantity movements can be given. The corresponding price series are shown in Table 15, and the actual expenditures in Table 16. Finally, in Table 17, quantity and price series for each item or group of items are provided in a comparable index number form. The quantity series are base-weighted aggregate index numbers and the price series current-weighted aggregates. The product of these series is thus a simple index of expenditure. Each series has been multiplied through by actual expenditure in 1938 and is shown in this form in the diagrams of §1.

TABLE 14. ESTIMATED QUANTITIES OF HOUSEHOLD GOODS AND SERVICES PURCHASED FOR FINAL CONSUMPTION IN THE UNITED KINGDOM, 1920–38

	1920	1921	1922	1923	1924	1925	1926	1927	1928	1929	1930	1931	1932	1933	1934	1935	1936	1937	1938
Domestic service (ooo's employed)	1,256	1,267	1,291	1,315	1,341	1,365	1,389	1,415	1,439	1,464	1,489	1,513	1,538	1,562	1,586	1,610	1,635	1,659	1,683
Matches (million boxes)																			
Home-produced	1,557	1,498	1,341	1,278	1,295	1,207	1,100	994	1,085	1,156	1,191	1,213	1,251	1,218	1,233	1,237	1,227	1,229	1,216
Imported	679	722	817	930	1,010	1,161	1,378	1,423	1,260	1,255	1,250	1,238	980	1,041	1,053	1,092	1,156	1,179	1,138
Total	2,236	2,220	2,158	2,208	2,305	2,368	2,478	2,417	2,345	2,411	2,441	2,451	2,231	2,259	2,286	2,329	2,383	2,408	2,354
Soap (ooo's tons)																			
Hard	213·4	214·2	215·6	222·4	223·5	218·6	212·5	214·2	218·3	220·9	209·2	200·3	196·5	198·3	196·9	199·3	197·1	193·5	187·7
Soft	0·8	1·4	2·0	2·7	3·3	3·9	4·4	5·1	5·8	6·6	7·0	7·0	7·2	7·7	8·1	8·4	8·1	7·8	7·4
Toilet	22·6	22·2	21·8	21·9	21·5	20·5	19·3	18·9	18·6	18·2	16·6	18·9	21·7	25·4	29·0	29·8	31·4	32·9	34·1
Powders	40·9	42·7	44·6	47·7	49·7	50·3	50·7	52·9	55·8	58·5	57·3	62·9	70·4	80·5	90·4	95·0	102·2	109·2	115·2
Flakes	5·0	6·9	8·8	11·0	13·1	14·9	16·5	18·8	21·3	23·9	24·8	25·5	26·8	29·0	30·9	32·8	37·4	41·9	46·2
Scourers	18·7	18·6	18·7	19·1	19·1	18·6	18·0	18·0	18·2	18·3	17·2	18·0	19·4	21·4	23·3	23·9	24·5	25·0	25·3
Shaving and others	2·3	2·7	3·2	3·7	4·2	4·6	5·0	5·5	6·1	6·7	6·9	5·9	5·1	4·4	3·5	3·6	3·7	3·7	3·7
Total	303·7	308·7	314·7	328·5	334·4	331·4	326·4	333·4	344·1	353·1	339·0	338·5	347·1	366·7	382·1	392·8	404·4	414·0	419·6
Polishes and other cleaning materials (1929 = 100·0)	78·1	84·7	79·6	86·1	92·0	91·2	89·1	93·4	96·4	100·0	93·4	91·2	88·3	85·4	89·8	85·4	91·2	97·8	102·2
Laundry, cleaning and dyeing services (1929 = 100·0)	69·0	66·7	70·0	73·9	76·6	80·9	84·3	89·6	95·0	100·0	105·9	109·3	110·8	118·6	128·1	139·1	137·1	135·3	133·9
Other household services (1929 = 100·0)	94·3	85·5	93·1	92·9	93·1	95·4	96·0	100·0	97·9	100·0	99·4	101·0	100·0	105·5	105·9	110·7	113·8	114·9	115·3

TABLE 15. ESTIMATED AVERAGE PRICES OF HOUSEHOLD GOODS AND SERVICES PURCHASED FOR FINAL CONSUMPTION IN THE UNITED KINGDOM, 1920–38

	1920	1921	1922	1923	1924	1925	1926	1927	1928	1929	1930	1931	1932	1933	1934	1935	1936	1937	1938
Domestic service (average earnings, £'s per year)	154·6	145·6	114·0	105·7	107·0	108·1	107·2	105·5	104·3	103·5	101·6	98·1	96·1	94·4	94·7	95·7	98·2	97·2	104·5
Matches (d. per dozen boxes)	12·65	12·73	12·47	12·28	12·07	11·75	11·30	11·68	12·03	12·03	11·96	11·89	11·91	11·92	11·95	11·91	11·81	11·82	11·89
Soap (d. per lb.)																			
Hard	10·7	8·6	7·1	6·5	6·5	6·4	6·3	6·3	6·3	6·3	6·0	5·9	5·4	5·0	5·0	4·0	4·1	4·8	5·0
Soft	12·3	9·9	8·2	7·5	7·5	7·4	7·3	7·3	7·3	7·3	7·0	6·9	6·4	6·0	6·0	5·0	5·1	5·8	6·0
Toilet	36·5	29·4	24·2	22·4	22·3	22·2	21·9	22·3	22·4	22·6	21·8	20·0	17·2	14·8	13·8	13·8	13·8	13·8	13·8
Powders	17·0	13·8	11·3	10·5	10·4	10·2	10·0	10·1	10·0	10·0	9·6	9·5	9·0	8·5	8·7	8·7	8·7	8·7	8·7
Flakes	27·5	22·2	18·3	16·9	16·8	15·6	14·3	13·4	12·3	11·3	9·8	9·8	9·1	8·6	8·8	8·8	8·8	8·8	8·8
Scourers	5·75	5·50	5·25	5·00	4·75	4·75	4·75	4·75	4·75	4·75	4·75	4·75	4·75	4·75	4·75	4·75	4·75	4·75	4·75
Shaving and others	72·0	69·0	66·0	63·0	60·0	60·0	60·0	60·0	60·0	60·0	60·0	60·0	60·0	60·0	60·0	60·0	60·0	60·0	60·0
Polishes and other cleaning materials (1929 = 100·0)	169·8	131·2	120·3	108·3	104·2	103·1	102·1	101·0	100·5	100·0	99·5	99·0	98·4	99·0	98·4	97·9	97·9	98·4	98·4
Laundry, cleaning and dyeing services (1929 = 100·0)	124·0	131·7	108·3	102·3	103·0	102·5	102·5	100·5	99·8	100·0	99·5	96·9	94·8	92·7	91·5	89·5	90·4	92·7	97·2
Other household services (1929 = 100·0)	175·2	140·6	114·4	105·3	104·0	103·0	101·2	98·2	102·1	100·0	94·7	88·4	82·8	79·4	79·1	79·4	78·5	83·2	85·2

TABLE 16. ESTIMATED EXPENDITURE ON HOUSEHOLD GOODS AND SERVICES PURCHASED FOR FINAL CONSUMPTION IN THE UNITED KINGDOM, 1920–38 (£ M.)

	1920	1921	1922	1923	1924	1925	1926	1927	1928	1929	1930	1931	1932	1933	1934	1935	1936	1937	1938
Domestic service	194·2	184·4	147·2	139·0	143·5	147·6	148·9	149·3	150·1	151·5	151·3	148·5	147·7	147·5	150·2	154·1	160·5	161·3	175·9
Matches	9·8	9·8	9·3	9·4	9·7	9·7	9·7	9·8	9·8	10·1	10·1	10·1	9·2	9·3	9·5	9·6	9·8	9·9	9·7
Soap																			
Hard	21·2	17·2	14·2	13·6	13·6	13·1	12·4	12·6	12·8	12·9	11·7	11·0	9·9	9·3	9·2	7·4	7·5	8·6	8·8
Soft	0·1	0·1	0·2	0·2	0·2	0·3	0·3	0·3	0·4	0·4	0·5	0·4	0·4	0·4	0·5	0·4	0·4	0·4	0·4
Toilet	7·7	6·1	4·9	4·6	4·5	4·2	3·9	3·9	3·9	3·8	3·4	3·5	3·5	3·5	3·7	3·8	4·0	4·2	4·4
Powders	6·5	5·5	4·7	4·7	4·8	4·8	4·7	5·0	5·2	5·5	5·1	5·6	5·9	6·4	7·3	7·7	8·3	8·8	9·3
Flakes	1·3	1·4	1·5	1·7	2·1	2·2	2·2	2·3	2·4	2·5	2·3	2·3	2·3	2·3	2·5	2·7	3·1	3·4	3·8
Scourers	1·0	1·0	0·9	0·9	0·8	0·8	0·8	0·8	0·8	0·8	0·8	0·8	0·9	0·9	1·0	1·1	1·1	1·1	1·1
Shaving and others	1·5	1·8	2·0	2·2	2·4	2·6	2·8	3·1	3·4	3·8	3·9	3·3	2·9	2·5	2·0	2·0	2·1	2·1	2·1
Total	39·3	33·1	28·4	27·9	28·4	28·0	27·1	28·0	28·9	29·7	27·7	26·9	25·8	25·3	26·2	25·1	26·5	28·6	29·9
Polishes and other cleaning materials	18·1	15·2	13·1	12·8	13·1	12·9	12·5	12·9	13·3	13·7	12·7	12·4	11·9	11·6	12·1	11·5	12·2	13·2	13·8
Laundry, cleaning and dyeing services	21·4	22·0	19·0	18·9	19·8	20·8	21·6	22·6	23·7	25·0	26·4	26·5	26·3	27·5	29·4	31·2	31·1	31·4	32·6
Other household services																			
Footwear repairs	55·9	42·0	37·1	33·3	32·5	32·5	32·4	32·6	33·3	32·9	30·2	28·4	25·7	26·1	25·5	27·0	27·1	29·2	30·0
Second-hand clothing and repairs	21·3	12·5	11·2	10·7	11·0	11·5	11·0	11·2	11·5	11·7	11·2	10·6	9·8	9·8	10·0	10·5	10·9	11·6	12·0
Second-hand furniture and removals	5·0	5·0	5·0	5·0	5·0	5·0	5·0	5·0	5·0	5·0	5·0	5·0	5·0	5·0	5·0	5·0	5·0	5·0	5·0
Other repairs	7·0	4·7	3·8	3·4	3·3	3·5	3·5	3·6	3·6	3·8	3·7	3·5	3·3	3·5	3·8	4·1	4·3	4·9	5·0
Miscellaneous household services	3·3	3·1	2·5	2·4	2·4	2·5	2·5	2·5	2·6	2·6	2·6	2·5	2·5	2·5	2·6	2·6	2·7	2·8	3·0
Total	92·5	67·3	59·6	54·8	54·2	55·0	54·4	54·9	56·0	56·0	52·7	50·0	46·3	46·9	46·9	49·2	50·0	53·5	55·0
All goods and services	375·3	331·8	276·6	262·8	268·7	274·0	274·2	277·5	281·8	286·0	280·9	274·4	267·2	268·1	274·3	280·7	290·1	297·9	316·9

TABLE 17. INDEX NUMBERS OF QUANTITIES AND AVERAGE PRICES FOR HOUSEHOLD GOODS AND SERVICES PURCHASED FOR FINAL CONSUMPTION IN THE UNITED KINGDOM, 1920–38

(Expenditure in 1938 is taken as the base for each series)

	1920	1921	1922	1923	1924	1925	1926	1927	1928	1929	1930	1931	1932	1933	1934	1935	1936	1937	1938
Domestic service																			
Quantity index	131·3	132·4	134·9	137·4	140·1	142·6	145·2	147·9	150·4	153·0	155·6	158·1	160·7	163·2	165·7	168·2	170·9	173·4	175·9
Price index	260·2	245·0	191·9	177·9	180·2	182·1	180·4	177·6	175·5	174·2	171·0	165·2	161·7	159·0	159·5	161·2	165·2	163·6	175·9
Soap																			
Quantity index	18·8	19·3	19·9	21·0	21·7	21·8	21·7	22·4	23·4	24·3	23·6	23·5	24·0	25·3	26·2	27·1	28·2	29·2	29·9
Price index	62·8	51·2	42·7	39·4	39·1	38·4	37·6	37·5	37·0	36·7	34·9	34·4	32·1	29·9	29·9	27·8	28·1	29·5	29·9
Matches, polishes, etc.																			
Quantity index	19·7	20·6	19·6	20·7	21·9	22·1	22·2	22·6	22·7	23·5	22·7	22·4	21·1	20·8	21·5	21·1	22·1	23·1	23·5
Price index	33·3	28·5	26·9	25·2	24·5	24·0	23·5	23·6	23·9	23·8	23·6	23·6	23·5	23·6	23·6	23·5	23·4	23·5	23·5
Laundry and other household services																			
Quantity index	61·8	57·0	61·4	62·3	63·0	65·2	66·3	69·5	69·8	72·0	73·2	74·8	74·7	79·2	81·7	86·7	87·7	87·7	87·6
Price index	161·4	137·2	112·1	103·6	102·9	101·8	100·4	97·7	100·0	98·6	94·7	89·6	85·1	82·3	81·8	81·2	81·0	84·8	87·6
All goods and services																			
Quantity index	231·6	229·3	235·8	241·4	246·7	251·7	255·4	262·4	266·3	272·8	275·1	278·8	280·5	288·5	295·1	303·1	308·9	313·4	316·9
Price index	513·5	458·6	371·7	345·0	345·2	345·0	340·2	335·1	335·3	332·2	323·6	311·9	301·9	294·5	294·6	293·5	297·6	301·2	316·9

CHAPTER IV

PERSONAL CARE AND HEALTH EXPENSES

1 GENERAL REMARKS

The estimates in this chapter cover the expenditures of consumers on personal care and health. Apart from expenditure on drugs and other medical supplies, these are service items: the services of hairdressers, doctors, dentists, voluntary hospitals, etc. Like most services they are of a composite nature and may be more, or less, strictly defined. The services of private doctors, for example, may be taken to cover either the total payments made by patients or, at the other extreme, merely the net remuneration of practitioners. In the present study, largely for reasons of expediency, the service items are for the most part narrowly defined. It would have been desirable to give the components from which estimates of both gross and net expenditures might have been derived, since the appropriate concept varies with the problem in hand, but this has not been possible to any great extent.

The precise scope of the estimates is of particular significance when comparisons are made with other items of consumers' expenditure or of government expenditure. It will be worth while, before considering the changes in this group of expenditures over the period, to set out briefly the definitions of the different items involved; they will be given in greater detail in the sections dealing with the methods of estimation.

Expenditure on personal care (hairdressing, etc.), as given here, excludes purchases of toilet wares and other counter sales which are often a part of the gross receipts of barbers' shops and beauty parlours. The valuation of the services of private doctors covers only the net remuneration of the practitioners. Not only are the receipts from dispensing excluded, but also the expenses of maintaining a surgery (rent, fuel and light, and domestic service) and running a car. The values of the services of dentists, opticians, private duty nurses and other auxiliary medical practitioners are similarly defined. For expenditure on voluntary hospitals the value of wages and salaries *plus* a few miscellaneous items not otherwise entering into final consumption is taken.

It may be noted that the various elements of the gross payment to doctors, dentists, etc., which are excluded by these definitions appear elsewhere under other headings of consumers' expenditure and are omitted here to avoid double-counting. Nevertheless, the definitions are not merely arbitrary; the value of medical services in this strictly defined sense is of use if comparisons are being made between countries and periods in which social institutions are different. It provides, in fact, a measure of the 'net output' of these services.

A large part of the cost of the health services during this period was not borne directly by the patient but was the responsibility of government, either through the National Health Insurance scheme or the municipal hospitals. This part of expenditure on health services is wholly excluded from the present reckoning. Even where the entire cost of the service is borne by the contributions of the insured, it is more usual to regard these transactions as a part of direct taxes rather than as payment for a service. The degree to which services are provided by government is a further point to be borne in mind when making comparisons over long periods or between different countries.

The total expenditure on personal services and health expenses, as defined here, was of the order of £99 m. in 1938, or a little more than 2 % of total consumers' expenditure during the year. A third of this total was expenditure on drugs and other medical supplies. About one-seventh, £14 m., was the net income of doctors from private practice, almost 35 % of personal expenditure on all health services. The value of services supplied by voluntary hospitals amounted to only £8 m., or 19 % of the total for health services. Expenditure on services associated with care of the person, in particular hairdressing, manicuring, chiropody and beauty parlours, was of the order of £25 m. As might be expected, expenditure on this item shows a steeper upward trend over the period than expenditure on the medical services; though a part, at least, of this difference in trend will be due to the increasing provision for medical care through compulsory health insurance schemes and local authority hospitals.

Apart from these general comparisons of relative level, there is not much to be said about the individual series. It is worth noting, however, that personal expenditure

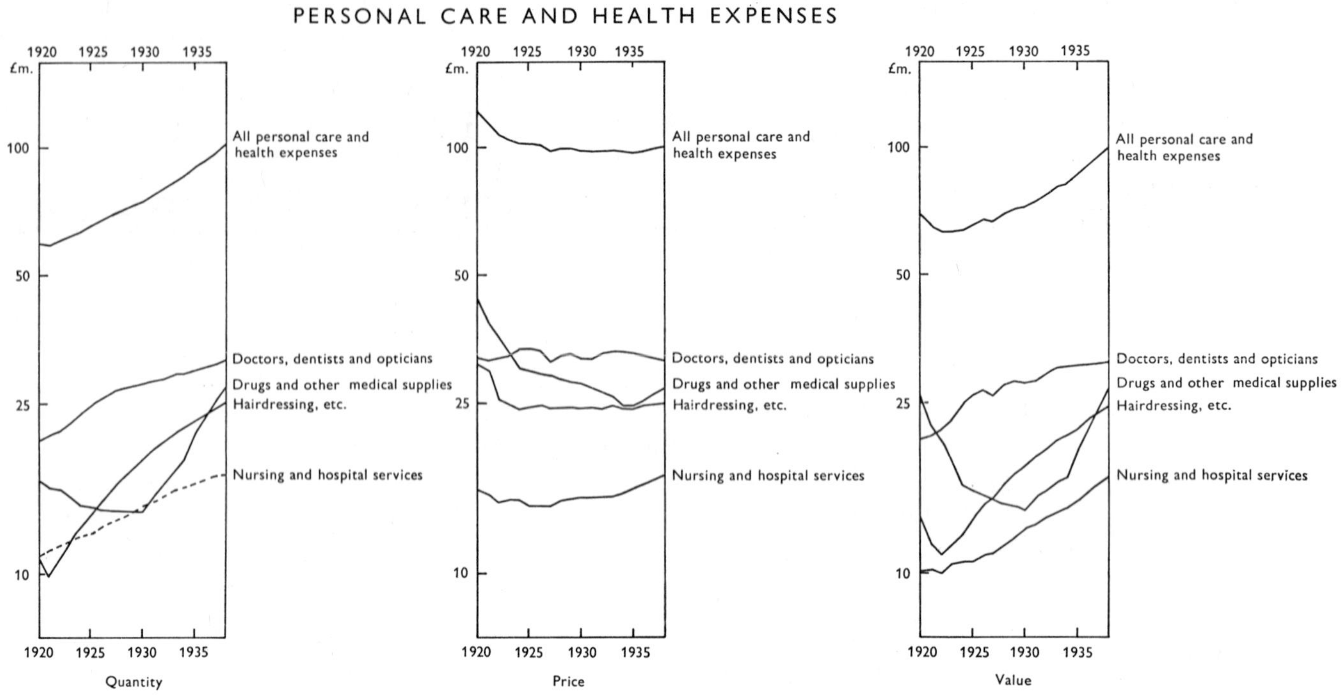

PERSONAL CARE AND HEALTH EXPENSES

Fig. 4. The variations in the quantities purchased, average prices and expenditure on personal care and health by final consumers in the United Kingdom, 1920–38.

per head of the population on this group of items increased markedly in comparison with average expenditure on all other goods and services. It is difficult to say how far this involved an actual quantitative increase, and even more difficult to determine how far any increase in welfare was involved. In part the problem is one of deciding what price indices are appropriate for deflating expenditure on service items. It is certain that the figures of average net earnings, which have been used for the present estimates, are not wholly adequate for this purpose. They would imply, for instance, that the number of doctors in practice was an appropriate index of the volume of medical services rendered by them in each year. Comparisons on this basis are likely to be especially misleading if they are interpreted in welfare terms.

2   METHODS OF ESTIMATION

Scope of the estimates. For most service items dealt with in this chapter, consumers' expenditure is narrowly defined to cover the net rather than the gross receipts. If the total payments had been included here, it would have been necessary to make many crudely estimated deductions elsewhere to avoid double-counting. Net expenditure in this case covers the wages and salaries paid and the appropriations for personal income by entrepreneurs, proprietors and those professionally engaged. In addition, certain miscellaneous expenses peculiar to these services are included. The cost of drugs and medical

supplies provided by hospitals, etc., is included with direct purchases in the estimate for this item. All other expenses, the cost of food and drink, rent, fuel, etc., are accounted for under these specific heads elsewhere in the estimates. Expenditure by the government sector, including the value of all benefits received under the National Health Insurance schemes, is wholly excluded.

A small part of the expenditures included here will represent payments by foreign residents. Similarly expenditure abroad on these services by United Kingdom residents will be omitted. It has not been possible to make detailed estimates of these expenditures for individual commodities but an estimate of the gross balancing items is given below in Chapter X.

General procedure. Essentially the same method has been employed for each of the service items: an estimate of the number engaged is multiplied by the average annual net earnings and from this total are deducted all payments from outside the personal sector. The employment series are based largely on the figures of registered membership in the various professional associations, but these numbers have been adjusted in the light of the census data for the two years 1921 and 1931. There is little information on net earnings during this period and it has usually been necessary to apply an average figure for the whole period. For the two most important groups, doctors and dentists, the results of sample inquiries are available; in other cases professional bodies have been consulted to establish a reasonable average figure. No direct estimate of expenditure on drugs and medical supplies can be made but it is possible to indicate the order of magnitude and the trend of quantities and prices through the period.

Methods employed. The methods employed for the different items of personal care and health expenditure are discussed below in the following order:

(a) Personal care (hairdressing, etc.).
(b) Doctors' services.
(c) Dentists' services.
(d) Optical services.
(e) Nursing services.
(f) Drugs and medical appliances.
(g) Voluntary hospitals.

(A) PERSONAL CARE (HAIRDRESSING, ETC.)

Included in this item are expenditures on hairdressing, chiropody, manicuring and similar services. The value of toilet requisites, cosmetics and other articles purchased in hairdressers' shops, is not included; the total consumption of these items is covered elsewhere.[1]

It has not been possible to make direct estimates of expenditure on these services but there are certain pieces of collateral evidence which serve to indicate an order of magnitude for 1938. Expenditure in other years was then derived from a series of employees' aggregate earnings.

The family budget inquiries for 1937–9 show the average weekly expenditure on hairdressing, etc., by different types of family to be as follows:[2]

	Expenditure per household per week
Agricultural working class	2¼d.
Industrial working class	6¼d.
Middle class	1s. 1d.

This is equivalent to a total annual expenditure of £21·1 m.[3] It must be remembered, however, that these were primarily inquiries into household expenditure and expenses of this kind, which are almost purely individual, would be likely to be understated.

A post-war inquiry was specifically directed to estimating expenditure on hairdressing.[4] In this case records of expenditure in November 1949 were collected from a representative sample of the whole population. Additional information on tips was also collected. The following estimates of average monthly expenditure per head were obtained:

Expenditure per head per month

	Hairdressing d.	Tips d.	Total d.
Men	19·5	2·5	22·0
Women	20·4	1·2	21·6
Children	5·7	—	5·7

If these expenditures are first deflated for the change in the average price of these services between 1938 and 1949 and then multiplied by the numbers in each class in 1938, a total expenditure of £25·1 m., of which £1·9 m. represents tips, is obtained. In the same inquiry it was also found that the average monthly expenditure by adults on chiropody was 2·7d. This is equivalent to a total annual expenditure of £3·0 m. at 1938 values.

Finally, the results of the Census of Distribution for 1950 indicate that employees' earnings amount to 30% of total takings in hairdressers' shops.[5] If this same ratio is applied to estimated employees' earnings in 1938,[6] a total expenditure of £24·1 m. is derived. This will include counter sales but will exclude expenditure on chiropody and tips.

It seems reasonable to conclude from these results that expenditure on this group of services in 1938 was of the order of £25 m. and that approximately 7½% of this total represented tips. Expenditure in other years of the period was estimated by varying this figure directly with the aggregate earnings of employees.[7]

An index of average earnings per employee has been taken as the price series for this item; the quantity series is, by implication, equivalent to the number employed.

(B) DOCTORS' SERVICES

The estimates discussed in this section cover personal expenditure on doctors' services, that is, payments to general practitioners and specialist consultants. They do not include expenditure on drugs dispensed by doctors, which are treated separately in §(f) below. They also exclude those items of doctors' expenses which are dealt with under other headings of this study; for example, rent of premises, fuel and light, travelling expenses, domestic service, etc. The remuneration of assistants to general practitioners is, of course, included. Treatment obtained under the public health services does not appear as an item of personal expenditure, and doctors' earnings from this source have to be excluded.

The number of doctors in private practice was estimated in the following way. The number of physicians, surgeons, and registered medical practitioners, engaged in 'medicine and care of the sick and infirm (not

---

[1] See Chapter I, §2 (e), p. 8 above.
[2] See [62] *Ministry of Labour Gazette*, December 1940 and February 1941; and [80] Massey, *J. R. Statist. Soc.* cv (1942), part III, p. 159.
[3] For weighting, see vol. I of this study, p. 168.
[4] [56] *Expenditure on Hairdressing, Cosmetics and Toilet Necessities*, by W. F. F. Kemsley and David Ginsburg (The Social Survey, 1950).
[5] [36] *Census of Distribution (1950)*, vol. I, table 3, p. 16: men's hairdresser-tobacconists are excluded from this calculation.
[6] [69] Chapman, *Wages and Salaries in the United Kingdom, 1920–1938*, table 86, p. 221.
[7] *Ibid.*

government or local authority)' in 1921 and 1931 is known from the Census of Population.[1] The ratio which these figures bear to the number of civilian doctors resident in Great Britain, recorded in the *Medical Directory*,[2] varies little between the two years; i.e. 72·9 and 74·1 %. Comparable figures for other years of the period were obtained by interpolating these ratios. Between 1921 and 1931 a linear trend in this ratio was assumed; before and after these years the ratio was kept constant.

In the 1931 Census 0·8 % of medical practitioners were recorded as unemployed. This same percentage was applied for all years.

Comparable figures are given for Northern Ireland in 1926.[3] The ratio of this figure to the estimate for Great Britain in 1926 was applied for other years to derive estimates for Northern Ireland. The Great Britain unemployment percentage was applied for Northern Ireland in all years.

The figures thus derived for the United Kingdom will be considerably in excess of the numbers engaged in private practice, which cannot be obtained directly from the census tables. For 1938, however, an estimate of the number of doctors in private practice has been made.[4] The number of principals in general practice was known almost completely from the National Health Insurance records, and the number of specialist consultants in private practice was obtained by direct inquiry of all those likely to be so engaged. The difference between this total and the estimate from the census data must comprise mainly assistants to general practitioners and the medical staff of hospitals, including full-time consultants. It probably also includes a number of those employed by the public health service, for whom the numbers appear to be understated in the census.[5] It was assumed that the size of this residual group would vary with the number of salaried doctors.[6] The number of assistants to general practitioners was then calculated as 15 % of those in private practice.[7]

From the figures thus derived, a number of small deductions were made for doctors employed part-time by public authorities, estimating the full-time equivalent of part-time work.

First, there are the private practitioners employed part-time in school medical service. For England and Wales, the number of full- and part-time doctors employed, and their full-time equivalent, is known for the years 1925–38.[8] From these figures the full-time equivalent of part-time school doctors who were also private practitioners could be estimated. It was assumed that part-time specialist medical officers gave the rest of their time to private practice, and the full-time equivalent of their part-time work was found by assuming that the time they gave to school medical work was one-

eighth of the time given by the non-specialist school medical officers. Roughly ten part-time non-specialist medical officers were equivalent to one full-time medical officer.

There are similar figures for Scotland for some of the years of the period;[9] they were converted into full-time equivalents on the basis of the data available for England and Wales. In the other years the England and Wales figures were raised by the ratio which Scotland's figures bear to them in given years. For Northern Ireland the Great Britain figure was raised by 2 %. For the years before 1925, the 1925 figure was taken.

Secondly, the private practitioners employed as part-time medical officers by local authorities must be deducted. For England and Wales there are figures for the years 1927–38.[10] Since the time devoted to such service is not known, but is likely to have varied considerably, it was assumed that eight part-time doctors were equivalent to one full-time. Approximately the same number was taken for 1920–6 as in 1927. These figures were raised by 6 % to cover Scotland and Northern Ireland.

Finally, there are the doctors employed part-time in local authority hospitals. For the later years of the period there are published figures for part-time doctors and specialists employed in each local authority hospital.[11] These figures were totalled separately for 1936. Since it is not known how much time on average was spent at hospital work, it was assumed that eight non-specialist doctors working part-time in hospitals gave time equal to that of one full-time doctor, and that specialists gave rather less time, ten part-time specialists being equivalent to one full-time specialist. The estimated full-time equivalent in 1936 was reduced slightly for earlier years of the period and raised for later years.

In 1947 a detailed inquiry was made into the earnings of general practitioners and consultants in the years

---

[1] [24] *Census of England and Wales, 1921*; [25] *1931*; [26] *Census of Scotland, 1921*; [27] *1931*.

[2] [99] *Medical Directory*, 1938 edition.

[3] [28] *Census of Northern Ireland, 1926*.

[4] See [72] A. Bradford Hill, 'The doctor's day and pay', *J. R. Statist. Soc.* series A, cxiv (1951), part 1, p. 1.

[5] For this purpose comparison was made with the returns for the British Medical Association plebiscite of 1948: see [96] *The Economist, Records and Statistics*, 21 February 1948.

[6] [69] Chapman, *Wages and Salaries in the United Kingdom, 1920–1938*, table 74, p. 201; the coverage of the two groups is very similar.

[7] See [43] *Report of the Inter-Departmental Committee on Remuneration of General Practitioners*, Cmd 6810 (1946), p. 25. In a sample for 1936–8 nearly 18 % of the general practitioners had assistants. If this proportion is applied to the total for 1938 it represents 15 % of all general practitioners and specialist consultants in private practice.

[8] [3] *Report of the Chief Medical Officer of the Board of Education*.

[9] [5] *Annual Report of the Department of Health for Scotland* (1926, 1929, 1930 and 1935–8); 1938 Report, p. 83.

[10] [4] *Annual Report of the Ministry of Health* (1926–7 to 1938–9); 1938–9 Report, p. 51.

[11] [97] *The Hospitals Year Book* (1938), p. 153.

1936–8.[1] Records of gross and net earnings were obtained from a large sample. The representativeness of this sample was thrown in doubt by the fact that only a two-thirds response was obtained, with an evident bias due to the larger preponderance of refusals from older men. It was nevertheless doubtful whether this bias in the returns would necessarily involve a corresponding bias in the figures of average earnings for the whole sample. It seems probable that if refusal was associated with income level it would be connected with both extremes, upper and lower, and thus be offsetting in the average. The inquiry was directed towards assessing *normal* income, and a number of special cases, involving prolonged illness, late entry, or special arrangements in a family practice, were rejected from the sample. This undoubtedly results in a small upward bias, but it is probably offset in the present calculations by some underestimation of the number of practitioners.

The inquiry found that the average annual gross earnings of general practitioners were £1,600, and average net earnings £1,000. For present purposes the appropriate figure is that of net earnings, since other expenditure—drugs and medicines, travelling expenses, rent, fuel and domestic service—is included elsewhere under these separate heads of expenditure.

In addition to payments to general practitioners, expenditure on consultants' and specialists' services must also be included. The earnings of doctors employed full-time by various non-profit-making bodies, whether hospitals, universities or research institutes, are included in the net expenditure of these bodies. The average annual net earnings of consultants and specialists from the sample inquiry were £2,000.

A figure of average net earnings for all general practitioners (principals only) and specialists in private practice was calculated by weighting these estimates of net earnings by the numbers in 1938. On this basis a figure of £1,150 was obtained for the whole group. The average earnings of assistants in this year have been estimated at £200–235.[2] If these are included, the average net earnings of all doctors in private practice are, in round terms, £1,000 per annum. This figure would vary with changes in both the rates of remuneration and the proportions in the three categories. In the absence of any information on these points, it seems best to assume the same figure throughout the period. There was little variation in professional salaries during this period and, for the degree of accuracy attained in this estimate, changes of a similar order would hardly be significant.

The number of doctors in private practice, excluding the full-time equivalent of those doing part-time work for public authorities, was multiplied by this average figure to obtain total net earnings.

Income received from the government sector must be deducted from total net earnings to obtain the figure of personal expenditure required: that is, the net income of doctors from private patients *less* expenses (rent, fuel, etc.) incurred in respect of National Health Insurance patients. This last item must be deducted here since it has not been possible to exclude these payments from the estimates of expenditure on the individual items of rent, etc. The required amount is identically equal to the total income from private practice *less* expenses and national insurance earnings; it has been obtained in this way here.

Accordingly, the remuneration received by doctors under the National Health Insurance schemes of England and Wales,[3] Scotland,[4] and Northern Ireland,[5] was deducted in each year. A further deduction was made of earnings received as District Medical Officers. The numbers of those acting as District Medical Officers are not known, but for England and Wales there are figures of persons in receipt of domiciliary medical relief.[6] It is not known what fees were paid for this kind of medical service by local authorities. Therefore a figure of £50,000[7] was taken for expenditure on this service in 1938. This figure was varied through the period with the numbers in receipt of domiciliary medical relief in England and Wales.

(c) DENTISTS' SERVICES

The estimates of personal expenditure on dental services cover the remuneration of dentists in private practice, including assistants and dental mechanics, and expenditure by dentists on purely dental supplies. Other expenses paid out of dentists' gross earnings—rent, fuel, etc. —are dealt with under their respective headings. That part of dental expenditure paid from National Health Insurance funds was deducted.

The number of dentists in private practice was estimated in the following way. The number of dentists in Great Britain, for all years from 1923 onwards, is known from *The Dentists' Register*.[8] Since the number registered

---

[1] [72] Hill, 'The doctor's day and pay', *J. R. Statist. Soc.* series A, cxiv (1951), sections 2 and 3, pp. 18–34; see also [43] *Report of the Inter-Departmental Committee on Remuneration of General Practitioners*, Cmd 6810 (1946) and [45] *Report of the Inter-Departmental Committee on the Remuneration of Consultants and Specialists*, Cmd 7420 (1948).

[2] [69] Chapman, *Wages and Salaries in the United Kingdom, 1920–1938*, p. 185.

[3] [4] *Report of the Chief Medical Officer of the Ministry of Health*; for the years 1920–3, the number of insured persons on doctors' lists and on lists of approved institutions was multiplied by the capitation fee of 11s. in force during these years.

[4] [5] *Annual Report of the Department of Health for Scotland*; before 1926 the number of persons entitled to benefit was multiplied by the capitation fee in force in each year.

[5] [22] *Ulster Year Book*; for 1920–1 the same figure as in 1922 was taken.

[6] [11] *Persons in Receipt of Poor Relief*.

[7] This figure assumes that the annual expenditure was about £2 per head of those receiving relief.

[8] [95] *The Dentists' Register*.

probably includes dentists no longer practising, a comparison was made between the figures in the *Register* and those in the 1931 Census of Population. The census figure was 93·2 % of the number registered. This percentage was applied in all years, including 1931, to the number registered, excluding dentists in the armed services.

Figures were derived for the years 1920–3 by first of all getting a figure for 1921 which would be comparable with the 1931 figure. This was done by applying the ratio of the 1921 to the 1931 figure in the Census of Population to the estimated figure for 1931. For the years 1920, 1922 and 1923 a linear interpolation was made between the 1921 and 1924 figures and the trend taken back for one year to 1920.

The number of dentists in Northern Ireland are given in the *Dentists' Register* for the years 1925 onwards. The number of dentists in the Census of Population for Northern Ireland in 1926 is 97 % of the figure in the *Register* for that year. This percentage was applied to the *Dentists' Register* figures to obtain estimates for the years 1925 onwards. For the early years of the period the percentage which the Great Britain 1920 figure forms of the 1926 figure was applied to the Northern Ireland figures for 1926. The figure obtained in this way for 1920 was linearly interpolated between this year and 1926 to derive figures for Northern Ireland's dentists in the intervening years.

By this method were obtained figures of the dentists in the United Kingdom in private practice and in public service, including those unemployed but excluding those in the Armed Services.[1] From these figures the numbers unemployed were deducted. The only data on dentists' unemployment are those given in the 1931 Census of Population for England and Wales[2] and for Scotland, when the number unemployed was only 1 % of the total. This 1 % was deducted from the estimated total in the United Kingdom in 1931; for the other years of the period the 1931 figure was very roughly adjusted according to changes in the general level of employment.

The next deduction to be made is of those dentists employed in public services. There are published figures for England and Wales for the years 1925–38.[3] These figures give the number of dentists employed full-time in schools and the full-time equivalent of those employed part-time. As well as school dentists, there are dentists employed by the Ministry of Health. There are figures of full-time dental officers of the Ministry of Health for the last three years of the period for England and Wales. The total number of dentists to be deducted was estimated by assuming that in 1938 the figure for the United Kingdom was 1,000,[4] and for the other years varying this figure proportionately with the full-time equivalent

of school dentists employed in England and Wales. For the years before 1925, the 1925 figure was simply reduced by 20 in each year back to 1920.

Total expenditure on dentists was estimated under four heads: the earnings of dentists, the earnings of dentists' assistants, the earnings of dental mechanics, and the expenditure by dentists on purely dental supplies.

An inquiry to assess the average pre-war earnings of dentists was undertaken by the dental associations at the request of the Spens Committee in 1947.[5] For this purpose a questionnaire was sent to all dentists who had been in practice during this period. Although the response was disappointing, the results were held to reflect 'in a broad way, the financial position of the profession'. From this evidence it would appear that the average annual net income of fully established dentists in large towns in the years 1936–8 was £800–850.[6]

It is particularly unfortunate for the present purpose that the representativeness of this sample cannot be more accurately assessed. It is known that there was a wide variation in both professional skill and form of practice among dentists. Probably more than one-third were unqualified practitioners admitted to registration under the 1921 Act when academic qualifications were first made compulsory.[7] The average income of these unqualified practitioners was known to be much lower than for the qualified. Some indication of this can be seen in the income distribution for 1936–8. The distribution is markedly skewed to the right on account of the long tail of incomes of £1,000 and more; and the mode is only about £500, or 60 % of the mean income. It is probable that qualified practitioners are more fully represented than the others and that they account for most of the high incomes. The understatement of small incomes will therefore give an upward bias to the mean, and it is possible that the mode would give a better indication of the true mean income for all practitioners. Certainly some reduction should be made to allow for the lower incomes of the extreme age groups and for practices out-

---

[1] The total number of dentists in the Services, as given in [95] *The Dentists' Register* for the whole of the United Kingdom, was deducted from the figures in the *Register* for Great Britain. Therefore no deduction from the Northern Ireland figures was necessary. This was done merely to simplify the method of estimation and makes no appreciable difference to the figures of dentists obtained for the United Kingdom.

[2] [25] Occupation Tables.

[3] [3] Board of Education, *Chief Medical Officer's Report* (1938), p. 1.

[4] The total for England and Wales in equivalent of full-time dentists for the year 1938 for schools only was 783. The difference between this figure and 1,000 is assumed to cover all dentists employed full-time and part-time in Scotland and Northern Ireland, those employed in England and Wales by the Ministry of Health full- and part-time, and those dentists who may be giving part-time services in factories.

[5] [44] *Report of the Inter-Departmental Committee on the Remuneration of General Dental Practitioners*, Cmd 7402 (1948).

[6] Ibid. table B, p. 5; net income in the age group 35–54.

[7] For an account of the development of the dental profession see [68] A. M. Carr-Saunders and P. A. Wilson, *The Professions*, pp. 107–17.

side the large towns. For the present purpose an average figure of £800 has been taken as applicable to all dentists.

It seems necessary, also, to allow for some upward trend in average earnings with the decline in the proportion of unqualified men. In 1921 more than 9,000 out of a total of 12,000 were unqualified. By the end of the period the total had risen to 14,000 and the proportion unqualified was less than half. It has also been suggested to us that, as a result of the action of the Dentists' Association, earnings were raised considerably between 1924 and 1925. Accordingly a figure of £650 was taken for 1920, rising to £750 by 1925, and then more slowly to £800 in 1938.

It has been estimated that from 1930 onwards about one-third of the dentists had assistants.[1] In the 1921 Census of England and Wales[2] a figure for dentists' assistants is given which is 18 % of the number of dentists. No similar data are given for Scotland in 1921, nor are such figures given for either area in 1931. To derive figures of dentists' assistants for the United Kingdom for all the years of the period, the England and Wales percentages were interpolated linearly between 1921 and 1930; for 1920 the same figure was taken as for 1921; and the 1930 percentage was taken for the rest of the period. These percentages applied to the numbers of dentists in the United Kingdom give the number of dentists' assistants. The number of assistants was multiplied in each year by a salary of £100 to obtain the amount of their earnings.

The numbers of dental mechanics in 1921 and 1931 are recorded by the Census of Population for England and Wales[3] and for Scotland.[4] These numbers are 85 % and 69 % of the numbers of dentists in the two census years.[5] These figures were interpolated for inter-censal years. For 1920 the 1921 percentage was taken, and for years after 1931 the same percentage as in that year. These percentages, applied to the numbers of dentists in the United Kingdom, give the numbers of dental mechanics in each year.

A salary of about £3 to £3. 10s. per week has been suggested as a representative figure for dental mechanics. An annual salary of £170 was therefore taken, and from this the total earnings of dental mechanics in each year were calculated; in the years before 1925 the earnings of dental mechanics were varied in the same way as the earnings of dentists.

Average expenditure on purely dental supplies during this period is estimated at £240 per annum, about one-fifth of the turnover of an average practice.[6] This figure was multiplied by the numbers of dentists in each year to obtain total expenditure on supplies.

Finally, to arrive at the figure of personal expenditure on dental services it is necessary to deduct expenditure

on dental benefits under the National Insurance schemes which began in July 1921. Published figures are available for most years of the period;[7] for other years, dental expenditure was assumed to vary in proportion to total expenditure on additional benefits.

(D) OPTICAL SERVICES

With the information available it is not possible to do much more than suggest an order of magnitude for expenditure on this item. It covers the value of the services of oculists and opticians and the cost of the spectacles supplied. That part of the total represented by ophthalmic benefit provided under the National Health Insurance schemes has been excluded.

A rough estimate of the number of spectacles supplied in 1935 may be obtained from the Census of Production returns.[8] From the figures it is evident that the lenses accounted for about a quarter and the frames for more than a half of the manufacturing cost of each pair of spectacles. As both complete spectacles and component parts are recorded it is not possible to ascertain the total output free of duplication. It seems probable, however, that the total output for home sales was of the order of 4 million pairs at this period. The value of sales in 1935, including the output of small firms, net imports, the costs of distribution, an allowance for sight-testing and the value of repair work, probably amounted to £5 m. Of course, not all purchases would involve the cost of sight-testing as well; it was still possible to obtain a pair of spectacles very cheaply from the counter of a popular chain store. On the other hand there would be people requiring the expensive specialist services of oculists.

The Census of Production returns for earlier years suggest that expenditure on optical services approximately doubled between 1924 and 1935 and that the increase was maintained smoothly through the intervening years. It is also evident that the upward trend was continued to the end of the period. Accordingly there was assumed to be a uniform annual increase in expenditure

---

[1] These are intended to include receptionists, clerks, etc. While, of course, all dentists would have some person to let patients in, it is assumed that the main work of such persons was really private domestic service, their work for the dentist being a very small part of their duties.

[2] [24] Industry Tables.   [3] [24], [25] Industry Tables.

[4] [26], [27] Industry Tables.

[5] That the percentage fell in this way was due to the attempts made to train and use disabled of the First World War as dental mechanics. The scheme was not a success and the numbers of dental mechanics later settled to what might be regarded as a 'normal' percentage.

[6] It was suggested that there is no need to vary the figure during the period.

[7] See [6] Annual Report of the Ministry of Health for England and Wales; [5] Annual Report of the Department of Health for Scotland for Scotland; and the [22] Ulster Year Book for Northern Ireland.

[8] See [32] Fifth Census of Production (1935), part III, pp. 482–9.

from £2·5 m. in 1925 to £5 m. in 1935, continuing at the same rate to 1938. Before 1925 the figure has been kept constant to allow for the offsetting effect of higher prices in the earlier years.

In 1938 the total number of opticians registered by the Ophthalmic Benefit Approved Committee for National Health Insurance optical work in England and Wales was just over 7,000.[1] It is probable that this figure, which included employees as well as those working on their own account, represented some 6,000 separate establishments. The estimate of total expenditure obtained above implies an average annual turnover in the region of £900 for the United Kingdom; this is probably not unreasonable.

It is finally necessary to exclude the value of expenditure under the National Health Insurance schemes. This was never more than £0·5 m. even at its highest level in the latest years of the period. Though the accuracy of the estimates hardly warrants a correction of this order, it seems best to make the deduction to avoid a possible source of bias.

(E) NURSING SERVICES

The methods employed to estimate expenditure on nursing services are discussed separately under three headings: (i) private duty nurses, (ii) midwives, and (iii) masseurs.

(i) *Private duty nurses*

Under this heading is included the value of the services performed by private duty nurses (including district nurses) for private individuals. The method employed is simply to multiply the number of nurses in each year by an estimate of their average earnings. No more direct method from the expenditure side is available.

The number of private duty and district nurses in the United Kingdom has been estimated for the years 1921 and 1931 from the data of the Census of Population.[2] In the census returns the unemployed are separately distinguished; these must be excluded for the purpose of estimating gross annual earnings. It is evident, however, that the term unemployment may be variously interpreted. The conditions of employment for the majority of private duty nurses are a series of short-term contracts whose incidence in the short run is largely unforeseen. Many of those who were not currently engaged on census night, but had a firm expectation of an engagement in the near future, would probably not consider themselves to be unemployed. It seems likely that the degree of underemployment, in this sense, among private duty nurses was considerable; it is known that the profession was oversupplied and that for many it was only a part-

time occupation. A reduction of 20 % in the numbers is probably not too large to allow for this. For the other years of the period figures were obtained by simple interpolation and extrapolation.

The estimation of the level of earnings presents further difficulties. There is little evidence about the earnings of nurses outside hospitals during this period. In view of the variety of qualifications held and of cases treated, it is only too likely that the range was wide. It has been assumed that average cash earnings were £100 in 1938 and that since 1920 there had been a steady increase comparable with the rise in hospital pay. Income in kind, an important part of total remuneration, was added to this. The value of these emoluments was assumed to be £60 for district nurses and £40 for private duty nurses in 1938; these figures were varied with the cost of living for other years of the period.[3]

(ii) *Midwives*

The number of midwives in private practice has been estimated from the census data for 1921 and 1931. Those employed by local or central government authorities were excluded. Since they are included elsewhere in the estimates it is also necessary to exclude midwives employed in voluntary hospitals. In 1938 this number was 1,004.[4] This has been reduced to 950 for 1931, 15 % of the total in that year; the same proportion has been deducted from the 1921 figure. The adjusted census figures were interpolated and extrapolated to 1936. Under the Midwives Act 1936, compulsory registration was imposed and many former midwives retired as unable to qualify for registration. The total number registered is known for 1937 and 1940,[5] and the figure for 1938 was obtained by interpolation.

It has been suggested that in 1938 midwives fell into roughly two classes as regards average earnings.[5] The lower group, comprising some 30–45 % of the total, earned about £150 per year, while the rest probably earned about £200 on average. It has been assumed that this grouping was characteristic of the whole of the inter-war period. However, the level of earnings probably changed over the period and it seems not unreasonable to vary the average level for earlier years with the earnings of hospital nurses.[6]

[1] [6] *Nineteenth Annual Report of the Ministry of Health 1937–8*, Cmd 5801 (1938), p. 181.

[2] For the details of these estimates, see [69] Chapman, *Wages and Salaries in the United Kingdom, 1920–1938*, pp. 186–9.

[3] See [83] PEP, *Report on the British Health Services* (1937), p. 175; and [69] Chapman, *Wages and Salaries in the United Kingdom, 1920–1938*, pp. 191–2.

[4] [97] *The Hospitals Year Book* (1940), part III.

[5] Information supplied by the College of Midwives.

[6] See [69] Chapman, *Wages and Salaries in the United Kingdom, 1920–1938*, p. 202.

EXPENDITURE BY PRIVATE HOUSEHOLDS ON MEDICAL SERVICES, DRUGS AND APPLIANCES, ETC., IN THE UNITED KINGDOM, 1937–9

	Number of families (000's)	Average weekly expenditure per family (pence)		Total annual expenditure (£m.)	
		Medical services	Drugs, etc.	Medical services	Drugs, etc.
Middle class	2,770	58·25	15·0	35·1	9·0
Industrial working class	9,477	10·75	6·0	22·1	12·4
Agricultural working class	775	7·25	4·25	1·2	0·7
Total	13,022	..	..	58·4	22·1

(iii) *Masseurs*

Masseurs form the third group of sufficient importance to be distinguished separately in estimates of expenditure on the nursing services. The information available about the numbers and earnings of masseurs during this period derives from a professional body, the Chartered Society of Physiotherapy. It is estimated that the number employed in private practice in 1938 was about 3,500, or roughly one-quarter of the total number registered with the Society.[1] The annual turnover of a well-established practice at this date was said to be in the region of £500; about one-third to a half of this could be regarded as the net earnings of the masseur. The cost of maintaining the masseur's equipment was approximately £25 per annum. The remaining expenses were general costs, such as travelling and the upkeep of premises, which are included elsewhere in personal expenditure. On this basis expenditure in 1938 was estimated as £0·9 m. For 1920 a figure of £0·4 m. was taken and for the intervening years these figures were linearly interpolated.

(F) DRUGS AND MEDICAL APPLIANCES

Personal expenditure on drugs and medical supplies includes all purchases by households and by voluntary hospitals and other non-profit-making bodies. Included elsewhere in the estimates are dental supplies (see §(c) above) and spectacles (see §(d) above). The value of all drugs and medical appliances obtained under the National Health Insurance schemes is excluded.

The method used in making this estimate is briefly as follows. From the family budget data for 1937–8 and the published accounts of various public bodies the value of total sales of drugs and appliances in 1938 was calculated. The value of total sales in other years of the period was estimated on the basis of quantity and price indices derived principally from the Census of Production. The necessary deductions were then made to obtain an estimate of personal expenditure as defined above.[2]

From the figures of weekly expenditure on drugs and medicines by a sample of working- and middle-class families in 1937–8, it is estimated that annual expenditure by households amounted to £22·1 m. The reliability of this figure may be judged in the light of a comparison that can be made for the other categories of medical expenditure. Information from the preceding sections of this chapter may be combined to yield the following figures of household expenditure in 1938.

EXPENDITURE ON MEDICAL SERVICES IN THE UNITED KINGDOM, 1938 (£M.)

	Gross earnings	*Less* N.H.I. payments	Household expenditure
Doctors	36·6	9·6	27·0
Dentists	18·1	2·2	15·9
Opticians	5·8	0·5	5·3
Nurses	9·0	—	9·0
Total	69·5	12·3	57·2

The figure of £57·2 m. for household expenditure reached in this way may be compared with a comparable figure of £58·4 m. derived from family budget data. The details of this calculation are set out in the table above. In this table, for each of the three social classes into which the whole population has been divided, there are given an estimate of the number of families in the class,[3]

---

[1] There were, in addition, masseurs doing work for hospitals and others working privately, but as a very part-time occupation, whose' contribution is negligible for the present purpose.

[2] It does not seem possible to make any use of the returns to stamp duty charged on patent medicines for the purpose of estimating consumers' expenditure on drugs. These returns exhibit a strong downward trend over the period, said to be due to a growing knowledge of methods of securing legal exemption. It was also suggested that, instead of £0·75 m., the full yield in 1937 should have been £3·3 m., roughly equivalent to a total turnover of £16–20 m. (See **[49]** *Report of the Select Committee on Medicine Stamp Duties*, 1937.)

[3] See vol. I of this study, p. 168.

the average weekly expenditure on medical services and drugs, etc., recorded in the family budget inquiries of 1937–9,[1] and the estimated total annual expenditures derived from these figures. In spite of the uncertainty attaching to some of the component items the agreement between the two estimates of total expenditure on medical services is very close; it may be concluded that household expenditure on drugs and medicines may reasonably be assumed to be of the order of £22–23 m.

To obtain an estimate of total expenditure, additions must be made to this figure of expenditure by households to include both expenditure by others within the personal sector and also by the government sector through local authority hospitals and the National Health Insurance scheme. It may be estimated that in 1938 voluntary hospitals spent £1·9 m. on drugs and appliances.[2] Poor-law institutions run by local authorities spent a further £0·2 m.[3] Separate figures are not available for the expenditure of local authority hospitals on drugs and appliances but comparison with the figures for voluntary hospitals suggests that total public expenditure on drugs and appliances would be of the order of £4 m., of which the greater part is accounted for by hospitals. The payments made to chemists under the N.H.I. schemes amounted to £2·9 m., and a further £0·2 m. was paid to doctors who dispensed medicines in rural areas where no chemist was easily accessible.[4] Medical and surgical appliances paid for by the additional benefits cost a further £0·1 m.[5] The sum of these additions is £9·3 m.

Although it was the rule under the N.H.I. scheme for all medicines to be supplied by chemists wherever possible, many doctors undertook a certain amount of dispensing in connexion with their private practice. From a sample of returns for the immediate pre-war years it appeared that on average dispensing accounted for approximately 8% of the gross income of general practitioners. This would amount to a further £2·5 m. in addition to the small sum paid by the N.H.I. schemes. It is likely that for the most part the cost of this medicine would be included in the budget figures of payments to doctors; for present purposes the whole amount has been added to the figure for household expenditure on drugs and medicines, making £24·6 m. in all for this.

The total expenditure on drugs in 1938 estimated in this way amounts to £33·9 m. Finally, if the value of dental supplies and of spectacles is also added (see §§(c) and (d) above) the total becomes £40·3 m.

Comparable estimates of total expenditure for other years of the period were made by varying this figure with a roughly compiled index series. For this purpose the information on the output of drugs and medicines recorded by the Census of Production was used. It is not possible to derive any very precise data from this source;

only a part of drugs and chemicals used for medicinal purposes is separately distinguished in the census. However, the recorded output of specifically medical preparations and appliances in 1935 amounts to approximately £20 m.[6] Comparison with the estimate made above for 1938 suggests that in fact a large part of medical supplies is covered by these items. While the margin for distribution costs is known to be large for proprietary medicines, it is probably much smaller for medicines dispensed directly by the chemist, particularly through the National Health Insurance scheme, and for supplies going to hospitals. It seems reasonable, therefore, to base an estimate of the variation in total supplies on the data available for these specified items in the Census. Although the degree of coverage may have changed during the period, it seems unlikely that the change was large.

For each of the years 1924, 1930 and 1933–5, the Census provides estimates of the total output of medical supplies at current and constant prices—that is, the value and volume of output. From these figures an implied price index could be calculated. For the intervening years it has been necessary simply to interpolate the values for the census years; the trends have also been roughly extrapolated over the years at the beginning and end of the period.

The estimates of expenditure obtained in this way are figures of the total value of drugs and medical supplies. For expenditure in the personal sector, as defined here, it is necessary to deduct public expenditure (local authority hospitals, poor law, etc.) and N.H.I. payments as well as the value of dental supplies and spectacles already included under other headings of this chapter. The level of public expenditure in earlier years has been roughly estimated by varying the figure for 1938 with local authority expenditure on hospital services.[7] After these deductions the remainder represents the value of final expenditure required for the present purpose.

(G) VOLUNTARY HOSPITALS

The voluntary hospitals, that is those supported by patients' contributions and private charity, come within the category of private, non-profit-making institutions, which are treated as part of the personal sector under the

[1] [80] Massey, 'The expenditure of 1360 British middle-class households in 1938–39', J. R. Statist. Soc. cv (1942), part III, p. 159; and [62] 'Weekly expenditure of working-class households in the United Kingdom in 1937–38', Ministry of Labour Gazette, December 1940 and January 1941.

[2] [97] Hospitals Year Book.

[3] See [10] Local Government Financial Statistics.

[4] [4] Annual Report of the Chief Medical Officer of the Ministry of Health; [5] Annual Report of the Department of Health for Scotland; and [22] Ulster Year Book.

[5] Ibid.

[6] This includes medical preparations and appliances, surgical instruments, hot-water and air goods, spectacles, dental goods, bandages, etc.

[7] See [20] Statistical Abstract.

definitions adopted for this inquiry. The payments made by individuals and households to those institutions, whether in the form of voluntary gifts or payments for services received, must be considered merely as transfers between persons. What is required for the present purpose is the actual expenditure by the hospitals on goods and services. Much of this will already be included elsewhere: for example, food, fuel and light, rent, etc. It remains, therefore, to include here the expenditure on specifically medical services (drugs and other medical supplies are included in the preceding section of this chapter) and a number of miscellaneous items connected with administration and maintenance, namely fees for the professional services of lawyers, accountants, etc., and expenditure on advertising.

Annual returns of the income and expenditure of voluntary hospitals are collected and published.[1] Separate information is given for the four areas: London, the Provinces, Scotland, and Ireland. Information from all hospitals is not available, but the proportion of available beds covered by the returns is known for each area and estimates for the hospitals omitted were made on this basis.[2] In order to exclude Southern Ireland, only 30% of the estimated total for Ireland was taken in each year.[3]

Expenditures in each year are classified under six heads: provisions; surgery and dispensary; domestic; salaries and wages; other expenditure; and expenditure on maintenance. For the present purpose only the two items 'salaries and wages' and 'other expenditure', are required. The former covers the monetary remuneration of medical and nursing staff and other employees. However, a part of the gross earnings of nurses will be income in kind. Unless the value of these emoluments is also included expenditure on nursing services will be understated. It is not possible to extract these figures from the published returns, nor is the number of nurses employed by the voluntary hospitals recorded. The value of these emoluments has therefore been estimated indirectly in the following way. An estimate of the number of nurses employed in voluntary hospitals in 1921 and 1931, based mainly on census data, was varied for other years with the number of beds available, which are recorded annually. These figures were then multiplied by the estimated value of emoluments in each year.[4]

From the category 'other expenditure' it is necessary to make certain deductions to exclude the following: printing and stationery, postages, etc., insurance, and rents and rates; all these items are included elsewhere in the estimates. It has been suggested that apart from rent these expenditures only amounted to 1 or 2% of total expenditure on maintenance, £0·5 m. at most. The deduction for rent and rates will also be fairly small; most of the hospitals own their premises and it is only necessary to consider here the actual rent paid, not the annual value of the premises included in the main rent estimate. What little evidence there is suggests that some £0·2 m. should be taken at the beginning of the period and increased to £0·3 m. and £0·4 m. in later years.

With these adjustments the published figures of wages, salaries, and other expenses were summed for each year of the period. An index of the number of beds available was taken as the quantity series for this item; the corresponding price series was then obtained by simple division.

3 THE RELIABILITY OF THE ESTIMATES

The estimating procedures employed in the preceding section differ considerably between items. In order to assess the reliability of the results it is therefore necessary to consider each series separately. They are discussed in turn in the following paragraphs.

The level of expenditure on personal care (hairdressing, etc.) can be established approximately for the inter-war period on the basis of sample inquiries of household expenditure. It is known that estimates of total expenditure obtained in this way are generally biased. Difference of coverage is likely to be a source of further discrepancy in the present case. Any bias in the estimate for 1938 will extend to the figures for the earlier years as well. The series of aggregate earnings, taken as the basis for extrapolation, is probably more satisfactory in terms of trend than of the year-to-year variations. Errors, therefore, are as likely to be systematic as random in character, and are probably large.

The estimates of both doctors' and dentists' net earnings are undoubtedly subject to fairly wide margins of error. The number of practitioners is based primarily on the registration statistics and these are clearly fallible as a source for the number actively engaged in private practice. The deductions made for the retired or unemployed cannot be regarded as more than rough indications of the orders of magnitude involved. The further deductions, to exclude those in public service, are small compared with the probable margin of error, but would introduce a definite bias if neglected. The estimates of

---

[1] In [97] *The Hospitals Year Book*, published by the Central Bureau of Hospital Information.

[2] This is only an approximate adjustment but no serious error can be introduced in the present case.

[3] For the years before 1929 no returns are given for Ireland and a percentage of the figure for Great Britain was taken; the adjustment is very small.

[4] See [69] Chapman, *Wages and Salaries in the United Kingdom, 1920–1938*, pp. 186–92, for the details of these calculations.

net earnings are derived from sample surveys that are not wholly free from a suspicion of bias. For most years of the period it has been necessary either to assume no change in the figure of average net earnings or to make only the crudest adjustments. This is clearly the principal source of error in the resulting series of expenditure. It is also evident that a great part of the annual variation is lost, since it is unlikely that changes in the number of practitioners will fully reflect the short-term changes in total earnings; the estimates provide no evidence for or against the presence of any cyclical behaviour in expenditure on medical services. It is not unreasonable to assume a standard error of the order of 20 % for each series, apart from any bias that may also be present.

Very little is known regarding expenditure on optical services and it has not been possible to do more than indicate the order of magnitude for this item. The margin of error for this estimate could well be as large as 20 %.

For the nursing services the same method has been employed as for the services of doctors and dentists; that is, registration figures of the numbers engaged in the profession were multiplied by an estimate of average earnings. For these professions, however, registration was only enforced towards the end of the period and it has been necessary to make much cruder estimates of the numbers engaged in the earlier part of the period. Not much more can be claimed for the figures than that they represent an appropriate order of magnitude with some indication of the trend through the period.

Total expenditure on drugs and medical supplies is a relatively large item for which no particularly precise information is available. Again it is necessary to rely on family budget data, but the resulting figures are supported by information from other sources. While the trend of expenditure over the period may be adequately repre-sented, any year-to-year variations shown are very largely fortuitous. The margin of error will be greatest for the earlier years.

The principal source of error in the estimates for voluntary hospitals lies in the allowance that has to be made for non-reporting hospitals. The simple proportionate adjustment on the basis of the number of beds is probably the best in the circumstances but it is possible that some bias may be introduced. It may well be that among the hospitals who fail to make reports there is a higher proportion of the less efficient and of the less adequately staffed. It also seems likely that the level of expenditure per bed in these hospitals would be lower. This will not apply to all hospitals in this group, of course, but if any bias is introduced it is probable that this will tend to overestimate rather than underestimate the level of expenditure. The simple adjustment for wages in kind is too small to be the source of any considerable discrepancy.

4   THE MAIN TABLES

The following tables set out the estimates of expenditure on personal care and health discussed in the preceding sections. In Tables 18–20, details of the calculations regarding services of doctors, dentists and nurses are given; the supplementary information on numbers and earnings may have some independent interest. Estimated expenditures on all items are brought together in Table 21. Finally, in Table 22, quantity and price series for each item or group of items are given in a comparable index number form. While the quantity series are base-weighted aggregate index numbers, the price series are current-weighted aggregates; their product is thus a simple index of expenditure. Each index has been multiplied through by expenditure in 1938, the base year, and they are shown in this form in the diagrams of § 1.

TABLE 18. ESTIMATED NUMBER OF DOCTORS AND EXPENDITURE ON DOCTORS' SERVICES IN THE UNITED KINGDOM, 1920–38

	1920	1921	1922	1923	1924	1925	1926	1927	1928	1929	1930	1931	1932	1933	1934	1935	1936	1937	1938
Number of doctors[a] (000's)																			
Great Britain	31·16	31·30	31·37	31·82	32·75	34·15	35·40	36·47	37·06	37·58	37·84	38·17	38·48	39·18	39·70	40·39	41·24	41·73	42·61
Northern Ireland	0·84	0·85	0·85	0·86	0·89	0·93	0·96	0·99	1·00	1·02	1·03	1·03	1·04	1·06	1·08	1·09	1·12	1·13	1·15
United Kingdom	32·00	32·15	32·22	32·68	33·64	35·08	36·36	37·46	38·06	38·60	38·87	39·20	39·52	40·24	40·78	41·48	42·36	42·86	43·76
of which, doctors who were																			
retired, etc.	8·67	8·71	8·69	8·77	8·99	9·34	9·64	9·89	9·99	10·09	10·12	10·15	10·24	10·42	10·57	10·74	10·98	11·11	11·33
unemployed	0·19	0·19	0·19	0·19	0·20	0·21	0·21	0·22	0·23	0·23	0·23	0·23	0·23	0·24	0·24	0·25	0·25	0·25	0·26
salaried: full-time	8·64	8·64	8·74	8·74	8·95	9·05	9·46	9·76	9·96	9·96	9·96	10·07	10·47	10·57	10·88	10·98	11·18	11·29	11·49
part-time[b]	0·42	0·42	0·42	0·42	0·42	0·42	0·45	0·44	0·46	0·46	0·45	0·45	0·45	0·45	0·45	0·43	0·43	0·43	0·42
in private practice[c]	14·08	14·19	14·18	14·56	15·08	16·06	16·60	17·15	17·42	17·86	18·11	18·30	18·13	18·56	18·64	19·08	19·52	19·78	20·26
Earnings of doctors (£m.)	16·26	16·38	16·37	16·81	17·41	18·53	19·16	19·79	20·10	20·61	20·89	21·11	20·92	21·41	21·50	22·01	22·51	22·81	23·41
Less National Health Insurance payments, etc.	−7·56	−7·99	−7·91	−7·91	−7·25	−7·24	−7·43	−7·48	−7·68	−7·74	−8·08	−8·18	−7·73	−7·76	−7·84	−8·25	−8·74	−9·06	−9·47
Personal expenditure	8·70	8·39	8·46	8·90	10·16	11·29	11·73	12·31	12·42	12·87	12·81	12·93	13·19	13·65	13·66	13·76	13·77	13·75	13·94

[a] Doctors in the *Medical Directory*, excluding those resident abroad or serving in the Armed Forces.   [b] Full-time equivalent.   [c] Principals only.

TABLE 19. ESTIMATED NUMBER OF DENTISTS AND EXPENDITURE ON DENTISTS' SERVICES IN THE UNITED KINGDOM, 1920–38

	1920	1921	1922	1923	1924	1925	1926	1927	1928	1929	1930	1931	1932	1933	1934	1935	1936	1937	1938
Number of dentists (000's)																			
Great Britain	9·60	10·11	10·66	11·22	11·85	12·18	12·50	12·66	12·82	12·67	12·67	12·70	12·75	12·80	12·72	12·74	12·75	12·82	12·90
Northern Ireland	0·20	0·20	0·22	0·23	0·24	0·24	0·26	0·26	0·27	0·26	0·26	0·27	0·27	0·28	0·28	0·27	0·27	0·27	0·27
United Kingdom	9·80	10·31	10·88	11·45	12·09	12·42	12·76	12·92	13·09	12·93	12·93	12·97	13·02	13·08	13·00	13·01	13·02	13·09	13·17
of which, dentists who were																			
unemployed	0·06	0·10	0·09	0·10	0·10	0·10	0·11	0·11	0·11	0·11	0·12	0·13	0·13	0·13	0·12	0·11	0·10	0·09	0·10
in public service	0·36	0·37	0·39	0·41	0·43	0·45	0·47	0·51	0·56	0·62	0·66	0·70	0·71	0·72	0·77	0·82	0·90	0·95	1·00
in private practice	9·38	9·84	10·40	10·94	11·56	11·87	12·18	12·30	12·42	12·20	12·15	12·14	12·18	12·23	12·11	12·08	12·02	12·05	12·07
Average earnings (£ per head)	650	663	675	687	700	750	752	756	760	764	768	772	776	780	784	788	792	796	800
Earnings of dentists (£m.)	6·10	6·52	7·02	7·52	8·09	8·90	9·16	9·30	9·44	9·32	9·33	9·37	9·45	9·54	9·49	9·52	9·52	9·59	9·66
Earnings of dentists' assistants	0·17	0·18	0·21	0·24	0·27	0·29	0·32	0·33	0·36	0·37	0·40	0·40	0·40	0·40	0·40	0·40	0·40	0·40	0·40
Earnings of dental mechanics	0·90	1·03	1·14	1·27	1·41	1·50	1·59	1·59	1·56	1·52	1·49	1·42	1·43	1·43	1·42	1·42	1·41	1·41	1·42
Expenditure on dental supplies	2·25	2·36	2·50	2·63	2·77	2·85	2·92	2·95	2·98	2·93	2·92	2·91	2·92	2·94	2·91	2·90	2·89	2·89	2·90
Total expenditure	9·42	10·09	10·87	11·66	12·54	13·54	13·99	14·17	14·34	14·14	14·14	14·10	14·20	14·31	14·22	14·24	14·22	14·29	14·38
Less National Health Insurance payments	—	−0·01	−0·07	−0·17	−0·32	−1·09	−1·31	−2·95	−2·12	−1·93	−2·34	−2·29	−1·98	−1·76	−1·75	−1·72	−1·97	−2·04	−2·18
Personal expenditure	9·42	10·08	10·80	11·49	12·22	12·45	12·68	11·22	12·22	12·21	11·80	11·81	12·22	12·55	12·47	12·52	12·25	12·25	12·20

TABLE 20. ESTIMATED NUMBERS AND EARNINGS OF NURSES, MIDWIVES AND MASSEURS IN THE UNITED KINGDOM, 1920–38

	1920	1921	1922	1923	1924	1925	1926	1927	1928	1929	1930	1931	1932	1933	1934	1935	1936	1937	1938
Private duty nurses																			
Number (000's)	35·38	36·20	37·02	37·84	38·66	39·48	40·30	41·12	41·94	42·76	43·58	44·40	45·22	46·04	46·86	47·68	48·50	49·32	50·14
Average earnings[a] (£ per head)	152	149	139	138	138	138	137	136	136	135	135	132	132	132	133	135	137	141	143
Total earnings (£m.)	5·39	5·38	5·14	5·21	5·33	5·44	5·51	5·58	5·69	5·77	5·87	5·88	5·98	6·09	6·25	6·45	6·66	6·93	7·15
Midwives																			
Numbers (000's)	4·51	4·61	4·70	4·80	4·89	4·99	5·08	5·18	5·27	5·37	5·46	5·56	5·65	5·74	5·83	5·92	6·01	5·50	5·00
Average earnings (£ per head)	216	206	185	181	182	182	180	178	177	176	174	170	169	168	169	171	174	179	183
Total earnings (£m.)	0·97	0·95	0·87	0·87	0·89	0·91	0·92	0·92	0·93	0·95	0·95	0·94	0·95	0·96	0·99	1·01	1·05	0·98	0·91
Masseurs																			
Number (000's)	1·55	1·66	1·76	1·87	1·98	2·09	2·20	2·31	2·42	2·52	2·63	2·74	2·85	2·96	3·07	3·18	3·29	3·39	3·50
Average earnings (£ per head)	260	260	260	260	260	260	260	260	260	260	260	260	260	260	260	260	260	260	260
Total earnings (£m.)	0·40	0·43	0·45	0·48	0·51	0·54	0·57	0·60	0·63	0·66	0·68	0·71	0·74	0·77	0·80	0·83	0·86	0·88	0·91

[a] Including income in kind.

TABLE 21. ESTIMATED EXPENDITURE ON PERSONAL CARE AND HEALTH EXPENSES BY FINAL CONSUMERS IN THE UNITED KINGDOM, 1920–38 (£M.)

	1920	1921	1922	1923	1924	1925	1926	1927	1928	1929	1930	1931	1932	1933	1934	1935	1936	1937	1938
Hairdressing, etc.	13·4	11·7	11·0	11·7	12·3	13·4	14·4	15·1	16·1	17·1	17·8	18·8	19·5	20·6	21·2	21·9	23·0	24·0	25·0
Doctors' services	8·7	8·4	8·5	8·9	10·2	11·3	11·7	12·3	12·4	12·9	12·8	12·9	13·2	13·7	13·7	13·8	13·8	13·8	13·9
Dentists' services	9·4	10·1	10·8	11·5	12·2	12·5	12·7	11·2	12·2	12·2	11·8	11·8	12·2	12·6	12·5	12·5	12·3	12·3	12·2
Opticians' services	2·5	2·5	2·5	2·5	2·5	2·5	2·6	2·7	3·0	3·2	3·4	3·6	3·9	4·1	4·4	4·6	4·8	5·0	5·3
Nursing services																			
Private duty nurses	5·4	5·4	5·1	5·2	5·3	5·4	5·5	5·6	5·7	5·8	5·9	5·9	6·0	6·1	6·3	6·5	6·7	6·9	7·2
Midwives	1·0	0·9	0·9	0·9	0·9	0·9	0·9	0·9	0·9	0·9	0·9	0·9	1·0	1·0	1·0	1·0	1·0	1·0	0·9
Masseurs	0·4	0·4	0·4	0·5	0·5	0·5	0·6	0·6	0·6	0·7	0·7	0·7	0·7	0·8	0·8	0·8	0·9	0·9	0·9
Total	6·8	6·7	6·4	6·6	6·7	6·8	7·0	7·1	7·2	7·4	7·5	7·5	7·7	7·9	8·1	8·3	8·6	8·8	9·0
Drugs and other medical supplies	25·9	22·1	20·4	18·2	15·9	15·5	15·2	14·8	14·5	14·4	14·1	15·0	15·6	16·3	16·8	19·3	21·6	24·5	27·1
Voluntary hospitals	3·3	3·5	3·6	3·9	4·0	3·9	4·0	4·1	4·5	4·8	5·2	5·5	5·8	6·0	6·2	6·6	7·0	7·5	7·8
All goods and services	70·0	65·0	63·2	63·3	63·8	65·9	67·6	67·3	69·9	72·0	72·6	75·1	77·9	81·2	82·9	87·0	91·1	95·9	100·3

TABLE 22. INDEX NUMBERS OF QUANTITY AND AVERAGE PRICE FOR PERSONAL CARE AND HEALTH EXPENSES FOR FINAL CONSUMPTION IN THE UNITED KINGDOM, 1920–38

(Expenditure in 1938 is taken as the base for each series)

	1920	1921	1922	1923	1924	1925	1926	1927	1928	1929	1930	1931	1932	1933	1934	1935	1936	1937	1938
Hairdressing, etc.																			
Quantity index	10·9	9·8	10·8	11·8	12·7	13·7	14·6	15·6	16·5	17·4	18·4	19·3	20·2	21·0	21·8	22·6	23·4	24·2	25·0
Price index	30·7	29·7	25·4	24·9	24·1	24·4	24·6	24·3	24·4	24·5	24·3	24·4	24·2	24·6	24·3	24·2	24·6	24·8	25·0
Doctors, dentists and opticians																			
Quantity index	20·3	20·9	21·5	22·4	23·5	24·7	25·6	26·4	26·9	27·3	27·6	28·0	28·3	28·9	29·1	29·7	30·2	30·7	31·4
Price index	31·8	31·5	31·8	32·1	33·3	33·4	33·1	31·2	32·2	32·6	31·8	31·7	32·6	33·0	33·0	32·7	32·1	31·8	31·4
Nursing and hospital services																			
Quantity index	10·9	11·3	11·5	11·9	12·2	12·4	12·8	13·1	13·4	13·8	14·3	14·6	15·1	15·5	15·8	16·0	16·4	16·7	16·8
Price index	15·6	15·2	14·6	14·8	14·8	14·4	14·4	14·4	14·7	14·9	15·0	15·0	15·1	15·1	15·3	15·7	16·0	16·4	16·8
Drugs and other medical supplies																			
Quantity index	16·3	15·7	15·6	15·1	14·4	14·2	14·0	13·9	13·9	13·9	13·8	15·0	16·0	17·1	18·4	21·2	23·0	25·1	27·1
Price index	43·0	38·1	35·4	32·7	30·0	29·6	29·3	28·9	28·4	28·0	27·7	27·1	26·5	25·8	24·6	24·6	25·3	26·3	27·1
Total																			
Quantity index	58·4	57·7	59·4	61·2	62·8	65·0	67·0	69·0	70·7	72·4	74·1	76·9	79·6	82·5	85·1	89·5	93·0	96·7	100·3
Price index	120·1	112·9	106·6	103·7	101·9	101·6	101·0	97·9	99·2	99·8	98·3	97·9	98·3	98·7	97·7	97·5	98·2	99·4	100·3

CHAPTER V

PRIVATE TRANSPORTATION

1 GENERAL REMARKS

Expenditure on private transportation in 1938 amounted to £144 m. or 3·3 % of total personal expenditure in that year. The purchase of new motor-cars accounted for £39·4 m. of this, and new motor-cycles for a further £1·9 m. The value of running costs, including taxation, in that year was more than double the value of new motor vehicles; petrol and oil cost £47·9 m. and replacements and repairs a further £27·0 m.; direct taxation on private motor vehicles in 1938 amounted to £12·8 m. Expenditure on new bicycles was £8·2 m., and £2·1 m. was spent on replacements and repairs.

It will be seen that in the estimates of private transportation discussed in this chapter all vehicles are treated as single-use goods and not as a form of private capital. Thus annual expenditure includes the running costs, such as payments for fuel, replacements, taxation, etc., together with the value of new vehicles purchased during the year. The alternative procedure would be to include only the annual depreciation of the vehicles in use as consumption and to treat the difference between this and the value of new cars as private net investment. This would bring the figures more in line with those for public transportation. On the other hand the services performed by the driver of a private car are by convention not valued.

The variation over the period of the principal items is shown in the three diagrams of Fig. 5. The quantity movements are shown in the first diagram, and the corresponding average prices in the second. In both these drawings the series have been ranged according to the level of expenditure in 1938. The actual expenditures are shown in the third diagram.

Expenditure on new motor-cars, the largest single item of the group, doubled during the period. The number of new cars purchased each year, however, increased more than sixfold. Estimated purchases in 1920 were 33,900. Demand fell off in the slump of the following year but thereafter the trend was upwards until 1929, when 116,300 cars were bought. By 1931 purchases had fallen to 101,300, but the upward trend was soon resumed and reached a maximum of 220,200 in 1937. The subse-

quent fall to 187,400 in 1938 was the severest recession of the period.

This marked upward movement of demand was accompanied by a comparable but less pronounced fall in price. From £684 in 1920 the average price of motor-cars fell by a third to £430 in 1924 and again by a third to £294 in 1929. The downward trend continued until 1933 when the price was £215. In subsequent years there were variations about this level but no marked fall in price. It must be remembered that it is essentially a series of average values which is being considered here. On the one hand, although the standard price may be the same in two different years, the later model may show marked improvements in performance and appearance. On the other hand, smaller cars of lower horsepower became increasingly popular in the later years of the period and much of the fall in average price is due to the increase in the proportion of cheaper cars.

It was probably the introduction of the small cheap car which accounted for the decline in popularity of the motor-cycle. In the early post-war years demand for motor-cycles was increasing at a rate only slightly lower than that for motor-cars. The highest point was reached in 1925; 71,600 motor-cycles, almost twice the pre-war annual output, were purchased in that year. Thereafter purchases declined to a minimum of 26,900 in 1933. There was some recovery to 39,300 in 1937 but this was followed by a recession to 31,600 in 1938. The price of motor-cycles fell from £141·2 in 1920 to £62·4 in 1926. This downward trend was not continued, for the average level of later years was only slightly below this. The lowest average price was £56·4 in 1933, but in the last years of the period prices were rising again and reached £61·2 in 1938.

The number of new bicycles purchased annually rose from some 385,000 in 1920 to a maximum of 1,610,000 in 1935. Purchases appear to have fallen off slightly in the last three years of the period. The average price of bicycles fell rapidly in the first half of the period from £15·9 in 1920 to £9·6 in 1923 and £5·9 in 1929. Thereafter the trend was only slightly downwards. A minimum of £5·0 was reached in 1933 but by 1938 the average price had again risen to £5·5.

PRIVATE TRANSPORTATION

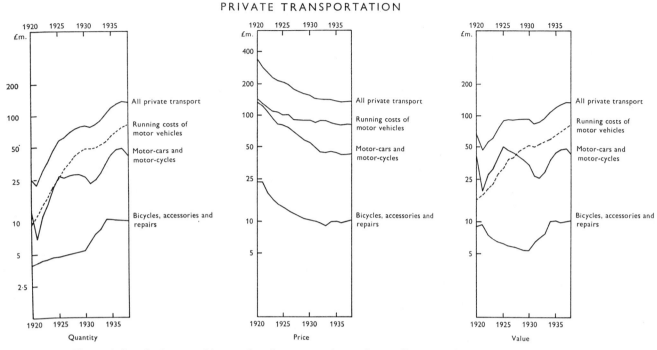

Fig. 5. The variations in the quantities purchased, average prices and expenditure on private transportation for final consumption in the United Kingdom, 1920–38.

The increase in the consumption of motor spirit and lubricating oil during the period mainly reflects the increase in the number of motor vehicles in use. However it also seems to be the case that during this period the average consumption of petrol per vehicle more than doubled. The average consumption of lubricating oil, on the other hand, only increased by 50 % above the 1920 level. The average price of motor spirit in 1920 was 3s. 9d. per gallon. This price included a government duty of 6d. which was cancelled at the end of the year. In the following years the price fell rapidly and in 1927 it was 1s. 3d. per gallon. In 1928 a duty of 4d. per gallon was introduced, which was raised to 6d. and then 8d. in 1931, and to 9d. in 1938. On account of these increases in duty the trend of prices was slightly upward in the second half of the period; in 1938 the price was 1s. 6d. per gallon. The price of lubricating oil fell from 7s. 6d. per gallon in 1920 to 5s. 6d. in 1923, and throughout the later years varied between this level and 6s. per gallon.

The number of replacement tyres purchased annually for motor vehicles rose from 371,000 in 1920 to 1,841,000 in 1938. The price varied comparatively little during the period from £4 at the beginning to £3 at the end. The average price of inner tubes appears to have been 10s. throughout the period. The cost of other replacements and repairs for motor vehicles rose from £4·2 m. in 1920 to £13·3 m. in 1929 and then to £21·0 m. by 1938.

Expenditure on replacements, repairs and accessories for bicycles fell steadily from £2·8 m. in 1920 to £1·5 m.

in 1933. In 1934 the value increased to £1·9 m. and by 1938 it had risen to £2·1 m. The principal item included is the cost of replacement tyres and inner tubes, which accounted for more than half the total value.

Of the other running expenses of motor vehicles the payments for driving licences, insurance, and garage accommodation varied directly with the number of vehicles in use; from £0·5 m. in 1920 they rose to £4·5 m. in 1938. Direct taxation on motor-cars took the form of a horsepower tax; this was levied at a rate of £1 per h.p. until 1934, when it was reduced to 15s. The increase in payments due to the rise in the number of vehicles in use was partly offset by the fall in their average horsepower. Between 1928 and 1938 the average horsepower of private cars in use fell from 13·5 to 11·6. The taxation paid on private motor vehicles rose from £4·0 m. in 1920 to £11·0 m. in 1933, and eventually to £12·4 m. in 1938.

2 METHODS OF ESTIMATION

Scope of the estimates. The estimates discussed in this chapter cover all forms of personal expenditure on private transportation, including purchases of new and second-hand vehicles, running costs and taxation. The purchases of new motor vehicles for purely business purposes by commercial travellers and others are not included. Similarly, the estimates for motor spirit, replacements, and repairs, cover only the requirements of personal users. It is not, however, possible to make detailed adjustments to exclude purchases by tourists and other non-residents. Similarly expenditures by United Kingdom residents abroad are not included. Estimates of the net balance for all items on these accounts are given in Chapter X.

General procedure. The number of new motor vehicles registered in each year is recorded from 1927 onwards. To complete the estimates for the earlier years of the period use was made of the statistics of total registrations and Census of Production data. Estimates of the number of bicycles purchased were based solely on the recorded output of census years. A price series for motor-cars was compiled from records of the selling prices of a number of popular makes in each year. The prices of motor-cycles and bicycles were derived from export average values. Estimates of the quantity and value of motor spirit, lubricating oil, and tyre replacements, were supplied by experts in the trade. These items depend mainly on the number of vehicles in use. Estimates of the cost of repairs were also supplied. An indication of the value of bicycle repairs and accessories could be obtained from the census data. Finally, the taxation paid on motor vehicles was obtained from the official returns. Nothing precise is known about business purchases or second-hand dealings during this period; no more than a simple proportionate adjustment could be made for these two elements, which are to some extent offsetting.

Methods employed. The methods of estimation employed for the different items of the group are discussed below in the following order:

(*a*) Motor-cars.
(*b*) Motor-cycles.
(*c*) Bicycles.
(*d*) Accessories, repairs, oil and petrol.
(*e*) Other running expenses of motor vehicles.

(A) MOTOR-CARS

The number of private cars newly registered in the United Kingdom is known for each of the years 1927–38.[1] The figures for 1927–9 relate to years ended September and were adjusted to calendar years by simple interpolation.

Estimates of the sales of private cars in the years 1920–6 are based on information regarding supplies for the home market—output adjusted for net imports. Three separate estimates of output,[2] deriving from the motor trade and covering different portions of the period, are in substantial agreement and enable a single continuous annual series to be constructed. These figures were then adjusted for exports and imports.[3] The movement of the adjusted series could be compared with the annual increase in the number of private cars in use.[4] While any close similarity is not possible—besides scrapping there was also re-

registration of cars after the war—the comparison appeared to confirm the reliability of the estimated series.

An estimate of the average retail value of new cars in the years 1928–38 is available.[5] This series has been calculated from the published statistics of the numbers of the new cars registered in each horsepower group and the prices of the most popular models as given in manufacturers' catalogues. It was found possible to apply a similar method for earlier years of the period. Two dozen of the most popular makes of car were selected from a published price list,[6] and the prices recorded for the different models in each year were arranged in the form of a frequency distribution. This was done separately for four different horsepower groups: up to 10 h.p., 11–12 h.p., 13–14 h.p., and over 14 h.p. The size of the frequency classes varied from intervals of £50 in the lower part of the range to £250 in the upper part. The midpoint of each interval was taken as the average price for the class. The number of quotations in each horsepower group varied from year to year as different models were introduced; there were altogether more than four times as many quotations in 1928 as in 1920. However, the number of quotations is less important than the fact that the prices selected are those of the most popular makes. For each year the average price in each horsepower group was calculated. A series of average prices for all motor-cars was obtained by weighting the four groups in proportion to the numbers of new cars registered in each group in 1928.

The published prices were probably current only until September in each year, since new models were usually introduced at the annual Motor Show in October. Accordingly the price series for the whole period was adjusted to calendar years by simple interpolation.

Finally, some allowance must be made to exclude business purchases and include second-hand dealings. As most second-hand cars were bought, directly or indirectly, from other consumers, only the value of the dealers' services is required here. In the absence of any more precise knowledge it has been assumed that a deduction of 30 % from the total value of new car sales in

---

[1] See [**101**] *The Motor Industry of Great Britain, 1951*, issued by the Society of Motor Manufacturers and Traders, table 61, p. 68.

[2] See [**54**] Committee on Industry and Trade, *Survey of Metal Industries* (1928), p. 217; [**65**] G. C. Allen, *British Industries and their Organization*, 2nd ed. (1935), p. 177; [**101**] *The Motor Industry of Great Britain, 1939*, table 8, p. 45.

[3] [**8**] *Annual Statement of the Trade of the United Kingdom*, vol. I, 1920–6. The figures for vehicles and chassis were taken together; in some cases second-hand and commercial vehicles were also included but the net discrepancy is probably not important.

[4] [**101**] *The Motor Industry of Great Britain, 1939*, table 20, p. 63.

[5] [**71**] K. F. Glover, *The Recent Course of Gross Investment in Inland Transport in Great Britain*, appendix IV, p. 133 (an unpublished thesis in London University Library).

[6] [**100**] *Motor Car Index* (Fletcher and Sons, Norwich, 1928 ed.).

each year would cover the net effect of these two adjustments; the number of cars purchased has been reduced in the same proportion. The numbers of new cars allotted to final consumption are shown in Table 23. The average prices and the corresponding estimates of expenditure are shown in Tables 24 and 25 respectively.

(B) MOTOR-CYCLES

The number of new motor-cycles registered each year is known from 1928 onwards.[1] The number of motor-cycles available for the home market in 1924 is also known.[2] For other years of the period only the total number of cycles in use is recorded.[3] In order to estimate the numbers of new vehicles purchased in these years it is necessary to proceed in the following way.

It is evident that in normal years the annual change in the total number of licences current is equal to the difference between the number of new vehicles purchased and the number scrapped. The relative importance of these two factors will vary with the progress of the industry. If demand is expanding rapidly the number of vehicles scrapped in each year will be relatively small compared with the number of new vehicles; when it reaches a limit and begins to decline the annual change in the number of vehicles in use will be determined largely by the number of vehicles scrapped during the year.

In the years before and after the First World War the number of motor-cycles in use was increasing rapidly. The rate of increase fell off during the 'twenties and after 1929 the total number in use decreased in each year. It is probable that many cycles which had been laid up during the war were re-registered for use in the immediate post-war years. In these years, therefore, the annual increase in registrations will considerably exceed the number of new vehicles purchased.[4]

The number of motor-cycles scrapped was 16,000 in 1924 and 53,500 in 1928. The number scrapped in each of the three intervening years was obtained by simple interpolation. The increase in the total number of registrations each year could then be added to these figures to derive an estimate of the number of new cycles purchased in the year. For the earlier years it was assumed that output in 1918 was at the average pre-war level of 40,000 vehicles and rose to 80,000 vehicles by 1923. Exports were deducted from these figures to obtain the number of new vehicles sold in the home market. To allow for the disturbed conditions of the years 1920–1 it was further assumed that in those years purchases of motor-cycles would show the same divergences from trend as sales of motor-cars.

The average factory value of motor-cycles is known for the four census years 1924, 1930 and 1934–5.[5] Estimates were made for the other years of the period on the basis of average export values. Since in most years as much as one-third of output was exported this series should at least provide a reliable indication of the trend of prices in the home market. Retail prices were obtained by adding 50 %[6] to the estimated average factory value in each year to cover distribution costs.

Finally, some allowance must be made to exclude motor-cycles purchased for business use and to include second-hand dealings. For this purpose the same proportion of total sales was taken as for motor-cars, 30 %. The number of motor-cycles bought by final consumers is shown in Table 23. The corresponding average prices and estimates of expenditure are shown in Tables 24 and 25.

(C) BICYCLES

The output of bicycles is known for the five census years 1924, 1930 and 1933–5,[7] and an estimate is available for 1938.[8] Exports[9] were deducted from these figures to obtain the quantity sold on the home market. The number of bicycles imported is negligible. Estimates of home consumption in other years of the period were derived from these figures by simple interpolation, the trend in consumption between 1924 and 1930 being carried back to 1920.

From the census data it was also possible to obtain the average factory value of bicycles sold for home consumption. Estimates were made for other years on the basis of the average value of bicycles exported. The ratios of the two prices in 1924, 1930 and 1933 were interpolated for the intervening years; before 1924 and after 1935 the ratios were kept constant. To these factory values 50 % was added in each year to cover the costs of distribution.

(D) ACCESSORIES, REPAIRS, OIL AND PETROL

The estimates of this section cover purchases of all commodities needed for the running or maintenance of motor vehicles and bicycles.

Tyres and inner tubes are the chief replacements required for motor vehicles and the value of these purchases is shown separately in Table 25. All other replacements are included in an overall estimate of the value of repair work. These figures relate only to maintenance repairs and not to repairs arising out of accidents, the cost of which is recovered from an insurance

[1] [19] Ministry of Transport, *Road Vehicles—Great Britain*.
[2] See [30] *Third Census of Production (1924)*, part II, p. 342.
[3] See [101] *The Motor Industry of Great Britain, 1939*, table 20, p. 63.
[4] The extent of the possible distortion may be judged from the fact that in normal years there is a seasonal variation in the number of cycles registered equivalent to roughly one-third of the total stock.
[5] The figure taken for this purpose was the average factory value of vehicles available for the home market.
[6] [73] Jefferys, *The Distribution of Consumer Goods* (1950), p. 363.
[7] [32] *Fifth Census of Production (1935)*, part II, p. 375, table V B.
[8] Supplied by the Board of Trade.
[9] [8] *Annual Statement of the Trade of the United Kingdom*, vol. I, 1920–38.

company. The quantity and value of motor spirit and lubricating oil purchased each year are also shown. The estimates for all these items were made by experts in the motor trade. They are based on the numbers of private cars and motor-cycles in use in each year and 30 % was deducted from the total figures to exclude business use.

Estimates of the value of bicycle accessories and repairs were made from Census of Production data. The output of inner tubes and tyres for bicycles is recorded by quantity and value for each of the five years, 1924, 1930 and 1933–5.[1] Exports were deducted from these figures and the small imports were added. The numbers of tyres purchased by cycle manufacturers were calculated on the basis of the output of cycles in these years. The remaining quantities, which were sold direct to consumers, were interpolated and extrapolated to obtain estimates for all years of the period. The average factory values in census years were varied for other years of the period on the basis of export values. Finally the factory values were raised by 50 % to include distribution costs. It is unnecessary to include the value of other cycle parts and accessories to the extent that they were used in repair work or were purchased by manufacturers. There is in fact considerable duplication in the census figures, which record both the output of vehicles and the output of component parts purchased from other firms. In view of this only 20 %[2] of the recorded value of accessories and parts of bicycles is included in the estimates of direct expenditure.[3] A margin of 50 % to cover distribution costs was added to factory value. The value of repair work for cycles done by large firms is approximately the same, £85,900, in each of the three census years, 1924, 1930 and 1935. Repair work done by small firms in 1924 was one-quarter of the total. On this basis £110,000 was added for the value of all repair work to cycles in each year of the period.

(E) OTHER RUNNING EXPENSES OF
MOTOR VEHICLES

In this final section are included the costs of taxation, driving licences, and garage accommodation for motor vehicles.

The figures of taxes paid on private motor-cars and motor-cycles are derived from the published returns.[4] For the years 1920–1 taxes on motor-cars and cycles are not separately enumerated; the amounts were estimated on the basis of the numbers of vehicles in use.

The amount paid for driving licences was calculated from the estimated number of private motor-cars and motor-cycles in use at a rate of 5s. per vehicle.

Finally, an estimate was made of the value of public garage accommodation used by motorists. It was assumed that 10 % of private cars were kept in public garages at an average annual cost per vehicle of £10.

In each case these estimates relate to all users of private cars and motor-cycles. To obtain estimates of personal consumption 30 % was deducted in each year to exclude expenditure by commercial travellers and others whose expenses are covered by their firm or business.

3 THE RELIABILITY OF THE ESTIMATES

From 1927 onwards the number of new cars is based on the registration figures and the estimates for these years should be substantially accurate. Estimates for earlier years are necessarily less reliable; while the trend will be adequately represented, the year-to-year variations are less accurate, particularly for the earliest years of the period.

The price series is similarly subject to a greater degree of error for the years before 1928. It is probable, because of inadequate weighting, that the values shown for these years represent modal prices rather than the true mean values. The price series used for the later years would appear to have a high degree of accuracy in its original form; the adjustment to calendar years may be expected to reduce some of the actual variation of the series.

As in the case of motor-cars, new registrations of motor-cycles are published for the years from 1927 onwards. The accuracy of the figures decreases considerably as the estimates are extended back to 1920. For the years 1924–7 the movement shown is probably satisfactory but it is likely that a random error of the order of 10 % has been introduced. The annual variations for the first four years of the period are merely an indication of the most likely course of events; the average level of the figures seems to be reasonably well founded and the errors involved, though fairly large, are probably random.

The trend of the price series is based on census data but the annual variations reflect only the movement of average export values. However, in most years of the period more than one-quarter of output was exported and it is reasonable to assume that the two series were closely correlated. The margin of error will be greatest in the early post-war years.

A uniform percentage adjustment was made to the total sales of both motor-cars and motor-cycles to exclude

---

[1] See, for example, [32] *Fifth Census of Production (1935)*, part III, p. 464.
[2] See [30] *Third Census of Production (1924)*, part II, p. 341; this is the relevant proportion suggested for the whole output for home consumption of the motor and cycle trade.
[3] [32] *Fifth Census of Production (1935)*, part II, p. 373.
[4] [19] Ministry of Transport, *Road Vehicles*.

business purchases and include second-hand dealings. This adjustment is not intended to be more than an indication of the order of magnitude involved.

Apart from a possible lag between output and sales, the consumption of bicycles may be said to be known accurately for the five census years and 1938. For other years of the period it has not been possible to indicate more than the probable trend of consumption, and only the average level of these figures is significant. Although based on average export values, the price series is probably a reliable indication of retail values. It is probably most accurate in the early half of the period when exports amounted to one-third of total output. In later years exports were less important and evidently represented a cheaper form of machine than was sold on the home market. The estimates of expenditure may be slightly overstated in that they include bicycles purchased for business purposes, but it is likely that this item would be so small as to be negligible compared with the probable margin of error of the estimates.

The estimates for motor accessories and repairs were made by experts in the trade and it is not possible to attach any particular margin of error to the figures. It may be presumed that they have a fair degree of accuracy but allowance must be made for the rough estimate of consumption by business users. Expenditure on bicycle accessories and repairs is a small item and little information is available for other than census years. The figures shown are probably a reliable indication of the average level of expenditure and the general trend.

For most of the period the reliability of the estimates of payments for taxation and driving licences for motor vehicles depends solely on the appropriateness of the deduction for business use. Since no official returns are available for 1920–1 the estimates for these years are less reliable. The estimates of expenditure on garage accommodation are probably of the right order of magnitude and should indicate the right trend movement through the period.

4 THE MAIN TABLES

The following tables give the annual estimates obtained by the methods described in the earlier sections of this chapter. The quantities purchased and average prices of private vehicles and the principal running costs are shown in Tables 23 and 24. The corresponding expenditures, including certain minor running costs for which no separate quantity and price series are available, are given in Table 25. Finally, in Table 26, index numbers are presented for all items or groups of items. The quantity series are base-weighted aggregate index numbers and the price series current-weighted aggregates. Their product is thus a simple index of expenditure. Each index, however, has been multiplied through by expenditure in 1938, the base year, and is shown in this form in the diagrams of §1.

TABLE 23. ESTIMATED PURCHASES OF MOTOR VEHICLES, BICYCLES, MOTOR SPIRIT, LUBRICATING OIL, MOTOR TYRES AND TUBES FOR FINAL CONSUMPTION IN THE UNITED KINGDOM, 1920–38

	1920	1921	1922	1923	1924	1925	1926	1927	1928	1929	1930	1931	1932	1933	1934	1935	1936	1937	1938
Motor-cars (000's)	33·9	27·2	39·0	56·4	79·5	95·4	101·3	113·1	114·5	116·3	107·4	101·3	108·4	134·0	162·8	195·5	215·8	220·2	187·4
Motor-cycles (000's)	39·1	24·3	45·3	44·8	57·8	71·6	69·9	62·0	58·9	58·9	54·5	36·8	35·1	26·9	32·1	32·4	38·4	39·3	31·6
Bicycles (000's)	385	410	435	460	485	510	535	560	585	610	635	828	1,021	1,213	1,554	1,610	1,573	1,535	1,498
Motor spirit (m. gal.)	37	49	65	78	105	127	158	184	222	248	265	265	279	300	338	391	431	466	499
Lubricating oil (m. gal.)	1·19	1·54	2·03	2·42	3·21	3·84	4·64	5·33	6·22	6·69	6·88	6·88	6·97	7·50	8·12	9·00	9·91	10·24	10·50
Motor tyres (000's)	371	448	560	672	798	959	1,106	1,288	1,407	1,498	1,540	1,540	1,554	1,498	1,568	1,631	1,680	1,771	1,841
Motor inner tubes (000's)	280	350	420	518	644	770	875	945	1,071	1,050	1,120	1,155	1,120	1,120	1,120	1,106	1,085	1,155	1,015

TABLE 24. ESTIMATED AVERAGE PRICES OF MOTOR VEHICLES, BICYCLES, MOTOR SPIRIT, LUBRICATING OIL, MOTOR TYRES AND TUBES PURCHASED FOR FINAL CONSUMPTION IN THE UNITED KINGDOM, 1920–38

	1920	1921	1922	1923	1924	1925	1926	1927	1928	1929	1930	1931	1932	1933	1934	1935	1936	1937	1938
Motor-cars (£)	684	632	553	475	430	424	406	356	322	294	279	246	219	215	220	213	208	207	210
Motor-cycles (£)	141·2	146·7	119·1	91·1	77·1	68·1	62·4	65·1	65·1	63·5	60·6	63·5	57·3	56·4	58·5	61·8	58·4	60·3	61·2
Bicycles (£)	15·9	16·0	11·5	9·6	8·5	7·8	7·0	6·7	6·3	5·9	5·9	5·7	5·3	5·0	5·3	5·2	5·0	5·3	5·5
Motor spirit (s. per gal.)	3·75	2·92	2·25	1·75	1·67	1·50	1·58	1·25	1·33	1·42	1·42	1·25	1·42	1·42	1·37	1·42	1·42	1·50	1·50
Lubricating oil (s. per gal.)	7·50	7·50	6·00	5·50	5·67	5·50	5·50	5·50	5·50	5·67	5·67	5·67	6·00	6·00	6·00	5·67	5·67	5·67	6·00
Motor tyres (£)	4·00	4·00	4·00	4·00	4·00	4·00	3·75	3·50	3·50	3·50	3·50	3·50	3·38	3·38	3·13	3·00	3·00	3·00	3·00
Motor tubes (£)	0·50	0·50	0·50	0·50	0·50	0·50	0·50	0·50	0·50	0·50	0·50	0·50	0·50	0·50	0·50	0·50	0·50	0·50	0·50

TABLE 25. ESTIMATED EXPENDITURE ON PRIVATE TRANSPORTATION BY FINAL CONSUMERS IN THE UNITED KINGDOM, 1920–38 (£M.)

	1920	1921	1922	1923	1924	1925	1926	1927	1928	1929	1930	1931	1932	1933	1934	1935	1936	1937	1938
Motor-cars	34·0	15·9	22·1	27·3	34·9	45·9	42·3	40·3	36·9	34·2	31·0	24·5	23·9	28·1	35·6	42·0	45·2	46·2	41·2
Motor-cycles	5·5	3·4	5·4	4·1	4·5	4·9	4·4	4·0	3·8	3·7	3·3	2·3	2·0	1·5	1·9	2·0	2·2	2·4	1·9
Bicycles	6·1	6·6	5·0	4·4	4·1	4·0	3·8	3·8	3·7	3·6	3·7	4·7	5·4	6·1	8·2	8·4	7·9	8·1	8·2
Accessories, repairs, oil and petrol																			
Motor spirit	7·0	7·1	7·3	6·8	8·8	9·6	12·5	11·5	14·8	17·6	18·7	16·5	19·7	21·3	23·2	27·7	30·5	34·9	37·4
Lubricating oil	0·4	0·6	0·6	0·7	0·9	1·1	1·3	1·5	1·7	1·9	1·9	1·9	2·1	2·3	2·4	2·5	2·8	2·9	3·2
Motor tyres	1·5	1·8	2·2	2·7	3·2	3·8	4·2	4·5	4·9	5·2	5·4	5·4	5·2	5·1	4·9	4·9	5·0	5·3	5·5
Motor inner tubes	0·1	0·2	0·2	0·3	0·3	0·4	0·4	0·5	0·5	0·5	0·6	0·6	0·6	0·6	0·6	0·6	0·5	0·6	0·5
Motor repairs	4·2	4·9	5·6	7·0	8·4	9·8	11·9	12·6	13·3	13·3	14·0	14·0	14·7	15·4	16·1	18·2	18·9	19·6	21·0
Bicycle accessories and repairs	2·8	2·7	2·5	2·4	2·3	2·2	2·1	2·0	1·9	1·8	1·7	1·6	1·6	1·5	1·9	1·8	1·9	2·0	2·1
Total	16·0	17·3	18·4	19·9	23·9	26·9	32·4	32·6	37·1	40·3	42·3	40·0	43·9	46·2	49·1	55·7	59·6	65·3	69·7
Other running expenses																			
Taxation	2·7	2·9	4·1	4·9	5·7	6·6	7·4	8·2	9·1	9·8	10·4	10·5	10·6	11·0	11·7	9·8	10·7	11·6	12·4
Driving licences	0·1	0·1	0·1	0·1	0·2	0·2	0·2	0·3	0·3	0·3	0·3	0·3	0·3	0·3	0·3	0·4	0·4	0·4	0·4
Garage accommodation	0·1	0·1	0·2	0·3	0·4	0·4	0·5	0·6	0·6	0·7	0·8	0·8	0·8	0·8	0·9	1·1	1·2	1·3	1·4
Total	2·9	3·1	4·4	5·3	6·3	7·2	8·1	9·1	10·0	10·8	11·5	11·6	11·7	12·1	12·9	11·3	12·3	13·3	14·2
All private transportation	64·5	46·3	55·3	61·0	73·7	88·9	91·0	89·8	91·5	92·6	91·8	83·1	86·9	94·0	107·7	119·4	127·2	135·3	135·2

TABLE 26. INDEX NUMBERS OF QUANTITY AND AVERAGE PRICE FOR PRIVATE TRANSPORTATION PURCHASED FOR FINAL CONSUMPTION IN THE UNITED KINGDOM, 1920–38

(Expenditure in 1938 is taken as the base for each series)

	1920	1921	1922	1923	1924	1925	1926	1927	1928	1929	1930	1931	1932	1933	1934	1935	1936	1937	1938
Motor-cars and motor-cycles																			
Quantity index	12·8	6·8	11·2	14·8	20·6	27·1	26·1	27·5	27·7	28·0	26·6	23·1	25·1	29·1	35·9	43·4	47·9	49·2	43·1
Price index	132·8	122·7	106·3	91·5	82·5	80·8	77·0	69·3	63·5	58·3	55·5	49·9	44·5	43·9	45·1	43·8	42·6	42·6	43·1
Running costs of motor vehicles																			
Quantity index	9·1	11·3	14·2	17·1	21·6	26·1	31·2	35·9	41·3	45·3	48·1	48·2	50·0	52·7	57·6	64·8	71·1	76·7	81·8
Price index	144·2	128·5	116·7	109·0	105·6	100·1	100·6	90·4	89·6	88·9	88·6	84·9	88·4	88·3	85·3	82·3	80·6	81·7	81·8
Bicycles, accessories and repairs																			
Quantity index	3·9	4·1	4·3	4·4	4·6	4·7	4·8	5·0	5·1	5·3	5·4	6·5	7·6	8·6	10·5	10·5	10·4	10·4	10·3
Price index	23·4	23·5	18·2	15·9	14·5	13·6	12·6	12·0	11·3	10·6	10·3	10·0	9·6	9·1	9·9	10·0	9·7	10·0	10·3
Total																			
Quantity index	25·8	22·2	29·7	36·3	46·8	57·9	62·1	68·4	74·1	78·6	80·1	77·8	82·7	90·4	104·0	118·7	129·4	136·3	135·2
Price index	336·6	282·7	252·3	227·1	212·9	207·7	197·8	177·4	167·1	159·3	154·9	144·4	142·2	140·6	139·9	136·0	132·9	134·3	135·2

CHAPTER VI

PUBLIC TRANSPORTATION

1 GENERAL REMARKS

Expenditure on all forms of public transport in 1938 amounted to £178 m. This represented 4% of total personal expenditure in that year. The largest component of this figure was expenditure on travel by bus and coach, £76 m., more than a third as big again as the next largest item, £56 m. spent on railway travel. The other main form of inland transport, tram and trolley bus, accounted for £21 m. Travel by taxi and hire car, which is also classed as public transport, cost £12 m. Sea travel by residents of the United Kingdom is also included and approximately £12 m. was spent in this way in 1938. Air travel was not yet of much importance and accounted for just over £0·5 m.

These values represent the costs of passenger travel paid for out of personal income, excluding all expenditure that would normally be charged to expense accounts of business. Of course a large part of expenditure on inland transport represents fares paid for journeys to and from work and might equally be reckoned as part of the costs of working in the same way as special clothes or tools bought by employees. On the other hand, those who travel farthest to their work probably enjoy a positive advantage in living away from the industrial area. Any attempt to estimate the proportion of the cost of the journey to work representing final consumption would probably be quite arbitrary, and for many important purposes it is probably unnecessary.[1]

The variations over the period in expenditure on the different forms of land transport are shown in Fig. 6. Quantity and price series for each item are also shown. These series represent the number of passenger-miles travelled and the average fare per mile. They are drawn on a logarithmic scale and ranged according to expenditure in 1938.

These estimates of the number of passenger-miles travelled and the average fare paid are useful for comparing the trend of development in the different forms of transport but too much significance should not be attached to the absolute values of the figures. In many cases the average fare represents a modal figure rather than a true weighted average value and consequently the estimates of passenger-miles will be subject to a definite upward or downward bias. More important, the passenger-mile is not a truly representative unit for comparing the services supplied by the different forms of transport.

Although expenditure on travel by railway took second place in 1938, this was a comparatively recent development. At the beginning of the period the railways were clearly the more important and the amount spent on train travel was more than twice that on buses or on trams. On a quantity basis the railways still held first place and accounted for the greatest number of passenger-miles travelled in 1938. The trend had been steadily rising throughout most of the period but demand was clearly responsive to variations in the level of general prosperity. The effect of the post-war slump, accompanied by a rise in price, was particularly severe. The figures reached their lowest level in 1932. The subsequent recovery was halted and demand again fell off in the last two years of the period when prices were rising. Apart from these last two years the trend in fares had been slowly downward throughout the period, from $1d.$ per mile in 1921 to less than $\frac{2}{3}d.$ per mile in 1936. The average fare paid for workmen's and season tickets had varied only slightly during the period about an average value slightly less than $\frac{1}{2}d.$ per mile.

Tramway services had continued to expand slowly during the first half of the period but declined with the onset of the depression in 1930 and in the last years were increasingly replaced by trolley buses. Although it offered the cheapest means of travel this form of public transport had failed to make any headway and total revenue fell by almost half. Average fares had tended downwards at a slightly slower rate than railway fares, falling from $0·8d.$ per mile in 1920 to $0·6d.$ per mile in 1938. Expenditure on travel by trolley bus was negligible at the beginning of the period and amounted to less than £1 m. in 1929. As trolley buses replaced trams during the second half of the period the value of expenditure rose to almost £6 m. by 1938.

Bus and coach services developed rapidly during the

---

[1] See the discussion on pp. 5–8 of Vol. I of this study.

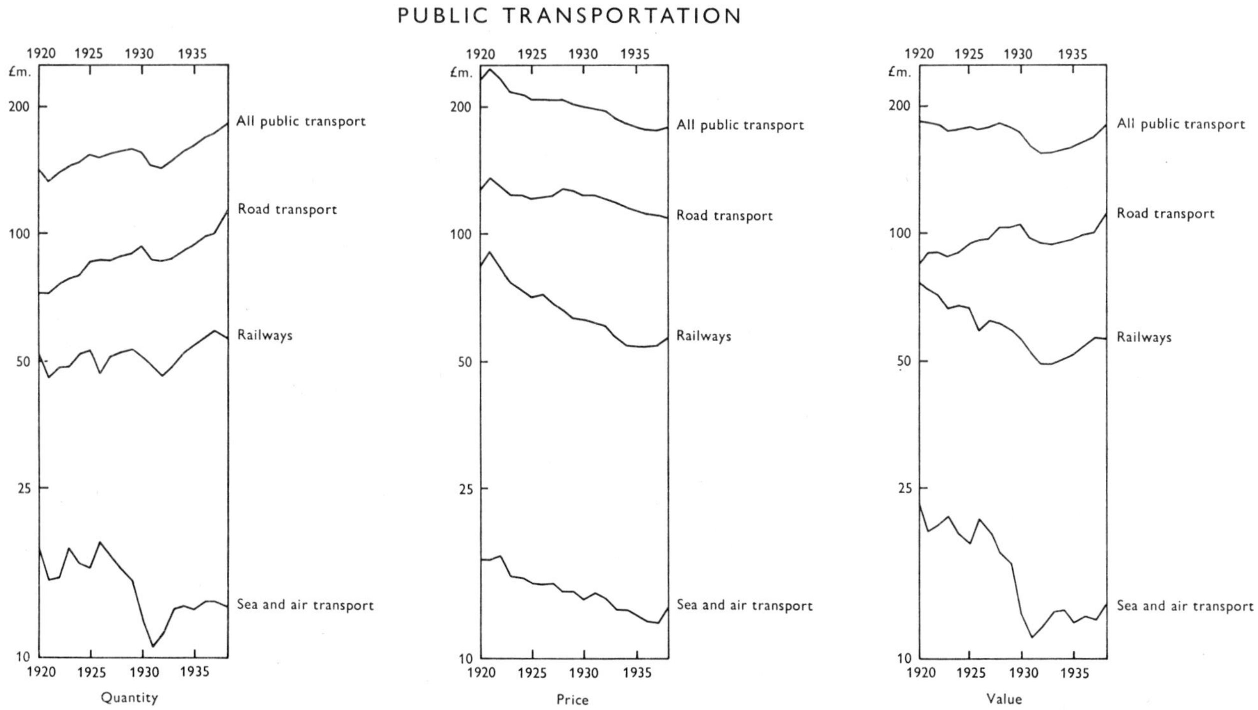

PUBLIC TRANSPORTATION

Fig. 6. The variations in the quantities purchased, average prices and expenditure on public transportation for final consumption in the United Kingdom, 1920–38.

period and expenditure on this form of transport increased from £28·5 m. in 1920 to £76·2 m. in 1938. The number of passenger-miles travelled rose from 3½ thousand million to more than 19 thousand million. The rise was continuous throughout the period apart from a slight setback in the slump years 1931–3. After a sharp rise in 1921 the average fare paid fell steadily from over 2¼d. per mile to just under 1d. per mile in 1938, becoming more and more competitive with the other forms of public transport. There seems little doubt, however, that a large part of the increase in bus services was due not so much to direct competition with other transport as to their reaching new sources of demand previously untapped.

Expenditure on travel by taxi cab and hire car amounted to as much as £23 m. in 1920 but had fallen to just half of this value by 1938. The average fare for this form of transport rose from 3·4d. per mile in 1920 to 4·9d. in 1932 and thereafter decreased slightly to 4·7d. in 1938. The number of passenger-miles travelled decreased from 1,624 million in 1920 to 587 million in 1938. There was also a small amount spent on horse-drawn hackney vehicles at the beginning of the period, £3·7 m. in 1920, but this had fallen to less than £1 m. by 1931 and to less than half this by 1938.

Although expenditure on sea travel is an item of considerable importance it is not possible to make more than a rough estimate of the order of magnitude involved. This was in the region of £10 m. in 1938. It seems

probable from a consideration of the passenger statistics that traffic had remained steady during the years up to 1929, fallen off severely during the slump, but regained its former level by 1938. However, while emigrants formed much the greater proportion of travellers in the earlier years it was the increase in tourism that was responsible for the recovery at the end of the period. Travel by steamboat on cross-channel passages, ferry services and pleasure-boat trips probably accounted for an additional £2 m. in 1938.

Air travel was still in its infancy and although the service developed rapidly during the period, expenditure was only just over £0·5 m. in 1938.

2 METHODS OF ESTIMATION

Scope of the estimates. The estimates discussed in this chapter cover expenditure on all forms of public passenger transport by land, sea, and air, paid for out of personal income. Expenditure for business purposes, which is normally charged to expense accounts, is excluded. As far as possible only the cost of travelling is reckoned here; the value of other goods and services purchased, such as meals served to travellers, is already included elsewhere in the estimates.

For most of the items in this group it is not possible to make detailed adjustments to exclude purchases by tourists and other non-residents. Similarly, expenditures by United Kingdom residents abroad are for the most part not included. Estimates of the net balance for all items on these accounts are given in Chapter X.

General procedure. For the principal forms of land transport fairly comprehensive statistics of receipts, and of passenger-miles travelled, are published for most or all of the period. From these sources the appropriate quantity, price, and value series, could be constructed for the whole period. The problem of consumer allocation had, for the most part, to be settled in rather arbitrary fashion. Expenditure on sea travel could be only approximately estimated on the basis of a value figure for 1936, the published passenger statistics, and an index of passenger fares. For the smaller items of travel expenditure, fewer data are available. The receipts from passenger travel on steamboats run by the railway companies are published, but no quantity or price estimates could be made. The number of passengers travelling by air is known for most years of the period and expenditure could be calculated by estimating the average fare paid.

Methods employed. The methods of estimation employed for the different items in the group are discussed below in the following order:

(a) Railways.
(b) Tramways and trolley vehicles.
(c) Buses and coaches.
(d) Taxis and hire cars.
(e) Horse-drawn hackney vehicles.
(f) Ocean-going shipping lines.
(g) Steamboat lines, ferries, etc.
(h) Airways.

(A) RAILWAYS

Receipts from passengers are published for the whole period.[1] The form of accounts was changed in 1928; the receipts as re-calculated for 1927 were £42,000 greater than those previously published and this amount was added to the published figures for the years 1920–6.[2] From 1933 the *Railway Returns* excluded the lines operated by the London Passenger Transport Board; the amounts which it was necessary to add for these lines were supplied by the L.P.T.B.

For the years after 1930 the *Railway Returns* give, as a percentage of the total passenger receipts excluding workmen's and season tickets, the receipts in the following categories of passenger travel:

At reduced fares
    Excursion
        Day and half-day
        Period
        Weekend
    Tourist
    Other reduced fares
At standard fares

Since the receipts from workmen's and season tickets are also given as a percentage of total receipts for these years, it was possible to calculate them as a percentage of receipts from ordinary passengers, that is, all those contained in the previous list. All these percentages exclude the L.P.T.B. for the whole period 1930–8.

As a result of special inquiries the *Railway Returns* also included average receipts per passenger-mile for the same types of ticket for September 1932 and September 1934, excluding the L.P.T.B., and for September 1930 and September 1932, including the L.P.T.B. The average for total traffic, excluding the L.P.T.B., was also published for September 1930. Since the relation of the two totals for 1930 was similar to that for 1932,[3] it was assumed that the same was true of the individual classes of ticket in order to calculate the average receipt per passenger-mile in the different categories for September 1930, excluding the L.P.T.B.

The fares calculated in this way were used as the annual average fares for the three years mentioned. For 1931 the average of 1930 and 1932 was taken for each group. For 1933 the average of 1932 and 1934 was taken for all categories except period tickets where the figures for these two years were 0·935*d.* and 0·979*d.* respectively. For 1933 the value 0·970*d.* was taken since the cheap monthly tickets at 1*d.* per mile, which greatly increased the percentage of traffic in this category, were introduced in 1933. The fares in the different groups in 1935 and 1936 were assumed to be the same as in 1934. As a result of the 5 % increase in fares as from 1 October 1937, fares were taken at 1·25 % higher in 1937 in each category except standard at 1·225 % and workmen's at 0·25 %, thus allowing for the cheaper tickets on which the 5 % increase had no effect. The increase in each group for 1938 as compared with 1934 was taken at four times that allowed for 1937.

If the receipts of a group taken as a percentage of ordinary receipts is r,[4] and p is the average receipts per passenger-mile in the group, the average fare per passenger-mile for all classes of travel is given by the formula $\Sigma r / \Sigma(r/p)$, the summation being over all groups. From the total passenger receipts and the average fare per passenger-mile, the total number of passenger-miles was

---

[1] **[14]** *Railway Returns*, published annually by the Ministry of Transport.

[2] In estimating average fares no allowance was made for this small adjustment.

[3] The actual average fares are:

	Including L.P.T.B. (*d.*)	Excluding L.P.T.B. (*d.*)
September 1930	0·737	0·743
September 1932	0·764	0·772

[4] Σr does not equal 100 since the figures are taken as a percentage of ordinary and not of total receipts.

calculated for the years 1930–8, excluding the L.P.T.B. from both receipts and passenger-miles.

Since the receipts of the L.P.T.B. (or, before July 1933, of the lines later taken over by the L.P.T.B.) are known,[1] only the average fare per passenger-mile for these lines was needed to get the total passenger-miles travelled in the years 1930–8. The total passenger-miles travelled and the average fare per passenger-mile were published for the months of September 1930, 1932, and 1934, both including and excluding the L.P.T.B. lines. From these figures it was possible to calculate the average fare per passenger-mile for the L.P.T.B. for these months. The resultant fares were 0·689d., 0·685d. and 0·670d.[2] It was assumed that these figures could be taken as the average fares for the whole year, that the average for 1931 was 0·687d., for 1933 was 0·675d., and for the years after 1934 remained at 0·670d.

The average fare per passenger-mile for all lines for the period so far considered could be calculated from the sum of receipts and passenger-miles for the L.P.T.B. and other lines.

For the years 1923 and 1929 data similar to those used above for non-L.P.T.B. lines are available for all lines. For 1927 the group 'At reduced fares' is only subdivided into 'Excursion and weekend' and 'Other'. The method described above was applied to each of these years, the September census being available for each. For 1924 and 1925 'Tourist' tickets are again shown separately and the census was taken in both February and September. To retain as much uniformity as possible only the September figures were used. For 1926 the figures are given in the same detail as for 1927 but only a February census was taken. The average fares in each group were raised to September levels by applying approximately the same ratio as existed between the two months in 1924 and 1925.[3]

For the years 1920–3 the only division of passenger receipts available is between ordinary, workmen's, and season tickets. There is also a division of passenger journeys at full, reduced, and workmen's fares, as a percentage of total passenger journeys, excluding those of season ticket holders. Taking the average fare for each of the four groups 'At full fares', 'At reduced fares', 'Workmen's', and 'Season tickets', as given (the method by which they were derived will be explained later), the method used to obtain the average fare for all travel was as follows.

By the method described above, the passenger-miles travelled in the two groups, 'At full fares' and 'At reduced fares', could be found for 1924 as a percentage of total passenger-miles. The percentage of passenger journeys, excluding those of season ticket holders, is also published for these two groups for 1924.[4] By dividing the percentage of passenger-miles in a group by the percentage of passenger journeys in the same group an index of the average length of a passenger journey in 1924 was found. The index was applied to the percentage of passenger journeys in the group for the years 1920–3, the product giving an index of passenger-miles in the group. Multiplying by the average fare in the group, a similar result could be obtained for receipts. Adding index numbers for receipts in the two groups, an index for all ordinary tickets was obtained, and the corresponding index for workmen's and season tickets could be calculated. The passenger-miles index for these groups was found by dividing by the average fare. Summing over all groups for both receipts and passenger-miles and dividing the former by the latter, the average fare for all travel was found.

It only remains to describe how the average fares in each group in these years were reached. In 1923 the census described above was taken in February and September. The September results were used as before. Earlier figures refer to July 1920, July 1921 and the year ending 31 August 1921, and do not include an estimate for season tickets. Since the figures for July 1921 and the year ending 31 August 1921 are almost identical they are taken as the average for 1921. The average of 1921 and 1923 was taken as the average fare in 1922. The average fare for 1920 was obtained from the July 1920 and July 1921 fares, the weighting being decided by the fact that there was an increase in fares in August and September 1920. Fares for season tickets for the three years were taken as about the same proportion of ordinary fares as in 1923.

An estimate of the proportion of total expenditure on passenger travel in 1938 which should be included under personal expenditure was made available for the purpose of this inquiry. This estimate is based on the experience of traffic officers and provides details of the proportion of business expenditure included in the returns for each class of ticket. The residual volume of personal expenditure represented 83·4% of the total in this year. Since

---

[1] The figures from 1933 were supplied by the L.P.T.B. Those for earlier years are simply the differences between the receipts given in the [**14**] *Railway Returns* before the formation of the L.P.T.B. and those given after that event for past years excluding L.P.T.B. lines. Even if the figures are not completely comparable, the total receipts will not be affected and the total passenger-miles only very slightly.

[2] If n, N are the number of passenger-miles excluding and including the L.P.T.B. respectively and p, P are the corresponding average fares, the average fare for the L.P.T.B. is $(NP - np)/(N - n)$.

[3] For workmen's and season tickets the difference between the two months is negligible. The ratio of September to February standard fares is taken at 1·01, being 1·017 in 1924 and 1·009 in 1925. The adjustment for reduced fares is greater, mainly because some fares of this type were current in the summer months.

[4] Since only the relative positions of full and reduced fares are relevant here the totals of which the percentage are taken are not important.

business expenditure was mainly at standard fares the proportion of passenger-miles represented by personal expenditure is slightly higher: in fact 85·8%. For want of other information these percentages were applied for each year throughout the period. Undoubtedly business travellers made increasing use of the motor-car during this period but this would not necessarily involve a fall in the proportion of railway travel represented by business travellers.

The estimates so far relate only to Great Britain. The data were not available to make similar detailed calculations for Northern Ireland and 2% was added to the estimates to cover this omission.

(B) TRAMWAYS AND TROLLEY VEHICLES

In the following discussion the years treated first are those which illustrate most effectively the general method employed. The methods used for other years can then be treated as modifications.

For the years 1925–32 figures are published[1] giving the passenger receipts separately for tramways and trolley undertakings in the following groups:

English and Welsh local authorities, April–March years;

Scottish local authorities, June–May years;

companies, calendar years.

From the same source, for each of these years except 1926 in the case of companies and 1926–7 in the case of local authorities,[2] average fares per mile for ordinary and, in most cases, workmen's travel were obtained for individual undertakings. The average fares in both categories for each of the groups mentioned above were calculated separately for trams and trolleys by weighting the average fares by the number of car-miles travelled.[3] The average fare in each group was obtained by combining ordinary and workmen's fares, using the following relative weights:[4]

Scottish local authorities, trams 95:5
Other 80:20

Fares and receipts in each group were adjusted to calendar years and by dividing receipts by fares the number of passenger-miles of travel was calculated.[5] The receipts and passenger-miles were summed for all groups and the average fares calculated separately for trams and trolleys.

For the years after 1932 the method described above was used for all undertakings not included in the L.P.T.B. For those undertakings which were included in the L.P.T.B. the passenger receipts and the passenger-miles travelled were calculated, in the way described above, for the years 1930–2. From the same source the number of passenger journeys on vehicles belonging to these undertakings could be found. The ratio of passenger-miles to passenger journeys gave the average distance of a journey for these three years. The distances were 2·39, 2·39 and 2·38 miles respectively on trams and 2·39, 2·40 and 2·40 miles on trams and trolleys combined. It was assumed that the average length of a journey on trams under the L.P.T.B. remained at 2·38 miles for the years 1933–8 and that the average length of a journey on trams and trolleys combined remained at 2·40 miles during the same years.[6] From the published figures for the number of passenger journeys[7] it was then possible to deduce the number of passenger-miles travelled on trams under the L.P.T.B. and on trams and trolleys combined. The difference gave the number of passenger-miles on trolleys. As the receipts of trams and trolleys belonging to the L.P.T.B. were known, both passenger receipts and passenger-miles could be added to those for other undertakings to complete the estimates described above.

From 1921–2 to 1923–4 the published figures give only the average ordinary fares for the different undertakings. It was assumed that the average fare, when allowance is made for workmen's travel, bears the same relation to average ordinary fares for the various groups as in the first year or two after the two sets of figures are published. The estimates were completed in the same way as for later years.

The earliest detailed figures of fares of individual undertakings which have been obtained relate to the year 1921 in the case of companies and 1921–2 in the case of local authorities. To complete estimates for the years 1920–2 it was necessary to estimate average fares for the earlier years. For 1920 for companies, and 1920–1 for local authorities, this was done on the basis of published figures of the average receipts per passenger. This is equivalent to an assumption that the average length of a passenger journey remained the same. The estimate for 1921 could now be completed as before. The average fare for local authorities in 1920 was taken to be the same as in 1920–1, thus enabling the 1920 estimate to be completed.

---

[1] [23] Ministry of Transport, *Tramways and Light Railways (Street and Road) and Trackless Trolley Undertakings*.

[2] The fares were estimated for these years on the basis of such statistics as were obtained.

[3] The actual weights are the nearest 100,000 car-miles.

[4] The lower percentage taken for Scotland is due to the fact that the largest undertakings in Scotland have no special workmen's fares.

[5] The number of passenger-miles calculated in this way represents the number which the passenger could travel for the fare and not the number actually travelled. The difference could be considered as waste by the consumer. Care must be taken in comparing the figures with passenger-miles for other forms of travel since this procedure could not be used in all cases.

[6] With the growing importance of trolleys this implies a reduction in the average length of journey on a trolley vehicle. The average length of such a journey in 1931–2 was much longer than on a tram but might be expected to approach this as trolleys became more general.

[7] [94] *Annual Reports* of the London Passenger Transport Board.

Ratios of personal to total travel on trams and trolleys were supplied by Mr E. J. Broster for the years 1923–1934. A rough estimate was made for other years.

(c) BUSES AND COACHES

The following basic data are known or can be readily estimated for the period:

(a) the total number of buses and coaches in service;
(b) the total number of vehicle-miles travelled;
(c) the total number of passenger journeys made;
(d) the total passenger receipts.

From these data estimates can be made of the receipts per passenger journey and per vehicle-mile. The number of passenger-miles cannot be directly estimated. It is necessary to make some assumption about either the average length of a passenger journey or the average number of people on board a bus at the same time.

For the calendar years 1931–7 the relevant figures for Great Britain of receipts, passenger journeys and vehicle-miles are published.[1] There are also figures of the number of vehicles owned at the end of these years. The figures are given separately for local authorities, London Passenger Transport Board, and other operators.

For all the years of the period there are for a few bus undertakings the same data separately for local authorities and for companies.[2] The number of undertakings providing such returns was much greater at the end of the period than at the beginning. For some further companies one or more of the data mentioned was provided but not all. The problem is to link the figures which are available to the complete figures for the later years.

The first step is to obtain the total figures in each financial year for those undertakings in the local authority sample for which all four figures are available. To the total of vehicle-miles are added the total for all other authorities for which the figures of vehicle-miles and the number of vehicles are available. This gives for as large a sample as possible in each year the average vehicle-miles per bus. By simple interpolation the figures were adjusted to calendar years. Similar figures for the average vehicle-miles per bus were worked out for the years 1931 to 1937 from the Traffic Commissioners' data. Suppose that the later figures are V while the figures for the sample are v. Then the estimates of V for other years were made by finding the ratio of V to v for each of the years 1931–7 and assuming that the average of these ratios applied to each of the other years of the period. The reasons why v is not the best estimate of V in each year are: in the first place, there is some doubt about the date to which the figures given in the sample refer, a doubt which should have as its main effect the making of v constantly a little too high or a little too low; secondly, the number of vehicles in the sample may in some cases

refer to the number in use and not to the number owned, as in the Traffic Commissioners' *Report*; finally, the sample may not be strictly random, since there might be some tendency for the undertakings with better figures to consent to their appearing separately. These estimates of V for earlier years are not the actual average number of miles travelled by a local authority bus during the year but they do provide a series of figures which, if multiplied by the number of vehicles corresponding in each year to the number as defined by the Traffic Commissioners, would give the best available estimate of the number of vehicle-miles travelled by the local authority buses during the course of the year. The way in which this number of vehicles was estimated is described later.

In a similar way the average number of passenger journeys made per local authority bus was estimated by first calculating for the sample the total passenger journeys and total number of vehicles for all authorities for which both sets of data were available and hence finding the average number of passenger journeys per vehicle for the sample. The corresponding figures for calendar years were obtained by simple interpolation and the average ratio of these figures to the Traffic Commissioners' data was used to extend the latter values backwards to cover the whole period. Similarly, using the total of passenger receipts for all those local authority undertakings for which both figures of the passenger receipts and the number of vehicles exist, the average passenger receipts per vehicle were found.

The figures for companies were treated in exactly the same way as the figures for the local authorities. There were, however, two differences. In the first place, the figures did not all relate to exactly the same years. This was dealt with by treating all the figures as if they related to the nearest calendar year. The total error involved should be small since in some cases it will be in one direction and in some in the other. Secondly, from the Traffic Commissioners' data the sum of the figures of the London Passenger Transport Board and of the figures of other operators was used. This assumes that all the undertakings which formed the London Passenger Transport Board were companies; while this may not be strictly true, it is the case that the largest of the undertakings were companies. The error involved should once more be small and it should tend to disappear in the total since all that will be involved will be the transference of some undertakings and vehicles from the category 'local authority' to the category 'company'.

The next point to be decided is the number of vehicles owned by local authorities and by companies before 1931 which will correspond to the number which were

---

[1] [7] *Annual Reports of the Traffic Commissioners.*
[2] See [102] *Motor Transport Yearbook.*

taken from the Traffic Commissioners' *Reports*. The figures used as the basis of this calculation are the figures for Great Britain of the numbers of coaches and buses owned at September in each of the years 1926 to 1938. For 1922 onwards there are figures of the approximate number of licences of motor hackneys current at various dates which include 31 August for each year. The estimate of the number of buses and coaches owned at September was made by roughly continuing the trend in the ratio of the buses and coaches figure to the motor hackney figure. A regression was fitted but was not successful—mainly, it is believed, because the conditions required before a motor-car could be registered as a motor hackney were made more stringent at various times. From the appearance of the figures for 1921 and 1922, as given for the highest quarter of the year,[1] it would appear that there was some such change between 1921 and 1922. In these circumstances the figure taken for hackneys in 1921 is little better than a guess. The figure for 1920 relates to the number of hackneys at 31 March.[2] This figure was multiplied by a correcting factor to adjust for seasonal variation and an interpolation was made between this estimate and the one for 1921 to get an estimate for the end of August 1920. The ratio of August figures in the two years was used as the basis for estimating the figure for 1920 from that for 1921.

The figures of buses owned at September for each year 1920–30 were adjusted to the level of the Traffic Commissioners' numbers of vehicles licensed by use of the average ratio of the two sets of figures for the years 1931–8. To obtain figures for the end of December simple interpolation was used.

The next problem is to divide the total number of buses and coaches into the number owned by local authorities and the number owned by other undertakings. For this purpose the number of buses owned by local authorities in the sample of undertakings mentioned above (the figure for the financial year being taken as the figure for the end of December in the financial year) was found for the end of each of the years 1931–7 as a ratio of the total number of vehicles owned by local authorities in these years, as given in the *Reports* of the Traffic Commissioners. The average of these ratios was applied to give estimates of the number of vehicles owned by local authorities in the other years. In making this calculation all the local authorities in the sample which gave figures for the number of vehicles were used, regardless of whether they gave any other information or not. This method assumes, of course, that the proportion of the local authority vehicles covered was the same throughout the period; this seems to be a reasonable assumption for most years since most of the local authorities do seem to be covered by the sample. If the

assumption is not justified, as it may not be in the earliest years, then the only effect will be to shift some of the buses from the group 'local authorities' to the group 'companies', and since it is intended to use only the figures of the total in further work there should not be very much error involved.

From the numbers of vehicles owned in the two groups and the sample figures of vehicle-miles per vehicle, passenger journeys per vehicle, and passenger receipts per vehicle, it is possible to calculate the total vehicle-miles, total passenger journeys and the total passenger receipts for the two groups. The figures for the two groups are then summed to provide the estimates of (*a*), (*b*), (*c*) and (*d*), which are needed as the first step in the calculation. The figures under (*d*) give, of course, the total value for expenditure on travel by buses and coaches to which the only corrections that have to be made are in respect of Northern Ireland and expenditure other than personal. These corrections, which apply equally to the quantity figures, will be dealt with later.

The problem then arises of how to make estimates of the price and quantity indices for travel by buses and coaches. The quantity measure required is an index number of passenger-miles. For this purpose it would be necessary to know for each year either the average number of passengers carried per mile, or the average length of the passenger journey. An estimate of the average seating capacity of a bus can be made but the average proportion of seats occupied remains unknown. Two assumptions seem the most reasonable that it is possible to make. The first is that the item most likely to vary rather slowly from year to year would be the average length of the passenger journey; this is likely to be affected less by either the level of general activity or the average fare than by the slow change in the average distance between place of residence and place of work and the gradual shift in taste governing the use of the bus or coach for journeys of different length. The second assumption is that the average proportion of seats occupied, while it might vary considerably from year to year with the change in the total number of people using buses, would be fairly stable in the long run.

If, as a first approximation, the average length of the passenger journey is assumed to be constant over the period, then the number of passenger-miles will vary proportionately with the number of passenger journeys. The ratio of the number of passenger journeys (equivalent to the number of passenger-miles, since the absolute level is not relevant) to the total number of seat-miles of all buses may then be taken as a preliminary estimate of the average proportion of seats occupied from year to year.

[1] **[101]** Society of Motor Manufacturers and Traders, *The Motor Industry of Great Britain, 1939*, table 20, p. 63.   [2] Ibid.

A corrected estimate of this proportion was obtained by eliminating the trend from this series. It was found that the best fit was given by fitting separate linear trends to the two periods 1920–30 and 1930–8. An index number of passenger-miles could then be calculated from the number of seat-miles. The probable reason for the break in trend was the coming into force of the Road Traffic Act 1930.

It remains to describe how the average seating capacity of a bus in each year was calculated. For each of the years from 1926 to 1938 the number of buses and coaches owned at September in Great Britain is given and the figures are classified according to the number of seats in nine size groups: from a minimum of eight seats to a final class of 64 seats and over. The averages of the groups were taken to be the mid-points of the class intervals and for the unclosed group at the end an average of 70 was taken. The average seating capacity of the buses was then found by multiplying the number in each group by the average size, including both light and heavy oil vehicles where these are shown separately. The mean proportional change of the first four years in the average number of seats per bus was used to obtain estimates of the September figures for the earlier years, since from graphical inspection this method seemed most suitable. The estimates for the average seating capacity in the middle of the year were made by linear interpolation.

The correction for Northern Ireland was made by taking the number of buses in use in Northern Ireland[1] as a percentage of the total for Great Britain, interpolating to get the percentage at the middle of the year and adding this percentage to the value and quantity for Great Britain. For the years 1923–34 estimates of the proportion of personal expenditure on travel by buses and coaches were supplied by Mr Broster. The percentage rises from 92·5 % in 1923 to 97·2 % in 1934. In view of the increase which his figures show in the early years, the figures 91·0, 91·5, and 92·0 were taken for the years 1920, 1921 and 1922, respectively. For the years after 1934 the percentage of 97·2 was kept. These percentages were applied both to the value and the quantity figures for the United Kingdom. The quantity figures were then reduced to an index. This index was divided into the value to get a price series, which was in its turn reduced to an index.

It has been estimated that the average fare on buses and coaches in 1938 was 0·96d. per mile.[2] At the level of expenditure calculated above, this implies that the number of passenger-miles travelled during the year was 19,037 million. Estimates for the other years of the period were obtained by applying the two index series already calculated.

(D) TAXIS AND HIRE CARS

From 1928 to 1938 the number of taxis in use in the United Kingdom in September of each year is known.[3] The average number in use during each calendar year was found by taking a weighted three-year moving average of these figures. The figures thus obtained were compared with an estimate by Mr Broster of the number of vehicles in the period 1923–35. Although the two series are not identical they are very similar, and the estimate was therefore carried back to 1923 on the basis of Broster's figures. From 1923 to 1920 the trend from 1926 to 1923 was continued.

Broster also provided estimates of the total mileage per vehicle, the total loaded mileage per vehicle, the loading coefficient, the price per passenger-mile and the proportion of travel by taxi charged to business expenditure. These estimates refer to the period from 1923 to 1935. For the other years of the period rough assumptions were made following the trend of his figures.

(E) HORSE-DRAWN HACKNEY VEHICLES

The estimates for the years 1923–35 for Great Britain were kindly provided by Mr Broster; the estimates for the remaining years of the period represent a guess. Two per cent was added to account for Northern Ireland.

No information about the methods employed can be given. The price figures were found by dividing the total personal expenditure by the total passenger mileage. The rough estimates for the periods not covered by Broster were made in accordance with the general trend of the expenditure and mileage figures.

(F) OCEAN-GOING SHIPPING LINES

The estimates under this heading relate only to long-distance sea voyages and exclude expenditure on cross-channel passages to Eire and the continent, which are discussed in the following section.

It is not possible to make a direct estimate of personal expenditure on this item since there are no comprehensive records of the number of United Kingdom residents who were passengers on ships sailing abroad, of the average fare paid, or of the average length of voyage taken. However, it is possible to fix the level of expenditure in 1936 and to derive estimates for other years of the period on the basis of a rough index of 'passenger-miles' travelled, compiled from the statistics of passenger movements, and an index of passenger rates.

It has been estimated that the total passenger receipts of United Kingdom shipping in 1936 were £22·5 m.;

---

[1] **[101]** *The Motor Industry of Great Britain, 1939*, table 21, p. 65.
[2] Ibid. p. 94.
[3] Ibid. p. 65.

expenditure by United Kingdom residents may be put at £11·8 m.[1] This figure will include the value of provisions purchased by ships in this country, which must be excluded from this estimate since it has already been accounted for in the estimate of food consumption. Net passenger receipts in this year may therefore be put at approximately £11 m. A further deduction must be made for the expenditure of those travelling on business. This may be assumed to be 10% of the total, leaving approximately £10 m. for personal expenditure in the year.

Although the number of travellers entering and leaving the country is officially recorded, the classification adopted for the published statistics[2] permits only a rough estimate of the actual number of residents going abroad in each year. The numbers travelling to Europe and to other countries are shown separately. Within these two groups passengers of British nationality (including those from the Dominions and Colonies) are separately distinguished. British passengers travelling to countries out of Europe are further divided between emigrants and other travellers. After 1930 the numbers going on pleasure cruises are also shown.[3]

In order to derive an estimate of the number of passenger journeys made by United Kingdom residents two assumptions were made. First, that 34% of British passengers, other than emigrants, travelling to countries out of Europe before 1933 were residents of the United Kingdom. This proportion is based on the results of a sample investigation for the year 1932.[4] From 1933 onwards there are published estimates of United Kingdom tourists.[5] Secondly, it was assumed that all British passengers to Europe travelled by the cross-channel route and could therefore be excluded from these estimates.

The estimated number of outward-bound United Kingdom tourists was divided according to destination in the same proportions as the recorded figures for all outward-bound British passengers other than emigrants. The numbers were then summed for each year after roughly weighting each class on the basis of the average length of voyage taken. The relative weights used for the four classes, Australia and New Zealand, British South Africa, United States and British North America, and other countries were 4, 2, 1, and 3. The number of emigrants was summed in the same way, applying the same weights as for tourists, and the two groups were then combined with weights of 2 and 1. The numbers going on pleasure cruises were also included with a weight of 1½. This combined series provides an index of the total 'passenger-miles' travelled in each year of the period.

A price index for the period was compiled on the basis of information from the principal shipping companies. The cost of passages at typical rates for all the main sailing routes was obtained for the whole or a part of the period. There are the inevitable difficulties in this sort of selection due to the varying standards of accommodation and the changing requirements of the traffic. To the extent that these are random factors they will cancel out in the total; there was also a fair degree of similarity in the movement of the different series which reduces the possible discrepancy due to errors of weighting. For each of the four classes distinguished above, the quotations in each year were simply averaged and a continuous, broadly consistent, series compiled. A single price index for all passages was then obtained by taking a weighted average of these four series, using fixed weights inversely proportional to the distance travelled.

The product of the index numbers of prices and quantities is then an index of expenditures. On the basis of this index and the figure for 1936 an estimate of expenditure in all years of the period was derived. It was not possible, however, to fix any absolute level for the price and quantity measures.

(G) STEAMBOAT LINES, FERRIES, ETC.

The receipts from passengers on steamboats run by railway companies are published for all years of the period.[6] It is assumed that these figures include the value of all cross-channel passages to the continent, the Channel Islands, Eire, etc. They will, however, also include, particularly for cross-channel traffic, a certain amount of expenditure by non-nationals and of business expenditure. On the other hand, some tourists will travel in foreign ships. The published figures were reduced by 20% to allow for this.

The *Railway Returns* exclude, of course, all travel by steamboats not run by railway companies. It is probable that the amount involved is quite small, the chief items being expenditure on ferries and pleasure boats. It seems reasonable to add £0·5 m. throughout the period to cover these additional items.

It is not possible to calculate separate price or quantity series for the items in this group.

---

[1] I.e. total receipts *less* fares paid by non-nationals *plus* expenditure in foreign ships. See [77] M. G. Kendall, 'United Kingdom merchant shipping statistics', *J. R. Statist. Soc.* series A (General), CXI (1948), part II, p. 143.

[2] See [53] *Board of Trade Journal, passim*; summary figures are also given in, for example, [20] *Eighty-second Statistical Abstract for the United Kingdom*, tables 9–15, pp. 9–13.

[3] For 1931 see [53] *Board of Trade Journal*, 9 March 1933, p. 371; figures for other years could be obtained from the [20] *Statistical Abstract*. The number in 1931 was not large and no estimates were made for earlier years.

[4] See [78] H. Leak and T. Priday, 'Migration from and to the United Kingdom', *J. R. Statist. Soc.* XCVI (1933), part II, p. 215.

[5] See, for example, [53] *Board of Trade Journal*, 9 March 1939, p. 359; i.e. the number of passengers for whom both last and intended future residence is the United Kingdom.

[6] See [14] Ministry of Transport, *Railway Returns*, account no. 12.

(H) AIRWAYS

From 1934 to 1938 the number of paying passengers carried by United Kingdom companies within the United Kingdom or Europe is known.[1] For the years prior to 1934 the yearly average of passengers carried on commercial cross-channel flights is given as an annual average for 1933–7, 1928–32, and 1923–7.[2] These averages were first turned into yearly figures by assuming an even growth within each period for which an average was given and by assigning the average to the middle year of the period.

The total number of passengers carried in 1934 was 80,285. The number of passengers on cross-channel flights for this year forms 72 % of the total. An estimate of the total number of passengers prior to 1934 was obtained by applying this proportion to the number of passengers on cross-channel flights.

Receipts from passengers are not published. The travel agents Thos. Cook and Sons, Ltd, kindly provided price figures, stating that before the war a flight to Paris, single, was £4. 10s., a return ticket £7. 10s., or under special conditions £6. 6s. It was assumed that the average price per flight in 1938 was £4. It was further stated that prices had roughly halved since the beginning of the passenger services in 1924, and that private flying before that date was negligible. The average price at the beginning of the period was therefore put at £8, and a gradual decrease over the period was assumed.

A proportion of the total obtained in this way will be business expenditure and some of the passengers carried will be foreigners making trips to this country. In each year 20 % was deducted from the total to obtain personal expenditure of United Kingdom residents.

3 THE RELIABILITY OF THE ESTIMATES

The figures of receipts for railway travel should be reliable except, possibly, for the small constant correction of £42,000 made for the first few years.

The fact that the division between different categories of ticket in the census months is not representative of the whole year does not matter except in so far as the actual average fare within a group is different in September from the average for the whole year. The only cases in which this is likely to be important is when there was some change in the course of the year in the fare-charging policy of the railway companies; for example, the increase in fares in October 1937 or the introduction of the cheap monthly return ticket in 1933. An attempt has been made to allow for such changes, the most important of which did not happen in years when the Sept-

ember census was taken. Such seasonal changes as occur in the fares within the categories are otherwise likely to be small. Even these are not important if the relation of the September fare to the annual average is the same in each year, since only comparisons of passenger-miles with other forms of transport would be affected and, as shown in the description of the estimates for tramways, such comparisons should only be made with great caution. The main sources of error in the calculation of fares lie in (a) the fact that the subdivision may not be sufficiently fine,[3] and (b) the interpolation and extrapolation of fares in years for which there was no September census. On account of (a) the figures become less reliable for the early years, although the error is unlikely to be great at any time. The same degree of confidence cannot be placed in the figures for the non-census years but they should give a fairly close picture of the true position.

The method applied to the L.P.T.B. figures is much cruder than that used in other cases. The only published subdivision of receipts in this case is for ordinary, workmen's and season tickets and even this relates to all railways in the London Passenger Pooling Scheme. It is unlikely that the variations among categories of tickets was great for L.P.T.B. lines, so there should not be much error on this score. From the method of calculating the fares for these lines in 1930, 1932 and 1934, there is some further possibility of error since a different method is applied. Even a fairly large percentage error here would, however, affect the total railway figures only slightly.

The extension of the series backwards from 1924 is probably less accurate than the estimates for other years since the number of subdivisions is less and the average fares within the groups are found less accurately. In addition, the method of deriving the percentage of passenger receipts from the percentage of passenger journeys was based on the assumption that the relative average length of journey was constant from 1920 to 1924, and this is an assumption which may not be justified. Even for these years, however, the estimate should not be wildly inaccurate; a conclusion which is supported by a comparison of the movement of passenger-miles in the 1921 slump with that in the later slump.

No assessment can be made of the accuracy of the percentage taken for conversion from total to personal travel.

Apart from small errors involved in the adjustment to calendar years and the allowance for Northern Ireland,

---

[1] [51] *The Civil Aviation Statistical and Technical Review, 1938*, Department of Civil Aviation, Air Ministry, table 4, p. 1.

[2] Ibid. p. 6.

[3] It is, for instance, always possible that there would be some change in the average fares if the different classes of ticket were treated separately.

the figures for total passenger receipts of tramways and trolley vehicles should be accurate.

The published figures for the average fares of individual undertakings are subject to error from the point of view of the present inquiry in so far as the fares for different journeys are not adequately weighted by the number of passengers. In addition, the use of car-miles instead of passenger-miles in combining the data for the various undertakings gives scope for error. These errors will not distort the year-to-year variations much unless there is significant correlation either between the errors and changes in fares or between the errors and the number of undertakings that cease to exist or change their relative size or change from trams to trolleys. The method used to deal with the L.P.T.B. for 1933–8 is necessarily rather crude.

From 1931 onwards the figures for expenditure on buses and coaches will have a high degree of accuracy since the only sources of error are the small adjustment for Northern Ireland and the proportion taken for personal travel. For earlier years of the period the movement of this series is calculated on the basis of sample values which become less reliable as the series is extended backwards towards 1920. The errors in those figures depend on a number of factors. The passenger receipts per vehicle were calculated separately for local authorities and for companies from the sample values and these were multiplied by estimates of the number of buses owned. The sample values are themselves less reliable in the earlier years of the period because of the smaller number of returns, and only rough estimates can be obtained of the total number of vehicles before 1922. The division of the total between local authorities and companies is not an important source of error; only the total figures are used and the small number that might be transferred from one group to the other would produce a negligible bias in the combined series. Similar sources of error are involved in the estimates of the number of vehicle-miles and passenger journeys and will therefore enter into the estimates of the price and quantity series, together with the further errors involved in the assumptions about the average seating capacity of a bus and the average proportion of seats occupied at the same time. The absolute level of the price series can only be approximately determined for 1938 and it is possible that it is not altogether comparable with the calculated index of prices. From a consideration of these sources of error it may be expected that the estimates are more likely to suffer from a proportionate bias or the

presence of a trend movement rather than from large random errors in each year. The bias will probably be more pronounced in the earlier years and the year-to-year variations will also be less reliable. The dangers involved in a comparison of the number of passenger-miles travelled and average fares for different forms of transport are more pronounced in this case on account of the probable bias in the component series, which must be used with caution for this purpose.

The estimates for taxis and hire cars are necessarily more satisfactory for the years after 1927 when published figures of the number of cars operating are available. It is not possible to estimate the margins of error for the other components of the estimate but they are unlikely to be large and the contribution to the total error of the group will be small.

The estimates of the expenditure on sea travel cannot provide more than an indication of the orders of magnitude involved for each year. Neither the number of passengers nor the average fare paid can be determined with much accuracy and the absolute level of expenditure is only approximately known for the restricted definition involved.

The two remaining items, travel by steamboat and travel by air, were both relatively small throughout the period and will contribute little to the total error of the group. The first is the more accurately known since a large proportion of the total is taken from published returns. The estimated fare paid by air travellers is only an indication of the average level during the period.

4 THE MAIN TABLES

The following tables present the annual estimates obtained by the methods described above. The estimated number of passenger-miles travelled on each form of inland transport are shown in Table 27. The corresponding average fares paid are given in Table 28. In Table 29 the estimated expenditures on all forms of public transport are shown. Finally, in Table 30, price and quantity index numbers are given in a comparable form for total transport and the three categories of rail, road and other transport. The quantity series are base-weighted aggregate index numbers and the price series current-weighted aggregates; their product is thus a simple index of expenditure. Each series has been multiplied through by expenditure in 1938, the base year, and is shown in this form in the diagrams of § 1.

TABLE 27. ESTIMATED NUMBER OF PASSENGER-MILES TRAVELLED BY FINAL CONSUMERS ON PUBLIC LAND TRANSPORT IN THE UNITED KINGDOM, 1920–38 (MILLIONS)

	1920	1921	1922	1923	1924	1925	1926	1927	1928	1929	1930	1931	1932	1933	1934	1935	1936	1937	1938
Railways																			
Workmen's and season tickets	8,177	7,296	7,559	7,770	7,442	7,474	6,953	7,131	7,212	7,206	7,179	6,945	6,785	6,848	7,107	7,244	7,423	7,598	7,549
Other travel	11,037	9,427	10,115	10,057	11,195	11,453	9,858	11,164	11,431	11,706	11,084	10,364	9,810	10,643	11,402	11,973	12,526	13,147	12,460
Total	19,214	16,723	17,674	17,827	18,637	18,927	16,811	18,295	18,643	18,912	18,263	17,309	16,595	17,491	18,509	19,217	19,949	20,745	20,009
Tramways and trolley vehicles																			
Tramways	8,041	7,968	8,267	8,373	8,432	8,619	8,532	9,041	9,276	9,310	9,099	8,534	8,005	7,823	7,785	7,616	7,311	6,875	6,196
Trolley vehicles	17	22	19	28	32	42	58	101	143	184	211	257	323	409	526	682	977	1,409	1,952
Total	8,058	7,987	8,289	8,401	8,464	8,661	8,590	9,142	9,419	9,494	9,310	8,791	8,328	8,232	8,311	8,298	8,288	8,284	8,148
Buses and coaches	3,457	3,451	4,240	4,606	5,193	6,574	7,870	9,075	10,579	11,307	12,922	12,124	12,545	12,866	13,695	14,551	15,625	16,363	19,037
Taxis and hire cars	1,624	1,645	1,662	1,691	1,686	1,693	1,532	1,225	1,014	929	832	720	667	684	691	677	655	624	587
Horse-drawn vehicles	216	206	196	186	161	138	117	93	81	63	53	46	40	35	26	22	19	16	13
Total	32,569	30,012	32,061	32,711	34,141	35,993	34,920	37,830	39,736	40,705	41,380	38,990	38,175	39,308	41,232	42,765	44,536	46,032	47,794

TABLE 28. ESTIMATED AVERAGE FARES PAID BY FINAL CONSUMERS TRAVELLING ON PUBLIC LAND TRANSPORT IN THE UNITED KINGDOM, 1920–38 (PENCE PER MILE)

	1920	1921	1922	1923	1924	1925	1926	1927	1928	1929	1930	1931	1932	1933	1934	1935	1936	1937	1938
Railways																			
Workmen's and season tickets	0·44	0·52	0·50	0·47	0·47	0·47	0·47	0·47	0·47	0·47	0·46	0·46	0·45	0·44	0·43	0·43	0·44	0·44	0·45
Other travel	1·34	1·45	1·30	1·20	1·12	1·07	1·09	1·02	0·98	0·92	0·92	0·90	0·88	0·82	0·78	0·77	0·77	0·77	0·80
Total	0·96	1·04	0·96	0·88	0·86	0·83	0·83	0·81	0·78	0·75	0·74	0·72	0·71	0·67	0·65	0·64	0·64	0·65	0·67
Tramways and trolley vehicles																			
Tramways	0·82	0·89	0·82	0·78	0·76	0·74	0·72	0·69	0·67	0·66	0·65	0·65	0·64	0·64	0·62	0·61	0·61	0·60	0·60
Trolley vehicles	1·06	1·07	1·00	0·95	1·04	1·06	1·04	1·00	0·95	0·95	0·96	0·97	0·93	0·84	0·83	0·81	0·77	0·74	0·72
Total	0·82	0·88	0·82	0·78	0·76	0·74	0·72	0·69	0·67	0·67	0·66	0·66	0·65	0·65	0·63	0·62	0·63	0·62	0·63
Buses and coaches	1·98	2·31	1·95	1·76	1·64	1·49	1·39	1·30	1·30	1·22	1·14	1·14	1·12	1·07	1·04	1·01	0·99	0·98	0·96
Taxis and hire cars	3·40	3·40	3·40	3·40	3·47	3·44	3·55	3·86	4·31	4·82	4·80	4·91	4·91	4·88	4·73	4·73	4·73	4·73	4·73
Horse-drawn vehicles	4·08	4·10	4·13	4·17	4·27	4·36	4·30	4·56	4·65	4·80	5·03	4·91	4·98	5·01	5·66	5·45	5·68	6·00	6·46

TABLE 29. ESTIMATED EXPENDITURE ON PUBLIC TRANSPORTATION BY FINAL CONSUMERS IN THE UNITED KINGDOM, 1920–38 (£ M.)

	1920	1921	1922	1923	1924	1925	1926	1927	1928	1929	1930	1931	1932	1933	1934	1935	1936	1937	1938
Railways																			
Workmen's and season tickets	14·8	15·7	15·8	15·3	14·7	14·7	13·6	14·0	14·1	14·1	13·8	13·2	12·8	12·6	12·9	13·1	13·4	13·9	14·2
Other travel	61·9	57·0	54·6	50·2	52·1	50·9	44·8	47·5	46·4	44·6	42·2	38·7	36·0	36·2	36·9	38·2	39·9	42·3	41·6
Total	76·7	72·7	70·4	65·5	66·8	65·6	58·4	61·5	60·5	58·7	56·0	51·9	48·8	48·8	49·8	51·3	53·3	56·2	55·8
Travel charges	0·7	0·7	0·7	0·6	0·6	0·6	0·5	0·6	0·6	0·5	0·5	0·5	0·4	0·4	0·4	0·5	0·5	0·5	0·5
Tramways and trolley vehicles																			
Tramways	27·4	29·2	28·4	27·0	26·8	26·5	25·6	26·1	25·9	25·6	24·7	23·1	21·5	20·9	20·1	19·3	18·5	17·2	15·4
Trolley vehicles	0·07	0·09	0·09	0·11	0·14	0·19	0·25	0·42	0·56	0·72	0·85	1·04	1·25	1·43	1·82	2·30	3·15	4·34	5·88
Total	27·5	29·3	28·5	27·1	26·9	26·7	25·8	26·5	26·5	26·3	25·5	24·1	22·7	22·3	21·9	21·6	21·6	21·5	21·3
Buses and coaches	28·5	33·3	34·5	33·7	35·5	40·9	45·8	49·1	57·2	57·3	61·7	57·5	57·4	57·3	59·3	61·4	64·3	66·6	76·2
Taxis and hire cars	23·0	23·3	23·6	23·9	24·4	24·3	22·7	19·7	18·2	18·6	16·7	14·8	13·7	14·0	13·6	13·3	12·9	12·3	11·5
Horse-drawn vehicles	3·67	3·52	3·37	3·22	2·87	2·50	2·10	1·76	1·56	1·26	1·11	0·94	0·83	0·72	0·60	0·52	0·46	0·41	0·36
Sea travel	22·3	17·9	18·6	19·5	17·6	16·4	19·2	17·7	15·3	14·3	10·3	9·0	9·9	10·7	10·8	9·8	10·0	9·5	10·5
Steamboats, ferries, etc.	1·6	1·9	1·9	1·9	2·0	2·1	2·1	2·1	2·2	2·2	2·2	2·0	1·8	1·8	1·8	1·9	1·9	2·2	2·2
Air travel	—	—	—	0·08	0·10	0·11	0·14	0·14	0·16	0·16	0·18	0·24	0·23	0·28	0·32	0·43	0·56	0·58	0·54
Total	184·0	182·6	181·6	175·5	176·8	179·2	176·6	179·1	182·3	179·4	174·2	160·9	155·7	156·3	158·5	160·7	165·6	169·8	178·9

TABLE 30. INDEX NUMBERS OF QUANTITY AND AVERAGE PRICE FOR PUBLIC TRANSPORTATION PURCHASED FOR FINAL CONSUMPTION IN THE UNITED KINGDOM, 1920–38

(Expenditure in 1938 is taken as the base for each series)

	1920	1921	1922	1923	1924	1925	1926	1927	1928	1929	1930	1931	1932	1933	1934	1935	1936	1937	1938
Railways																			
Quantity index	52·6	45·5	48·3	48·5	51·7	52·7	46·3	51·0	52·1	53·0	50·9	48·0	45·8	48·7	51·8	54·0	56·2	58·6	56·3
Price index	82·7	90·7	82·7	76·6	73·2	70·6	71·5	68·4	65·9	62·8	62·4	61·4	60·3	56·7	54·4	53·9	53·8	54·4	56·3
Road transport																			
Quantity index	71·8	71·7	75·7	77·8	79·5	85·1	86·3	85·9	88·1	89·1	92·9	86·0	85·4	86·7	90·1	93·2	97·1	99·6	109·4
Price index	125·9	136·2	129·9	123·7	123·3	121·4	122·1	123·7	128·4	127·1	123·7	123·7	121·3	119·1	115·8	113·6	111·7	110·7	109·4
Sea and air transport																			
Quantity index	18·6	15·3	15·5	18·2	16·8	16·3	18·9	17·5	16·2	15·3	12·3	10·5	11·4	13·0	13·2	12·9	13·5	13·5	13·2
Price index	17·1	17·1	17·5	15·6	15·5	15·1	15·0	15·1	14·4	14·4	13·7	14·2	13·8	13·0	12·9	12·5	12·2	12·1	13·2
Total																			
Quantity index	143·0	132·5	139·5	144·5	148·0	154·1	151·5	154·4	156·4	157·4	156·1	144·5	142·6	148·4	155·1	160·1	166·8	171·7	178·9
Price index	230·0	246·7	232·9	217·3	213·8	208·0	208·6	207·5	208·4	203·9	199·8	199·1	195·3	188·4	182·6	179·6	177·6	176·9	178·9

CHAPTER VII

COMMUNICATION SERVICES

1 GENERAL REMARKS

The services covered in this chapter are all operated by the General Post Office. Expenditure on postal, telephone and telegraph services in 1938 amounted to £29·5 m. Postal services represented 61 % of this total and telephone services a further 37 %. In 1920 expenditure on telephone services had been no more than expenditure on telegraph services, each accounting for about 8 % of the total.

The variations in consumption, average prices, and expenditure, for the three main types of service, are shown in the accompanying diagrams. The values are plotted on a logarithmic scale and the series are ranged according to the value of expenditure in 1938.

It can be seen that postal services dominate the picture in the early part of the period and show a gradual rise in the years before the war. Telephone services increased rapidly while telegraph services, always small, declined.

Postal services comprise three categories, correspondence, parcels, and remittance services, which varied differently over the period. The first, which is much the most important, showed in quantity terms little variation about an upward trend broken by a period of stability between 1928 and 1932 and resumed again in the later 'thirties. Postal rates, which cannot readily be summarized, were relatively high, around $1\frac{3}{4}d.$ per letter in the three years 1920–2 and then settled down to an average of a little less than $1\frac{1}{2}d.$ per letter for the remainder of the inter-war period. Parcels showed more variability in numbers. There was a fall to 1922, a gradual rise to 1930, a slow fall to a low point in 1934–5 and a recovery to a new high level in 1938. Again average values were high in the first three years, settled down to an average of a little less than $9d.$ per parcel between 1924 and 1934, and fell still further at the end of the period. Remittance services rose very rapidly after an initial decline, the rise being associated in part, at least, with pool betting.

The number of telephones installed (stations), local and trunk calls, rose at a fairly steady rate over the period apart from a slackening at the time of the great depression, especially the years 1931–3, and a fall between 1920 and 1921 in the case of calls. The number of calls

per station tended steadily downward over the period after a sudden drop between 1920 and 1921 and by 1938 had reached a daily average of a little more than 1·8. The method of charging and the services available changed considerably over the period.

Telegraph service is the only component of this group to show a substantial fall in quantity over the period. There was a gradual decline until 1935, when a recovery set in. The variations appear to have been associated with changes in the relative price of telegrams. From 1920 to 1922 telegram rates rose slightly at a time when retail prices generally were falling. Between 1925 and 1935 telegram rates were practically stationary while prices drifted downwards, and the fall in rates in 1935 was far greater than the gradual recovery of retail prices in general at that time. Added to this, there were undoubtedly factors at work tending to diminish the demand for telegrams. The telegraph service formed the subject of an exhaustive investigation by the Lever Committee in 1927;[1] while the Bridgeman Committee in 1932,[2] commenting on the fact that the service is run at a heavy loss, remarked:[3] 'It is in the unfortunate position of lying between the upper and nether millstones of an expanding Telephone Service and of a Postal organization which, with relatively minor exceptions, ensures the delivery of a letter anywhere within the boundaries of the British Isles within 24 hours of posting. No close comparison with the American telegraph system is therefore possible. In the United States a large part of the profit is derived from night letter telegrams, the equivalent of which can in this country be sent by post at a cost of $1\frac{1}{2}d.$' A sample inquiry into the uses of telegrams led to the conclusion that it is not only in the field of short-distance messages but also in the social sphere generally that the telegraph service has felt the most drastic effect of telephone competition.[4]

---

[1] **[37]** *Report of the Committee on the Inland Telegraph Service*, Cmd 3058, 1928.

[2] **[38]** *Report of the Committee of Enquiry on the Post Office, 1932*, Cmd 4149, August 1932.

[3] Ibid. p. 11.

[4] See **[63]** *Telegraph Census* (1935) by Elsie M. Tostevin and F. W. Fox, being no. 14 of the Post Office Green Papers, for the results of a sample survey of nearly 606,000 inland telegrams conducted in October 1934.

COMMUNICATION SERVICES

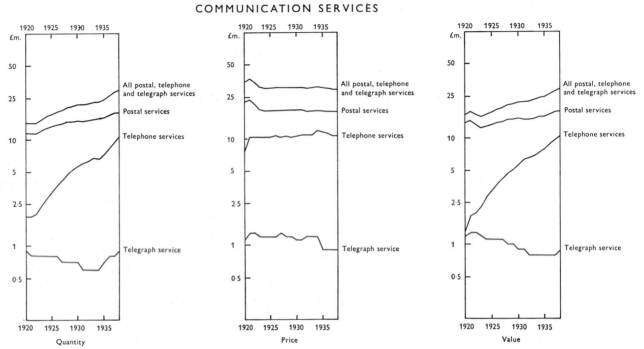

Fig. 7. The variations in the quantities purchased, average prices and expenditure on communication services for final consumption in the United Kingdom, 1920–38.

2   METHODS OF ESTIMATION

Scope of the estimates. The estimates given in this chapter represent personal expenditure in the United Kingdom on the postal, telephone and telegraph services provided by the General Post Office.

General procedure. Figures of total traffic and expenditure in each group are readily available for financial years:[1] the main problem is consumer allocation. This was made on the basis of sample investigations relating to the later years of the period. The estimates are derived from information supplied by experts, except in the case of the telephone and telegraph services over the years 1920–4 which must be regarded as especially rough. Average values, which in their major movements reflect price changes, were derived.

Methods employed. There is not much that can be added to the above brief description except for the early period in the case of telephone and telegraph services.

Sums payable by persons for telephone rentals were compiled as follows. The mean number of personal stations as a percentage of the total number of stations[2] shows a clear trend over the period. This trend was extrapolated freehand to 1921 and the percentage applied to the total number of stations in these years. An average rental of £5 per station was assumed.

The trend of personal to total local calls was extrapolated to 1921 and an average value per call was taken

equal to that obtaining in 1925. A similar method was adopted for trunk calls.

In 1920 rentals and rates in all categories were at a higher level. Accordingly a percentage of total telephone expenditure compatible with later years was taken as personal and this value was split proportionately between the three categories, rentals and local and trunk calls.

In the case of telegrams, personal traffic as a percentage of total traffic[3] showed no well-defined trend over the period 1925–38. Accordingly the percentage for 1925 was taken for the earlier years. The total value of personal expenditure was estimated in a similar way from total telegraph revenue[3] and an average value per telegram was derived.

3   THE RELIABILITY OF THE ESTIMATES

Since accurate information is available on total traffic and expenditure the principal source of error lies in consumer allocation. For the latter part of the period the available information, though not perfect, should suffice to give a fairly reliable subdivision of the total. As the

---

[1] In the [20] *Statistical Abstract* or in the annual [12] *Post Office Commercial Accounts.*

[2] [20] *Eighty-second Statistical Abstract for the United Kingdom*, pp. 328–9. All figures have been simply adjusted to calendar years for these calculations.

[3] Ibid. pp. 326–7.

estimates are pushed further and further back, however, more reliance must be placed on assumptions and qualitative information with a consequent loss of precision. No means is known of correcting or checking the estimates given here.

4 THE MAIN TABLES

The final estimates are brought together in Tables 31–34. The first of these shows the quantities purchased, in considerable detail, the second shows the movement of average values, the third the movement of expenditure, while the final table provides a summary in the form of index numbers of quantities and average values for the whole group of services. The quantity series are aggregate base-weighted index numbers and the price series current-weighted aggregates; their product is thus a simple index of expenditure. Each series has been multiplied through by expenditure in 1938, the base year, and is shown in this form in the diagrams of § 1.

TABLE 31. ESTIMATED QUANTITIES OF POSTAL, TELEPHONE AND TELEGRAPH SERVICES PURCHASED FOR FINAL CONSUMPTION IN THE UNITED KINGDOM, 1920–38

	1920	1921	1922	1923	1924	1925	1926	1927	1928	1929	1930	1931	1932	1933	1934	1935	1936	1937	1938
Postal services																			
Letters, etc. (millions)	1,500	1,552	1,570	1,682	1,758	1,808	1,865	1,918	1,982	1,948	1,998	1,945	1,980	2,022	2,068	2,080	2,162	2,265	2,268
Parcels (millions)	51	46	43	44	48	51	51	54	55	57	59	58	57	55	55	55	59	64	65
Remittances (millions)	120	113	110	118	128	134	146	150	158	175	195	208	218	231	261	293	330	385	411
Telephone services																			
Local calls (millions)	134	120	126	148	174	199	226	256	285	313	342	365	383	399	449	503	587	671	741
Trunk calls (millions)	8	8	9	10	12	14	15	17	19	22	23	24	25	27	20	20	23	26	28
Rentals (thousands)	143	159	176	204	238	274	321	369	419	468	514	551	580	609	667	757	882	1,024	1,143
Telegraph service																			
Telegrams (millions)	21	19	19	19	19	19	18	17	17	16	16	15	14	14	14	17	18	18	20

TABLE 32. ESTIMATED AVERAGE VALUES OF POSTAL, TELEPHONE AND TELEGRAPH SERVICES PURCHASED FOR FINAL CONSUMPTION IN THE UNITED KINGDOM, 1920–38

	1920	1921	1922	1923	1924	1925	1926	1927	1928	1929	1930	1931	1932	1933	1934	1935	1936	1937	1938
Postal services																			
Letters, etc. (d.)	1·74	1·85	1·65	1·43	1·39	1·40	1·42	1·42	1·43	1·44	1·44	1·44	1·40	1·41	1·42	1·43	1·43	1·43	1·43
Parcels (d.)	10·49	10·48	10·61	9·43	9·01	8·89	8·85	8·89	8·97	9·08	8·90	8·79	8·78	8·90	8·95	8·13	7·66	7·58	7·71
Remittances (d.)	1·74	1·76	1·77	1·73	1·68	1·68	1·62	1·62	1·60	1·56	1·53	1·53	1·51	1·49	1·47	1·45	1·45	1·42	1·39
Telephone services																			
Local calls (d.)	..	..	1·35	1·35	1·35	1·35	1·40	1·31	1·35	1·28	1·31	1·41	1·41	1·42	1·38	1·46	1·34	1·17	1·15
Trunk calls (d.)	..	..	11·20	11·20	11·20	11·25	11·15	11·03	11·23	11·72	11·62	11·70	11·66	11·84	15·98	18·23	19·18	19·50	19·57
Rentals (£)	..	..	5·00	5·00	5·00	5·01	5·24	5·01	5·13	4·97	5·11	5·18	5·18	5·15	5·12	4·21	4·21	4·14	4·11
Telegraph service																			
Telegrams (d.)	13·71	15·44	15·70	14·61	14·01	14·07	14·41	15·43	14·39	14·40	13·69	13·90	14·06	14·12	14·12	11·22	10·39	10·43	10·38

TABLE 33. ESTIMATED EXPENDITURE ON POSTAL, TELEPHONE AND TELEGRAPH SERVICES PURCHASED FOR FINAL CONSUMPTION IN THE UNITED KINGDOM, 1920–38 (£M.)

	1920	1921	1922	1923	1924	1925	1926	1927	1928	1929	1930	1931	1932	1933	1934	1935	1936	1937	1938
Postal services																			
Letters, etc.	10·9	11·9	10·8	10·0	10·2	10·5	11·0	11·4	11·8	11·7	12·0	11·7	11·6	11·6	12·2	12·4	12·9	13·5	13·5
Parcels	2·2	2·0	1·9	1·7	1·8	1·9	1·9	2·0	2·1	2·2	2·2	2·1	2·1	2·1	2·1	1·9	1·9	2·0	2·1
Remittances	0·9	0·8	0·8	0·8	0·9	0·9	1·0	1·0	1·1	1·1	1·2	1·3	1·4	1·4	1·6	1·8	2·0	2·3	2·4
Telephone services																			
Local calls	··	·7	·7	·8	1·0	1·1	1·3	1·4	1·6	1·7	1·9	2·2	2·3	2·4	2·6	3·1	3·3	3·3	3·6
Trunk calls	··	·4	·4	·5	·6	·7	·7	·8	·9	1·1	1·1	1·2	1·2	1·3	1·4	1·6	1·8	2·1	2·3
Rentals	··	0·8	0·9	1·0	1·2	1·4	1·7	1·9	2·2	2·3	2·6	2·9	3·0	3·1	3·4	3·2	3·7	4·2	4·7
Telegraph service																			
Telegrams	1·2	1·3	1·3	1·2	1·1	1·1	1·1	1·1	1·0	1·0	0·9	0·9	0·8	0·8	0·8	0·8	0·8	0·8	0·9
Postal services	14·0	14·7	13·5	12·5	12·9	13·3	13·9	14·4	15·0	15·0	15·4	15·1	15·1	15·4	15·9	16·1	16·8	17·8	18·0
Telephone services	1·3	1·9	2·0	2·3	2·8	3·2	3·7	4·1	4·7	5·1	5·6	6·3	6·5	6·8	7·4	7·9	8·8	9·6	10·6
Telegraph service	1·2	1·3	1·3	1·2	1·1	1·1	1·1	1·1	1·0	1·0	0·9	0·9	0·8	0·8	0·8	0·8	0·8	0·8	0·9
All services	16·5	17·9	16·8	16·0	16·8	17·6	18·7	19·6	20·7	21·1	21·9	22·3	22·4	23·0	24·1	24·8	26·4	28·2	29·5

TABLE 34. INDEX NUMBERS OF QUANTITY AND AVERAGE PRICE FOR POSTAL, TELEPHONE AND TELEGRAPH SERVICES PURCHASED FOR FINAL CONSUMPTION IN THE UNITED KINGDOM, 1920–38

(Expenditure in 1938 is taken as the base for each series)

	1920	1921	1922	1923	1924	1925	1926	1927	1928	1929	1930	1931	1932	1933	1934	1935	1936	1937	1938
Postal services																			
Quantity index	11·3	11·4	11·4	12·1	12·8	13·2	13·6	14·0	14·5	14·5	14·9	14·7	14·9	15·2	15·6	15·9	16·7	17·8	18·0
Price index	22·3	23·3	21·4	18·7	18·2	18·2	18·3	18·4	18·5	18·7	18·5	18·6	18·1	18·2	18·3	18·2	18·1	18·0	18·0
Telephone services																			
Quantity index	1·9	1·9	2·0	2·4	2·8	3·2	3·7	4·1	4·7	5·2	5·6	6·0	6·2	6·6	6·5	7·2	8·3	9·5	10·6
Price index	7·4	10·4	10·4	10·3	10·3	10·3	10·7	10·3	10·6	10·3	10·6	10·9	10·9	10·9	11·9	11·5	11·2	10·6	10·6
Telegraph service																			
Quantity index	0·9	0·8	0·8	0·8	0·8	0·8	0·8	0·7	0·7	0·7	0·7	0·6	0·6	0·6	0·6	0·7	0·8	0·8	0·9
Price index	1·1	1·3	1·3	1·2	1·2	1·2	1·2	1·3	1·2	1·2	1·1	1·1	1·2	1·2	1·2	0·9	0·9	0·9	0·9
All services																			
Quantity index	14·1	14·1	14·2	15·3	16·4	17·2	18·1	18·8	19·9	20·4	21·2	21·3	21·7	22·4	22·7	23·8	25·8	28·1	29·5
Price index	34·5	37·2	34·6	30·9	30·0	30·1	30·4	30·3	30·4	30·4	30·3	30·6	30·1	30·3	31·1	30·4	30·1	29·4	29·5

CHAPTER VIII

ENTERTAINMENT AND RECREATION

1 GENERAL REMARKS

Expenditure on this group of services amounted to £200–£250 m. on average during the period and represented approximately 5 % of total consumers' expenditure. This proportion is probably less than the relative importance these items would appear to have in the average family budget. The difference arises mainly from the treatment of expenditure on hotel services and betting. In the treatment adopted for this study, expenditure in hotels has been spread over the different component items such as food, fuel and lighting, rent, furnishings, etc. The part included under the present head consists only of the earnings of employees and the gross profits of the proprietors, which clearly cannot be allocated elsewhere. The figure of gross expenditure in hotels is therefore considerably larger than that included here. It is probable that gross expenditure in hotels would be about three times as large and would raise the total given above to some £400 m., or nearer 10 % of consumers' expenditure.

The discrepancy with regard to betting expenditure arises for different reasons. For consumers as a whole the betting losses of individuals will be offset by the gains of other individuals and the actual cost of betting will be the net receipts of the industry, the balance between bettors' gains and losses. By the nature of the activity, however, losses are much more common than gains and it is probable that the average individual would unhesitatingly regard the gross value of bets placed as his expenditure on betting. It has also been argued that this is a much better indicator of the true social cost. Gross expenditure on betting, in this sense, is in fact ten times the net figure included in the present estimates. If this too were added to the total above it would be raised to approximately £525 m., or more than 12–15 % of total expenditure.

Bearing these qualifications in mind, the relative importance of the different items of entertainment and recreation expenditure may be considered.

Expenditure on admissions to theatres, cinemas, other shows and sporting events increased by 15 % from £56·2 m. in 1920 to £64·9 m. in 1938. In the same period the number of admissions per year rose from 1,124 millions to 1,497 millions, an increase of 33 %. The accompanying fall in the average price per admission was from 1s. to 10½d. The upward trend in the number of admissions was not continuous through the period. From 1920 to 1923 the number fell off by 8 % but then rose again at a similar rate until 1930. In the slump, admissions fell off by some 10 % between 1930 and 1933, after which there was a continued rise to the end of the period. A notable discontinuity is apparent in 1930 when the number of admissions increased by more than 10 % over the level of the preceding year. There seems little doubt that this was due to the introduction of talking films. This is a particularly marked example of a quality change in consumption, but apart from this novelty effect its significance in broader, welfare terms is difficult to assess. The average price per admission fell by 1d. between 1920 and 1922, and in subsequent years fluctuated mostly between 11d. and 10½d. These figures, however, provide only a rough indication of price movements over the period. If, for example, an all-round reduction in cinema prices leads more people to prefer the dearer seats, it is possible that there will be relatively little or no change in the average price. For this reason it is likely that prices actually fell much more during this period than is apparent from the average values.

The largest of the items in this group, in spite of the restrictive definition adopted here, is expenditure on hotels, restaurants, etc. To obtain a comparison in real terms, expenditure at current prices may be reduced to figures at constant prices by deflating by an average retail price index. It is assumed for the present purpose that the ratio of labour costs and profits to the total receipts of hotels has remained fairly constant over the period. On this basis, expenditure on hotels, in real terms, appears to have increased by approximately a third over the period. Practically the whole of this increase appears to have occurred since 1930. In the first decade of the period consumption fell off after 1920 and only regained this level again in 1930. Through the early 'thirties, however—the period of slump—consumption continued to rise. It seems probable that these varia-

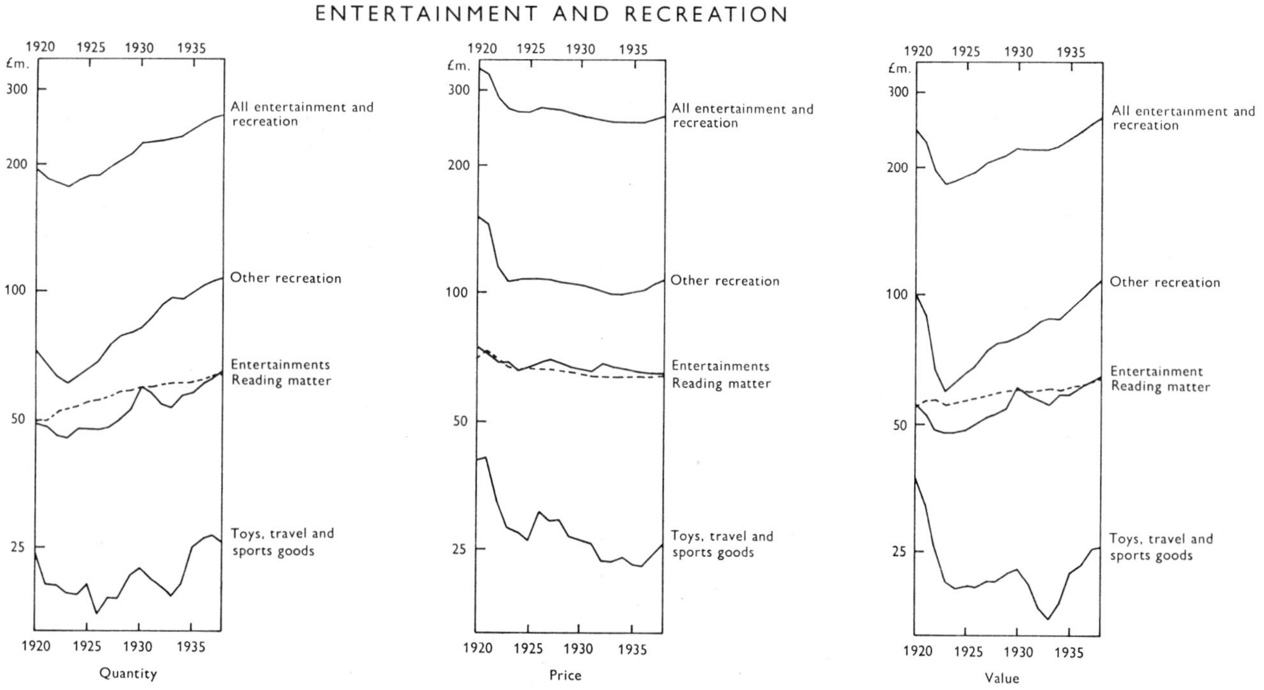

ENTERTAINMENT AND RECREATION

Fig. 8. The variations in the quantities purchased, average prices and expenditure on entertainment and recreation for final consumption in the United Kingdom, 1920–38.

tions reflect changes in social habits rather than the direct impact of economic factors.

Both the total value of bets staked and the very much smaller figure of net expenditure on betting, which is of principal concern here, rose markedly over the inter-war period. In both cases the value has more than trebled over the whole period. In 1920, however, the level was probably still below normal as a result of the war and a full recovery does not appear to have been made until 1922. Even so, expenditure more than doubled in subsequent years. Much of this increase was due to the introduction of new forms of betting, offering new opportunities and inducements to a much wider class. These innovations were dog racing, tote betting, football pools and sweepstakes. Each in turn appears to have grown rapidly without any compensating reduction in the receipts of other forms. The only noticeable decreases occurred as a result of legal sanctions. In 1933, for instance, tote betting at dog tracks was pronounced illegal, though later reinstated, and in the following year the sale of tickets for the Irish Sweep was forbidden in this country. In spite of the growth of many new forms, betting on horse races, particularly off-the-course betting with the bookmaker, remained the most conspicuous form of betting activity. In 1938 the turnover on football pools, for instance, was only one-fifth of that on horse racing. Dog racing was relatively much more important, the turnover having increased by 1938 to be more than three-fifths of that on horse racing. After the reinstate-

ment of tote betting on dog tracks in 1935, this type of betting increased particularly rapidly and by 1938 the turnover had outstripped that of the bookmakers at the tracks. For horse racing, on the other hand, tote betting remained relatively unimportant, accounting for less than 10 % of the total.

So far as the information goes, it appears that expenditure on books, newspapers and magazines varied very little during the period apart from a steady upward trend of just over 1 % per annum. The absence of any marked year-to-year variation is partly a reflexion of the inadequacies of the estimates. Expenditure on newspapers accounts for two-thirds of the total, but the increase in newspaper reading appears to have been accompanied by a similar rate of growth in the other two branches.

Expenditure on toys, travel goods and sports equipment is the remaining item of any importance included in this group. While expenditure at current prices showed no marked trend over the period, in real terms there was an upward trend in consumption of 1·5 % per year. This was a rather less rapid rate of increase than for consumption as a whole.

2 METHODS OF ESTIMATION

Scope of the estimates. The estimates discussed in this chapter cover the various items of expenditure on different forms of recreation and entertainment. This group includes expenditure on both goods and services, in the case of hotels and restaurants a composite commodity of considerable importance. To ensure that the estimates are consistent with those made elsewhere in this study it is necessary to adopt, in regard to certain items, a definition of consumers' expenditure which is at variance with what might seem immediately reasonable. Expenditure on betting, as estimated here, includes only the costs of operation, that is, the gross profits of bookmakers. In so far as losses by some bettors are offset by the gains of others, only a transfer between persons is involved. Again, expenditure on the services of hotels and restaurants has been estimated in this study under many different heads: for example, food, drink, fuel, etc. In this section only the residual items of expenditure, namely: labour costs and the gross profits of the proprietors, are included. Purchases by business users are excluded, though in most instances the allocation between personal and business use has to be made on a fairly arbitrary basis. It is not possible, however, to make detailed adjustments to exclude purchases by tourists and other non-residents. Similarly, expenditures by United Kingdom residents abroad are not included. Estimates of the net balance for all items on this account are given separately in Chapter X.

General procedure. Many different sources and methods have been employed for the items dealt with in this chapter. For the most part there is a lack of continuous annual data in this field. It is always possible, however, to establish a reasonable order of magnitude and to indicate the general trend of expenditures through the period. The basic information is partly derived from post-war inquiries and some discrepancy may arise through reading back more recent developments into the earlier period.

The estimates of expenditure on entertainments are derived from the entertainment tax returns, with adjustments for tax-free admissions. The figure for hotels and restaurants consists in large part of the value of employee earnings, for which fairly reliable estimates are available. The value of gross profits, which is possibly more variable, can only be determined within broad limits. It is a matter of considerable difficulty to establish even a reliable order of magnitude for expenditure on betting. The various official inquiries into the betting question are the main source of information for this item and an attempt has been made to trace the changing pattern of expenditure over the period. For magazines and newspapers much information, of varying degrees of reliability, is available regarding circulations and prices. The field is so large and heterogeneous, however, that even a complete enumeration of publications is difficult to make. Estimates of annual changes must

be made on a sample basis, though the sample cannot be truly representative but must be determined by the availability of the data. Finally, for the other goods dealt with in this chapter, books, toys, and sport and travel equipment, benchmark figures derived from the Census of Production have been variously interpolated to cover the whole period.

Methods employed. The methods employed in making the estimates for the different items of entertainment and recreation are discussed below in the following order:

(*a*) Public entertainments.
(*b*) Hotels, restaurants, boarding and lodging houses.
(*c*) Betting.
(*d*) Books, newspapers and magazines.
(*e*) Toys, travel goods and sports equipment.
(*f*) Other recreation expenditure.

(A) PUBLIC ENTERTAINMENTS

Included under this heading are all forms of public entertainment which involve payment for admission: cinemas, theatres, racing, and other sports. The estimates of expenditure are based on the returns for the entertainment duty charged on each admission; the various problems of estimation arise because of changes in the rates and incidence of the duty.

By the end of the period the most important form of public entertainment was undoubtedly the cinema, accounting for almost two-thirds of admissions and 60 % of gross takings, and much of the upward trend throughout the period must have been due to the rapidly growing popularity of this form of entertainment. Unfortunately, apart from the last five years of the period, separate figures are not available for the different types of entertainment.

Annual estimates of expenditure on taxed entertainments were made by applying estimated average proportions of the duty included in prices of admission to the entertainment duty returns. An estimate was made for tax-free admissions[1] and 2 % was added to account for Northern Ireland.

For each of the scales of duty in force during the period an estimate of the average ratio of duty to price of admission was supplied by H.M. Customs and Excise. Up to 1 June 1924 a common scale for all admissions was in force. The Finance Act of 1924 provided that from 2 June 1924 duty on payments for admission not exceeding 6*d.* should be abolished; duty on payments exceeding 6*d.* but not exceeding 1*s.* 3*d.*, exclusive of duty, were

---

[1] There is a further class of exempted entertainments—performances for charity or by non-profit-making bodies—but for the present purpose these involve merely transactions within the personal sector and are excluded by definition from the present reckoning.

reduced. This Act was modified from 9 November 1931, when the limit for complete exemption was reduced to 2d., and other duties were increased. On 1 July 1935 the exemption from duty for payments not exceeding 6d. was restored. At the same time a distinction was made between two types of duty: the full duty and the reduced duty, the latter applying at entertainments 'where all the performers whose works or actions constitute the entertainment are actually present and performing, and the entertainment consists solely of one or more of the following items, namely, a stage play, a ballet (whether a stage play or not), a performance of music (whether vocal or instrumental), a lecture, a recitation, a music hall or other variety entertainment, a circus or a travelling show'. These conditions applied to the end of the period.

For the years 1920–3 and 1932–4 the expenditure on taxed admissions to entertainments in Great Britain was derived from figures supplied by H.M. Customs and Excise for receipts from entertainment duty in calendar years,[1] and the average ratio of duty to price already mentioned. For the two years 1924 and 1931, during which changes in the rate of duty took place, the same method could be applied to the two parts of the years separately, using estimates of receipts of entertainment duty before and after the change.[2] In the years when two scales of duty were in force, the receipts from entertainment duty were divided into those from full duty, those from reduced duty, and unclassified.[3] On the suggestion of H.M. Customs and Excise, unclassified receipts were divided equally between full and reduced. The method described above could then be applied to both sections, the sum giving the total amount spent on taxed admissions to entertainments.

The addition to be made for tax-free admission was based on a survey of the cinema industry in 1934.[4] From an estimated distribution of all cinema admissions it was possible to calculate the number 'not over 2d.' and 'not over 7d.' respectively, that is 'not over 2d.' and 'not over 6d.' excluding tax. From a finer division of a slightly smaller sample of admissions the average price, exclusive of duty, in each of the two groups was calculated. Applying this to the distribution of all cinema admissions, an estimate was made of the receipts in the two classes, exclusive of tax. The ratios of these receipts to total cinema receipts excluding duty were then found. Assuming these ratios to hold for all entertainments and for all years, the total expenditure on tax-free admissions was estimated.

For the years 1934–8 estimates have been made of the total expenditure on and number of admissions to cinemas alone.[5] Expenditure on other entertainments can therefore be obtained as a residual for these years. Some indication of the relative importance of different entertainments within this combined group is given by the

duty returns for 1937–8, where they are separately distinguished.[6] No exact comparison can be made, since the figures are only approximate and the ratio of duty to receipts for the different entertainments is not known. However, making use of the information mentioned above, the following distribution is obtained.

ESTIMATED EXPENDITURE ON ENTERTAINMENTS IN GREAT BRITAIN, 1937–8

	£m.	%
Taxed admissions		
Cinemas	32·24	51·5
Theatres	8·00	12·8
Racing	3·10	5·0
Football	2·69	4·3
Cricket	0·12	0·2
Other	3·52	5·6
Tax-free admissions		
Cinema	8·06	12·9
Other	4·81	7·7
Total	62·54	100·0

A series of estimated average prices of taxed admissions, based on analyses of duty receipts, in certain selected weeks of the years 1922–36 was also supplied by H.M. Customs and Excise. From this series for taxed admissions, and the average prices of cinema seats 'not over 2d.' and 'not over 6d.' for tax-free admissions, it was possible to construct a series of the annual average price of admission to all entertainments in these years. Reasonable estimates could then be made for other years of the period allowing for duty changes. Total expenditure was divided by these average prices to obtain the number of admissions. For the years 1934–8 separate figures were calculated for cinemas and other entertainments.

(B) HOTELS, RESTAURANTS, BOARDING AND LODGING HOUSES

For the purposes of the present inquiry hotels, restaurants and other catering establishments are regarded as supplying a composite service which is included under

---

[1] Estimates of the correction necessary to exclude Southern Ireland in 1920 and 1921 were supplied by H.M. Customs and Excise. The figure for 1922 is approximate.

[2] Supplied by H.M. Customs and Excise.

[3] Supplied by H.M. Customs and Excise.

[4] **[88]** S. Rowson, 'A statistical survey of the cinema industry in Great Britain in 1934', *J. R. Statist. Soc.* XCIX (1936), part I, p. 67.

[5] **[67]** H. E. Browning and A. A. Sorrell, 'Cinemas and cinema-going in Great Britain', *J. R. Statist. Soc.* series A, CXVII (1954), part II, p. 133.

[6] **[16]** *Twenty-ninth Report of the Commissioners of H.M. Customs and Excise*, p. 102.

many separate heads throughout the estimates. Thus the value of the food and drink served is included under the different items of those sections; the crockery, cutlery and furnishings bought are included in the purchases of household durables; and rent, fuel, and other items, are similarly treated. The residual costs remaining to be included specifically in this section are the wages and salaries paid, including payments in kind, and the gross profits (before tax) of the proprietors.

The nature of the information available requires the present indirect treatment of these expenditures. There are no comprehensive statistics for the hotel and catering industry in this country during the period under review and it would only be possible to obtain an estimate of total consumers' expenditure on this item within a wide margin of error. This uncertainty would involve a comparable, though compensating, discrepancy for all those items where it was necessary to allocate total purchases between households and caterers.

The catering establishments covered in these estimates include all hotels, restaurants, cafés, boarding and lodging houses. Many shops serving light refreshments also sell bakery goods or confectionery and tobacco, but only the value of the catering service is included here. Fried fish and chip shops are excluded since the total value of their sales is included in food expenditure. The catering by railway companies in station buffets and restaurant cars is included. Public houses, in so far as they do no catering apart from snacks sold over the bar, are excluded.

There are four principal sources of information. First, there are estimates of the total wages and salaries paid by the hotel and catering industry throughout the period.[1] These estimates are based largely on census data and cover employees in lodging and boarding houses, restaurants, hotels, inns and public houses, and in political, social and working-men's clubs. This coverage is not exactly what is required for the present purpose but these figures form a useful basis for extrapolation over the period.

Secondly, there are the statistics of the catering done by the railway companies during this period.[2] These figures relate to receipts and expenditure in respect of hotels, refreshment rooms, and cars, where catering is carried on by the companies. A total turnover of £6 m. is recorded for 1938, and expenditure in each year is analysed under nine heads. Although not typical of the industry as a whole, these data may be combined with other information to give a more representative picture.

The third source of information consists of a broad sample of returns from a large number of hotels, giving details of their receipts and expenditures in the years immediately preceding the war.[3] While the statistics of the railway companies will be more typical of the purely catering side of the industry, this may be corrected by reference to the sample returns, which are confined to hotels.

Finally, further information for the catering side of the industry is available in the Census of Distribution for 1950,[4] which covers all non-residential catering establishments except public houses. Separate figures are given for fried fish shops and industrial canteens and they may be easily excluded for the present purpose; otherwise the coverage is virtually complete. Information on receipts and purchases, numbers employed, and wages and salaries paid, is given in considerable detail. The absolute values recorded, however, can only be used for the inter-war period subject to considerable qualification. Some indication of the changes taking place during the intervening years may be gained from the records, maintained for rationing purposes by the Ministry of Food, of the number of catering establishments and meals served. They are first available for May 1941.[5] A further small piece of information relating to hotels and boarding houses is available in the sample inquiries into holiday expenditure undertaken in 1949.[6]

The proportionate distribution of expenditure between the different items of costs may be compared for the railway companies, the sample of hotels, and the catering establishments covered by the Census of Distribution. For this purpose total expenditures may be divided between four principal categories: the cost of provisions, other expenses, wages and salaries, and gross profit or the balance between expenditures and receipts. It is found that for both hotels and railway companies the sum of wages, salaries and profits accounts for one-third of total receipts in the immediately pre-war years. The proportion paid out in wages and salaries is higher for the railway companies, as might be expected; many of the small independent hotels have working proprietors whose remuneration will be counted as a part of profits. For hotels the cost of provisions accounts for one-third of total receipts, while for railway companies the proportion rises to 47 %, an indication of the greater emphasis on catering by the railway companies. For other caterers, the census returns suggest that wages and salaries were approximately one-quarter of the total. It seems likely, however, that in this case other costs were correspondingly lower.

---

[1] [69] Chapman, *Wages and Salaries in the United Kingdom, 1920–1938*, pp. 210–11.

[2] See, for example, [14] *Railway Returns, 1938*, Account no. 15, p. 18.

[3] Private source; information supplied confidentially for the purpose of the present inquiry.

[4] [36] Board of Trade: *Census of Distribution, 1950*, vol. II.

[5] See [2] *Annual Abstract of Statistics*.

[6] [57] The Social Survey, *Holidays and Holiday Expenditure*, by W. F. F. Kemsley and David Ginsburg, n.s. 709/2 (1949).

From these figures it can be seen that earnings and gross profits together probably represented between 35 and 45 % of total turnover. An average of 40 % may be taken for the whole industry.

It is further necessary to determine how this sum was divided between earnings and profits. For the sample of hotels, profits were one-fifth of total receipts, or 60 % of earnings and profits together. For the railway companies, however, profits were only one-tenth of total receipts. It is probable that the sample figures are more representative of the small privately owned business that must be characteristic of the industry. The census data appear broadly to confirm this view, and on this evidence it seems more reasonable to assume an even split between earnings and profits for caterers. For the industry as a whole, therefore, the ratio of earnings to profits would probably be in the region of 45:55.

Before applying these proportions to the series of estimated total earnings in the industry, it is necessary to exclude the earnings of those serving behind bars, since they will already be included in the value of alcoholic drinks. In 1931 there were 46,725 barmen and barmaids in work in England and Wales.[1] This figure was raised by 12 % to include Scotland and Northern Ireland, that is 52,300 or 15 % of all wage-earners in the hotel and catering industry. This percentage was deducted from wage payments in all years.

With this adjustment to the earnings figures, an estimate of gross profits in all years may be obtained by applying the proportion calculated above. However, not the whole of this item is required for the present purpose. The other costs which go to make up the total of hotel expenditure (food, fuel, etc.) have been valued at retail prices throughout the present study. But at least part will have been obtained at wholesale prices, and it is necessary to make some deduction from the present item in order to avoid double-counting. An approximate adjustment may be made in the following way. The retailer's margin on food as a whole was found to be 24 % of the retail value in 1938; for other goods it was slightly higher.[2] It was estimated above that purchases of provisions and other expenses accounted for 60 % of total receipts for the industry as a whole. By no means all of this represents purchases at wholesale prices. Many small establishments must have bought their supplies retail, and for certain items, rent for example, no overvaluation is involved. The actual extent of the double-counting is probably much less than the average retail margin on all purchases. It has been assumed that this expenditure has been overvalued by one-sixth, that is 10 % of total receipts or one-quarter of the sum of earnings and profits. The estimates were reduced by one-quarter in each year to exclude this element of double-counting.

Finally, allowance must be made for that part of expenditure in hotels and restaurants which is not met out of personal incomes. This will be very largely expenditure chargeable as a business expense. As with the estimate of duplication made above, the deduction to be made here is in respect of all expenditure on hotels and restaurants. It is assumed that it would amount to 5 % of the total or one-eighth of earnings and profits; this proportion was deducted in each year.

(c) BETTING

Expenditure on betting, as an item of total consumers' expenditure, includes only that part of the total turnover which is retained by the bookmaker or promoter to cover his costs and profits (including tax). In so far as bets lost are offset by the winnings of other bettors the only transaction involved is a transfer between persons which, under the definitions adopted for the present study, is excluded from personal expenditure. Clearly, the balance established between losses and gains in this case is a purely monetary one; the question of how far any real cost is involved is outside the scope of the present inquiry.

The moral and social issues involved, however, have been the principal impulse behind the frequent public inquiries into gambling activities, and it is their reports that form the main source of evidence for any estimate of expenditure in this field. The inquiries relevant to the present purpose are: the Select Committee on Betting Duty of 1923,[3] the Royal Commission of 1932–3,[4] and the Royal Commission of 1949–51.[5] The last of these appears to give the most reliable estimate of (consumers') expenditure on betting and provides a useful summary of the available evidence.[6] In addition, there are the reports of the Racehorse Betting Control Board,[7] and an independent survey of the betting industry in 1936.[8] Some further indication of the volume of betting may be obtained from the returns under the betting duty,[9] in force from 1 November 1926 to 31 March 1929.

An estimate of the total volume of betting and of the gross profits retained must be built up from these diverse pieces of information. The method adopted here will be to consider each form of betting in turn and to construct

[1] [25] Census of England and Wales, 1931, General Report, 1950, p. 116.
[2] See [73] Jefferys, The Distribution of Consumer Goods, p. 69.
[3] [48] Report of the Select Committee on Betting Duty (1923).
[4] [39] Interim Report of the Royal Commission on Lotteries and Betting, 1932–3, Cmd 4234 (1933); and [40] Final Report, Cmd 4341 (1934).
[5] [47] Report of the Royal Commission on Betting, Lotteries and Gaming, 1949–51, Cmd 8190 (1951).
[6] Ibid. p. 19 and appendix II, p. 146. See also [84] A. W. Peterson, 'The statistics of gambling', J. R. Statist. Soc. series A, CXV (1952), part II, p. 179.
[7] [13] Annual Report of the Racecourse Betting Control Board (1929–39).
[8] [96] Economist, 29 February and 7 March 1936.
[9] See [16] Customs and Excise Reports.

estimates of turnover and takings which are as reliable as the evidence permits. However, a wide margin of error is common to all estimates for this period. There were a number of developments in the inter-war years which make the process of extrapolation from later experience particularly hazardous. It was during this period that organized greyhound racing first became popular, that totalisator betting was introduced on racecourses, and that football pools developed on a national scale. Account must also be taken of the short-lived betting duty and of the sudden growth in popularity and subsequent prohibition of the Irish Sweepstake in this country. There is very little evidence to decide whether the new forms of gambling developed alongside or at the expense of older forms. The basis for the estimates must therefore be to a large extent conjectural, but it is nevertheless possible to establish an order of magnitude and to give some indication of the general trend through the period.

In the sections which follow, expenditure on betting is examined under four heads: (i) betting on horse races; (ii) betting on dog races; (iii) football pools; and (iv) other forms of betting.

(i) *Betting on horse races*

Betting on horses accounted for by far the greater part of total betting activity during the inter-war years. At the beginning of the period it was the only form of betting of any importance and throughout the period accounted for practically the whole of the great volume of off-the-course betting with bookmakers. The totalisator was introduced on horse racecourses in 1928 but probably never accounted for more than one-quarter of betting on the course. Betting on horse races is done predominantly with the bookmaker, and mostly off the course.

The earliest data available are the assessments of bookmakers' incomes in the years 1919–20 to 1922–3, as submitted to the Select Committee on Betting Duty.[1] The Board of Inland Revenue suggested that these figures should be raised by one-third to obtain the net profits of all bookmakers. It was further suggested that the gross profits of bookmakers were on an average four times their net profits. On the basis of the findings of later Royal Commissions it has been assumed for the present purpose that net and gross profits would be 1·5 and 7·0 % respectively of gross turnover. On this basis estimates of gross turnover in these years could be made; these figures, adjusted to calendar years 1920–2, are shown in Table 37.

A duty on all bets was in force from 1 November 1926 until 31 March 1929. There were two rates of duty, of which the lower applied in the first five months to bets made on horse racecourses and subsequently to all on-the-course betting. From the returns of duty paid the total amount charged at the two rates in each financial year may be calculated.[2] There was undoubtedly considerable evasion, but it may be supposed that this was largely confined to off-the-course betting, where it was believed that only 40 % of bookmakers were doing wholly legitimate (credit) business. The total turnover calculated in this way, and adjusted to calendar years, is £77 m. in 1927 and £93 m. in 1928. In the first five months of the duty on-the-course betting on horse races alone accounted for one-third of the total, while in the financial year 1927–8 all on-the-course betting accounted for almost 45 %. Applying these proportions to the figures for 1927, it may be estimated that on-the-course betting on horse races was £26 m. and on dog races was £10 m. in this year. In the last financial year of the duty on-the-course betting contributed 55 % of the total turnover. In 1928, therefore, it has been assumed that the turnover of on-the-course betting was £49·5 m. It has been estimated (see (ii) below) that dog racing accounted for £22·5 m. in this year, leaving £27 m. as the turnover on horse racecourses. It has further been assumed that 40 % of the total turnover of off-the-course bookmakers evaded the duty in these years. Thus it may be estimated that off-the-course turnover was £70 m. in 1927 and £77·5 m. in 1928. Total betting on horse races was, therefore, £95·0 m. and £104·5 m. respectively in the two years.

The Royal Commission of 1949–51 estimated that in 1938 the gross profits of bookmakers were £10 m.[3] If gross profits are 7 % of turnover, this is equivalent to a total turnover of £145 m. It is estimated that £35 m. of this total was taken by bookmakers at dog tracks.[4] The remaining £110 m., plus £9·1 m. received by the totalisator, may be divided between on- and off-the-course betting on horse races in the same proportions as in 1927–8; that is, one-quarter on the course and three-quarters off the course. The estimates for the earlier years 1920–2 have been similarly divided.

Totalisators were introduced on horse racecourses in this country in 1928. Their operation is subject to government control and records of their transactions are published.[5] Though primarily concerned with cash betting, they also handle a certain amount of credit betting both on and off the course. The volume of totalisator betting on and off the course is shown in Table 37. It may be noted that in 1938 the totalisator accounts for 20 % of

[1] [47] *Royal Commission 1949–51, Report*, p. 160.
[2] See [15] *Annual Reports of Inland Revenue*, and [47] *Royal Commission 1949–51, Minutes of Evidence*, p. 53.
[3] Ibid. *Report*, p. 160.   [4] See § (ii) below.
[5] See [13] *Annual Reports of the Racecourse Betting Control Board*; a summary of accounts for the years 1929–48 is given in [47] *Royal Commission 1949–51, Minutes of Evidence*, p. 98.

betting on the course; for post-war years the Royal Commission of 1949–51 suggested a figure of something over 25 %.

For the intervening years 1923–6 and 1929–37, for which no data are available, the total volume of betting on horse races has been assumed to vary with an index of money incomes adjusted for trend. The volume of totalisator betting is known and the proportions taken by bookmakers on and off the course were assumed to be constant throughout the period.

For bets taken by bookmakers it has been assumed that throughout the period gross profits amounted to 7 % of total turnover (less tax). This figure is based on the findings of the Royal Commission of 1949–51 and corresponds to an average net profit of $1\frac{1}{2}$ %. The value of the betting duty paid was added to gross profits for 1926–9.

The operations of the totalisator are governed by law and accounts are published annually. For the present purpose, gross profit has been taken to include the total amount retained and other revenue receipts.

(ii) *Betting on dog races*

From its introduction to this country in 1926 greyhound racing grew rapidly in popularity and by 1938 attracted a volume of betting equal to almost 70 % of that on horse races. The facts that the most important tracks are situated in the main industrial areas and hold meetings throughout the year, that almost all betting is transacted on the course, and that the greater part of the persons attending do so regularly, on an average more than once a week, indicate that it caters for a special public somewhat distinct from that of horse racing.

The development of totalisator betting on dog tracks is a further indication of this. The licensing of totalisator betting in 1928 was intended to apply only to horse racing, where it was under the control of the Racecourse Betting Control Board. However, between 1929 and 1932 privately owned totalisators were introduced tentatively on greyhound tracks until they were declared illegal in December 1932. Total turnover on totalisators at this time was about £8 m. The ban continued until the new provisions of the Betting and Lotteries Act 1934 came into force in July 1935, when totalisators were permitted to operate at greyhound races under licence from the local authority and subject to certain controls on gross profits. By 1938 gross turnover had risen to more than £40 m.[1] It may be assumed that the volume of betting with the totalisator increased gradually to £8 m. in 1932; and then rapidly from £4 m. in 1935, for the first half-year of operation after the ban, to £40 m. in 1938.

The Royal Commission of 1949–51 estimated that in the post-war period bets with bookmakers at dog tracks amounted to 80 % of the volume of betting on the totalisator. It is unlikely that the figure would be much different in 1938 and it has been assumed that the volume of betting with bookmakers in this year was £35 m. For other years of the period it has been assumed that the volume of betting with bookmakers varied with the number of persons attending. For this purpose we have used a series of the estimated numbers present at N.G.R.S. tracks in each year 1927–38.[2]

Since the 1934 Act the amount of total turnover retained by the totalisator operator has been limited to 6 %, and the same proportion may be applied for the earlier years. As for horse racing, the gross profits of bookmakers are assumed to be 7 % of total turnover (less tax). On this basis figures of consumers' expenditure were obtained for all years, including duty paid in 1927–9.

(iii) *Football pools*

Although introduced to this country in 1922, organized pool betting on football matches did not at first spread widely. It was still 'in its infancy' at the time of the Royal Commission of 1932–3. In subsequent years, however, development was rapid. In 1934, when the Football Pool Promoters' Association was founded, total turnover was said to be about £8 m. By 1938 it had risen to £22 m.

For the years 1935–8 the volume of betting on football pools may be estimated on the basis of sales of postal orders, by which the greater part of the transactions are made.[3] For 1934 the figure of £8 m. put forward by the F.P.P.A. has been adopted.[4]

Before 1934 football pools, it is generally admitted, were on a much smaller scale, though there was a certain amount of similar activity carried on through newspaper competitions, which are dealt with in the following section. Rough guesses have been made for a diminishing turnover back to the middle of the 'twenties.

The amount retained by promoters of football pools is estimated to be on the average 'rather more than 20 %'.[5] Accordingly, 22 % of turnover in each year has been taken as consumer expenditure.

(iv) *Other forms of betting*

The other forms of betting are numerous and, for the most part, individually of little importance. Small lotteries, raffles, whist drives and the like, run for private or charitable purposes, are by definition excluded from the present account. The net costs of running these

---

[1] The figures of turnover in this year were collected from the local authorities by the Churches' Committee on Gambling.
[2] Information supplied by the National Greyhound Racing Society.
[3] See [47] *Royal Commission 1949–51, Report*, appendix II, p. 149.
[4] See [96] *The Economist*, 29 February 1936, p. 457.
[5] [47] *Royal Commission 1949–51, Report*, p. 17.

activities are included in the estimates of the general expenses of clubs and charitable organizations, etc. (see §§ (*f*) and (*h*) of Chapter IX below). The most important forms of betting considered here are large-scale lotteries, in particular the Irish Hospitals Sweepstake, newspaper competitions, and gaming machines. After the 1934 Act restrictions were much more stringently enforced and expenditure on these forms of gambling declined considerably.

Following its inception in 1930 the Irish Hospitals Sweepstake became rapidly popular in the three years 1931–3 and it is estimated that annual subscriptions from this country rose from £0·5 m. in 1930 to an annual level of £10 m.[1] Since 1934 probably no more than £2 m. a year has been subscribed from this country.

It has been suggested that annual expenditure on gaming machines during this period may have been as much as £15 m.[2] This figure is undoubtedly much too high, even allowing for the freer conditions before 1934. Newspaper competitions at this time appear to have attracted a further £3 m. annually in entrance money. For the present purpose it has been assumed that these miscellaneous forms of gambling accounted for £5 m. annually up to 1934 and £3 m. in subsequent years.

The gross profit on these forms of gambling is much larger than on other forms. Only half of the Sweepstake takings are distributed in prize money and it is probable that a similar proportion applies for the other forms. An estimate of personal expenditure has been made on this assumption.

(D) BOOKS, NEWSPAPERS AND MAGAZINES

The methods employed for the different items of this group are discussed separately under the three headings: (i) books, (ii) newspapers, and (iii) magazines.

(i) *Books*

Estimates of the output of printed books in the United Kingdom may be made for the three years 1924, 1930 and 1935 from the Census of Production. The whole output is not given explicitly in these figures and an allowance must be made for this. These estimates and the corresponding value of retail sales to the home market in these years are summarized in the following table.[3]

Imports and exports of books are recorded by quantity (total weight) and value throughout the period.[4] Exports amount to almost one-third of the home output and, as they are likely to be fairly representative of the total product, export average values have been used to deflate the value of home sales. Between 1924 and 1935 the average value of exports fell by 27 %. If this figure is applied to home sales, consumption would appear to

ESTIMATES OF THE OUTPUT AND RETAIL SALES OF BOOKS IN THE UNITED KINGDOM IN 1924, 1930 AND 1935 (£M.)

	1924	1930	1935
Census output of printed books, etc.	4·5	5·0	5·1
Census output of bookbinding	2·6	2·2	2·1
Allowance for small firms (and Northern Ireland in 1930)	—	0·3	0·2
	7·1	7·5	7·4
'Unrecorded output'	2·5	2·5	2·5
	9·6	10·0	9·9
Less Net exports	−3·5	−3·3	−2·9
Wholesale value	6·1	6·7	7·0
Plus Distribution costs	2·7	2·9	3·0
Retail value	8·8	9·6	10·0

have risen by more than half during this period. The values at constant prices for the three census years lie close to a straight-line trend and this has been simply interpolated and extrapolated for other years of the period. Expenditure at current prices was then obtained by multiplying by the index of average values.

These figures are estimates of the total home sales of books; in addition to purchases by final consumers they will include sales to public libraries, schools, and business. For want of any precise information, it has been assumed that sales outside the personal sector amounted to 10 % of the total in each year, and this proportion has been deducted to obtain the value of consumers' expenditure.

(ii) *Newspapers*

The estimates of circulation and sales revenue for newspapers given here are taken directly from the work of Kaldor and Silverman.[5] In the course of an inquiry into advertising expenditure and the revenue of the press they have compiled annual figures of sales revenue for all newspapers through the period 1920–44. The methods

[1] [96] *The Economist*, 29 February 1936, p. 457.

[2] Ibid.

[3] In compiling this estimate we have had the advice of experts in the trade.

[4] [8] *Annual Statement of the Trade of the United Kingdom*, vol. I, 1920–1938. The trade figures exclude books sent through the post and include some printed matter other than books, but the size of the net discrepancy is not known. See [70] Marjorie Deane, 'United Kingdom publishing statistics', *J. R. Statist. Soc.* series A, CXIV (1951), part IV, p. 468.

[5] [76] Nicholas Kaldor and Rodney Silverman, *A Statistical Analysis of Advertising Expenditure and of the Revenue of the Press*, National Institute of Economic and Social Research, Economic and Social Studies, no. VIII (Cambridge, 1948).

used in making these estimates may be briefly indicated here. Full details are given in the original source.[1]

Five separate categories of newspapers were distinguished: national and London morning, London evening, provincial daily, national and provincial Sunday, and suburban and provincial weekly. For each of the first four groups chain base indices of circulations and average prices were built up essentially from the individual records of circulations. For the smaller groups this information was very nearly complete although it was necessary to make allowance for some overstatement in unaudited figures. Where individual figures were missing estimates were made by interpolation or by reasoned guesses. Care was taken to determine the exact date of price changes and amalgamations since this materially affected the estimate of sales revenue in a particular year. The reliability of the estimates is judged to have increased during the period, particularly as a result of the greater number of audited figures in later years. For the fifth group, which comprised by far the largest number of publications, although comparatively small in total sales, it was not possible to make estimates on the basis of recorded circulations since the figures available appeared not to be representative of the whole group. In this case the total circulation of these papers in 1938 was calculated from the quantity of newsprint used and the average size per copy. For other years of the period an index of circulation was compiled from sample data. Similarly, an average price was calculated for the whole group in 1938 and this was extended to other years on a sample basis. The reliability of this series is somewhat less than the others, but it is believed that the general trend shown by the figures gives a reasonably true picture of events.

It seems unnecessary to make any allowances for purchases outside the personal sector. Purchases by clubs and similar private non-profit-making bodies are included by definition as part of personal consumption. Purchases by public libraries should be excluded but are too small, compared with the probable margin of error of the estimates, for there to be any real precision obtained by making this adjustment; purchases by purely business users must also be very small.

(iii) *Magazines*

The number of magazines published in this country far exceeds the number of newspapers. Very many of them have only a small circulation and are of purely local or specialist interest. Any allocation of purchases between final consumers and business must be largely arbitrary. It is not possible in these circumstances to make a very precise estimate of consumers' expenditure for this item.

Fortunately there is a comprehensive and detailed analysis of periodical sales in 1935[2] which may be used as a basis for the estimates of consumers' expenditure required here. In this analysis some 4,080 periodicals were enumerated, covering a multiplicity of interests. They are cross-classified by type and frequency of publication. Four types are distinguished: general interest, special interest, technical journals, and trade journals. It may be assumed for the present purpose that purchases by final consumers comprise the first two of these groups while the last two are allotted wholly to business purchasers. The third group clearly includes some publications, particularly those of learned bodies, which are likely to be purchased by final consumers, but these omissions will be offset by business purchases in the first two groups.

The different types of periodicals are further subdivided according to whether they are published weekly, monthly, or quarterly. The group of general interest periodicals published weekly is of predominant importance. In 1935 expenditure on this group accounted for almost 60 % of the total for all periodicals of the two types allotted to final consumption. The number of periodicals in this group, however, is less than one-tenth of the total. Further information about this group is available on a sample basis for other years of the period. For a varying number of publications from 1923 onwards there are published figures of circulations and price per issue.[3] The size of the sample increases threefold from 24 to 72 during this period. In 1935 approximately two-thirds of total expenditure on the group is covered by the sample, though allowance must be made for possible overstatement in the unaudited figures. Although circulations are not recorded for every year in all cases, estimates have been made by interpolation where a trend was apparent in the published figures. In this way observations are available for a continually expanding sample through the period.

Information on circulations was also collected for the special interest periodicals published weekly and the two groups of general and special interest periodicals published monthly. For these groups information is scantier, particularly before 1930, but a sufficiently representative sample may be compiled to give a reasonable indication of the development of the group as a whole.

This information was used in the following way. The year-to-year changes were calculated by obtaining the proportionate change between each pair of adjacent years for those publications for which figures were given

[1] Ibid. pp. 57–70. [2] Ibid. pp. 85–97.
[3] The earlier figures were taken from the [93] *Advertisers A.B.C.*; for later years more exactly comparable, audited figures were obtained from the Audit Bureau of Circulations.

in both years. The year-to-year links were then multiplied out and the estimates for 1935 were taken as a base to derive total sales.

It seems probable that this method fails to estimate the trend of the series adequately. On the one hand, it is generally suspected that there is a reluctance to declare a fall in circulation and this factor would tend to give an upward bias to the series. On the other hand, the method makes no proper allowance for the introduction of new publications, which is likely to have outweighed the effect of any decline in the circulation of existing magazines. Comparison with the Census of Production data[1] suggests that there was in fact an upward trend in sales, which was not apparent in the calculated series, but that it was fairly moderate. Accordingly the calculated series has been adjusted to the census trend, making allowances for the increasing reliability of the estimated year-to-year changes towards the end of the period as the coverage improves. For the years before 1923 the series was roughly extrapolated on the basis of the trend.

Expenditure on quarterlies amounted to only 4% of expenditure on other periodicals in 1935. In the absence of any other information this same percentage was taken in all years for expenditure on this group.

Because of the changing composition of the sample from year to year it was not possible to obtain more than a rough indication of the movement of average prices. The prices of individual periodicals altered only rarely and it did not appear from the circulation figures that there was any marked shift towards the more expensive or the less expensive publications. In view of this it seemed not unreasonable to make use of a series of average prices calculated for weekly newspapers.[2] The average level is certainly lower for newspapers but the movement appeared to be consistent with the sample figures and is likely to reflect the general conditions of periodical publishing.

(E) TOYS, TRAVEL GOODS AND SPORTS EQUIPMENT

The estimates discussed in this section cover all forms of children's toys and games (including fireworks); sports requisites of various forms, rackets, fishing tackle, guns and ammunition; and miscellaneous travel goods, mostly trunks, travelling bags and cases, etc.

The basic data for the estimates were obtained for the five years 1924, 1930 and 1933–5 from the returns of the Census of Production and the Import Duties Act Inquiries. The details are given in the notes to Table 35. Problems of consumer allocation are of very little importance. The factory values of home-produced and imported supplies available for home consumption were raised by the appropriate distribution margins[3] to

obtain estimates of retail sales in the census years. The distribution of expenditures between the three principal groups in the years 1924, 1930 and 1935 are shown in Table 35.

TABLE 35. ESTIMATED CONSUMERS' EXPENDITURE ON TOYS, TRAVEL GOODS AND SPORTS EQUIPMENT IN THE UNITED KINGDOM IN 1924, 1930 AND 1935 (£ M.)

	1924	1930	1935
Toys and games	9·1	10·6	10·6
Travel goods	4·4	4·1	4·0
Sports equipment	6·9	8·1	7·7
Total	20·4	22·8	22·3

The composition of the different groups of toys, etc., shown in Table 35 is described in the following notes.

Toys and games: includes all output recorded for the *games and toys trade*, *plus* an estimate of the output of all small firms; rubber toys from the *rubber trade*, and toy balls of rubber from the *sports requisites trade*; rockets and other pyrotechnic products from the *explosives and fireworks trade*. Imports and exports of toys and games are recorded in the trade statistics for all years of the period, rubber toys being given separately in most years; imports and exports of fireworks are also recorded throughout the period.

Travel goods, etc.: includes, as well as trunks, travelling bags and cases from the *leather goods trade*, half of saddlery and harness, horse clothing, and whips, *plus* an estimate of the output of these goods by all small firms. Trunks and suitcases of metal are included with hardware and hollow-ware (see § (e) of Chapter II). Imports and exports of trunks, etc., and saddlery and harness, are recorded for all years in the trade statistics.

Sports requisites: includes all goods from *sports requisites trade* (except toy balls), *plus* an estimate of the output of all small firms; fishing tackle and fish-hooks from the *needle, pin, etc., trade*; sporting guns from the *small arms trade*, including small firm output; small arms ammunition for sporting purposes from the *explosives and fireworks trade*; and bathing caps and football bladders from the *rubber trade*. Imports and exports of these goods, so far as recorded separately, were taken from the trade statistics.

For other years of the period the estimates of output for census years have been interpolated and extrapolated on the basis of employment series. Output at constant prices in these years was calculated from the quantity figures when these were available, and in other cases by use of the indices of production which are given for various census groups.

An index of the numbers employed was constructed for this purpose in the following way. From the unemployment insurance records[4] the numbers employed in

---

[1] See [32] *Fifth Census of Production* (*1935*), part IV, §II, the printing and publication of newspapers and periodicals, p. 59. Publishers who did their own printing were required to record their total receipts, including those from sales, subscriptions and advertising. The comparison cannot, therefore, be very precise, except in so far as other costs and receipts vary proportionately with sales.

[2] See [76] Kaldor and Silverman, *A Statistical Analysis of Advertising Expenditure and of the Revenue of the Press*, p. 69.

[3] See [73] Jefferys, *The Distribution of Consumer Goods*, pp. 370–6.

[4] See [20] *Statistical Abstract for the United Kingdom.*

the toys, games and sports requisites industry and in the leather goods industry were combined with weights of 2 and 1. These figures are not available before 1924 and for these years rough estimates were made on the basis of estimates for a group of miscellaneous manufacturing industries;[1] for this purpose the ratio of the two series in subsequent years was roughly extrapolated.

From these figures the ratio of employment to output was calculated for each of the census years. These ratios show a downward trend throughout the period, except for the final year 1935. This trend is, of course, no indication of productivity changes, since the output figures relate to the gross output for final consumption, but a uniform trend over the period is some confirmation of a systematic, but undetermined, relation between output and employment, which is all that is required for the present purpose. Accordingly, the observed trend in the ratios was interpolated and extrapolated to cover other years of the period and on this basis estimates of output were calculated.

An index of prices was compiled from the census data and the average values of exports falling within this group. The goods for which information on quantities as well as expenditures is available in the foreign trade statistics are: dolls and soft toys, sporting guns, ammunition, and saddlery and harness. The average export values were roughly weighted according to their importance in final consumption, and the combined series was then adjusted to the trend shown for all goods in the group by the census data, the trend being roughly extended before 1924 and after 1935.

The estimates of output at current prices in each year were adjusted for exports and imports, inclusive of duty,[2] and raised by the appropriate margin for distribution costs to obtain an estimate of retail sales in all years. Relative changes in the composition of the group were small enough during this period for the average distribution margin to be assumed constant. Accordingly, the index of prices previously calculated may serve equally for retail sales.

(F) OTHER RECREATION EXPENDITURE

The remaining items of recreation expenditure discussed here are: (i) licences, and (ii) pets and pet foods.

(i) *Licences*

Included here is the cost of licences for wireless sets, dogs, guns, etc. These are licences which are charged directly to the consumer and do not enter into the price of any other consumption article. The figures are taken directly from the official statistics.

The number of wireless receiving licences issued in each year is recorded for the whole period.[3] These

figures are for fiscal years ending 31 March; for the present purpose they have been simply adjusted to calendar years by taking one-quarter and three-quarters of the figures for consecutive years. The numbers of licences in each calendar year were then multiplied by the price, which was 10s. throughout the period.

The returns for gun licences, game (including gamekeepers') licences, and dog licences, also relate to fiscal years.[4] They were adjusted to calendar years in the same way as for wireless licences.

(ii) *Pets and pet foods*

Dogs probably account for much the greater part of expenditure under this heading. Though the keeping of cage-birds may have been equally widespread, the costs involved are much smaller. The cost of keeping backyard poultry is excluded, since the value of their output has already been included in food expenditure.

From Census of Production data, expenditure on manufactured dog foods would appear to have increased approximately from £2 m. to £3 m. between 1924 and 1937. There was, however, no corresponding increase in the number of dog licences.

In the absence of any more precise information, it is not possible to do more than state an order of magnitude for this item. It seems reasonable to assume that expenditure was £5 m. in each year.

3 THE RELIABILITY OF THE ESTIMATES

The substantial accuracy of the estimates of expenditure on entertainments is guaranteed by the tax data on which they are based. There is, of course, a considerable degree of uncertainty regarding both the average ratio of price to tax and the allowance for tax-free admissions. But the average level of the figures is clearly well established and the year-to-year variations should be generally significant. It seems probable that systematic bias is the most serious component of error; while the true level of expenditure may well lie 10 % above or below the estimated level, it is unlikely that the random error amounts to more than 5 %.

The main source of uncertainty in the figures for hotels, restaurants, etc., is the estimate of gross profits, since this has simply been assumed to be a fixed proportion

---

[1] See [69] Chapman, *Wages and Salaries in the United Kingdom, 1920–1938*, table 44, 'other manufacturing industries', p. 100.

[2] See [8] *Annual Statement of the Trade of the United Kingdom*, vols. I and II, 1920–1938.

[3] See [20] *Eighty-second Statistical Abstract for the United Kingdom*, table 243, pp. 328–9; for the year 1938–9 the figure was taken from the [42] *12th Annual Report of the B.B.C.*, p. 3.

[4] [15] *Reports of the Commissioners of H.M. Customs and Excise*; see, for example, the 1939 Report, Cmd 6098, p. 173.

of the labour cost. While it is probable that the general trend over the period is adequately represented, the random error for any particular year is likely to be large. The systematic bias in the series is perhaps of the order of 10–20 %, though the direction of the bias, of course, is unknown; the component of random error may not be more than 10 %. A much larger error would have been involved in estimating the total receipts of hotels, but there would also have been compensating errors in other commodity estimates wherever hotel consumption was deducted.

Many separate scraps of information have been brought together in order to compile an estimate of the gross turnover of the betting industry. The reliability of much of this material may be questioned and many assumptions are involved in putting together a coherent story for the whole period. While these assumptions are thought to be the most reasonable in the circumstances, it is fully realized that alternative assumptions might well be made from which a different pattern would emerge. Even if the general trend is well founded, there may be a sizeable systematic error in the estimates of personal expenditure, as the net operating costs of bookmakers must be largely inferred from estimated turnover.

The estimates of expenditure on books are probably reliable as regards both trend and the average level within a margin of error of 10 %; but little significance can attach to the year-to-year variations of these figures. Very much more information is available about the sales of newspapers and these estimates probably have a high degree of accuracy; though even here there is a sizeable group of suburban and provincial newspapers for which it is less than certain that coverage is complete. This is even more likely to be so with regard to the estimates of expenditure on magazines. The basic estimates for 1935 are undoubtedly the most reliable, the margin of error increasing as the figures are projected backwards for earlier years. Since, even for 1935, it is only possible to estimate the level of expenditure within fairly broad limits, the presence of some systematic bias is highly probable. The estimate of trend for this series is hardly more than a reasonable conjecture in the earlier part of the period. For later years, however, the series are based on more data and the year-to-year variations are more likely to be significant.

The basic estimates for toys, travel goods and sports equipment are derived from census data. This should ensure a reasonably complete coverage and the absolute level of the figures should be substantially correct. The extrapolation to other years of the period, based on employment series, is likely to introduce an appreciable degree of error in the year-to-year variations, though the long-term trend will be less affected. A further component of error in the estimates of current expenditure is due to the price index, based on export average values, but this is a random error rather than an element of systematic bias.

A part of other recreation expenditure consists of licence fees paid to government departments, which are known from the published records. For the rest, a rough order of magnitude was included to cover items for which no more detailed estimate could be made.

4 THE MAIN TABLES

The estimates for entertainment and recreation, obtained by the methods described in the preceding sections, are set out in the following tables. In view of the approximate nature of the estimates for some of the items, no attempt has been made to provide quantity and price figures for each item separately. Details of the estimates for public entertainments, including, so far as they are available, figures of attendances and prices paid, are given in Table 36. The estimates for betting, classified by type, are given in the form both of gross expenditures, Table 37, and of net expenditures, Table 38. Expenditures on all items of entertainment and recreation are brought together in Table 39. Finally, in Table 40, quantity and price series are provided for all items, individually or collectively, in a comparable index number form. The quantity series are base-weighted aggregate index numbers and the price series are current-weighted aggregates; their product is thus a simple index of expenditure. Each series has been multiplied through by expenditure in 1938, the base year, and is shown in this form in the diagrams of § 1.

TABLE 36. ESTIMATED NUMBER OF ADMISSIONS, AVERAGE PRICE AND EXPENDITURE ON PUBLIC ENTERTAINMENTS IN THE UNITED KINGDOM, 1920–38

	1920	1921	1922	1923	1924	1925	1926	1927	1928	1929	1930	1931	1932	1933	1934	1935	1936	1937	1938
Cinemas																			
Number of admissions (millions)	..	..	..	..	..	..	..	..	..	..	..	..	..	..	903	907	917	946	987
Average price (d. per admission)	..	..	..	..	..	..	..	..	..	..	..	..	..	..	10·3	10·2	10·1	10·1	10·1
Expenditure (£m.)	..	..	..	..	..	..	..	..	..	..	..	..	..	..	38·8	38·7	38·6	39·9	41·5
Other entertainments																			
Number of admissions (millions)	..	..	..	..	..	..	..	..	..	..	..	..	..	..	412	425	483	501	510
Average price (d. per admission)	..	..	..	..	..	..	..	..	..	..	..	..	..	..	11·5	11·2	11·0	10·9	11·0
Expenditure (£m.)	..	..	..	..	..	..	..	..	..	..	..	..	..	..	19·7	19·9	22·2	22·8	23·4
All entertainments																			
Number of admissions (millions)	1,124	1,105	1,050	1,034	1,090	1,086	1,086	1,106	1,150	1,216	1,378	1,333	1,253	1,234	1,315	1,332	1,400	1,447	1,497
Average price (d. per admission)	12·0	11·5	11·1	11·0	10·5	10·7	11·0	11·2	11·0	10·8	10·6	10·5	11·0	10·8	10·7	10·6	10·4	10·4	10·4
Expenditure (£m.)	56·2	53·0	48·4	47·5	47·7	48·4	49·8	51·6	52·7	54·7	60·9	58·5	57·2	55·4	58·5	58·6	60·8	62·7	64·9

TABLE 37. ESTIMATED GROSS EXPENDITURE ON BETTING IN THE UNITED KINGDOM, 1920–38 (£M.)

	1920	1921	1922	1923	1924	1925	1926	1927	1928	1929	1930	1931	1932	1933	1934	1935	1936	1937	1938
Horse racing																			
(i) On the course																			
Tote	—	—	—	—	—	—	—	—	—	0·5	2·8	3·4	3·2	3·3	3·9	4·6	5·4	5·8	6·2
Bookmaker	15·1	19·8	23·6	23·4	23·8	24·3	24·5	25·0	27·0	26·0	24·0	22·6	21·6	21·8	21·7	22·4	23·0	24·3	25·0
(ii) Off the course																			
Tote	—	—	—	—	—	—	—	—	—	—	0·4	0·5	0·8	1·1	1·2	1·6	2·0	2·1	2·9
Bookmaker	43·1	56·4	67·1	66·5	67·6	69·3	69·8	70·0	77·5	75·6	75·8	73·6	69·6	70·3	71·7	75·4	78·8	83·6	85·0
Dog racing																			
Tote	—	—	—	—	—	—	—	—	—	2·0	4·0	6·0	8·0	—	—	4·0	16·0	28·0	40·3
Bookmaker	—	—	—	—	—	—	—	10·0	22·5	26·5	28·0	30·0	32·0	32·5	32·0	33·5	33·5	34·0	35·0
Football pools	—	—	—	—	—	—	—	0·5	1·0	3·0	5·5	7·5	8·5	9·7	12·5	16·0	18·5	20·5	22·0
Irish Sweepstake	—	—	—	—	—	—	—	—	—	—	0·5	6·0	9·0	10·0	2·0	2·0	2·0	2·0	2·0
Other forms	5·0	5·0	5·0	5·0	5·0	5·0	5·0	5·0	5·0	5·0	5·0	5·0	5·0	5·0	3·0	3·0	3·0	3·0	3·0
Total	63·2	81·2	95·7	94·9	96·4	98·6	99·3	110·5	133·0	138·6	146·0	154·6	157·7	153·7	148·0	162·5	182·2	203·3	221·4

TABLE 38. ESTIMATED PERSONAL EXPENDITURE ON BETTING IN THE UNITED KINGDOM, 1920–38 (£ M.)

	1920	1921	1922	1923	1924	1925	1926	1927	1928	1929	1930	1931	1932	1933	1934	1935	1936	1937	1938
Bookmakers	4·1	4·6	6·3	6·3	6·4	6·6	6·9	9·4	11·1	9·2	8·9	8·8	8·6	8·7	8·8	9·2	9·5	9·9	10·2
Horse tote	—	—	—	—	—	—	—	—	—	—	0·3	0·4	0·5	0·5	0·6	0·7	0·8	0·9	1·0
Dog tote	—	—	—	—	—	—	—	0·1	—	0·1	0·2	0·4	0·5	—	—	0·2	1·0	1·7	2·4
Football pools	—	—	—	—	—	—	—	—	0·2	0·7	1·2	1·7	1·9	2·1	2·8	3·5	4·1	4·5	4·8
Other forms	2·5	2·5	2·5	2·5	2·5	2·5	2·5	2·5	2·5	2·5	2·8	5·5	7·0	7·5	2·5	2·5	2·5	2·5	2·5
Total	6·6	7·1	8·8	8·8	8·9	9·1	9·4	12·0	13·8	12·5	13·4	16·8	18·5	18·8	14·7	16·1	17·9	19·5	20·9

TABLE 39. ESTIMATED EXPENDITURE ON ENTERTAINMENT AND RECREATION BY FINAL CONSUMERS IN THE UNITED KINGDOM, 1920–38 (£ M.)

	1920	1921	1922	1923	1924	1925	1926	1927	1928	1929	1930	1931	1932	1933	1934	1935	1936	1937	1938
Public entertainments	56·2	53·0	48·4	47·5	47·7	48·4	49·8	51·6	52·7	54·7	60·9	58·5	57·2	55·4	58·5	58·6	60·8	62·7	64·9
Hotels, restaurants, etc.	88·6	76·8	51·9	44·4	46·9	49·8	51·8	54·2	55·8	57·8	58·1	57·1	58·6	60·1	63·3	65·7	69·0	73·6	76·0
Betting	6·6	7·1	8·8	8·8	8·9	9·1	9·4	12·0	13·8	12·5	13·4	16·8	18·5	18·8	14·7	16·1	17·9	19·5	20·9
Reading matter																			
Books	9·4	9·5	9·2	8·0	7·9	8·2	8·6	8·5	8·7	8·8	8·6	8·4	8·3	8·5	8·6	9·0	9·1	9·3	9·7
Newspapers	28·8	30·4	31·1	30·5	30·9	31·1	31·3	32·1	32·8	33·2	33·7	33·2	33·8	34·2	33·5	33·9	34·2	35·0	35·7
Magazines	16·2	16·4	16·6	16·7	17·1	17·4	17·5	17·6	17·7	17·7	17·9	17·8	17·8	17·7	18·0	18·2	18·2	18·4	18·7
Total	54·4	56·3	56·9	55·2	55·9	56·7	57·4	58·2	59·2	59·7	60·2	59·4	59·9	60·4	60·1	61·1	61·5	62·7	64·1
Toys, travel goods and sports equipment	38·1	32·4	25·4	21·1	20·4	20·8	20·5	21·3	21·3	22·2	22·8	21·1	18·4	17·3	18·9	22·3	23·2	25·4	25·7
Other recreation expenditure																			
Licences	1·1	1·1	1·2	1·5	1·9	2·2	2·6	2·7	2·8	3·0	3·2	3·6	4·1	4·5	4·9	5·2	5·5	5·7	5·9
Pets and pet foods	5·0	5·0	5·0	5·0	5·0	5·0	5·0	5·0	5·0	5·0	5·0	5·0	5·0	5·0	5·0	5·0	5·0	5·0	5·0
Total	6·1	6·1	6·2	6·5	6·9	7·2	7·6	7·7	7·8	8·0	8·2	8·6	9·1	9·5	9·9	10·2	10·5	10·7	10·9
All entertainment and recreation	250·0	231·7	197·6	183·5	186·7	192·0	196·5	205·0	210·6	214·9	223·6	221·5	221·7	221·5	225·4	234·0	242·9	254·6	262·5

TABLE 40. INDEX NUMBERS OF QUANTITY AND AVERAGE PRICE FOR ENTERTAINMENT AND RECREATION PURCHASED FOR FINAL CONSUMPTION IN THE UNITED KINGDOM, 1920–38

(Expenditure in 1938 is taken as the base for each series)

	1920	1921	1922	1923	1924	1925	1926	1927	1928	1929	1930	1931	1932	1933	1934	1935	1936	1937	1938
Entertainments																			
Quantity index	48·7	47·9	45·5	44·8	47·2	47·1	47·1	47·9	49·8	52·7	59·7	57·8	54·3	53·5	57·0	57·7	60·7	62·7	64·9
Price index	74·9	71·8	69·0	68·8	65·6	66·7	68·6	69·9	68·7	67·4	66·2	65·7	68·4	67·2	66·6	65·9	65·0	64·9	64·9
Reading matter																			
Quantity index	49·9	49·4	51·9	52·6	53·6	54·9	55·4	56·4	57·8	58·6	59·7	59·6	60·2	60·8	60·8	61·5	62·2	63·2	64·1
Price index	69·9	73·1	70·3	67·3	66·8	66·2	66·4	66·1	65·7	65·3	64·6	63·9	63·8	63·7	63·4	63·7	63·4	63·6	64·1
Toys, travel and sports goods																			
Quantity index	24·3	20·3	20·2	19·4	19·1	20·4	17·2	18·9	18·8	21·3	22·3	21·1	20·3	19·0	20·4	25·0	26·2	26·8	25·7
Price index	40·3	41·0	32·3	28·0	27·5	26·2	30·6	29·0	29·1	26·8	26·3	25·7	23·3	23·4	23·8	22·9	22·8	24·4	25·7
Other recreation																			
Quantity index	72·2	67·0	62·8	60·5	63·0	65·7	68·4	74·2	78·3	79·9	82·1	86·6	92·4	96·1	95·4	99·0	103·2	106·4	107·8
Price index	151·2	144·8	114·8	106·4	107·3	108·5	108·4	107·4	106·6	105·6	104·7	102·7	100·6	99·2	99·3	100·2	101·7	105·2	107·8
Total																			
Quantity index	195·1	184·6	180·4	177·3	182·9	188·1	188·1	197·4	204·7	212·5	223·8	225·1	227·2	229·4	233·6	243·2	252·3	259·1	262·5
Price index	336·4	329·5	287·5	271·7	268·0	267·9	274·2	272·6	270·1	265·5	262·3	258·3	256·1	253·5	253·3	252·6	252·7	257·9	262·5

CHAPTER IX

MISCELLANEOUS SERVICES

1 GENERAL REMARKS

A number of miscellaneous service items, which have not found a place in earlier chapters, are dealt with here. They include expenditure on insurance, private education, trade unions, religion, charities, fees paid to local authorities, legal and financial services and funeral expenses. Together they accounted for £153·8 m. in 1938, or 3½ % of total expenditure in the year. The proportion was generally lower in earlier years.

For a number of the items the value of consumers' expenditure as defined here is very much less than the actual outlay by households. There are two reasons for this. First, certain services (insurance, charities) involve a large transfer element, by which funds are merely redistributed between persons. These transfers within the personal sector count as gifts and form no part of national output or income. Secondly, there are services of a composite nature (education, religion), for which a large part of expenditure has already been included under other headings, so that only the residual elements of employees' earnings and net profits remain for inclusion here.

For most of the services covered there is no obvious unit in terms of which changes in volume might reasonably be assessed and the concept of expenditure at constant prices is far from unambiguous. The measures adopted for the present purpose are determined as much by the information available as by purely theoretical considerations. Where part of a composite service is concerned, a valuation on the basis of costs has usually been adopted; it is then natural enough to divide the total value of wages and salaries, the principal component included here, by an index of average earnings. The same method has been adopted in other cases where the justification is not so strong. A special problem arises in connexion with the two kinds of insurance business. It seemed necessary to adopt a different treatment for life assurance and other insurance. In both cases the current value of the service, as defined here, is equal to the sum of costs and profits, excluding the transfers between persons. Life assurance, however, includes a large element of saving and the service performed by assurance companies might best be regarded as being the management of these funds. An index of average earnings was used to derive estimates at constant prices. For general insurance this element of saving is absent and the benefit derived is much more nearly the coverage provided during the year, which may be regarded as proportional to the value of the goods covered. Accordingly it seems reasonable to deflate expenditure on general insurance by an index of consumer prices rather than employees' earnings.

A further qualification of the series discussed in this chapter concerns their reliability. Many of the figures given here are at best only indications of the order of magnitude involved and the probable trend through the period.

As regards the trend in expenditure, the items fall into two groups. Those which have increased most (insurance, private education, and fees paid to local authorities) are perhaps the items most closely associated with the process of economic growth during this period. The other items (expenditure on trade unions, religion, charities and funeral expenses), which have shown no particular upward trend, are only marginally related to the main stream of economic advance.

2 METHODS OF ESTIMATION

Scope of the estimates. The estimates of this chapter cover a residual group of miscellaneous services. They include such items as insurance, education, religion, charities and funeral expenses. The particular definitions adopted have been chosen to be consistent with those used in other sections of this study and with the general framework of social accounts to which they belong. For this reason the estimated expenditures differ somewhat from the actual outlays by households in respect of a number of these items. In general, the amounts included here are net expenditures, excluding any transfers within the personal sector and, in the case of composite services, any double-counting of expenditures already included under other headings.

As far as possible business expenditures are excluded. Except for insurance business, however, it is not possible

MISCELLANEOUS SERVICES

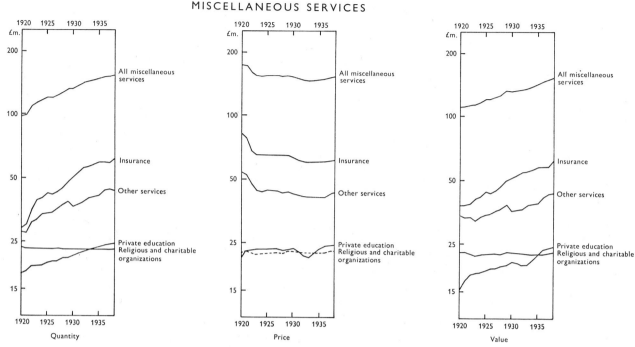

Fig. 9. The variations in the quantities purchased, average prices and expenditure on miscellaneous services for final consumption in the United Kingdom, 1920–38.

at this stage to exclude purchases made by tourists and other non-residents. Similarly, any expenditures abroad by United Kingdom residents are not included. An estimate of the net balance for all items on these accounts is made in Chapter X.

General procedure. Estimates of insurance business have been made on the basis of the published accounts, care being taken to exclude insurance done in respect of those abroad and for business users. For education, trade unions, religion, and charities, the expenditures required here are principally the net earnings of those engaged, and the figures are based on estimates of wages and salaries for those in corresponding occupational groups. The chief problem in estimating fees paid to local authorities was again that of consumer allocation, the published data providing little indication of the sources of receipts; for the present purpose the allocation was made largely in terms of the type of service. Legal and other expenses were roughly estimated on the basis of Stamp Duty returns. Finally, burial expenses were calculated by multiplying the number of deaths in each year by the estimated average cost of a funeral.

Methods employed. The methods of estimation employed for the different items of the group are discussed below in the following order:

(*a*) Life assurance.
(*b*) General insurance.
(*c*) Private education.
(*d*) Trade unions.

(*e*) Religion.
(*f*) Charity organizations.
(*g*) Fees paid to local authorities.
(*h*) Other miscellaneous services.
(*i*) Funeral expenses.

(A) LIFE ASSURANCE

The amounts to be included under this heading are the expenses and profits, including miscellaneous reserves, of life assurance companies and collecting societies. This is the sum which is taken from the aggregate contribution made by assured persons for the purpose of providing the service of life assurance. The remaining portion of transactions between the private sector and assurance businesses represents either saving by individuals through the medium of life assurance or simply transfers within the sector from premium payers to persons making claims.

The consolidated accounts of life assurance companies and collecting societies provide the necessary data.[1] Some adjustment is required for the overseas transactions of ordinary life assurance. The expenses and profits of British companies in respect of overseas business must be excluded, while the expenses and profits of overseas companies in respect of British business must be included. For companies established within the United

---

[1] See, for example, [20] *Eighty-second Statistical Abstract for the United Kingdom*, tables 197–8, pp. 270–3. Further details are available in the [9] *Assurance Companies Returns*, Board of Trade, and the [17] *Reports of the Industrial Assurance Commissioner*.

Kingdom the value of premiums, of consideration for annuities, and of commission, is given in respect of business both within and outside the United Kingdom. Expenses and profits are not so distinguished. Similarly, for companies established outside the United Kingdom the value of premiums, consideration for annuities, and commission for business within the United Kingdom is given. It has been assumed that in each year the sum of expenses, profits, etc., for all business within the United Kingdom would bear the same proportion to the value of premiums and consideration for annuities as it does for the total business of companies established within the United Kingdom. The net adjustment is quite small, only 4% at most of the total expenses, profits, etc., of companies within the United Kingdom. The value of commission in respect of business in the United Kingdom has then been added to these adjusted figures of expenses, profits, etc.

For industrial assurance companies and collecting societies no adjustment for overseas transactions is necessary; the recorded values of commission, expenses, and profits, were taken in each year.

Two further adjustments are required. From 1924 onwards the miscellaneous outgoings of industrial assurance companies include income tax payments, interest received being given gross of tax for these years. The value of tax paid may be calculated from the returns and can then be deducted to give a consistent series over the whole period. Secondly, for both ordinary and industrial life assurance companies, miscellaneous expenditure included transfers to investment and other reserves. These were particularly large in 1920 and 1931, miscellaneous income in subsequent years being inflated by transfers back from reserves. Since this is a purely financial transaction and does not represent a real expense of management occurring in these years, it seems reasonable to smooth the series by spreading these excessive allowances over later years. This was done for the subsequent five years in each case, the total readjustment amounting to £7·4 m. and £14·0 m. in 1920 and 1931 respectively. Finally, it may be noted that, although cash bonuses and other benefits included in the miscellaneous expenditure of industrial assurance companies should rightly be excluded for the present purpose, the values recorded separately for 1934 onwards are quite small and they may reasonably be ignored.

The total expenditure on life assurance obtained in this way is shown for each year of the period in Table 41.

For the purpose of converting this series to real terms the only deflator available is a series of the average earnings of employees in insurance, banking and finance.[1] This is perhaps not inappropriate since what is being measured is the cost of insuring and not the volume of

cover provided. On the other hand, while a series of average earnings may be an appropriate deflator for management expenses, it is less obviously so for the profit component.

(B) GENERAL INSURANCE

For other forms of insurance (accident, fire, motor vehicle, etc.) since there is no appreciable accumulation of reserves against future claims, as with life assurance, the element of saving involved is negligible. Consumers' expenditure may be taken simply as the difference between premiums and claims paid, this being equivalent to the expenses and profits of management, which constitute the costs of insuring for the consumer.

Summary accounts are available annually for the principal categories of insurance business.[2] There are separate accounts for companies established in the United Kingdom and companies established outside the United Kingdom carrying on business here. In both cases the figures relate to the total business transacted, whether within or outside the United Kingdom. For this reason the latter group is hardly relevant to the present purpose. Even for the United Kingdom companies it is known that a large part of the business is transacted overseas. It is also certain that much of the remainder will be with the business sector. In the absence of any precise information only rough orders of magnitude can be given for the proportion of total business due to final consumers. The following figures are considered to be representative for the period as a whole: accident 15%, fire 20%, motor vehicle 40%, and miscellaneous 25%.

It may be noted that not all the general insurance of the personal sector is transacted through insurance companies. Some friendly societies also transact general insurance, usually sickness insurance, though others pay a death benefit. Lloyd's underwriters also do a certain amount of motor vehicle and other business. The amounts involved are very small and it is unlikely that their omission will contribute any significant discrepancy to the estimates made here.

The most important of the four categories is fire insurance; although in later years motor vehicle insurance is of equal importance for the personal sector. Before 1931, the year when insurance against third party risk was made compulsory, motor vehicle insurance was included with other unspecified forms in 'miscellaneous insurance'. An estimate of motor vehicle insurance for these years was made on the basis of the number of vehicles in use,[3] and the average cost of insurance per

---

[1] [69] Chapman, *Wages and Salaries in the United Kingdom, 1920–1938*, pp. 152–5.
[2] See [9] Board of Trade, *Assurance Companies Returns* (1921–39).
[3] [101] *The Motor Industry of Great Britain, 1939*, table 20, p. 63.

vehicle, which was assumed to have had a downward trend throughout the period. The proportions given above were then applied in each year.

To obtain estimates at constant prices these expenditures were divided through by an index of average retail prices. This seems a more reasonable procedure than the use, say, of an index of average earnings of the employees of insurance companies or of the prices of items insured; the value of the insurance cover obtained is regarded simply as the value, in real terms, of the sum insured.

(c) PRIVATE EDUCATION

The definition of private education adopted for the present purpose includes: private schools in the usual sense of those receiving no State aid; all other privately owned educational establishments such as commercial colleges, language schools, etc.; and all universities. Although the universities as a whole received large and increasing government grants during this period, it is more convenient to treat them as part of private education, while grant-aided secondary schools, for instance, are regarded as part of the public system.

Education is a composite service, which, for lack of adequate data to undertake a more coherent treatment, has to be dealt with under its component items. The fees paid for a child at boarding school, for example, will cover, apart from more strictly scholastic expenses, expenditure on food, fuel and light, rent, and other items, including the remuneration of the proprietors. The greater part of this expenditure has been accounted for elsewhere in the present estimates. It remains, therefore, to make an estimate here of the residual unallocated expenditures: that is, teachers' salaries and the profits of proprietors. No attempt is made to measure the total outlay on private education.[1] This restricted definition, however, is not without economic significance. It is equivalent to the net output of the (private) education industry, and may be more useful than a gross figure for certain comparisons.

Any precise information about private schools during this period is limited to those schools recognized (that is, open to inspection) by the Board of Education. They represent only a minor part of the total. It is thought that the total number of private schools was of the order of 10,000.[2] In scope they varied from the most expensive type of public boarding school to the smallest, least satisfactory kind of private day school. It does not seem feasible, in this field, to collect reliable and representative information from which a direct estimate of expenditure might be made. Nevertheless, it is possible to establish an approximate order of magnitude on the basis of the numbers engaged and their average earnings.

Estimates of teachers' salaries are taken from Chap-

man,[3] and the full details of their compilation are to be found in the original source. For private, non-aided schools, they are based on an estimate of numbers derived from census data and an average salary related to that for public education. The number of teachers in private schools was obtained as a residual, deducting from the census total the numbers known to be employed by local education authorities, in private grant-aided schools, and in universities. The figures in the two census years, 1921 and 1931, were then interpolated and extrapolated on a straight-line trend to cover all other years of the period. The average earnings of these teachers have been taken to be equal to the average salary of all those engaged in public elementary and secondary schools. While rates of remuneration were almost certainly lower in private primary schools, where many unqualified teachers were employed, it is thought that this would be offset by a relatively larger proportion of the more highly paid secondary school teachers.

The salaries of teachers in universities were calculated directly from the returns of the University Grants Committee.[4]

Finally, an estimate must be made of the remuneration of the proprietors of private schools, etc. In the census returns the number of teachers classified as employers or self-employed, and therefore excluded from the estimates above, was equal to between 70 and 80 % of the number of teachers employed in private schools. It is probable that very many were working proprietors. For the present purpose it has been assumed that the average remuneration in this group was much the same as for employees. It is known that many of the higher-class schools are essentially non-profit-making and it seems likely that the relatively low standard of many others would depress the average rate of return to proprietors. An amount equal to three-quarters of total teachers' salaries has been taken in each year to cover the remuneration of proprietors.

Estimates of expenditure at constant prices were obtained by dividing through by an index of the average salary of teachers.[5]

(d) TRADE UNIONS

The estimates under this heading relate to that part of expenditure on trade unions which is not included in savings or transfer of income (benefits paid by trade

---

[1] For estimates of gross expenditure on education in private schools, see [79] G. C. Leybourne and K. White, *Education and the Birthrate* (London, 1940); and [90] J. Vaizey, *The Costs of Education* (London, 1958).

[2] See [52] Board of Education, *Report of the Departmental Committee on Private Schools* (1932), p. 15.

[3] See [69] Chapman, *Wages and Salaries in the United Kingdom, 1920–1938*, table 73, p. 199.

[4] Ibid. p. 197.   [5] Ibid. table 75, p. 202.

unions, for example) or accounted for under other headings (heating and lighting of offices, etc.).

The expenditure of registered trade unions forms the greater part of this item. Small additions were made to this figure to cover the expenditure of unregistered unions and the Trades Union Congress.

The expenditure of all registered trade unions is recorded annually[1] and classified under various headings, amongst them an item 'management and other expenditure' which contains probably the bulk of expenditure within the scope of the definition given above. The working expenditure of unions with a membership over 10,000 is analysed in further detail by the Chief Registrar under the headings: salaries of officers, expenses of committee, other working expenditure. In 1926 the item 'salaries of officers' amounted to 52 % of total working expenditure; in 1931 the figure was 56 %; in 1936 it was 57 %. As salaries cover most but not all of the expenditure needed here, it was assumed that two-thirds of management and other working expenditure of all registered trade unions would be a more adequate proportion for the present purpose, and this figure was applied in all years.

Registration with the Chief Registrar of Friendly Societies is on a voluntary basis and covers less than half of the total number of unions, though most of the large unions are included. In 1937 there were 1,033 unions registered and unregistered, with a total membership of 5·9 millions;[2] for the same year the Chief Registrar accounts for 426 unions with a total membership of 4·9 millions. It was assumed that the average annual expenditure, as defined above, of the unregistered unions was about £300; that is, together they had an expenditure of £0·2 m. annually. This same figure was taken for all years of the period.

A small addition was made to cover the corresponding expenses of the Trades Union Congress.

Figures at constant prices have been obtained by deflating with an index of average earnings for those employed in comparable organizations.[3]

(E) RELIGION

Churches and associated religious organizations are essentially non-profit-making bodies, which are classified for present purposes as part of the personal sector. Their purchases of goods and services, therefore, have been included in the estimates of expenditure throughout this study. The voluntary contributions of individuals to church funds are treated simply as gifts between persons. It remains, however, to take into account that part of expenditure by religious bodies which does not fall under any other commodity heading, in effect the incomes of clergy and others specifically employed in religious activities.

The total earnings of all ministers of religion, monks, nuns, itinerant preachers, scripture readers, mission workers, etc., have been estimated by Chapman for the inter-war period.[4] The full details of the methods used are available in the original source, but a brief summary may be given here.

From census data and church statistics the approximate number of earners in all denominations could be calculated for all years of the period. Comprehensive financial statistics, from which an estimate may be made of the average earnings of clergy, are available only for the Church of England, representing a third of the total. The earnings of other denominations were estimated from these data on the basis of certain assumptions about the relative levels of incomes. Allowances for income in kind, the rental value of the parsonage for example, are of considerable importance in evaluating total incomes. It was assumed that the earnings of monks and nuns would consist only of income in kind.

The estimates of total incomes obtained in this way are reproduced in Table 41.

(F) CHARITY ORGANIZATIONS

The estimates to be compiled under this head relate neither to the total contributions to charity made by persons, nor to the total expenditure of charitable bodies. On the one hand, the effect of charitable activity is merely redistributive, transferring income between different groups within the personal sector, and as such these contributions are excluded from the present account. On the other hand, whether a charity distributes goods or money payments to its beneficiaries, the ultimate purchases of commodities are mostly included already under other heads in the present estimates. The only expenditures remaining for inclusion here are the particular administrative expenses of the organizations themselves.

There is a very real difficulty in this field of establishing even a reliable order of magnitude for the expenditures involved. The number of charities in existence at any time is largely a matter of guess-work. Compulsory registration was required only for war charities and those for the blind. Endowed charities are subject to the supervision of the Charity Commissioners, to whom they are obliged to send annual accounts, and their number was estimated to be approximately 80,000 during the inter-war period. There were also some 29,000 educational endowed charities under the jurisdiction of the Board of Education. The number of collecting charities, both with

---

[1] [18] *Report of the Chief Registrar of Friendly Societies, part 4, Trade Unions*; e.g. 1936, table 9, p. 19.
[2] [62] *Ministry of Labour Gazette*, October 1938, p. 402.
[3] See [69] Chapman, *Wages and Salaries in the United Kingdom, 1920–1938*, p. 221.
[4] Ibid. pp. 177–80.

and without endowment income, was variously estimated to be between 15,000 and more than 80,000.[1]

In scope they range from small local collections of a merely temporary nature, as for instance many war charities, to large national organizations. There seems little doubt that the small charities predominate in the total number, while representing a very much smaller proportion of the total income. It is probable that these small charities are of very little importance for the present purpose, in that they are more likely to rely on voluntary unpaid help and to incur very few other costs. Furthermore, that group of charities which probably accounts for a larger share of the total income than any other, the voluntary hospitals, is particularly well documented, and has already been discussed.[2]

The proportion of income expended on administration may vary considerably between different charities, from almost negligible amounts to as much as 25 %. The Charity Commissioners stipulate a maximum of 5 % of the income of a charitable trust, of which they are trustees, for expenditure on costs of administration of the charity. The exact significance of this figure, however, is extremely ambiguous, practice varying considerably between institutional and non-institutional charities. For the majority of charities a much higher proportion is probably involved. The cost of street collections alone amounted on average to 12½ % of the amount collected.[3] The figures compiled by the Charity Organization Society for charities in or available for London[4] suggest a figure of 15 %. But this is probably not wholly typical and 20–25 % would perhaps be more representative for the general run of charities recorded in the *Register*.

It seems likely that for most charities administrative expenses consist largely of three main items: wages and salaries; rent, light and heating; stationery, postage and telephones. Under the definitions adopted for this study, expenditure by charities on the last two groups has already been included in the estimates for the particular commodities. For the remaining item, wages and salaries, together with any miscellaneous expenses not covered elsewhere, it seems reasonable to take 5 % of the endowment income controlled by the Charity Commissioners and 15 % of the other income of charities.

The total income of charities in any year can only be roughly assessed. It has been estimated that 'if the income of purely endowed charities and of purely religious and political organizations is excluded, the total receipts of all charitable organizations in 1934 were probably between £35 million and £50 million'.[5] Since it is not wished to exclude endowed charities here, a figure of £45 m. probably provides the best estimate for the present purpose. Of this total £15 m. represents the income of voluntary hospitals, and must be excluded.

The remaining £30 m. may be assumed to comprise £5 m. endowment income[6] and £25 m. other income. Applying the proportions suggested above, therefore, yields a figure of £4 m. for expenditure on wages and salaries, etc.

The greater part of this sum will undoubtedly represent employees' earnings, and these will be very largely salaried officers and social welfare workers. For other years of the period, therefore, this figure has been simply varied with the estimated salary payments in a group of miscellaneous service industries including charitable service and other personal services.[7] While the year-to-year variations will have no particular significance because of the wide margin of uncertainty attaching to the estimate, some allowance for the long-term trend is probably justified.

(G) FEES PAID TO LOCAL AUTHORITIES

Numerous fees and similar payments are made to local authorities by households and others in the personal sector. Such items, for example, as fees paid for education and hospital treatment, to libraries and museums, for the use of baths and wash-houses, parks, and public conveniences, are all included here. These transactions are distinguished from the purchase of services such as water, gas, electricity, transport, etc., supplied by local authorities, in that the payment made in most cases is not determined by the cost of the service provided. The main cost of these services is borne by the rates and a further large part is paid for by government grants. The expenditure figures given here, therefore, are only an indication of the extent to which the services are paid for directly and do not reflect the relative benefit enjoyed.

The specific income from fees, rents, and recoupments, etc., of local authorities in England and Wales is recorded annually throughout the period,[8] with details for each service. By no means the whole of this item falls within

---

[1] See [66] Constance Braithwaite, *The Voluntary Citizen* (London, 1938), pp. 151–2; see also a contribution by the same author to [81] *Voluntary Social Services since 1918*, by Henry A. Mess (London, 1947), pp. 195–203.

[2] See Chapter IV, §(g), p. 46 above.

[3] See [66] Braithwaite, *The Voluntary Citizen*, p. 156; this figure relates to street collections in the metropolis.

[4] See [92] *Annual Charities Register and Digest*; the figures are also reprinted in [98] *London Statistics*.

[5] [66] Braithwaite, *The Voluntary Citizen*, p. 163.

[6] The income from securities held by the Official Trustees of Charitable Funds was £3 m.; see the [41] *Eighty-second Report of the Charity Commissioners*, Cmd 4857 (1935).

[7] See [69] Chapman, *Wages and Salaries in the United Kingdom, 1920–1938*, p. 221.

[8] See [10] *Local Government Financial Statistics*; summary accounts for all local authorities in a consolidated form, which exclude transfers between and within authorities, are published in the [6] *Annual Reports of the Ministry of Health*; the summary accounts for the two years 1937–8 and 1938–9 were published separately in 1941 and 1942.

the category of payments by the personal sector as defined above. There are clearly some services, public slaughterhouses for instance, which are used only by business. A further part of the total represents the rent of private dwellings and has already been included elsewhere in consumers' expenditure.

Apart from the classification by service there is no evidence in the accounts themselves to indicate the proportion to be allocated to personal consumption. It is only possible to make a rough assessment of the amounts required, on the basis of reasonable guesses. Fortunately, for the present purpose it is not necessary to justify each percentage adopted, service by service, since considerable allowance can be made for the cancellation of individual errors in the aggregate.

There are certain services that are clearly personal, for which the whole amount of fees, etc., may be included with little hesitation: education and health services, the use of public baths, wash-houses, parks and conveniences, the care of the mentally deficient, and relief of the poor. There are also certain general services such as the collection of refuse, administration of justice, valuation expenses, etc., of which only a part has been taken here. Finally, a half of the figure for miscellaneous services and administrative expenses, not allocated to specific services, was also included. These are all rate fund services. From the trading services it seemed reasonable to include payments in respect of cemeteries and half the figure for other unspecified services.

The total payments obtained in this way were first adjusted to a calendar year basis and an addition was then made to cover Scotland and Northern Ireland. In the financial year 1938–9 current income, other than rates or government grants, of local authorities in Scotland and Northern Ireland amounted to 13% of the figure for England and Wales.[1] Comparison with earlier years suggests that this proportion changed only slightly during the period under review. Accordingly this same percentage was added in each year to the total derived for England and Wales. An approximate adjustment of this kind seems quite adequate in view of the lack of precision for the estimate as a whole.

Estimates at constant prices were obtained by deflating these expenditures by an index of wages of those employed in local government service.[2]

(h) OTHER MISCELLANEOUS SERVICES

There are a number of other service items, each very small, for which individually no adequate estimates can be made. For many of them personal expenditure represents only a small part of the total, and little or no information is available on which to base a direct estimate. They include legal fees, bank charges, stamp duties payable on financial transactions, cheques, etc., and miscellaneous professional services.

Expenditure on stamp duties, which is known from the revenue returns,[3] is the only component of this group for which anything more than fragmentary information can be obtained. Much the greater part of these duty payments, of course, relate to transactions within the business sector and form no part of personal expenditure. But the figures are available annually throughout the period, and may reasonably be regarded as a rough index of expenditure on the whole group of services dealt with here. A figure of £5 m. was taken for 1938 and this was varied for other years with total stamp duty receipts.

Estimates at constant prices were obtained by dividing through by an index of all consumer prices.

This estimate makes no claim to exactness but is merely an indication of the appropriate order of magnitude. There would be nothing to be gained for the present purpose by a more laborious attempt at greater precision.

(i) FUNERAL EXPENSES

The estimates made under this heading cover only specifically funeral expenditure and do not extend to such incidental expenses as the cost of mourning clothes or the entertainment of mourners, etc., which are included in other categories of expenditure. The figures are based on the statistics published in connexion with the valuations for estate duty.

The allowances for funeral expenses deducted from the total gross capital value of estates liable to estate duty in Great Britain are published annually for most years of the inter-war period.[4] This total divided by the number of estates liable to duty[5] in the year gave an average figure varying around £19 for the expenses of each funeral. Although these data relate only to the higher income groups of the community, the widespread habit of insuring for funeral costs, and the disproportionately high expenditure of the lower income groups on this item,[6] suggest that a figure of this order would not be unreasonable as a general average. Accordingly these figures, adjusted to calendar years, were multiplied by the number of deaths[7] in the United Kingdom in each year to obtain an estimate of total expenditure on funerals.

---

[1] [2] *Annual Abstract of Statistics*, no. 89 (1952), tables 267, 271 and 274.

[2] [69] Chapman, *Wages and Salaries in the United Kingdom, 1920–1938*, p. 175.

[3] See [15] *Reports of the Commissioners of H.M. Inland Revenue*.

[4] Ibid., e.g. *Eighty-second Report*, for the year ended 31 March 1939, Cmd 6099, p. 19.

[5] Ibid. p. 16.

[6] See [91] Sir Arnold Wilson and Hermann Levy, *Burial Reform and Funeral Costs* (Oxford, 1938), pp. 130–2.

[7] See [20] *Statistical Abstract for the United Kingdom*.

Comparable figures of funeral expenses are not available for 1920 or 1921, and the same average expenditure as in 1922 was taken for both years. Furthermore, the number of deaths in Northern Ireland are not recorded separately for these two years. They were estimated on the basis of the figures for Great Britain by simply applying the ratio found for the total number of deaths in the United Kingdom to the total for Great Britain in the years 1922–5.

Expenditure at constant prices was calculated by multiplying the number of deaths in each year by the average expenditure in 1938.

3 THE RELIABILITY OF THE ESTIMATES

It will be evident from the account of the methods used that most of the estimates presented in this chapter are subject to fairly wide margins of error. Even where the basic data are published series of unimpeachable reliability, the assumptions involved in deriving the estimates introduce a large element of conjecture. Some indication of the degree of reliance to be placed on the figures can be briefly indicated here. This may appear rather slight for many of the items, but by making full use of the little information available for these separate estimates, the proportionate error in the total may be considerably reduced.

Although the estimates of insurance business are derived from published accounts, and to this extent can be regarded as firmly based, the assumptions required to obtain an estimate of purely personal expenditure are hardly more than rough guesses, which will necessarily lead to a wide proportionate margin of error. In absolute terms, however, it seems unlikely that the order of magnitude is mistaken.

For private education, trade unions, religion and charities, the figures are based chiefly on estimates of employees' earnings. For the most part these are derived from census figures of numbers employed, interpolated and extrapolated to cover other years of the period, and estimates of average earnings. The reliability of the basic series varies a good deal, and further scope for error is given by the special adjustments required for the present purpose: for example, to estimate proprietors' earnings in private schools. For all these items, little significance can attach to any of the year-to-year changes shown. At most, it may be hoped that their relative magnitudes are satisfactorily established.

The estimates of fees paid to local authorities also derive from published accounts. But here again the question of consumer allocation presents difficulties. The itemization of services, however, allows for the cancellation of errors between separate components, and the proportionate error in the total will be considerably less than that of individual items.

The figures for other miscellaneous services are only a very rough indication of the approximate magnitude. If they had been omitted altogether, it would certainly have introduced an element of bias into the estimates; even a very rough estimate is preferable to no estimate at all.

The fact that the estimate of average expenditure on funerals is derived solely from information relating to those with higher incomes might suggest that the figure must be overstated. However, it is known that the practice of insuring to cover funeral costs was widespread and it is not thought that the level of expenditure by the lower income groups would be much below the figure adopted here.

4 THE MAIN TABLES

The estimates for the miscellaneous services, described in the preceding section, are set out in the following tables. Expenditures on all items are brought together in Table 41. In view of the fairly considerable margins of error attaching to many of the series, as well as the inherent ambiguity of the concepts, it does not seem useful to give separate price and quantity figures for each item. Collectively, the estimates are more reliable and meaningful. In Table 42, price and quantity series for four groups of items are shown in a comparable index number form. The quantity series are base-weighted aggregate index numbers and the price series are current-weighted aggregates; their product is thus a simple index of expenditure. Each series has been multiplied through by expenditure in 1938, the base year, and is shown in this form in the diagrams of §1.

TABLE 41. ESTIMATED EXPENDITURE ON MISCELLANEOUS SERVICES BY FINAL CONSUMERS IN THE UNITED KINGDOM, 1920–38 (£ M.)

	1920	1921	1922	1923	1924	1925	1926	1927	1928	1929	1930	1931	1932	1933	1934	1935	1936	1937	1938
Insurance																			
Life assurance	28·1	29·0	28·9	29·5	30·3	31·7	30·4	31·4	33·0	36·1	38·3	40·9	42·3	42·2	42·5	43·4	43·1	42·4	46·0
Other	10·1	9·3	10·0	11·5	12·0	13·0	13·5	13·8	14·2	14·1	13·6	12·3	12·7	13·2	14·1	14·8	15·4	16·4	16·1
Total	38·2	38·3	38·9	41·0	42·3	44·7	43·9	45·2	47·2	50·2	51·9	53·2	55·0	55·4	56·6	58·2	58·5	58·8	62·1
Private education	15·2	17·0	18·1	18·4	18·5	19·0	19·4	19·5	19·8	20·1	20·8	20·6	20·1	20·2	21·3	22·7	23·8	24·4	24·7
Trade unions	3·0	3·0	2·6	2·2	2·3	2·2	2·2	2·0	1·9	1·9	2·0	2·0	1·9	1·8	1·8	1·9	2·0	2·2	2·4
Religion	16·7	17·7	17·9	17·8	18·0	18·2	18·3	18·4	18·3	18·8	18·8	18·7	18·7	18·7	18·6	18·7	18·7	19·1	19·2
Charity organizations	6·3	5·5	4·8	4·5	4·5	4·4	4·4	4·4	4·3	4·3	4·2	4·2	4·1	4·0	4·0	4·0	4·0	3·9	3·9
Fees paid to local authorities	15·3	15·5	15·4	15·6	15·8	16·4	17·1	18·0	19·0	19·7	20·0	20·2	20·7	21·4	21·8	22·5	23·7	25·5	26·3
Other services	5·0	4·0	4·0	4·0	4·5	5·0	5·0	5·0	6·0	5·0	4·0	3·5	4·0	4·5	5·0	5·0	6·0	5·0	5·0
Funeral expenses	10·9	10·7	11·5	10·4	11·0	10·9	10·5	11·3	10·1	12·0	10·1	10·7	10·2	10·6	10·0	9·9	10·0	11·0	10·2
Total	110·6	111·7	113·2	113·9	116·9	120·8	120·8	123·8	126·6	132·0	131·8	133·1	134·7	136·6	139·1	142·9	146·7	149·9	153·8

TABLE 42. INDEX NUMBERS OF QUANTITY AND AVERAGE PRICE FOR MISCELLANEOUS SERVICES PURCHASED FOR FINAL CONSUMPTION IN THE UNITED KINGDOM, 1920–38

(Expenditure in 1938 is taken as the base for each series)

	1920	1921	1922	1923	1924	1925	1926	1927	1928	1929	1930	1931	1932	1933	1934	1935	1936	1937	1938
Insurance																			
Quantity index	28·7	30·1	35·4	39·1	40·2	42·4	41·7	43·1	45·0	48·0	50·5	53·2	55·9	56·7	57·9	59·4	59·5	59·2	62·1
Price index	82·7	79·0	68·2	65·1	65·3	65·5	65·4	65·1	65·1	64·9	63·8	62·1	61·1	60·7	60·7	60·8	61·1	61·7	62·1
Private education																			
Quantity index	17·6	18·1	19·1	19·2	19·3	19·9	20·2	20·3	20·9	21·0	21·5	22·1	22·6	23·0	23·3	23·7	24·1	24·5	24·7
Price index	21·3	23·2	23·4	23·7	23·7	23·6	23·7	23·7	23·4	23·6	23·9	23·0	22·0	21·7	22·6	23·7	24·4	24·6	24·7
Religious and charitable organizations																			
Quantity index	23·6	23·1	23·2	23·1	23·2	23·2	23·2	23·3	23·2	23·2	23·1	23·2	23·2	23·1	23·1	23·1	23·1	23·0	23·1
Price index	22·5	23·2	22·6	22·3	22·4	22·5	22·6	22·6	22·5	23·0	23·0	22·8	22·7	22·7	22·6	22·7	22·7	23·1	23·1
Other services																			
Quantity index	27·6	27·5	30·6	31·6	33·5	33·9	34·2	35·9	37·4	38·7	36·7	37·5	38·7	40·4	40·7	41·6	44·0	44·6	43·9
Price index	54·4	53·0	48·1	44·7	44·0	44·7	44·7	44·4	43·4	43·8	43·2	42·6	41·7	41·6	41·6	41·5	41·6	43·0	43·9
Total																			
Quantity index	97·5	98·8	108·3	113·0	116·2	119·4	119·3	122·6	126·5	130·9	131·8	136·0	140·4	143·2	145·0	147·8	150·7	151·3	153·8
Price index	174·5	173·9	160·8	155·0	154·7	155·6	155·7	155·3	153·9	155·1	153·8	150·5	147·6	146·7	147·5	148·7	149·7	152·4	153·8

CHAPTER X

ADJUSTMENT ITEMS

1 GENERAL REMARKS

To complete the estimates of consumers' expenditure, two further items are required: payments in kind to the Armed Forces, not so far included in the commodity estimates, and the net balance of travellers' expenditures.

Income in kind of the Armed Forces must be included as part of consumers' expenditure in order to balance the corresponding addition to military pay and allowances on the income side of the national accounts. Other elements of income in kind already included, servants' keep and emoluments of nurses, differ in being a part of consumers' expenditure on these particular services.

The estimates of expenditure for individual goods and services throughout this study relate to total purchases in the United Kingdom and include the expenditure not only of residents but also of visitors from other countries. Similarly, the expenditure of United Kingdom residents travelling abroad is excluded. To preserve the national basis of the estimates it is necessary to deduct the expenditure of non-residents and to add that part of expenditure abroad which is not chargeable as a business expense. This cannot be done for each item separately but it is possible to make estimates of the total expenditures involved.

The figures of tourist expenditure are not without some interest of their own. Though the margin of error in the calculations is necessarily large, the general trend shown by the series should be reliable. By far the greater number of United Kingdom tourists abroad were travellers to the continent. From just over 400,000 in 1920 they increased to 960,000 in 1930 and, after a quite considerable falling off in the slump, had risen to well over 1 million by 1938. Though their average expenditure was relatively small, about £25 in 1938, in total they accounted for more than 85 % of expenditure abroad. The number of tourists to other countries was less than 5 % of those going to the continent and showed a similar movement over the period. A new development in the later years was the growth in popularity of pleasure cruises. The number of passengers increased particularly rapidly in the early 1930's, rising to 50,000 in 1933. This may have been partly at the expense of other forms of tourism; by the end of the period the number had fallen off to less than half this level.

While the expenditure of United Kingdom tourists increased over the period, though much more slowly in the 'thirties, expenditure by visitors from abroad tended to decline. Visitors from the continent, representing somewhat over half of the total, increased from 173,000 in 1920 to 256,000 in 1929. The drop in the early 'thirties was again marked, with a recovery in subsequent years to 290,000 by the end of the period. Average expenditure by these visitors is low (about £30 in 1938) and they accounted for less than 20 % of the total expenditure by non-residents. Visitors from countries outside Europe are likely to have travelled a considerable distance and both their length of stay and expenditure are likely to be proportionately greater. Those coming from British and Commonwealth countries include many colonial officials on leave and their numbers did not vary greatly during the period. The number of visitors from foreign countries, however, fell off by more than half between 1929 and 1933, and remained below its former level to the end of the period. Average expenditure by these visitors was estimated to be £200 in 1938.

An estimate of spending by United Kingdom troops serving overseas completes the total of expenditures abroad. In the immediate post-war years this was equal to tourist expenditure but for the rest of the period accounted for less than a third of the total.

2 METHODS OF ESTIMATION

Scope of the estimates. Unlike the preceding estimates of this study, the items dealt with here do not relate to individual commodities but to a whole group of goods and services for which only an estimate in total can reasonably be made. Income in kind of the Armed Forces covers principally those items of food and clothing issued to members of the services both at home and abroad which are omitted from the individual commodity estimates. Expenditure by non-residents includes all purchases by foreigners, whether visiting tourists, businessmen, diplomatic staffs, seamen, or military personnel. The figures of expenditure abroad by United

Kingdom travellers, on the other hand, are restricted to spending by the personal sector, excluding any business or government expenditure. Personal expenditure by members of the Armed Forces serving abroad is included, however, and a separate estimate is made to cover this.

General procedure. Estimates of the value of allowances in kind to the Armed Forces were obtained from the published government accounts. A proportion of the figure of pay and cash allowances from the same source was taken for expenditure abroad by members of the services. Other expenditure abroad by the personal sector and expenditure in this country by non-residents were calculated from the records of passenger movements and estimates of average expenditure.

Methods employed. The methods employed to estimate these adjustment items are discussed below in the following order:

(*a*) Income in kind of the Armed Forces.
(*b*) Tourist expenditure.
(*c*) Personal expenditure abroad of the Armed Forces.

(A) INCOME IN KIND OF THE ARMED FORCES

The figures of allowances in kind given here are taken directly from Chapman's estimates of military pay and allowances,[1] compiled from the government Appropriation Accounts. They relate to provisions, including naval soap and tobacco, and clothing. Some cash allowances in lieu of provisions and clothing, not separately shown in the accounts, are also included.

To obtain estimates at constant prices the series was deflated by a price index combining indicators for food and clothing prices in the ratio 2:1.

(B) TOURIST EXPENDITURE

From the statistics of passenger movements it is possible to estimate the numbers of travellers to and from the United Kingdom, distinguishing certain broad categories: that is, trippers, tourists, and long-term visitors. This cannot be done more than approximately with the available statistics which, at most, record only the country of origin and destination of passengers. Some distinction is necessary, however, since the average amounts spent differ considerably for the different categories. Rough estimates of average expenditures could be made, with some indication of the trend over the period; on this basis the total expenditures could be calculated, a certain proportion of expenditure abroad being allocated to business expense.

With certain minor qualifications, the tourist expenditures to be calculated here are also components in the nation's balance of payments, and it is in this connexion that certain official estimates have been made from 1930 onwards.[2] The method used is similar to that described above, but only figures of the year-to-year changes in the net balance are actually published. Estimates of the actual net balance may be obtained by cumulating these figures from the initial year, 1930, for which it was stated that credit and debit payments were approximately equal. For the present purposes, in particular the exclusion of business expenditure abroad, it is necessary to re-work these estimates, so far as possible, from the original data. The similarity of the methods used ensures a broad agreement between the estimates, and comparable figures for the earlier years of the period may also be obtained.

Estimates for the earlier years are also available in the very valuable pioneer work of Ogilvie.[3] In fact, the official figures appear to be very largely a continuation, with some revision, of Ogilvie's series. Much of the difference turns on the best interpretation of the passenger statistics and Ogilvie was well aware of the limitations of his knowledge in this respect. In making the present estimates an attempt has been made to incorporate these revisions and provide a consistent set of figures for the whole of the inter-war period.

The nature and classification of the passenger statistics have been discussed above in connexion with the estimates of expenditure on overseas travel.[4] The main facts may be briefly recapitulated here. Both inward and outward movements are recorded but the latter are held to be probably the more reliable for the present purposes.[5] Separate information is available with respect to passenger traffic with the continent and with countries outside Europe, the latter being treated in greater detail. This distinction, however, refers only to the immediate and not the ultimate destination. Thus Americans returning home via the continent are recorded only in the first category.

In both groups British subjects are distinguished from aliens. Unfortunately, 'British' in this context includes not only the residents of the United Kingdom, but also those of the colonies, the Dominions, and the Irish Republic. This statistical anomaly largely nullifies the usefulness of the figures for the present purpose and without further information estimates of tourist traffic would be highly arbitrary.

Some additional information is given for travellers to countries out of Europe. There is a classification of

---

[1] [**69**] Chapman, *Wages and Salaries in the United Kingdom, 1920–1938*, pp. 165–9.

[2] See, for example, 'The Balance of Payments' in the [**53**] *Board of Trade Journal*, vol. CXLII, 23 February 1939, pp. 284–9; a summary of the estimates for 1930–8 is given in [**64**] *Balance of Payments 1938*, Economic Intelligence Service, League of Nations (Geneva, 1939), pp. 128–9.

[3] See [**82**] F. W. Ogilvie, *The Tourist Movement* (London, 1933).

[4] See Chapter VI, §(*f*), above.

[5] See the [**53**] *Board of Trade Journal, passim*; for example, 9 March 1939, pp. 358–68.

British passengers according to country of destination, distinguishing a number of British countries, the United States and other foreign countries; and emigrants are shown separately from other travellers. From 1933 onwards further detail was given in the form of a cross-classification of the figures according to both last and intended future residence, whether in the United Kingdom, British possessions, or foreign countries. From these figures it was possible for the first time to distinguish United Kingdom tourists from foreign visitors.

For the years from 1931 onwards there are also figures for the numbers of passengers going on pleasure cruises. These were almost entirely residents. Finally, from 1921 foreign visitors were subject to much closer surveillance under the Aliens Order and detailed statistics were published annually.[1]

To obtain estimates of expenditure the total number of tourists and visitors in each year has been divided into categories which are most likely to reflect differences in the average length of stay and consequent levels of expenditure. Very little is known about actual expenditures and the estimates are based largely on the experience of other countries together with some fragmentary information about special classes of visitors.

It will be evident from the preceding account that the estimates cannot pretend to any high degree of accuracy. But the methods adoped may claim to make the best use of the available information and there will clearly be some scope for cancellation of errors between different components of the total.

United Kingdom residents travelling abroad are divided into three categories:

(i) *Visitors to the continent.* The recorded number of British passengers to the continent includes both day trippers and overseas-British visitors, as well as United Kingdom residents going to European countries on holiday or business. The expenditure of day trippers is so very small that they may be wholly excluded for the present purpose. While many colonial officers on leave and other overseas-British visitors entering this country travel by the overland route, the number who return this way is believed to be much smaller. In the period 1930–8, the proportion of United Kingdom residents, other than day trippers, varied between 80 and 90 %. It has been assumed that a constant figure of 85 % could be applied for the earlier years. Average expenditure per head was estimated to have been £30 for 1930–5 and to have fallen in 1937–8 with the devaluation of the franc and the reduction in rail fares.[2] For the earlier years of the period the figure has been varied with the index of retail prices; for 1937–8 a figure of £25 was taken.

(ii) *Visitors to countries outside Europe.* The greater part of the British passengers to ports outside Europe, ex-

cluding emigrants, consists of overseas-British visitors returning home. In the years 1933–8, these visitors represented on average two-thirds of the total. It has been assumed that in all earlier years of the period one-third of the total represented United Kingdom residents travelling abroad. There seems little doubt that these travellers would be likely to stay much longer than visitors to the continent and that their expenditure would be correspondingly greater. Evidence of tourist receipts in a number of these countries suggests an average figure of £100 in 1930.[3] For other years of the period this figure has been simply varied with the index of retail prices.

(iii) *Travellers on pleasure cruises.* The number going on pleasure cruises in 1931, the first year for which figures are available, was only 10,000, although it increased rapidly in the next two years. It seems probable that the figure was much smaller in earlier years and may be ignored for the present purpose. The expenditure of these travellers, apart from the fare and expenses on board, is judged to be relatively small, since only brief visits are paid in most ports. An average figure of £25 has been taken for each year.

Visitors to the United Kingdom are also divided into three categories:

(i) *Visitors from the continent.* From the recorded number of alien passengers to the continent it is necessary to exclude both day trippers, whose expenditure is so small as to be negligible for present purposes, and foreign visitors from countries outside Europe travelling via continental ports. The remainder are European visitors to this country. In the years 1930–8 these visitors represented between 64 and 72 % of the total. For the earlier years a constant average figure of 68 % has been taken in all years. The average expenditure of these visitors was estimated to be £30 for the period 1930–8. This figure has been roughly varied with an index of retail prices for earlier years of the period.

(ii) *Overseas-British visitors.* The greater part of these visitors come from British and Commonwealth countries and many are colonial officers coming on leave. As indicated above, these visitors were estimated to be two-thirds of the British passengers to ports outside Europe throughout the period. As a whole these visitors are likely to be relatively wealthy and to make a fairly extended stay in this country. Their expenditure, therefore, is likely to be correspondingly large. From an annual sample of colonial officials in the years 1933–8,[4] it was found that average expenditure was £170–200, declining slightly until 1936 and rising again in the last two years.

---

1 See [21] *Statistics in regard to Alien Passengers.*
2 The [53] *Board of Trade Journal,* 23 February 1939, p. 287.
3 See [82] Ogilvie, *The Tourist Movement,* p. 133.
4 See [53] *Board of Trade Journal,* 23 February 1939, p. 288.

The upper limit of this range has been taken for 1938 and varied for other years of the period with a general index of retail prices.

(iii) *Other foreign visitors.* This final category of visitors represents foreigners coming from countries outside Europe. As with most overseas-British visitors, they will usually have travelled a considerable distance and it is likely that their stay will be relatively long and expenditure comparatively large. It has already been noted that many of these visitors, particularly those from the United States, travel via European ports and are not therefore recorded as alien passengers to countries outside Europe. It is evident from the figures for 1930–8, however, that all alien visitors included in the present estimates are a fairly constant proportion of the total recorded alien passengers in each year. For the years before 1930 an average figure of 80 % has been taken. The estimated number of visitors from the continent was then deducted and the number of other foreign visitors was obtained as a residual. Average expenditure in each year was assumed to be the same as for overseas-British visitors.

On the basis of these estimates of numbers and average expenditure for each category of traveller total expenditure could be calculated. The whole of the expenditure by visitors must be deducted from consumers' expenditure. The corresponding addition for expenditure abroad, however, must exclude any expenditure incurred for business purposes. It has been assumed that two-thirds of the total in each year represents personal expenditure.

The estimates are shown in Table 43.

(c) PERSONAL EXPENDITURE ABROAD OF THE ARMED FORCES

Estimates of the total pay and cash allowances received by the Armed Forces have been compiled by Chapman[1] from the Appropriation Accounts. It is not possible to make more than a very rough estimate of the proportion that is spent abroad. For the present purpose a figure of £10 m. was taken in 1938 and the same fraction, one-fifth, of total pay and cash allowances in all other years of the period.

The estimates of expenditure under each of these three headings, and the annual net adjustment, are shown at current and constant (1938) prices in Table 44.

3 THE RELIABILITY OF THE ESTIMATES

The figures of allowances in kind are taken from the published accounts and, apart from small discrepancies in coverage, are not likely to be subject to any appreciable error. The deflator used to derive estimates at constant prices, though not based on a detailed calculation, should also have a high degree of reliability.

The classification of the passenger statistics is not sufficiently detailed for it to be possible to make more than a broad estimate of tourist traffic. The discrepancy between the inward and outward figures is an indication of inherent ambiguity in the data, but it is believed that the latter offer the better basis for the present calculations. The additional information available from 1930 onwards, and particularly after 1933, renders the estimates for these later years much more reliable. For the earlier years it has usually been necessary to make a fixed proportionate allocation, to separate United Kingdom residents from other British travellers for instance, and this is likely to introduce sizeable, largely systematic, errors. Little is known about the average expenditure of tourists or other travellers. While the average level shown is probably of the right order of magnitude, the yearly variations will have little significance.

There is clearly some scope for offsetting errors and the expenditure totals should be relatively more reliable than the components. The net balance, however, which is obtained as a difference, will be subject to particularly large proportionate errors.

The estimate of expenditure abroad by the Armed Forces does not aim at any degree of precision, but the size of the error is clearly limited by the accurately known total pay and allowances.

---

[1] **[69]** Chapman, *Wages and Salaries in the United Kingdom, 1920–1938*, pp. 165–9.

TABLE 43. ESTIMATED EXPENDITURE BY TOURISTS TO AND FROM THE UNITED KINGDOM, 1920–38

	1920	1921	1922	1923	1924	1925	1926	1927	1928	1929	1930	1931	1932	1933	1934	1935	1936	1937	1938
U.K. tourists to the continent																			
Number (000's)	417	470	543	660	690	785	816	830	930	930	960	910	660	780	711	805	896	1,160	1,126
Average expenditure (£ per head)	45	40	35	32·5	32·5	32·5	32·5	30	30	30	30	30	30	30	30	30	30	25	25
Expenditure (£m.)	18·8	18·8	19·0	21·5	22·4	25·5	26·5	24·9	27·9	27·9	28·8	27·3	19·8	23·4	21·3	24·2	26·9	29·0	28·2
U.K. tourists to other countries																			
Number (000's)	23	23	25	27	36	37	39	41	45	46	43	38	34	31	37	39	51	48	45
Average expenditure (£ per head)	145	135	115	110	110	110	110	105	105	105	100	95	95	90	90	90	95	95	100
Expenditure (£m.)	3·3	3·1	2·9	3·0	4·0	4·1	4·3	4·3	4·7	4·8	4·3	3·6	3·2	2·8	3·3	3·5	4·8	4·6	4·5
U.K. tourists on pleasure cruises																			
Number (000's)	—	—	—	—	—	—	—	—	—	—	—	10	35	50	44	36	32	25	22
Average expenditure (£ per head)	—	—	—	—	—	—	—	—	—	—	—	25	25	25	25	25	25	25	25
Expenditure (£m.)	—	—	—	—	—	—	—	—	—	—	—	0·3	0·9	1·2	1·1	0·9	0·8	0·6	0·5
Total expenditure (£m.)	22·1	21·9	21·9	24·5	26·4	29·6	30·8	29·2	32·6	32·7	33·1	31·2	23·9	27·4	25·7	28·6	32·5	34·2	33·2
Less Business expenses, etc. (£m.)	−7·4	−7·3	−7·3	−8·2	−8·8	−9·9	−10·3	−9·7	−10·8	−10·9	−11·0	−10·4	−8·0	−9·1	−8·5	−9·6	−10·8	−11·4	−11·1
Total consumers' expenditure abroad (£m.)	14·7	14·6	14·6	16·3	17·6	19·7	20·5	19·5	21·8	21·8	22·1	20·8	15·9	18·3	17·2	19·0	21·7	22·8	22·1
Visitors from the continent																			
Number (000's)	173	194	182	184	225	216	208	227	247	256	265	235	195	190	230	237	276	296	288
Average expenditure (£ per head)	45	40	35	32·5	32·5	32·5	32·5	30	30	30	30	30	30	30	30	30	30	30	30
Expenditure (£m.)	7·8	7·8	6·4	6·0	7·3	7·0	6·8	6·8	7·4	7·7	8·0	7·1	5·9	5·7	6·9	7·1	8·3	8·9	8·6
Visitors from other British countries[a]																			
Number (000's)	45	46	50	54	66	66	71	76	83	86	82	76	67	70	76	76	83	85	80
Average expenditure (£ per head)	300	275	240	220	220	220	220	215	215	210	205	195	190	185	185	190	190	195	200
Expenditure (£m.)	13·5	12·6	12·0	11·9	14·5	14·5	15·6	16·4	17·8	18·0	16·8	14·8	12·7	12·9	14·1	14·5	15·8	16·6	16·0
Visitors from other foreign countries																			
Number (000's)	97	120	106	131	124	120	130	148	143	138	125	90	75	62	66	78	96	118	91
Average expenditure (£ per head)	300	275	240	220	220	220	220	215	215	210	205	195	190	185	185	190	190	195	200
Expenditure (£m.)	29·1	33·0	25·4	28·8	27·3	26·4	28·6	31·8	30·8	29·0	25·6	17·5	14·2	11·5	12·2	14·8	18·2	23·0	18·2
Total expenditure of non-residents (£m.)	50·4	53·4	43·8	46·7	49·1	47·9	51·0	55·0	56·0	54·7	50·4	39·4	32·8	30·1	33·2	36·4	42·3	48·5	42·8

a Includes British visitors from other foreign countries.

14·2

TABLE 44. ESTIMATES OF INCOME IN KIND, TOURIST EXPENDITURE AND PERSONAL EXPENDITURE ABROAD OF THE ARMED FORCES, 1920–38 (£ M.)

	1920	1921	1922	1923	1924	1925	1926	1927	1928	1929	1930	1931	1932	1933	1934	1935	1936	1937	1938
At current prices																			
Income in kind of the Armed Forces	40·8	22·3	13·5	9·9	9·4	9·4	9·5	8·9	8·6	8·4	7·8	6·8	6·3	6·4	6·6	7·3	8·3	10·8	14·7
Expenditure abroad																			
by tourists	14·7	14·6	14·6	16·3	17·6	19·7	20·5	19·5	21·8	21·8	22·1	20·8	15·9	18·3	17·2	19·0	21·7	22·8	22·1
by the Armed Forces	21·0	13·0	10·0	9·0	9·0	8·0	8·0	8·0	8·0	8·0	8·0	8·0	7·0	7·0	7·0	8·0	8·0	8·0	10·0
Total	35·7	27·6	24·6	25·3	26·6	27·7	28·5	27·5	29·8	29·8	30·1	28·8	22·9	25·3	24·2	27·0	29·7	30·8	32·1
Less Expenditure by non-residents	−50·4	−53·4	−43·8	−46·7	−49·1	−47·9	−51·0	−55·0	−56·0	−54·7	−50·4	−39·4	−32·8	−30·1	−33·2	−36·4	−42·3	−48·5	−42·8
Net balance	−14·7	−25·8	−19·2	−21·4	−22·5	−20·2	−22·5	−27·5	−26·2	−24·9	−20·3	−10·6	−9·9	−4·8	−9·0	−9·4	−12·6	−17·7	−10·7
Total adjustment	26·1	−3·5	−5·7	−11·5	−13·1	−10·8	−13·0	−18·6	−17·6	−16·5	−12·5	−3·8	−3·6	1·6	−2·4	−2·1	−4·3	−6·9	4·0
At constant (1938) prices																			
Income in kind of the Armed Forces	21·2	14·0	10·6	8·3	7·9	7·8	8·1	7·9	7·6	7·5	7·3	7·0	6·8	7·1	7·3	7·9	8·9	11·0	14·7
Net balance	−9·8	−18·8	−16·3	−19·3	−20·4	−18·3	−20·5	−25·7	−24·6	−23·6	−19·8	−10·8	−10·3	−5·1	−9·6	−10·0	−13·2	−18·0	−10·7
Total adjustment	11·4	−4·8	−5·7	−11·0	−12·5	−10·5	−12·4	−17·8	−17·0	−16·1	−12·5	−3·8	−3·5	2·0	−2·3	−2·1	−4·3	−7·0	4·0

CHAPTER XI

TOTAL EXPENDITURE, 1920–1938

1 INTRODUCTION

The estimates for all items of consumers' expenditure are brought together in this chapter and summary tables setting out the series for the main commodity groups and for total expenditure are provided. It is not proposed at this stage to present any detailed analysis of the figures. In the following chapter the course of consumers' expenditure over the whole period 1900–55 is surveyed and some aspects of the changing pattern of consumption are briefly discussed.

It is of interest to compare the present estimates with other figures from the same field of inquiry. In the following section a number of comparisons are made: first, the results obtained in this study are compared with the information from the family budget inquiries of 1937–9; secondly, the aggregate price series is compared with the cost-of-living index, a commonly used price deflator for the period; and thirdly, a comparison is made with the official estimates of consumers' expenditure in 1938.

The significance of these comparisons will depend on the accuracy of the figures being compared; small differences could be due to estimation errors. In assessing these errors it is important to take account of the fact that the main expenditure groups in this study are aggregates of a number of independently estimated items; it is reasonable to expect that there will be some cancelling of errors between components. This should apply especially to the estimates of total expenditure. A discussion of the degree of reliability that may be attributed to the estimates appears in §3.

Finally, in §4, there is a reconciliation of the series in this volume with the estimates for the earlier years 1900–19. These links are required in order to make valid comparisons over the whole period 1900–38.

The estimates for the main commodity groups of consumers' expenditure are brought together in Table 45. The series for total expenditure shows the familiar cyclical pattern of the inter-war period. Between 1920 and 1923 the level of expenditure fell by more than one-quarter. The subsequent rise lasted until 1929 and was followed by a further fall to a level in 1932–3 slightly below that of ten years earlier. The recovery was more rapid than

before and by 1938 expenditure had reached a level only less than in 1920. These are expenditures at current prices, however, and are affected by variations in the value of money. In real terms the pattern is different. Expenditures at constant (1938) prices are shown in Table 46. Here an upward trend through the period is clearly apparent, the fall in expenditure being more than offset by the fall in prices. The recession in the 'twenties is less marked and the level of 1920 had been regained by 1923. By 1938 expenditure had risen 31 % above this level, an average annual rate of growth of 1·8 %. The depression of the 'thirties appears only to have slowed down the rate of growth and not to have produced an actual decline. Among the component groups there was a marked decrease in the consumption of alcoholic drink at this time, a somewhat smaller decline in public transportation, and slighter lapses in a few other groups. For most groups consumption continued to increase during these years. In part the differences in movement between component groups will be due to the effect of changes in relative prices on demand. Price index numbers are shown in Table 47. They were obtained simply as the ratio of the expenditures at current and constant prices and are therefore current-weighted (Paasche) index numbers. It can be seen from these figures that alcoholic drinks became much more expensive in the early 'thirties and this will account for much of the decline in their consumption. The fall in food prices, on the other hand, did much to sustain the standard of living during these years.

2 COMPARISONS WITH OTHER ESTIMATES

The family budget inquiries of 1937–9 were undertaken to provide information on the pattern of consumers' expenditure at that time. They are chiefly valuable, perhaps, as evidence about the variations in expenditure associated with changes in income. But it is not without interest to compare the average expenditures derived from these inquiries with the estimates obtained, for the most part by quite different methods, in this study.

TABLE 45. ESTIMATED EXPENDITURE AT CURRENT PRICES ON ALL GOODS AND SERVICES PURCHASED FOR FINAL CONSUMPTION IN THE UNITED KINGDOM, 1920–38 (£ M.)

	1920	1921	1922	1923	1924	1925	1926	1927	1928	1929	1930	1931	1932	1933	1934	1935	1936	1937	1938
Food	1,739·3	1,574·6	1,317·0	1,304·2	1,321·6	1,354·5	1,329·7	1,311·3	1,332·0	1,327·0	1,285·7	1,213·4	1,164·2	1,129·1	1,156·2	1,186·8	1,221·6	1,284·9	1,308·8
Alcoholic drinks and table waters	463·3	421·2	364·7	340·7	354·3	347·1	332·1	329·6	319·7	320·9	310·4	292·5	274·7	269·5	273·8	284·9	295·2	309·4	306·4
Tobacco products	119·8	116·2	111·7	109·2	111·9	116·1	117·3	124·0	131·4	135·5	139·5	140·4	138·7	142·4	146·2	153·0	160·9	168·9	175·8
Rent, rates and water charges	292·5	340·1	353·1	346·8	345·2	348·7	360·2	374·2	382·2	392·1	402·9	409·8	414·8	422·8	431·6	446·8	462·0	475·1	488·4
Fuel and light	182·7	175·2	163·6	153·6	166·4	164·9	150·9	173·0	159·7	169·5	169·5	169·4	164·3	165·7	169·5	172·0	184·1	193·4	197·2
Clothing and other personal effects	919·6	593·6	523·6	485·3	491·3	508·1	501·7	508·5	522·1	521·8	502·6	478·5	439·0	448·8	462·0	481·2	501·2	542·9	567·4
Furniture, furnishings, etc.	308·7	217·0	198·0	192·3	191·5	200·1	196·9	210·2	217·3	224·4	224·9	218·0	208·9	217·6	237·0	249·4	260·2	277·0	263·7
Household operation	375·3	331·8	276·6	262·8	268·7	274·0	274·2	277·5	281·8	286·0	280·9	274·4	267·2	268·1	274·3	280·7	290·1	297·9	316·9
Personal care and health expenses	70·0	65·0	63·2	63·3	63·8	65·9	67·6	67·3	69·9	72·0	72·6	75·1	77·9	81·2	82·9	87·0	91·1	95·9	100·3
Private transportation	64·5	46·3	55·3	61·0	73·7	88·9	91·0	89·8	91·5	92·6	91·8	83·1	86·9	94·0	107·7	119·4	127·2	135·3	135·2
Public transportation	184·0	182·6	181·6	175·5	176·8	179·2	176·6	179·1	182·3	179·4	174·2	160·9	155·7	156·3	158·5	160·7	165·8	169·8	178·9
Communication services	16·5	17·9	16·8	16·0	16·8	17·6	18·7	19·6	20·7	21·1	21·9	22·3	23·0	23·0	24·1	24·8	26·4	28·2	29·5
Entertainment and recreation	250·0	231·7	197·6	183·5	186·7	192·0	196·5	205·0	210·6	214·9	223·6	221·5	221·7	221·5	225·4	234·0	242·9	254·6	262·5
Miscellaneous services	110·6	111·7	113·2	113·9	116·9	120·8	120·8	123·8	126·6	132·0	131·8	133·1	134·7	136·6	139·1	142·9	146·7	149·9	153·8
Income in kind of Armed Forces	40·8	22·3	13·5	9·9	9·4	9·4	9·5	8·9	8·6	8·4	7·8	6·8	6·3	6·4	6·6	7·3	8·3	10·8	14·7
Less Expenditure by non-residents	−50·4	−53·4	−43·8	−46·7	−49·1	−47·9	−51·0	−55·0	−56·0	−54·7	−50·4	−39·4	−32·8	−30·1	−33·2	−36·4	−42·3	−48·5	−42·8
Consumers' expenditure in the U.K.	5,087·2	4,393·8	3,905·7	3,771·3	3,845·9	3,939·4	3,892·1	3,946·8	4,000·4	4,042·9	3,989·7	3,859·8	3,744·6	3,752·9	3,861·7	3,994·5	4,141·2	4,345·5	4,456·7
Consumers' expenditure abroad	35·7	27·6	24·6	25·3	26·6	27·7	28·5	27·5	29·8	29·8	30·1	28·8	22·9	25·3	24·2	27·0	29·7	30·8	32·1
Total expenditure	5,122·9	4,421·4	3,930·3	3,796·6	3,872·5	3,967·1	3,920·6	3,974·3	4,030·2	4,072·7	4,019·8	3,888·6	3,767·5	3,778·2	3,885·9	4,021·5	4,170·9	4,376·3	4,488·8

TABLE 46. ESTIMATED EXPENDITURE AT CONSTANT (1938) PRICES ON ALL GOODS AND SERVICES PURCHASED FOR FINAL CONSUMPTION IN THE UNITED KINGDOM, 1920–38 (£(1938) M.)

	1920	1921	1922	1923	1924	1925	1926	1927	1928	1929	1930	1931	1932	1933	1934	1935	1936	1937	1938
Food	940·7	970·6	1,020·3	1,075·2	1,090·5	1,100·7	1,109·3	1,132·7	1,155·8	1,165·1	1,199·8	1,241·2	1,252·1	1,258·2	1,281·0	1,273·0	1,293·5	1,304·6	1,308·8
Alcoholic drinks and table waters	426·5	370·4	323·9	326·7	341·9	344·0	329·5	327·2	316·5	317·5	307·3	281·3	247·1	258·9	272·0	283·4	293·9	308·3	306·4
Tobacco products	117·8	114·8	111·4	109·2	111·9	116·5	117·8	122·7	128·3	132·7	136·2	136·6	134·4	138·6	143·3	150·2	159·1	167·9	175·8
Rent, rates and water charges	364·3	364·7	367·5	371·2	373·6	377·7	385·1	394·1	401·8	408·4	417·3	422·7	428·4	433·7	442·3	454·1	465·9	478·2	488·4
Fuel and light	143·3	124·7	140·1	144·6	154·3	156·6	137·1	168·7	163·4	171·3	170·3	168·8	165·1	168·7	173·3	179·6	188·5	195·1	197·2
Clothing and other personal effects	461·1	383·3	427·6	430·9	435·5	449·1	446·2	472·1	476·8	487·5	487·1	495·7	477·5	499·7	510·9	531·1	553·7	561·7	567·4
Furniture, furnishings, etc.	182·8	149·9	174·9	187·6	189·3	198·7	202·4	220·7	228·9	239·2	242·1	245·6	254·2	265·3	285·3	300·6	303·5	289·6	263·7
Household operation	231·6	229·3	235·8	241·4	246·7	251·7	255·4	262·4	266·3	272·8	275·1	278·8	280·5	288·5	295·1	303·1	308·9	313·4	316·9
Personal care and health expenses	58·4	57·7	59·4	61·2	62·8	65·0	67·0	69·0	70·7	72·6	74·1	76·9	79·6	82·5	85·1	89·5	93·0	96·7	100·3
Private transportation	25·8	22·2	29·7	36·3	46·8	65·0	62·1	68·4	74·1	78·6	80·1	76·9	82·7	90·4	104·0	118·7	129·4	136·3	135·2
Public transportation	143·0	132·5	139·5	144·5	148·0	154·1	151·5	154·4	156·4	157·4	156·1	144·5	142·6	148·4	155·1	160·1	166·8	171·7	178·9
Communication services	14·1	14·1	14·2	15·3	16·4	17·2	18·1	18·8	19·9	20·4	21·2	21·3	21·7	22·4	22·7	23·8	25·8	28·1	29·5
Entertainment and recreation	195·1	184·6	180·4	177·3	182·9	188·1	188·1	197·4	204·7	212·5	223·8	225·1	227·2	229·4	233·6	243·2	252·3	259·1	262·5
Miscellaneous services	97·5	98·8	108·3	113·0	116·2	119·4	119·3	122·6	126·5	130·9	131·8	136·0	140·4	143·2	145·0	147·8	150·7	151·3	153·8
Adjustment items	11·4	−4·8	−5·7	−11·0	−12·5	−10·5	−12·4	−17·8	−17·0	−12·5	−12·5	−3·8	−3·5	2·0	−2·3	−2·1	−4·3	−7·0	4·0
Total expenditure	3,413·4	3,212·8	3,327·3	3,423·4	3,504·3	3,586·2	3,576·5	3,713·4	3,773·1	3,850·6	3,909·8	3,949·5	3,930·0	4,029·9	4,146·4	4,256·1	4,380·7	4,455·0	4,488·8

TABLE 47. ESTIMATED PRICE INDEX NUMBERS FOR ALL GOODS AND SERVICES PURCHASED FOR FINAL CONSUMPTION IN THE UNITED KINGDOM, 1920–38

(1938 = 100·0)

	1920	1921	1922	1923	1924	1925	1926	1927	1928	1929	1930	1931	1932	1933	1934	1935	1936	1937	1938
Food	184·9	162·2	129·1	121·3	121·2	123·1	119·9	115·8	115·2	113·9	107·2	97·8	93·0	89·7	90·3	93·2	94·4	98·5	100·0
Alcoholic drinks and table waters	108·6	113·7	112·6	104·3	103·6	100·9	100·8	100·7	101·0	101·1	101·0	104·0	111·2	104·1	100·7	100·5	100·4	100·4	100·0
Tobacco products	101·7	101·2	100·3	100·0	100·0	99·7	99·6	101·1	102·4	102·1	102·4	102·8	103·2	102·7	102·0	101·9	101·1	100·6	100·0
Rent, rates and water charges	80·3	93·3	96·1	93·4	92·4	92·3	93·5	95·0	95·1	96·0	96·5	96·9	96·8	97·5	97·6	98·4	99·2	99·4	100·0
Fuel and light	127·5	140·5	116·8	106·2	107·8	105·3	110·1	102·5	97·7	98·9	99·5	99·8	99·5	98·2	97·8	95·8	97·7	99·1	100·0
Clothing and other personal effects	199·4	154·9	122·5	112·6	112·8	113·1	112·3	107·7	109·5	107·0	103·2	96·5	91·9	89·8	90·4	90·6	90·5	96·7	100·0
Furniture, furnishings, etc.	168·9	144·8	113·2	102·5	101·2	100·7	97·3	95·2	94·9	93·8	92·9	88·8	82·2	82·0	83·1	83·0	85·7	95·6	100·0
Household operation	162·0	144·7	117·3	108·9	108·9	108·9	107·4	105·8	105·8	104·8	102·1	98·4	95·3	92·9	93·0	92·6	93·9	95·1	100·0
Personal care and health expenses	119·9	112·7	106·4	103·4	101·6	101·4	100·9	97·5	98·9	99·4	98·0	97·7	97·9	98·4	97·4	97·2	98·0	99·2	100·0
Private transportation	250·0	208·6	186·2	168·0	157·5	153·5	146·5	131·3	123·5	117·8	114·6	106·8	105·1	104·0	103·6	100·6	98·3	99·3	100·0
Public transportation	128·7	137·8	130·2	121·5	119·5	116·3	116·6	116·0	116·6	114·0	111·6	111·3	109·2	105·3	102·2	100·4	99·3	98·9	100·0
Communication services	117·0	127·0	118·3	104·6	102·4	102·3	103·3	104·3	104·0	103·4	103·3	104·7	103·2	102·7	106·2	104·2	102·3	100·4	100·0
Entertainment and recreation	128·1	125·5	109·5	103·5	102·1	102·1	104·5	103·9	102·9	101·1	99·9	98·4	97·6	96·6	96·5	96·2	96·3	98·3	100·0
Miscellaneous services	113·4	113·1	104·5	100·8	100·6	101·2	101·3	101·0	100·1	100·8	100·0	97·9	95·9	95·4	95·9	96·7	97·3	99·1	100·0
Total expenditure[a]	149·8	137·5	118·1	110·9	110·5	110·6	109·6	107·0	106·8	105·8	102·8	98·5	95·9	93·8	93·7	94·5	95·2	98·2	100·0

[a] Excluding adjustment items

TOTAL EXPENDITURE

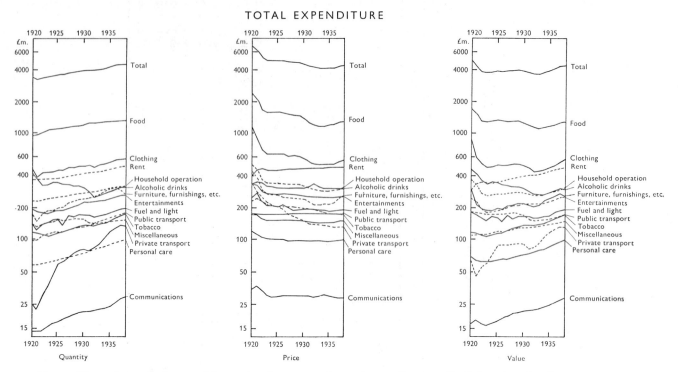

Fig. 10. The variations in the quantities purchased, average prices and expenditure on all goods and services for final consumption in the United Kingdom, 1920–38.

The inquiry conducted by the Ministry of Labour between October 1937 and July 1938 collected some 10,396 budgets from households of (employed) industrial and agricultural workers.[1] There was a comparable inquiry into middle-class expenditure, based on 1,360 budgets obtained from families of civil servants, local government officers, and teachers, between April 1938 and January 1939.[2] While it cannot be claimed that a combination of material from these two surveys is equivalent to a properly representative sample from the whole population, it should provide a reasonably satisfactory comparison for the present purpose.

The results of the comparison are given in Table 48, in which all the figures have been reduced to a common basis of expenditure per head per week. The first three columns show the recorded expenditures for each category of household: middle-class, industrial working-class, and agricultural working-class. The fourth column, obtained as a weighted average of the other three,[3] shows the corresponding average expenditures for all classes. These figures may be directly compared with the estimates from the present inquiry which are given in the final column.

Only those items are shown for which comparable estimates are available. Thus it has been necessary to exclude a number of budget items such as payment of insurance premiums, trade union subscriptions, and contributions to hospital funds, for which there is no

corresponding item in the estimates of this study. On the other hand, certain adjustments have been made to the present estimates to conform with the budget definitions: the value of income in kind has been excluded from expenditure on domestic service, and an estimate has been made of the gross income (*less* National Health Insurance payments) of doctors, dentists, etc.[4] No correction has been made for the different treatment of expenditure in hotels, restaurants, etc. In the present study this has been distributed over the particular commodities involved, whereas in the budgets it will be mostly included in 'meals eaten out' and 'holiday expenditure'. This latter item is very small—on average only 2*d*. per head—and it is certainly understated as families were not asked to keep budgets while on holiday. It is probable that the budget records of travel expenditure are also understated for the same reason.

In view of these inconsistencies, and the approximate

---

[1] [**62**] 'Weekly expenditure of working-class households in the United Kingdom in 1937–38', *Ministry of Labour Gazette*, December 1940 and January 1941.

[2] [**80**] Massey, 'The expenditure of 1360 British middle-class households in 1938–39', *J. R. Statist. Soc.* cv (1942), part III, p. 159.

[3] The weights used are: middle class 0·19, industrial working class 0·75, and agricultural working class 0·06. These weights were derived from an income distribution of families in Great Britain in 1937, as described in Vol. 1 of this study, p. 168.

[4] No corresponding deductions are made from the other items (fuel and light, rent, etc.) under which part of these gross incomes is included in the treatment adopted for this study, but the amounts involved will be relatively small.

TABLE 48. ESTIMATED WEEKLY EXPENDITURES IN 1938 (PENCE PER HEAD)

	Family budget data				This study
	Middle class	Industrial working class	Agricultural working class	All classes	
Food	154·5	109·1	87·6	116·4	124·0
Drink	6·8	2·5	1·2	3·2	29·9
Tobacco	11·8	8·1	6·1	8·7	17·1
Fuel and light	37·2	20·5	15·6	23·3	20·2
Clothing	78·0	26·0	16·3	35·3	42·6
Furniture, furnishings and household equipment	42·6	9·5	4·6	15·5	25·7
Domestic service	13·4	0·7	0·3	3·1	10·3
Other household goods and services	18·3	9·3	5·4	10·7	11·7
Hairdressing, etc.	4·0	1·7	0·6	2·1	2·4
Medical expenses	22·5	4·5	3·0	7·8	8·2
Travel	20·5	7·2	2·8	9·5	16·4
Postages, telephones and telegrams	8·4	1·3	1·1	2·6	2·9
Entertainments	9·8	4·4	1·1	5·2	6·3
Newspapers and periodicals	5·6	3·2	2·6	3·6	5·3
Licences	5·6	1·6	1·4	2·3	1·8
Other goods	34·9	9·4	5·4	14·0	28·9

weighting applied to the three categories of household, no very precise comparison can be made. Nevertheless, certain features are conspicuous. The largest discrepancies are for drink and tobacco expenditure, which are grossly understated in the budgets. Hardly more than one-tenth of expenditure on drink is recorded and only half of tobacco expenditure. The difficulty of obtaining accurate budget information about these expenditures, due perhaps to both deliberate concealment and imperfect memory, is notorious. It is interesting that expenditure on entertainments does not appear to be understated to anything like the same extent. The relatively low figures for domestic service shown by the budgets reflect the fact that the highest incomes are unrepresented; it may also be partly due to the fact that the estimates of this study include domestic help in boarding houses and similar small catering establishments. The residual group of 'other goods' also shows a large discrepancy. The contents of this group are not too well defined in the budgets but would appear to include principally books and stationery, chemists' goods, sports and travel goods, and expenditure on motoring and cycling. This last item is likely to be the most seriously understated, particularly in respect of purchases of vehicles, and if it is excluded altogether from the estimates of this study the two figures are brought much closer together.

It has long been recognized that family budget data are likely to suffer from some bias simply because the pattern of expenditure is affected by the act of keeping

a record. There is a tendency to make 'typical' expenditures, buying in those items which are usually bought and postponing exceptional outlays. It seems likely that this bias will have affected the budget figure for household durable goods, of which a large part consists of those large infrequent outlays which would be regarded as untypical. In this context the comparison for clothing is of particular interest. When the budget inquiries were planned it was thought that because expenditure on clothing was so variable it might be misrepresented if figures were collected for only 4 weeks, as with other items. Accordingly, a number of households were asked to keep records of clothing expenditure over a whole year. It was found that the expenditure recorded by those keeping records for 52 weeks was, surprisingly, lower than for those who kept budgets for only 4 weeks.[1] The values shown in Table 48 are averages for all budgets collected in the 4 weeks of the main inquiry, including families who kept records for the whole year. While the error present in the estimates of this study must not be overlooked, the comparison suggests a strong downward bias in the figures from the 52 weeks' records. It seems most likely that this bias is the result of omissions

---

[1] The corresponding figures for expenditure on clothing and repairs are as follows:

	(Pence per head per week)	
	Middle class	Working class
4-week budgets	94·2	30·7
52-week budgets	57·2	26·0

These figures are given by [86] Prais and Houthakker, *The Analysis of Family Budgets*, p. 40.

due to fatigue in keeping records over so long a period. It is noticeable that the bias is greatest for the middle-class households who had probably both a larger number and a greater variety of purchases to record.[1]

The cost-of-living price index offers a second field for comparison with the results obtained in this study. The price index numbers for the different categories of expenditure which emerge from the present investigations are set out in summary form in Table 47. Further details are given in the separate commodity chapters and the total series shown is a weighted average of all the individual series used in the compilation of the estimates. For comparison with the cost-of-living index the series have been grouped into two categories of food and non-food items. The results are shown in Table 49. Although in this table each series is presented in terms of a common base, 1938 = 100, the two index numbers are not exactly comparable in the method of construction employed. While the cost-of-living index is a simple aggregative (Laspeyres) index with fixed weights, the price index numbers of this study are current-weighted (Paasche) aggregates. Thus, apart from any difference in weighting, the former is an arithmetic and the latter a harmonic average of price ratios. The cost-of-living index, moreover, was designed to measure the changing cost of the working-class standard of living and this is reflected in the weighting, based on the pattern of 1914, and the restricted number of series involved. The emphasis is on the basic necessities of food, rent, fuel and clothing, which together account for 96 % of the total weight; food alone accounts for 60 %. The differences between the two index numbers must not be overstressed, however, since they also have much in common. In compiling the estimates of this study much use has necessarily been made of the component price series of the cost-of-living index. This was generally the most reliable, and often the only, indicator available for a particular commodity, and these items together account for a large part of expenditure. There is also, of course, a considerable degree of correlation between most prices during this period. In Table 49 it can be seen that in fact the series from the two sources show very similar movements. The difference in weighting is apparent in the way that the cost-of-living index for all items is much more nearly a reflexion of the food component, and this both alters the trend slightly and increases the amplitude of variation. It can also be seen that, although both components of the cost-of-living index have less downward trend than the estimates of this study, the combined series shows a slightly steeper slope.

A final comparison may be made with the figures of consumers' expenditure which form part of the official estimates of national income and expenditure compiled for the years from 1938 onwards. Though the definitions adopted are not precisely the same, this will not greatly affect the comparison, which may serve as a basis for linking the inter-war series of this study to the official series for subsequent years.

TABLE 49. ALTERNATIVE INDEX NUMBERS OF RETAIL PRICES IN THE UNITED KINGDOM, 1920-38

(1938 = 100·0)

	Food		Non-food		Total	
	Cost-of-living index	This study	Cost-of-living index	This study	Cost-of-living index	This study
1920	182·2	184·9	131·8	136·4	159·6	149·8
1921	163·3	162·2	121·8	126·8	144·9	137·5
1922	125·3	129·1	106·7	113·2	117·3	118·1
1923	120·3	121·3	100·4	106·1	111·5	110·9
1924	121·0	121·2	100·6	105·7	112·2	110·5
1925	121·7	123·1	100·8	105·1	112·8	110·6
1926	116·7	119·9	102·5	105·0	110·3	109·6
1927	113·9	115·8	99·3	103·2	107·4	107·0
1928	111·7	115·2	98·6	103·1	106·4	106·8
1929	109·6	113·9	99·0	102·2	105·1	105·8
1930	103·2	107·2	98·0	100·9	101·3	102·8
1931	93·2	97·8	95·7	98·8	94·6	98·5
1932	89·7	93·0	94·2	97·2	92·3	95·9
1933	85·4	89·7	93·6	95·6	89·7	93·8
1934	86·8	90·3	94·0	95·3	90·4	93·7
1935	89·0	93·2	94·2	95·0	91·7	94·5
1936	92·5	94·4	95·4	95·5	94·2	95·2
1937	98·9	98·5	98·2	98·1	98·7	98·2
1938	100·0	100·0	100·0	100·0	100·0	100·0

The latest revision of the official estimates of consumers' expenditure in 1938, apart from reclassification, was made in 1955.[2] These figures are shown in Table 50 together with the corresponding estimates of this study. For this purpose two adjustments were made to the Blue Book figures: food supplied to caterers has been revalued at retail prices, as in the estimates of this study;[3] and expenditure on maintenance and repairs of houses has been excluded.[4] For the rest the estimates of this study

---

[1] For a discussion of recording fatigue and other sources of bias in family budget data, see [85] S. J. Prais, 'Some problems in the measurement of price changes with special reference to the cost of living', *J. R. Statist. Soc.* series A (General), CXXI (1958), part III, pp. 312–23.

[2] [59] Central Statistical Office, *National Income and Expenditure 1955*: referred to here as the Blue Book.

[3] See Vol. I of this study, pp. 170–1. To balance this addition to food a corresponding deduction was made from the Blue Book item 'Other services'.

[4] The figure of rent, etc., excluding maintenance costs, was taken from [58] *Statistical Digest of the War* (1951), table 186, p. 203.

have been adjusted as nearly as possible to the Blue Book definitions. Certain minor differences still remain. In particular, whereas the Blue Book allocates expenditure on hotels between two items, 'food' and 'other services', in the estimates of this study the non-food components of this composite service are distributed over several items—rent, fuel, furniture and furnishings, etc.

TABLE 50. ALTERNATIVE ESTIMATES OF CONSUMERS' EXPENDITURE IN 1938 (£ M.)

	Blue Book	This study
Food	1,310[a]	1,301
Alcoholic drink	285	294
Tobacco	177	176
Rent, rates and water charges	491[b]	488
Fuel and light	197	189
Durable household goods	234	264
Other household goods	54	53
Clothing	446	438
Reading matter	64	64
Private motoring and cycling	141	142
Travel	167	178
Communication services	29	30
Entertainments	64	65
Domestic service	121	176
Other services	382[a]	405
Other goods	197	193
Income in kind not included elsewhere	17	15
Less Expenditure by non-residents	−43	−43
Consumers' expenditure in the United Kingdom	4,333	4,428
Consumers' expenditure abroad	34	32
Total	4,367[c]	4,460

[a] Adjusted figure.   [b] Figure from [58] *Statistical Digest of the War.*
[c] The published figure, including occupiers' maintenance costs, is 4,394.

Allowing for these marginal differences in treatment, the comparison in Table 50 reveals the very large measure of agreement between the two estimates. For most items the discrepancies are less than 5 %. The large differences in the figures for domestic service simply reflect alternative, equally plausible interpretations of the few data available for making the estimate.[1]

The discrepancy for total consumers' expenditure can be seen to be no more than 2 %. This is well within the margin of error which may be reasonably attributed to these aggregates. It should be noted, moreover, that the error attaching to year-to-year changes in the series is likely to be much smaller, since much of this discrepancy will represent systematic bias.

3 THE RELIABILITY OF THE ESTIMATES

Throughout this study an attempt has been made to assess the reliability of the estimates in each chapter. In the present section these assessments are summarized and presented in terms of a common numerical scale. They are also used to derive margins of error for the main expenditure groups and for total consumers' expenditure.

The initial assessment of the errors attaching to the individual series is very largely subjective, reflecting merely the degree of confidence felt by the compilers. This is inevitable where so much of the basic material has to be taken from miscellaneous sources and adapted to the purpose in hand. But it has seemed reasonable to assume that the probable error of the derived series could be obtained by more objective procedures.

Much attention has been given throughout the study to distinguishing between random and systematic errors in the estimates. Recording and sampling errors are the chief sources of random error. Systematic error may take the form of a simple bias (causing the estimates to lie above or below the true level), an error in the amplitude of the fluctuations shown by the estimates, or an error in trend. While the presence of systematic error may often be suspected, because of difficulties in allocating supplies between consumers and business, for instance, and its magnitude may be surmised, its direction will be unknown. In assigning estimates to error classes, these elements of systematic error have been taken into account as well as the components of random error. When the expenditures for a number of items in any year are added together, the elements of systematic error may be regarded as randomly distributed between items and can be combined accordingly.

It is frequently the case that the magnitude of the error in a series is believed to vary from year to year. In part this will be due simply to the fact that the discrepancy varies proportionately with the level of the series. More important, however, are the changes in the quality of the information on which the estimate was based. It was often found that the quality of the data improved for later years of the period; but this was not always a uniform process. In certain years, such as those for which census information was available, the reliability of the estimates was much greater. Moreover, interpolation between census years is probably much more reliable than extrapolation to years outside these benchmarks. To provide some indication of the variation in reliability the calculations have been made for both 1920 and 1938.

---
[1] See footnote 4 on p. 141 below.

TABLE 51. ERROR CLASSES[a] OF THE COMPONENTS OF EXPENDITURE,
1920 AND 1938

	1920			1938		
	Quantity	Price	Value[b]	Quantity	Price	Value[b]
Bread and cereals						
Flour	C	A	C	B	A	B
Bread, cakes and biscuits	B	B	C	B	B	C
Other cereals	C	C	C	C	C	C
Meat, poultry and eggs						
Beef and veal	B	B	C	A	B	B
Mutton and lamb	B	B	C	A	B	B
Pork	C	B	C	C	B	C
Meat products	B	B	C	B	B	C
Poultry, rabbits and game	C	C	C	B	C	C
Eggs	B	B	C	B	B	C
Fish						
Fresh fish	C	C	C	C	C	C
Cured fish	B	C	C	B	C	C
Shell fish and salmon	C	C	C	C	C	C
Canned fish	B	B	C	B	B	C
Dairy products						
Fresh milk	C	A	C	C	A	C
Condensed milk	C	C	C	C	C	C
Cream	C	D	D	C	D	D
Butter	B	B	C	A	B	B
Cheese	B	B	C	B	B	C
Margarine and other fats						
Margarine	B	A	B	A	A	A
Lard and lard substitutes	B	B	C	A	B	B
Dripping	D	D	D	D	D	D
Edible oils	D	D	D	D	D	D
Vegetables						
Producers' consumption: potatoes	C	B	C	C	B	C
other fresh vegetables	D	C	D	D	C	D
Home-produced: potatoes	B	B	C	B	B	C
other fresh vegetables	C	C	C	C	C	C
Imported fresh vegetables	B	C	C	B	C	C
Dried and canned vegetables	B	B	C	B	B	C
Fruit and nuts						
Producers' consumption	D	C	D	D	C	D
Home-produced fresh fruit	C	B	C	C	B	C
Imported fresh fruit and nuts	B	B	C	B	B	C
Canned and bottled fruit	B	B	C	B	B	C
Imported dried fruit	C	C	C	C	C	C
Sugar, chocolate and confectionery						
Sugar	B	A	B	B	A	B
Chocolate and chocolate confectionery	B	B	C	B	B	C
Sugar confectionery	B	B	C	B	B	C
Tea, coffee and cocoa						
Tea	B	A	B	B	A	B
Coffee	B	C	C	B	C	C
Cocoa	B	B	C	B	B	C
Other foods						
Jam and marmalade	C	C	C	C	C	C
Other preserves	D	D	D	D	D	D
Fish and chips	C	C	C	C	C	C
Miscellaneous manufactured foods	D	D	D	D	D	D

TABLE 51 (CONT.)

	1920			1938		
	Quantity	Price	Value[b]	Quantity	Price	Value[b]
Alcoholic drinks and table waters						
Beer	A	A	A	A	A	A
Spirits	A	A	A	A	A	A
Wine	B	B	C	B	B	C
Cider and perry	C	C	C	C	C	C
Table waters	C	C	C	C	C	C
Tobacco products						
Cigarettes	A	A	A	A	A	A
Pipe tobacco	A	A	A	A	A	A
Other products	B	B	C	B	B	C
Rents, rates and water charges						
Rents	B	C[c]	B	B	B[c]	A
Rates	B	C[c]	B	B	B[c]	A
Water charges	B	C[c]	C	B	C[c]	B
Fuel and light						
Coal	B	A	B	B	A	B
Coke	B	C	C	B	C	C
Gas	C	C	C	B	B	C
Electricity	A	B	B	A	A	A
Kerosene	B	B	C	B	B	C
Candles and night lights	B	B	C	B	B	C
Clothing and other personal effects						
Apparel	C[d]	B	C	C[d]	B	B
Dress materials	D[d]	C	D	D[d]	C	D
Footwear	B	B	C	B	B	C
Other personal effects	C[d]	C	C	C[d]	C	C
Furniture, furnishings and household equipment						
Furniture and furnishings	C[d]	B	C	C[d]	B	B
Household textiles	D[d]	C	D	D[d]	C	D
China and pottery	C[d]	C	C	C[d]	C	C
Glassware	C[d]	C	C	C[d]	C	C
Hardware and hollow-ware	C[d]	C	C	C[d]	C	B
Household operation						
Domestic service	D	D	D	D	D	D
Matches	C	B	C	C	B	C
Soap	C	B	C	B	B	C
Polishes and cleaning materials	D	D	D	D	D	D
Laundry, etc.	C[d]	C	C	C[d]	C	C
Other household services	D	D	D	D	D	D
Personal care and health expenses						
Hairdressing	D[d]	D	D	D[d]	D	C
Doctors' services	C	C	C	C	C	C
Dentists' services	C	C	C	C	C	C
Opticians' services	D	D	D	D	D	D
Nursing services	C	D	D	C	D	D
Drugs and medical supplies	D	D	D	D	D	D
Voluntary hospitals	C[d]	C	C	C[d]	C	C
Private transportation						
Motor-cars	C	C	C	B	B	C
Motor-cycles	C	C	C	B	C	C
Bicycles	C	C	C	B	C	C
Petrol and oil	C	B	C	B	B	C
Tyres and tubes	C[d]	C	C	C[d]	C	C
Repairs	C[d]	C	C	C[d]	C	C
Other running expenses	D[d]	D	D	C[d]	C	C

TABLE 51 (CONT.)

	1920			1938		
	Quantity	Price	Value[b]	Quantity	Price	Value[b]
Public transportation						
Railways	C[d]	B	B	B[d]	B	A
Tramways and trolley vehicles	C[d]	B	B	C[d]	B	B
Buses and coaches	C	C[c]	C	B	C[c]	B
Taxis and hire cars	C	D	D	B	C	C
Other travel	D	D	D	D	D	D
Communication services						
Postal services	B	C[c]	B	B	C[c]	B
Telephone services	C	C[c]	C	B	C[c]	B
Telegraph services	C	C[c]	C	B	C[c]	B
Entertainment and recreation						
Entertainments	C[d]	B	B	C[d]	B	B
Hotels	D[d]	D	D	D[d]	D	D
Betting	D[d]	D	D	D[d]	D	C
Books	C[d]	C	C	C[d]	C	C
Newspapers	B	B	C	B	B	C
Magazines	C	C	C	B	C	C
Toys, travel and sports goods	C[d]	C	C	C[d]	C	B
Other recreation expenditure	D[d]	D	D	D[d]	D	D
Miscellaneous services						
Life assurance	D[d]	D	C	D[d]	D	C
General insurance	D[d]	D	D	D[d]	D	D
Private education	D[d]	C	D	D[d]	C	D
Trade unions	D[d]	D	C	D[d]	D	C
Religion	C	D	D	C	D	D
Charity organizations	D[d]	D	D	D[d]	D	D
Fees paid to local authorities	D[d]	D	C	D[d]	D	C
Legal services, etc.	D[d]	D	D	D[d]	D	D
Funeral expenses	A	B	B	A	B	B
Adjustment items						
Income in kind	C[d]	B	B	C[d]	B	B
Expenditure by non-residents	C[d]	B	C	C[d]	B	C
Expenditure abroad	C[d]	C	C	C[d]	C	C

ᵃ For the definition of the different error classes, see p. 119.

ᵇ Except where otherwise stated, the error class for expenditure has been derived from the relation $a_v = \sqrt{(a_q^2 + a_p^2)}$, where a_q and a_p are the proportionate errors for quantity and price respectively.

ᶜ In this case the expenditure and quantity series were allotted

directly to error classes and the error class for price was then derived, using the same method as in (b).

ᵈ In this case the expenditure and price series were allotted directly to error classes and the error class for quantity was then derived, using the same method as in (b).

Though these two years are not always representative, the comparison should give a broad indication of the trend through time.

It will be evident that the margins of error ascribed to the estimates cannot be more than a general indication of the reliability of the figures; they are far from being the purely sampling errors of conventional statistical practice. The assessment of error will, moreover, vary with the purpose for which the figures are used. The gradings ascribed here, for example, do not adequately represent the reliability of year-to-year changes or any other time comparison. For this purpose it would be necessary to

discount those elements of bias which are common to all years of the period. In general, this would upgrade many of the items, in some cases quite considerably. This will not always be the case, however, since errors in the amplitude or trend of the series will increase the discrepancy for any comparison over time.

The methods used can be described quite briefly.[1] The quantity and price series for each item were first assigned to an error class. For this purpose four error classes were distinguished and defined as follows:

[1] They are the same as those devised and applied by [69] Chapman, *Wages and Salaries in the United Kingdom, 1920–1938*, pp. 230–6.

Error class	Margin of error[a] (%)	Standard error (%) Range	Standard error (%) Mean
A. Firm figure	0–5	0–2½	1¼
B. Good estimate	5–10	2½–5	3¾
C. Rough estimate	10–25	5–12½	8¾
D. Conjecture	>25	>12½	20

[a] I.e. at 95% probability level.

Not every estimate was assessed separately. Many of the minor food items, in particular, have been assessed as a single group, with due allowance for cancellation of error between components where this seemed plausible. Substituting the numerical values shown, an estimate of the error in expenditure could be obtained from the formula

$$a_v = \sqrt{(a_q^2 + a_p^2)}, \qquad (1)$$

where a_v, a_q and a_p are the mean proportionate errors for value, quantity and price, respectively. In a few cases, where this was required by the method of estimation, expenditure has been assigned directly to an error class and the error in price, or quantity, estimated by a formula similar to (1).

The next stage was to derive estimates of error for the main expenditure groups. While it is reasonable to assume that there will be no correlation between the errors in price and quantity series, and this assumption is in fact implicit in (1), it cannot always be supposed that different quantity estimates are similarly uncorrelated. Where a given total is allocated between alternative uses, for example, some negative correlation may be expected between the errors in the two estimates. This arises particularly among the food groups. On the other hand, a common source of information may lead to significant positive correlation, as for the estimates of rent and rates. Allowing for these interactions, an estimate of the error variance for an expenditure aggregate, Σv_i, may be obtained from the formula

$$V(\Sigma v_i) = \Sigma v_i^2 (a_{qi}^2 + a_{pi}^2) + 2 \sum_{i<j} r_{ij} v_i v_j a_{qi} a_{qj} \qquad (2)$$

where r_{ij} is the correlation between the errors in two quantity estimates. On this basis each expenditure group could also be assigned to an error class. The results are shown for a number of food subgroups in Table 52, and for all the main expenditure groups and for total expenditure in Table 53. If a comparison is made with the initial assessments set out in Table 51, it can be seen how large a reduction in the proportionate error of the aggregates is obtained through the cancellation of errors.

TABLE 52. ERROR CLASSES OF FOOD EXPENDITURE GROUPS, 1920 AND 1938

	1920	1938
Bread and cereals	B	B
Meat, poultry and eggs	B	A
Fish	C	C
Dairy products	C	B
Margarine and other fats	B	C
Vegetables	C	C
Fruit and nuts	B	B
Sugar, chocolate and confectionery	A	A
Tea, coffee and cocoa	B	B
Other foods	C	D
All food	A	A

TABLE 53. ERROR CLASSES OF MAIN EXPENDITURE GROUPS, 1920 AND 1938

	1920	1938
Food	A	A
Alcoholic drinks and table waters	A	A
Tobacco products	A	A
Rents, rates and water charges	B	A
Fuel and light	B	A
Clothing and other personal effects	C	B
Furniture, furnishings and household equipment	C	B
Household operation	D	D
Personal care and health expenses	C	C
Private transportation	C	B
Public transportation	C	B
Communication services	B	B
Entertainment and recreation	C	C
Miscellaneous services	C	C
Adjustment	D	D
Total expenditure	A	A

4 A RECONCILIATION WITH THE ESTIMATES FOR 1900–19

While the particular definitions adopted, as well as the underlying framework of social accounts, are the same for the estimates of this study and those made for the earlier period,[1] there are also a number of minor differences in treatment and classification due to the nature of the data available. It will be useful, therefore, to present here a reconciliation of the two series and the subsidiary

[1] [87] A. R. Prest, *Consumers' Expenditure in the United Kingdom, 1900–1919* (1954).

TABLE 54. COMPARABLE ESTIMATES OF CONSUMERS' EXPENDITURE IN 1919 (£ M.)

	Great Britain and Ireland (at current prices)	Differences in classification, etc. (at current prices)	Southern Ireland (at current prices)	United Kingdom (Great Britain and Northern Ireland)		
				At current prices	At 1938 prices	Price index 1938 = 100
Clothing and other personal effects						
Apparel	597·4	—	..	..	..	..
Boots and shoes	71·8	—	..	..	..	..
Other goods	102·3	−4·0[a]	..	..	..	..
Total	771·5	−4·0	−38·4	729·1	410·1	177·8
Furniture, furnishings, etc.						
Furniture and soft furnishings	113·9	—	..	..	..	..
Pottery, hardware, etc.	96·9	4·0[a]	..	..	..	..
Total	210·8	4·0	−10·7	204·1	135·2	151·0
Household operation						
Domestic service	145·0	—	..	..	..	..
Other household goods	56·0	—	..	..	..	..
Other household services	20·9	92·0[b]	..	..	..	..
Total	221·9	92·0	−15·7	298·2	255·6	116·7
Personal care and health expenses						
Hairdressing	13·1	—	..	..	..	..
Medical services	37·8	—	..	..	..	..
Drugs and medical supplies	26·9	—	..	..	..	..
Total	77·8	—	−3·9	73·9	62·8	117·7
Private transportation						
Vehicles	44·2	−3·2[c]	..	..	..	..
Running expenses	39·9	−21·9[d]	..	..	..	..
Total	84·1	−25·1	−3·0	56·0	22·7	246·7
Public transportation						
Railways	68·6	—	..	..	..	..
Other public transport	85·6	—	..	..	..	..
Total	154·2	—	−7·7	146·5	117·4	124·8
Communication services	13·0	—	−0·7	12·3	10·9	112·8
Entertainment and recreation						
Entertainments	48·7	—	..	..	..	..
Hotels, etc.	109·3	—	..	..	..	..
Betting	5·5	—	..	..	..	..
Books, newspapers and magazines	38·8	—	..	..	..	..
Travel and sports goods	32·9	—	..	..	..	..
Other recreation expenditure	1·1	5·0[e]	..	..	..	..
Total	236·3	5·0	−12·1	229·2	202·2	113·4
Miscellaneous services						
Insurance	19·4	10·0[f]	..	..	..	..
Private education	23·5	—	..	..	..	..
Trade unions	2·5	—	..	..	..	..
Religion and charities	20·1	—	..	..	..	..
Other miscellaneous services	127·2	−107·0[g]	..	..	..	..
Funeral expenses	11·7	—	..	..	..	..
Total	204·4	−97·0	−5·4	102·0	99·4	102·6

information required to link the two sets of estimates together both at current and constant prices.

A reconciliation for the commodity groups dealt with in Volume I of this study has already been given.[1] In Table 54 similar information is provided for the remaining categories of expenditure covered by the present volume.

For this purpose it has seemed best to show the adjustments needed to put the 1919 figures into a form comparable with those for 1920. In the earlier study the adjustments required by the 1920 estimates to provide figures comparable with those given for the earlier period were shown. The alternative procedure is followed here in view of the slightly different grouping of commodities in the two volumes. The classification adopted for the present study is more in accord with that recommended for general use to facilitate international comparisons.[2] It has seemed more useful, therefore, to show the adjustments required to put the figures for the earlier years into a similar form.

A simple proportionate correction was made to exclude expenditure in Southern Ireland. The amount involved is small and no attempt has been made to do more than show the order of magnitude involved; 5 %[3] of expenditure in each main category was deducted. While this figure cannot be taken as more than a very rough estimate of expenditure in Southern Ireland, the consequent error in the estimate for the United Kingdom will be virtually negligible. For the rest, the adjustments involved are almost entirely a matter of reclassification of items; the details are given in the notes to Table 54.

While the calculation made here is adequate for present purposes, it does not aim to provide the best possible estimate of the change between 1919 and 1920, or of consumption in Southern Ireland in 1919.

---

[1] [87] Prest, *Consumers' Expenditure in the United Kingdom, 1900–1919*, pp. 183–5.
[2] See [64a] *A System of National Accounts and Supporting Tables*, United Nations (New York, 1953).
[3] This is the average proportion found for the other categories in 1920.

NOTES TO TABLE 54

[a] Expenditure on perambulators and garden equipment transferred from 'other goods' to 'hardware'.

[b] Expenditure on dry cleaning and dyeing, repairs, removals and other household services, included by Prest with 'other miscellaneous services'.

[c] Expenditure on bicycle repairs transferred to 'running expenses'.

[d] Prest includes £25·1 m. for the running costs of carriages. This appears to involve both an overestimate and a mistaken allocation.

As no comparable item appears in the estimates for 1920, it is omitted here.

[e] Expenditure on pets, included by Prest with 'other miscellaneous services'.

[f] Expenditure on general insurance, included by Prest with 'other miscellaneous services'.

[g] The remaining items are fees paid to local authorities, and stamp duties, legal services, etc.

CHAPTER XII

A SURVEY OF CONSUMERS' EXPENDITURE, 1900–1955

1 INTRODUCTION

In this final chapter the scope of the inquiry is widened to include a review of the changing pattern of consumers' expenditure in the United Kingdom during the half-century since 1900. The primary aim has been to present the available data in a comparable form for the whole period, and this essential statistical foundation is provided by the tables. Some comments on the nature of the figures and their interpretation are presented in the following sections.

The development of total consumers' expenditure is first considered. Ten major commodity groups are distinguished; expenditures at current and constant prices are given, together with the implied movements in average prices (Tables 55–58). A few of the more salient features of the long-term pattern which emerges from these figures are discussed in §2.

Almost one-third of total expenditure throughout this period is accounted for by expenditure on food. It seems worth while, therefore, to present the data for this important group in greater detail. Ten subgroups of food are distinguished and the data are presented in a similar form to those for total expenditure (Tables 59–62). Some brief comments on the figures are given in §3.

An alternative classification of the items of expenditure is according to their durability in use. In this approach it is conventional to distinguish a few broad classes of commodities such as perishables, semi-durables, durables and services. The distinctions can hardly be very strictly determined but are nevertheless useful, both as a summary statement of the changing pattern of consumption and because of their implications for economic policy. In §4 the results of this reclassification of consumers' expenditure are discussed and a set of tables covering the whole period on this basis is presented (Tables 63–66).

The recognition that commodities have different degrees of durability in use leads to a new concept of consumption. The satisfaction, or use, to be derived from durable goods, whether furniture, hardware, or articles of clothing, is usually spread over a number of years. It has been suggested, therefore, that the purchase of these goods should be regarded as additions to consumers' stocks and that consumption be equated with their annual depreciation. A simple method of making this adjustment is set out in §5 and the resulting estimates of stocks, net investment and consumption of consumer durables are shown for the whole period in Tables 67–70.

2 TOTAL EXPENDITURE, 1900–55

Consumers' expenditures on ten major groups of commodities are summarized for the period 1900–55 in Tables 55–58. In money terms, as shown in Table 55, expenditure increased sixfold during this period. The individual groups that have increased most rapidly are tobacco, durable household goods, and miscellaneous other goods, which have each shown a more than tenfold increase. Alcoholic drinks, rents, etc., and miscellaneous other services, have risen less than the average. These divergences resulted in changes in the proportionate distribution of expenditure between the different groups as shown in the lower half of the table.

Expenditure on food is the largest group distinguished, accounting for one-third of total expenditure. This proportion has remained almost constant and at the end of the period was virtually the same as it had been in 1900. A similar stability was shown by expenditure on clothing and on fuel and light. The proportion spent on rent and rates, however, has declined, but this is clearly due in a large part to the operation of rent control. Together these basic necessities accounted for more than half of total expenditure, the proportion showing a slight downward trend over the whole period. The pattern of expenditure on other groups has been more variable, although in total the change has been only slight. Alcoholic drink has accounted for a declining proportion of expenditure, apart from the abnormal war periods, but this has been more than counterbalanced by the great increase in tobacco expenditure. The proportion spent on durable household goods, though only a small part of the total,

TABLE 55. CONSUMERS' EXPENDITURE AT CURRENT PRICES: UNITED KINGDOM, 1900–55

(£M. AND PERCENTAGES)

	1900–4	1905–9	1910–14	1915–19	1920–4	1925–9	1930–4	1935–8	1939–45	1946–50	1951–5
£ million											
1 Food	552·9	596·7	663·0	1,137·2	1,432·7	1,317·4	1,180·4	1,242·0	1,511·9	2,357·2	3,681·4
2 Alcoholic drink	181·6	166·1	172·5	241·9	376·5	320·6	273·7	286·8	546·0	766·0	818·2
3 Tobacco	28·8	32·6	39·3	73·3	113·8	124·9	141·4	164·7	394·4	714·8	838·6
4 Rents, rates and water charges	189·6	211·3	226·3	244·8	335·5	371·5	416·4	468·1	516·3	598·6	753·8
5 Fuel and light	73·2	71·3	75·2	120·2	164·6	158·4	161·4	179·1	236·7	317·0	452·4
6 Clothing	154·2	164·7	191·7	321·6	508·3	429·5	382·9	413·6	486·4	870·4	1,145·4
7 Durable household goods	57·8	60·9	68·6	123·6	221·5	209·8	221·3	262·6	187·3	479·2	771·0
8 Transport and communications	92·6	100·8	115·7	155·8	257·1	289·6	276·6	325·3	292·9	555·8	877·4
9 Other goods	79·8	93·4	105·9	187·7	259·9	236·1	235·8	279·8	333·3	559·6	742·0
10 Other services	260·7	285·5	311·9	406·4	529·4	527·8	562·5	624·2	581·0	843·0	913·0
11 Total	1,671·2	1,783·3	1,970·1	3,012·5	4,199·3	3,985·6	3,852·4	4,246·2	5,086·2	8,061·6	10,993·2
Percentages											
1 Food	33·1	33·5	33·7	37·7	34·1	33·1	30·6	29·2	29·7	29·2	33·5
2 Alcoholic drink	10·9	9·3	8·8	8·0	9·0	8·0	7·1	6·8	10·7	9·5	7·4
3 Tobacco	1·7	1·8	2·0	2·4	2·7	3·1	3·7	3·9	7·8	8·9	7·6
4 Rents, rates and water charges	11·3	11·8	11·5	8·1	8·0	9·3	10·8	11·0	10·2	7·4	6·9
5 Fuel and light	4·4	4·0	3·8	4·0	3·9	4·0	4·2	4·2	4·7	3·9	4·1
6 Clothing	9·2	9·2	9·7	10·7	12·1	10·8	9·9	9·7	9·6	10·8	10·4
7 Durable household goods	3·5	3·4	3·5	4·1	5·3	5·3	5·7	6·2	3·7	5·9	7·0
8 Transport and communications	5·5	5·7	5·9	5·2	6·1	7·3	7·2	7·7	5·8	6·9	8·0
9 Other goods	4·8	5·2	5·4	6·2	6·2	5·9	6·1	6·6	6·6	6·9	6·7
10 Other services	15·6	16·0	15·8	13·5	12·6	13·2	14·6	14·7	11·4	10·5	8·3

has doubled since 1900; somewhat smaller increases were shown for expenditure on transport and 'other goods'. These increases were offset by the decreasing proportion spent on 'other services'.

The great increase in expenditure during this period is to a large extent of course a reflexion of the decline in the value of money. The prices of individual goods have also varied relatively to one another. In Table 56 all expenditures have been revalued at 1938 prices. In real terms total expenditure rose during the period by almost exactly 50 %; the pattern of demand, as shown in the lower half of the table, is also a good deal different to that of expenditure at current prices. The proportion devoted to food increased during the period, indicating that the demand for food rose more than demand as a whole. There was a similar marked increase in the share of rents and rates, while the shares of neither fuel and light, nor clothing, showed any clear tendency to fall. As a result, the 'basic necessities', which accounted for just one-half of the total in 1900, took a quite significantly larger proportion at the end of the period. This increase is much less marked, however, if the figures for alcoholic drink are excluded from the reckoning. The consumption of alcoholic drink decreased by half during the period, the share falling from 18 to 6 %. The offsetting increase in the demand for tobacco was proportionately much greater but less in absolute terms, so that the share of drink and tobacco together fell from one-fifth to one-tenth of the total. The proportion taken by durable goods and transport more than doubled but was offset by a corresponding fall in 'other services'.

The rise in consumption during this period must be seen in relation to the increase in population; real expenditure per head provides a more meaningful indicator of economic welfare. Expenditures per head, at constant prices, are shown in Table 57; in the lower half of this table the series are converted to index numbers with a common base year. Total real expenditure per head is seen to have increased by less than one-quarter (22 %). Practically the whole of this increase took place in the second half of the period, although interrupted for a decade by the Second World War and the subsequent period of shortages. In the years from 1900 to 1914 consumption of most items was very nearly constant, certain small increases being more than offset by the declining consumption of alcoholic drink. The war brought a positive fall, particularly in food and clothing, and the recovery was not complete until late in the 'twenties. The great depression of the 'thirties appears to have had only a small effect on average consumption compared with the marked changes in the war periods. In the years 1930–4, for all commodity groups except alcoholic drink, real expenditure per head was higher

than in the preceding five years. It is clear, however, that the rate of growth had been generally reduced during this period, and the decline in drink consumption was certainly accelerated. In the case of food consumption there was hardly any slackening in the rate of growth; this must be accounted for by the great relative fall in agricultural prices which occurred during the recession. The Second World War period was marked by a greater proportionate decrease in total consumption than the first, though a higher absolute level was maintained. The purchase of durable goods, especially, was affected and fell to a lower level than at any other time during the whole period; a slow post-war recovery followed and the pre-war level had not been regained at the end of the period under review. This also applies to clothing, though not to other groups, except where the long-term trend was downward. Total consumption at the end of the period showed an increase of only 5 % over the pre-war level.

That the pattern of consumption should change as the level of real income rises is to be expected. As the demand for the basic necessities approaches saturation, an increasing surplus is available for the purchase of luxuries. This process is disturbed, however, by the impact of changing prices and by shifts in the underlying structure of tastes. The figures in Table 56, for instance, display none of the orderliness apparent in family budget data, which show average consumption for different levels of income at a single point of time.

The importance of the price factor can be seen from Table 58. In the upper half of this table the implied price index for each group is shown, the figures being obtained simply as the ratios of expenditures at current prices (Table 55) and at constant prices (Table 56). They are therefore current-weighted aggregate (Paasche) index numbers. The lower part of the table shows a relative price index for each group. These figures are calculated as the ratio of the index for the particular group to the average index for all other groups.[1]

While the average price level increased more than fourfold during the period, the relative variation of the individual groups was on a much smaller scale. Nevertheless, the relative changes have been sufficiently large to produce considerable shifts in demand between groups. The relative price of alcoholic drink, for instance, largely as a result of increasing duty, rose by 127 % during the period. There seems little doubt that this contributed significantly to the downward trend of drink

---

[1] It may be noted that these figures may also be readily obtained from the preceding tables. Writing w_1 for the proportion of total expenditure at current prices represented by the particular group (Table 55) and w_0 for the proportion at constant prices (Table 56), then the relative price index is given by the formula:

$$100 \, (w_0^{-1} - 1)/(w_1^{-1} - 1).$$

TABLE 56. CONSUMERS' EXPENDITURE AT CONSTANT (1938) PRICES: UNITED KINGDOM, 1900–55

(£ M. AND PERCENTAGES)

	1900–4	1905–9	1910–14	1915–19	1920–4	1925–9	1930–4	1935–8	1939–45	1946–50	1951–5
£ million											
1 Food	898·4	944·6	981·9	900·6	1,002·3	1,116·7	1,231·1	1,285·9	1,180·6	1,450·8	1,596·8
2 Alcoholic drink	594·8	536·7	502·5	388·2	351·8	320·5	264·6	286·4	291·3	289·2	293·2
3 Tobacco	72·5	77·5	84·0	100·0	113·0	123·6	137·8	163·3	199·4	204·4	206·4
4 Rents, rates and water charges	293·2	315·2	333·7	345·1	368·3	393·4	428·9	471·7	502·6	525·4	550·4
5 Fuel and light	134·3	133·0	137·3	139·4	138·7	155·0	163·7	182·7	197·6	221·6	254·0
6 Clothing	338·9	333·2	367·2	289·5	356·7	388·8	403·1	434·8	315·7	421·6	448·8
7 Durable household goods	123·5	127·2	134·7	119·6	176·9	218·0	258·5	289·4	117·6	213·0	282·6
8 Transport and communications	107·3	114·0	131·5	137·3	188·5	241·9	258·2	326·1	256·7	383·8	472·2
9 Other goods	132·6	148·5	164·1	176·2	204·3	219·9	243·6	293·4	250·0	309·8	349·8
10 Other services	558·2	573·3	591·0	530·2	458·5	515·4	584·0	643·4	474·4	521·6	471·8
11 Total	3,253·7	3,303·2	3,427·9	3,126·1	3,359·0	3,693·2	3,973·5	4,377·1	3,785·9	4,541·2	4,926·0
Percentages											
1 Food	27·6	28·6	28·6	28·8	29·8	30·2	31·0	29·4	31·2	31·9	32·4
2 Alcoholic drink	18·3	16·2	14·7	12·4	10·5	8·7	6·7	6·5	7·7	6·4	6·0
3 Tobacco	2·2	2·3	2·5	3·2	3·4	3·3	3·5	3·7	5·3	4·5	4·2
4 Rents, rates and water charges	9·0	9·5	9·7	11·0	11·0	10·7	10·8	10·8	13·3	11·6	11·2
5 Fuel and light	4·1	4·0	4·0	4·5	4·1	4·2	4·1	4·2	5·2	4·9	5·2
6 Clothing	10·4	10·1	10·7	9·3	10·6	10·5	10·1	9·9	8·3	9·3	9·1
7 Durable household goods	3·8	3·9	3·9	3·8	5·3	5·9	6·5	6·6	3·1	4·7	5·7
8 Transport and communications	3·3	3·5	3·8	4·4	5·6	6·5	6·5	7·5	6·8	8·5	9·6
9 Other goods	4·1	4·5	4·8	5·6	6·1	6·0	6·1	6·7	6·6	6·8	7·1
10 Other services	17·2	17·4	17·2	17·0	13·6	14·0	14·7	14·7	12·5	11·5	9·6

TABLE 57. CONSUMERS' EXPENDITURE PER HEAD AT CONSTANT (1938) PRICES: UNITED KINGDOM, 1900–55

(£ (1938) PER HEAD AND INDEX NUMBERS)

	1900–4	1905–9	1910–14	1915–19	1920–4	1925–9	1930–4	1935–8	1939–45	1946–50	1951–5
£ (1938) per head											
1 Food	21·43	21·59	21·59	20·86	22·61	24·60	26·59	27·25	26·28	29·72	31·54
2 Alcoholic drink	14·20	12·27	11·05	8·97	7·94	7·06	5·72	6·07	6·49	5·94	5·79
3 Tobacco	1·73	1·77	1·84	2·32	2·55	2·72	2·98	3·46	4·45	4·20	4·08
4 Rents, rates and water charges	6·99	7·20	7·34	8·00	8·31	8·67	9·26	10·00	11·20	10·77	10·87
5 Fuel and light	3·20	3·04	3·02	3·23	3·13	3·42	3·54	3·87	4·40	4·54	5·02
6 Clothing	8·09	7·61	8·08	6·69	8·05	8·56	8·71	9·22	7·00	8·63	8·87
7 Durable household goods	2·94	2·91	2·96	2·77	3·99	4·80	5·58	6·13	2·59	4·36	5·58
8 Transport and communications	2·56	2·60	2·89	3·18	4·25	5·33	5·58	6·91	5·72	7·87	9·32
9 Other goods	3·16	3·39	3·61	4·08	4·61	4·84	5·26	6·22	5·55	6·34	6·91
10 Other services	13·31	13·10	13·00	12·28	10·35	11·35	12·61	13·63	10·55	10·71	9·32
11 Total	77·61	75·48	75·38	72·38	75·79	81·35	85·83	92·76	84·23	93·08	97·30
Index numbers (1938 = 100·0)											
1 Food	78·2	78·8	78·8	76·1	82·5	89·8	97·0	99·5	95·9	108·5	115·1
2 Alcoholic drink	229·4	198·2	178·5	144·9	128·3	114·1	92·4	98·1	104·8	96·0	93·5
3 Tobacco	46·8	47·8	49·7	62·7	68·9	73·5	80·5	93·5	120·3	113·5	110·3
4 Rents, rates and water charges	68·0	70·0	71·4	77·8	80·8	84·3	90·1	97·3	108·9	104·8	105·7
5 Fuel and light	80·4	76·3	75·8	81·1	78·6	85·9	88·9	97·2	110·6	114·1	126·1
6 Clothing	87·7	82·5	87·6	72·6	87·3	92·8	94·5	100·0	75·9	93·6	96·2
7 Durable household goods	53·0	52·4	53·3	49·9	71·9	86·5	100·5	110·5	46·7	78·6	100·5
8 Transport and communications	35·4	35·9	39·9	43·9	58·7	73·6	77·1	95·4	79·0	108·7	128·7
9 Other goods	48·2	51·8	55·1	62·3	70·4	73·9	80·3	95·0	84·7	96·8	105·5
10 Other services	96·9	95·3	94·6	89·4	74·4	81·6	90·7	98·0	76·8	77·9	67·8
11 Total	82·7	80·4	80·3	77·1	80·6	86·5	91·3	98·7	89·8	99·2	103·7

TABLE 58. INDEX NUMBERS OF ACTUAL AND RELATIVE PRICES: UNITED KINGDOM, 1900–55

(1938 = 100·0)

	1900–4	1905–9	1910–14	1915–19	1920–4	1925–9	1930–4	1935–8	1939–45	1946–50	1951–5
Actual prices											
1 Food	61·5	63·2	67·5	126·3	143·0	118·0	95·9	96·6	128·1	162·5	230·5
2 Alcoholic drink	30·5	30·9	34·3	62·3	107·0	100·0	103·4	100·1	187·4	264·9	279·1
3 Tobacco	39·7	42·1	46·8	73·3	100·7	101·1	102·6	100·9	197·8	349·7	406·3
4 Rents, rates and water charges	64·7	67·0	67·8	70·9	91·1	94·4	97·1	99·2	102·7	113·9	137·0
5 Fuel and light	54·5	53·6	54·8	86·2	118·7	102·2	98·6	98·0	119·8	143·1	178·1
6 Clothing	45·5	49·4	52·2	111·1	142·5	110·5	95·0	95·1	154·1	206·5	255·2
7 Durable household goods	46·8	47·9	50·9	103·3	125·2	96·2	85·6	90·7	159·3	225·0	272·8
8 Transport and communications	86·3	88·0	88·0	113·5	136·4	119·7	107·1	99·8	114·1	144·8	185·8
9 Other goods	60·2	62·9	64·5	106·5	127·2	107·4	96·8	95·4	133·3	180·6	212·1
10 Other services	46·7	49·8	52·8	76·7	115·5	102·4	96·3	97·0	122·5	161·6	193·5
11 Total	51·4	54·0	57·5	96·4	125·0	107·9	97·0	97·0	134·3	177·5	223·2
Relative prices											
1 Food	129·8	125·8	126·9	149·6	121·8	113·9	98·5	99·4	93·4	88·0	105·0
2 Alcoholic drink	54·6	53·0	56·0	61·4	84·1	92·0	107·2	103·4	144·3	154·4	127·1
3 Tobacco	76·9	77·9	79·6	74·4	80·0	93·4	106·1	104·1	151·2	206·4	188·8
4 Rents, rates and water charges	128·8	127·4	121·0	71·3	70·5	86·2	100·2	102·6	73·8	61·3	58·5
5 Fuel and light	107·7	100·0	94·8	88·4	94·7	94·5	101·8	101·0	88·7	79·8	78·9
6 Clothing	87·3	90·2	89·7	116·9	115·9	102·7	97·7	97·8	116·2	118·3	116·0
7 Durable household goods	91·8	86·7	89·4	108·2	100·1	88·5	87·6	93·1	119·3	128·4	123·9
8 Transport and communications	170·5	166·7	158·7	119·2	109·6	111·8	111·3	103·1	84·0	80·2	81·8
9 Other goods	117·9	116·4	113·2	111·4	101·8	99·4	99·8	98·2	99·2	101·9	94·7
10 Other services	89·0	90·4	90·3	76·2	91·6	93·4	99·2	100·0	90·1	90·0	85·5

consumption. On the other hand, a comparable increase in the price of tobacco was accompanied by an upward trend in consumption and it is clear that in this case some change in the structure of preferences must be taken into account. The relative fall in average rent is largely a reflexion of rent control which maintained controlled rents at a constant money level in the face of a persistent rise in the general price level. The relative decrease in transport prices goes some way to account for the increasing importance of travel during the period. But a comparable fall in the price of 'other services' after 1938 did not prevent a continuing decline in demand for these services.

A more precise analysis would be required to say what proportion of the change in demand was due to income or price effects and how much to some residual factor of changing tastes and habits. To some extent changes in tastes will be expressed by shifts in the composition of a group and these hidden quality changes are very difficult to assess. The composition of the food group, for instance, includes not only the volume of foodstuffs consumed but also manufacturing and distributive services involved in the processing, packaging and retailing of foods. It is known that there has been a considerable expansion of these services which has transferred much of the preparation of food from the home to the factory; the increasing importance of these services goes some way to account for the fact that the proportion of expenditure devoted to food has shown no tendency to decline with the rising standard of living. Changes in the opposite direction, where the housewife now performs for herself tasks which previously she had paid others to do, have also taken place. Examples are readily found in the field of domestic equipment; new appliances operated by the housewife herself have taken the place of hired domestic help. Similarly, the private motor-car is taking over the function of the public passenger services. Important changes may also be seen in the field of entertainment with the successive introduction during this period of cinemas, sound broadcasting and television.

It is beyond the scope of the present inquiry to pursue the investigation of these social and technical changes and their economic implications in any detail. It may be concluded that while significant variations in the pattern of consumption may be traced to the direct effect of income and price changes, in the long run there are also important factors of changing tastes and habits to be taken into account. The infiltration of new products and the introduction of new methods of marketing continually disturb the expected sequence of economic development. For the most part these changes work relatively slowly; the effect of innovations is limited to a small sector of the whole field of consumption and the most

marked substitutions are likely to take place within the main groups of expenditure where like replaces like. In this connexion it is worth while considering a little more closely the changing pattern of food consumption during the period; this is undertaken in the following section.

3 FOOD EXPENDITURE, 1900–55

Detailed information for ten categories of food is set out in Tables 59–62. In Table 59 the actual expenditures are shown, together with the percentages of total expenditure on food taken by each category. In considering the changing pattern revealed by these figures, allowances must be made, of course, for the effects of the food rationing introduced during both wars. In the Second World War period rationing was much more comprehensive and also maintained for a far longer period (derationing was not complete until the middle of 1954). As a result all the figures for the years after 1938 have to be used with caution if an attempt is made to assess long-term trends.

The largest of the individual groups distinguished is meat and bacon, accounting for almost a third of total expenditure at the beginning of the period, though the proportion tended to decline. Bread and cereals, about one-sixth of the total, remained a fairly constant proportion. The share of dairy products and eggs tended to increase; partly, it would seem, at the expense of oils and fats. Together these four groups accounted for two-thirds of total expenditure throughout the period 1900–38. In later years, the years of war and rationing, the proportion fell. The corresponding increases were in the share taken by fruit and vegetables and by the residual group of 'other foods'.

As the standard of living rises, it is to be expected that a declining proportion of food expenditure would be devoted to cheap, bulky foods, such as bread and potatoes, and that there would be greater variety in the diet with increased consumption of the more expensive fresh fruits and vegetables. Both these tendencies may be discerned in Table 59, but they emerge more clearly in Table 60, in which purchases have been revalued at 1938 prices. A comparison of the pattern in 1900–4 with that in 1935–8 reveals a more even distribution between groups in the later period, indicative of more variety in the average diet; there is also a marked proportionate gain in the share of fruit and vegetables. These tendencies appear most markedly in the final two periods, but here the effect of rationing on demand may be held to be partly responsible. Changes have also taken place within groups, with a shift towards the more expensive foods; for example, an increased demand for the more expensive cuts of meat and for poultry and

TABLE 59. CONSUMERS' EXPENDITURE ON FOOD AT CURRENT PRICES: UNITED KINGDOM, 1900–55

(£ M. AND PERCENTAGES)

	1900–4	1905–9	1910–14	1915–19	1920–4	1925–9	1930–4	1935–8	1939–45	1946–50	1951–5
£ million											
1 Bread and cereals	88·5	101·3	112·2	189·9	206·9	189·9	165·4	186·1	270·7	412·0	560·8
2 Meat and bacon	172·9	177·3	196·0	352·4	439·4	412·1	359·8	358·8	357·1	417·2	835·2
3 Fish	19·6	20·4	24·4	47·0	58·5	53·4	48·7	50·0	73·3	114·6	133·2
4 Dairy products and eggs	71·1	79·0	85·4	131·5	188·9	173·0	165·2	183·5	240·3	390·4	569·6
5 Oils and fats	47·3	52·7	57·5	92·1	100·6	103·6	85·4	91·7	62·6	89·2	191·8
6 Vegetables	41·7	42·5	48·0	87·5	102·7	93·3	94·2	101·9	165·1	304·0	403·4
7 Fruit and nuts	22·8	25·9	27·9	51·1	89·1	90·6	84·6	80·4	64·3	203·2	286·8
8 Sugar, preserves and confectionery	52·7	58·9	70·6	119·5	166·5	123·5	101·7	101·4	119·9	183·8	348·6
9 Beverages	32·6	34·7	36·6	58·6	72·7	69·2	62·0	67·9	74·7	113·8	178·8
10 Other food	3·7	4·0	4·4	7·6	7·4	8·8	13·4	20·3	83·9	129·0	173·2
11 Total	552·9	596·7	663·0	1,137·2	1,432·7	1,317·4	1,180·4	1,242·0	1,511·9	2,357·2	3,681·4
Percentages											
1 Bread and cereals	16·0	17·0	16·9	16·7	14·4	14·4	14·0	15·0	17·9	17·5	15·2
2 Meat and bacon	31·3	29·7	29·6	31·0	30·7	31·3	30·5	28·9	23·6	17·7	22·7
3 Fish	3·5	3·4	3·7	4·1	4·1	4·1	4·1	4·0	4·8	4·9	3·6
4 Dairy products and eggs	12·9	13·2	12·9	11·6	13·2	13·1	14·0	14·8	15·9	16·6	15·5
5 Oils and fats	8·6	8·8	8·7	8·1	7·0	7·9	7·2	7·4	4·1	3·8	5·2
6 Vegetables	7·5	7·1	7·2	7·7	7·2	7·1	8·0	8·2	10·9	12·9	11·0
7 Fruit and nuts	4·1	4·3	4·2	4·5	6·2	6·9	7·2	6·5	4·3	8·6	7·8
8 Sugar, preserves and confectionery	9·5	9·9	10·6	10·5	11·6	9·4	8·6	8·2	7·9	7·8	9·5
9 Beverages	5·9	5·8	5·5	5·2	5·1	5·3	5·3	5·5	4·9	4·8	4·9
10 Other food	0·7	0·7	0·7	0·7	0·5	0·7	1·1	1·6	5·5	5·5	4·7

TABLE 60. CONSUMERS' EXPENDITURE ON FOOD AT CONSTANT (1938) PRICES: UNITED KINGDOM, 1900–55

(£M. AND PERCENTAGES)

	1900–4	1905–9	1910–14	1915–19	1920–4	1925–9	1930–4	1935–8	1939–45	1946–50	1951–5
£ million											
1 Bread and cereals	136·5	142·1	151·0	156·2	150·8	156·6	173·1	185·6	..	214·2	209·8
2 Meat and bacon	316·1	318·7	323·0	305·4	326·2	359·1	380·2	375·6	..	291·4	342·4
3 Fish	39·2	44·2	48·8	35·3	44·9	47·3	49·1	51·3	..	82·4	62·6
4 Dairy products and eggs	123·2	133·9	138·7	112·1	143·9	163·0	182·4	197·1	..	271·8	289·0
5 Oils and fats	56·2	60·3	62·6	57·3	62·7	75·2	90·0	97·8	..	73·6	82·4
6 Vegetables	54·5	60·7	61·3	52·0	77·0	85·0	98·7	101·7	..	157·6	162·8
7 Fruit and nuts	44·4	51·2	50·6	45·8	61·4	77·7	87·1	83·4	..	112·2	135·6
8 Sugar, preserves and confectionery	82·5	85·9	96·0	85·2	72·4	84·5	91·6	103·7	..	94·2	138·4
9 Beverages	42·6	44·7	46·8	48·1	58·9	62·4	68·1	70·9	..	75·4	82·4
10 Other food	3·2	2·9	3·1	3·2	4·0	5·9	10·7	18·9	..	78·0	91·4
11 Total	898·4	944·6	981·9	900·6	1,002·2	1,116·7	1,231·0	1,286·0	1,180·6	1,450·8	1,596·8
Percentages											
1 Bread and cereals	15·2	15·0	15·4	17·3	15·0	14·0	14·1	14·4	..	14·8	13·1
2 Meat and bacon	35·2	33·7	32·9	33·9	32·5	32·2	30·9	29·2	..	20·1	21·4
3 Fish	4·4	4·7	5·0	3·9	4·5	4·2	4·0	4·0	..	5·7	3·9
4 Dairy products and eggs	13·7	14·2	14·1	12·4	14·4	14·6	14·8	15·3	..	18·7	18·1
5 Oils and fats	6·3	6·4	6·4	6·4	6·3	6·7	7·3	7·6	..	5·1	5·2
6 Vegetables	6·1	6·4	6·2	5·8	7·7	7·6	8·0	7·9	..	10·9	10·2
7 Fruit and nuts	4·9	5·4	5·2	5·1	6·1	7·0	7·1	6·5	..	7·7	8·5
8 Sugar, preserves and confectionery	9·2	9·1	9·8	9·5	7·2	7·6	7·4	8·1	..	6·5	8·7
9 Beverages	4·7	4·7	4·8	5·3	5·9	5·6	5·5	5·5	..	5·2	5·2
10 Other food	0·4	0·3	0·3	0·4	0·4	0·5	0·9	1·5	..	5·4	5·7

TABLE 61. CONSUMERS' EXPENDITURE PER HEAD ON FOOD AT CONSTANT (1938) PRICES: UNITED KINGDOM, 1900-55 (£ (1938) PER HEAD AND INDEX NUMBERS)

	1900–4	1905–9	1910–14	1915–19	1920–4	1925–9	1930–4	1935–8	1939–45	1946–50	1951–5
£ (1938) per head											
1 Bread and cereals	3·26	3·25	3·32	3·62	3·40	3·45	3·74	3·93	..	4·39	4·14
2 Meat and bacon	7·54	7·28	7·10	7·08	7·36	7·91	8·21	7·96	..	5·98	6·76
3 Fish	0·93	1·01	1·07	0·82	1·01	1·04	1·06	1·09	..	1·69	1·24
4 Dairy products and eggs	2·94	3·06	3·05	2·59	3·25	3·59	3·94	4·18	..	5·57	5·71
5 Oils and fats	1·34	1·38	1·38	1·33	1·42	1·66	1·94	2·07	..	1·50	1·63
6 Vegetables	1·30	1·39	1·35	1·20	1·74	1·87	2·13	2·16	..	3·23	3·22
7 Fruit and nuts	1·06	1·17	1·11	1·06	1·38	1·71	1·88	1·77	..	2·29	2·68
8 Sugar, preserves and confectionery	1·97	1·96	2·11	1·97	1·63	1·86	1·98	2·20	..	1·93	2·73
9 Beverages	1·02	1·02	1·03	1·11	1·33	1·37	1·47	1·50	..	1·54	1·63
10 Other food	0·08	0·07	0·07	0·07	0·09	0·13	0·23	0·40	..	1·60	1·81
11 Total	21·44	21·59	21·59	20·85	22·61	24·59	26·58	27·26	26·28	29·72	31·55
Index numbers (1938 = 100·0)											
1 Bread and cereals	81·1	80·8	82·6	90·0	84·6	85·8	93·0	97·8	..	109·2	103·0
2 Meat and bacon	95·0	91·7	89·4	89·2	92·7	99·6	103·4	100·3	..	75·3	85·1
3 Fish	86·1	93·5	99·1	75·9	93·5	96·3	98·1	100·9	..	156·5	114·8
4 Dairy products and eggs	69·7	72·5	72·3	61·4	77·0	85·1	93·4	99·1	..	132·0	135·3
5 Oils and fats	65·4	67·3	67·3	64·9	69·3	81·0	94·6	101·0	..	73·2	79·5
6 Vegetables	58·8	62·9	61·1	54·3	78·7	84·6	96·4	97·7	..	146·2	145·7
7 Fruit and nuts	63·9	70·5	66·9	63·9	83·1	103·0	113·3	106·6	..	138·0	161·4
8 Sugar, preserves and confectionery	88·7	88·3	95·0	88·7	73·4	83·8	89·2	99·1	..	86·9	123·0
9 Beverages	67·5	67·5	68·2	73·5	88·1	90·7	97·4	99·3	..	102·0	107·9
10 Other food	16·3	14·3	14·3	14·3	18·4	26·5	46·9	81·6	..	326·5	369·4
11 Total	78·2	78·8	78·8	76·1	82·5	89·7	97·0	99·5	95·9	108·5	115·1

game within the meat and bacon group, and an increase in the consumption of fresh milk and cream at the expense of the cheaper forms of condensed milk. These changes are reflected in the values given here; the actual weight of food consumed would show a slower rate of growth in these groups.

In Table 61 expenditures at constant prices are shown per head of the population; the index numbers given in the lower half of this table make it easier to compare rates of change in the different groups. The groups that have increased at a slower rate than the average—bread, meat, fish, and sugar—comprise mainly the bulky energy-producing foods. The existence of rationing, of course, accounts for the fact that consumption of meat and bacon and of oils and fats was lower at the end of the period than during the inter-war years. The exceptional increase in fish consumption in the immediate post-war years, 1946–50, is clearly a consequence of the shortage of meat. Similar compensatory movements may be observed in earlier years, though on a much smaller scale. The other groups, which have shown a rate of increase above the average, all exhibit a similar pattern of development through the period: a constant level of consumption during the early years is followed by a fall during the First World War, then in the inter-war years consumption begins to rise at a steady rate, and the level reached by the end of the period appears as an extrapolation of this earlier rate of growth, as if unaffected by the second war interim. The fact that the trend appears to have persisted through the war period suggests an underlying change in tastes. It must not be forgotten, however, that rationing would tend to force up consumption of the unrestricted foods. The marked increase in the consumption of 'other foods' since the early 'twenties reflects the growing popularity of items such as ice cream, canned soup, and specially prepared infant and invalid foods. These are foods which reduce the housewife's labour by substituting factory processing for preparation in the home.

Price movements are shown in Table 62. The fourfold increase in the average price of food is to a large extent common to each of the component groups. There are, nevertheless, differences between groups and these are brought out in the lower half of the table which shows the price index for each group as a ratio of the average index for all other groups. Close substitutes for individual foods are more likely to be found among other foods than among commodities outside the food group. There will certainly be some substitution between foods and other commodities, but it is probable that the most marked price effects will be manifest in the substitution of one food for another. The variation in relative prices shown in Table 62 will explain many of the deviations from

trend in the pattern of demand. The marked fall in the relative price of 'other foods', for instance, would be a strong incentive to increase the consumption of these foods. Similarly the fact that consumption of oils and fats has risen at a faster rate than the average may be due in a large part to the relative fall in price of this group. The consumption of fruit might have expanded more rapidly than it did if the price had not been rising relatively to that of other foods through much of the period.

In conclusion, it may be said that, although there have been some significant changes in the average diet during this period, the dominant impression must be of the long-term stability of food habits.

4 THE DURABILITY OF COMMODITIES

The items of consumers' expenditure may be grouped in different ways in order to bring out special aspects of the changing pattern of demand. One important classification, by degree of durability, is considered here. While some goods have a useful life of several years, others are used up almost immediately. The extent to which some allowance is made for the satisfaction to be derived from past purchases of consumer durable goods will affect any assessment of economic wealth and welfare. Differences in durability are also likely to be of some significance in determining consumers' behaviour.

There is a wide range in degrees of durability extending from items of furniture, which may last a number of decades, through articles of clothing, surviving one or two years, to most foodstuffs, which are consumed practically instantaneously. Durability in use is the relevant concept here. Coal, for instance, which may be stored indefinitely, is regarded as being as perishable as bread or milk. The distinction is far from precise; a large stock of coal or of canned food, for example, which is drawn upon over a long period, might more properly be treated as a durable good. In practice it is necessary to adopt a classification which most nearly reflects the common usage of the time.

For the present purpose total expenditure has been divided between five groups; perishable goods lasting up to six months in use; semi-durable goods, which last more than six months but less than three years; durable goods, which last longer than three years; rent, including rates and water charges; and other services.

To some extent the allocation of items between the different groups has been dictated by the nature of the information available. All furniture and furnishings, for instance, have been classed as durable goods, even though certain items, such as household linens, etc., might be more properly considered as semi-durables.

TABLE 62. INDEX NUMBERS OF ACTUAL AND RELATIVE PRICES OF FOOD: UNITED KINGDOM, 1900–55

(1938 = 100·0)

	1900–4	1905–9	1910–14	1915–19	1920–4	1925–9	1930–4	1935–8	1939–45	1946–50	1951–5
Actual prices											
1 Bread and cereals	64·8	71·3	74·3	121·6	137·2	121·3	95·6	100·3	..	192·3	267·3
2 Meat and bacon	54·7	55·6	60·7	115·4	134·7	114·8	94·6	95·5	..	143·2	243·9
3 Fish	50·0	46·2	50·0	133·1	130·3	112·9	99·2	97·5	..	139·1	212·8
4 Dairy products and eggs	57·7	59·0	61·6	117·3	131·3	106·1	90·6	93·1	..	143·6	197·1
5 Oils and fats	84·2	87·4	91·9	160·7	160·4	137·8	94·9	93·8	..	121·2	232·8
6 Vegetables	76·5	70·0	78·3	168·3	133·4	109·8	95·4	100·2	..	192·9	247·8
7 Fruit and nuts	51·4	50·6	55·1	111·6	145·1	116·6	97·1	96·4	..	181·1	211·5
8 Sugar, preserves and confectionery	63·9	68·6	73·5	140·3	230·0	146·2	111·0	97·8	..	195·1	251·9
9 Beverages	76·5	77·6	78·2	121·8	123·4	110·9	91·0	95·8	..	150·9	217·0
10 Other food	115·6	137·9	141·9	237·5	185·0	149·2	125·2	107·4	..	165·4	189·5
11 Total	61·5	63·2	67·5	126·3	143·0	118·0	95·9	96·6	128·1	162·5	230·5
Relative prices											
1 Bread and cereals	106·4	115·5	112·1	95·6	95·3	103·2	99·6	104·4	..	122·3	118·8
2 Meat and bacon	83·8	83·0	85·6	87·5	91·7	96·0	98·1	98·5	..	85·6	107·5
3 Fish	80·7	72·1	73·0	105·6	90·8	95·5	103·6	101·0	..	84·9	91·9
4 Dairy products and eggs	92·9	92·4	89·9	92·0	90·6	88·5	93·6	95·8	..	86·1	82·8
5 Oils and fats	140·3	142·1	139·5	129·7	113·2	118·3	98·9	96·8	..	73·6	101·1
6 Vegetables	126·3	111·6	117·1	136·1	92·8	92·5	99·4	104·1	..	121·5	108·5
7 Fruit and nuts	82·7	79·2	80·8	87·7	101·5	98·8	101·4	99·9	..	112·5	91·1
8 Sugar, preserves and confectionery	104·3	109·5	110·0	112·3	168·8	126·3	117·3	101·4	..	121·9	110·2
9 Beverages	125·9	124·1	116·8	96·3	85·7	93·6	94·5	99·1	..	92·5	93·8
10 Other food	186·1	216·1	209·4	186·1	130·0	126·4	130·7	111·4	..	101·9	81·4

For most of the period, however, no separate information for the components was available and it was necessary to treat them alike. In a few instances, where a single estimate for a group of much less homogeneous goods had to be split between different categories, it was generally assumed that the proportions remained constant over the period. The most important items for which it was necessary to make arbitrary assumptions were: running costs of vehicles, and the group of miscellaneous goods comprising stationery, fancy goods, chemists' goods, and sports and travel equipment. For the most part, the major groups fall naturally into separate categories: food, drink and tobacco into perishables; clothing into semi-durables; and household furnishings and equipment into the durable group.

The results which emerge from this classification by degree of durability are presented in Tables 63–66. Throughout the greater part of the period the share of perishables was falling while that of durables was rising; the share of the intermediary group of semi-durables remained practically constant. This pattern is the same for expenditure at constant prices and at current prices. Services show a much less uniform pattern of development and were the most severely affected by the disturbances of the wars. Expenditure on domestic service, in particular, has been influenced both by changing social patterns and by the alternative demands for women's labour which developed during the period, especially in wartime. In contrast to the long-term decline in domestic service, however, there has been a marked growth in other services such as travel and entertainments.

The relative rates of growth of the different groups conform to the usual expectations as regards income elasticities in that perishables, semi-durables, and durables, might be expected to represent an ascending order of luxury and to be increasingly responsive to income changes. This orderly development was disrupted by the widespread shortages and the rationing of the Second World War, which caused a marked shift in the relative importance of the different groups in total consumption. The post-war period was largely one of readjustment, rather than a continuation of earlier trends. In Table 65 it can be seen that the proportion of real expenditure taken by perishables fell continuously from the beginning of the century up to the time of the Second World War; during the war period this proportion showed a marked increase; in the post-war years it fell again, but still remained above the average for the whole of the inter-war period. By contrast, the share of semi-durables, which had remained constant up to the war period, fell during the war years and subsequently remained below its previous level. Durables show a similar movement, but in this case there appears to have been an underlying upward trend and a more marked recovery occurs in the post-war period. The share of expenditure on services, at constant prices, shows relatively little variation, even in the war period, amounting to approximately one-fifth of the total in all years.

In Table 66 the implied price index for each group is shown. In the lower half of this table the relative price is given: that is, the price of the particular group relative to the prices of all other goods. A difference in pattern between goods and services is apparent. The movements in relative prices are complementary with respect to each other, with a marked negative correlation between the two groups. The reason for this may be seen by considering the actual price series in the upper half of the table. The prices of both service groups have varied little compared with goods prices. For rents this is clearly due to the operation of rent control. During the First World War period average rents rose only very slightly compared with the very marked rises in most other prices. After the war, with some permitted increases and some relaxation of controls, the average rent continued to rise slightly throughout the inter-war period. In the Second World War, rent control was reimposed and the average increase was again very small; subsequently there were permitted increases comparable to those following the First World War. The long-term rise in the prices of other services has been more marked than for rents, but is also much less than for most goods items. In part this may reflect the deficiencies of the estimates. It is possible, for instance, that there were changes in the quality of some services which are not reflected in the average price series used. Nevertheless, the differences apparent here probably do reflect a real divergence in pattern between the two groups. The prices of goods rose precipitately through the two war and post-war periods, falling to a comparable extent during the inter-war period. In the estimates of relative prices, therefore, the large movements in the goods series are simply reflected in the relative prices of the service items.

It is unlikely that the inverse movement in the relative prices of goods and services has failed to have its effect on the pattern of consumption. There are a number of reasons, however, why the degree of substitution will have been less than might have been expected. The low controlled rents were associated with a restricted supply of new houses and expenditure on rent was held down below the equilibrium level. The decline in domestic service was also an offsetting factor. The associated increase in the use of domestic appliances resulted in certain household operations being transferred from the services to the durables category. The growth of private transport will have had a similar effect. It is also possible that, as working hours have shortened, certain services

TABLE 63. CONSUMERS' EXPENDITURE AT CURRENT PRICES CLASSIFIED BY DURABILITY: UNITED KINGDOM, 1900–55 (£M. AND PERCENTAGES)

	1900–4	1905–9	1910–14	1915–19	1920–4	1925–9	1930–4	1935–8	1939–45	1946–50	1951–5
£ million											
1 Perishables	868·8	905·1	993·4	1,661·5	2,211·3	2,039·9	1,881·6	2,031·0	2,825·3	4,398·0	6,141·6
2 Semi-durables	173·0	186·3	216·9	366·8	564·3	477·6	428·4	465·4	541·6	966·6	1,272·6
3 Durables	78·9	85·9	100·0	165·4	305·6	297·7	296·9	366·2	260·9	661·8	1,108·2
4 Rent	189·6	211·3	226·3	244·8	335·5	371·5	416·4	468·1	516·3	598·6	753·8
5 Other services	360·9	394·8	433·5	574·0	782·5	798·9	829·0	915·3	942·1	1,436·6	1,717·0
6 Total	1,671·2	1,783·4	1,970·1	3,012·5	4,199·2	3,985·6	3,852·3	4,246·0	5,086·2	8,061·6	10,993·2
Percentages											
1 Perishables	52·0	50·8	50·4	55·2	52·7	51·2	48·8	47·8	55·5	54·6	55·9
2 Semi-durables	10·4	10·4	11·0	12·2	13·4	12·0	11·1	11·0	10·6	12·0	11·6
3 Durables	4·7	4·8	5·1	5·5	7·3	7·5	7·7	8·6	5·1	8·2	10·1
4 Rent	11·3	11·8	11·5	8·1	8·0	9·3	10·8	11·0	10·2	7·4	6·9
5 Other services	21·6	22·1	22·0	19·1	18·6	20·0	21·5	21·6	18·5	17·8	15·6

TABLE 64. CONSUMERS' EXPENDITURE AT CONSTANT (1938) PRICES CLASSIFIED BY DURABILITY: UNITED KINGDOM, 1900–55 (£M. AND PERCENTAGES)

	1900–4	1905–9	1910–14	1915–19	1920–4	1925–9	1930–4	1935–8	1939–45	1946–50	1951–5
£ million											
1 Perishables	1,768·6	1,769·1	1,791·1	1,619·4	1,709·5	1,834·3	1,932·8	2,086·2	1,964·9	2,270·4	2,468·6
2 Semi-durables	366·5	364·3	402·3	327·1	398·7	433·0	451·1	490·0	353·3	465·6	500·0
3 Durables	150·3	157·0	169·6	150·3	226·2	283·9	333·2	395·9	171·7	300·0	409·0
4 Rent	293·2	315·2	333·7	345·1	368·3	393·4	428·9	471·7	502·6	525·4	550·4
5 Other services	675·1	697·6	731·2	684·2	656·2	748·6	827·5	933·0	793·4	979·8	998·1
6 Total	3,253·7	3,303·2	3,427·9	3,126·1	3,358·9	3,693·2	3,973·5	4,376·8	3,785·9	4,541·2	4,926·0
Percentages											
1 Perishables	54·4	53·6	52·3	51·8	50·9	49·7	48·6	47·7	51·9	50·0	50·1
2 Semi-durables	11·3	11·0	11·7	10·5	11·9	11·7	11·4	11·2	9·3	10·3	10·2
3 Durables	4·6	4·8	4·9	4·8	6·7	7·7	8·4	9·0	4·5	6·6	8·3
4 Rent	9·0	9·5	9·7	11·0	11·0	10·7	10·8	10·8	13·3	11·6	11·2
5 Other services	20·7	21·1	21·3	21·9	19·5	20·3	20·8	21·3	21·0	21·6	20·3

TABLE 65. CONSUMERS' EXPENDITURE PER HEAD AT CONSTANT (1938) PRICES CLASSIFIED BY DURABILITY: UNITED KINGDOM, 1900–55 (£ (1938) PER HEAD AND INDEX NUMBERS)

	1900–4	1905–9	1910–14	1915–19	1920–4	1925–9	1930–4	1935–8	1939–45	1946–50	1951–5
£ (1938) per head											
1 Perishables	42·19	40·43	39·39	37·48	38·58	40·41	41·75	44·21	43·75	46·54	48·76
2 Semi-durables	8·74	8·32	8·85	7·56	9·00	9·54	9·74	10·39	7·83	9·53	9·87
3 Durables	3·59	3·59	3·73	3·48	5·10	6·25	7·19	8·39	3·78	6·14	8·07
4 Rent	6·99	7·20	7·34	8·00	8·31	8·67	9·26	10·00	11·20	10·77	10·87
5 Other services	16·10	15·94	16·07	15·86	14·81	16·49	17·87	19·77	17·67	20·10	19·73
6 Total	77·61	75·48	75·38	72·38	75·80	81·36	85·81	92·76	84·23	93·08	97·30
Index numbers (1938 = 100·0)											
1 Perishables	93·7	89·8	87·5	83·2	85·7	89·7	92·7	98·2	97·2	103·4	108·3
2 Semi-durables	83·9	79·8	84·9	72·5	86·4	91·6	93·5	99·7	75·1	91·5	94·7
3 Durables	46·0	46·0	47·8	44·6	65·3	80·0	92·1	107·4	48·4	78·6	103·3
4 Rent	68·0	70·0	71·4	77·8	80·8	84·3	90·1	97·3	108·9	104·8	105·7
5 Other services	79·3	78·6	79·2	78·2	72·3	80·6	87·3	96·6	87·1	99·1	97·1
6 Total	82·7	80·4	80·3	77·1	80·6	86·5	91·3	98·7	89·8	99·2	103·7

TABLE 66. INDEX NUMBERS OF ACTUAL AND RELATIVE PRICES FOR CONSUMERS' EXPENDITURE CLASSIFIED BY DURABILITY: UNITED KINGDOM, 1900–55

(1938 = 100·0)

	1900–4	1905–9	1910–14	1915–19	1920–4	1925–9	1930–4	1935–8	1939–45	1946–50	1951–5
Actual prices											
1 Perishables	49·1	51·2	55·5	102·6	129·4	111·2	97·4	97·4	143·8	193·7	248·8
2 Semi-durables	47·2	51·1	53·9	112·1	141·5	110·3	95·0	95·0	153·3	207·6	254·5
3 Durables	52·5	54·7	59·0	110·0	135·1	104·9	89·1	92·5	152·0	220·6	271·0
4 Rent	64·7	67·0	67·8	70·9	91·1	94·4	97·1	99·2	102·7	113·9	137·0
5 Other services	53·5	56·6	59·3	83·9	119·2	106·7	100·2	98·1	118·7	146·6	172·0
6 Total	51·4	54·0	57·5	96·4	125·0	107·9	96·9	97·0	134·3	177·5	223·2
Relative prices											
1 Perishables	90·8	89·4	92·7	114·7	107·1	106·2	100·8	100·8	115·6	120·3	126·3
2 Semi-durables	91·1	93·9	93·3	118·4	115·5	102·9	97·0	98·0	115·6	118·8	115·5
3 Durables	102·3	100·0	104·3	115·4	109·7	97·2	91·0	94·0	114·1	126·4	124·1
4 Rent	128·8	127·4	121·0	71·3	70·5	86·2	100·2	102·6	73·8	61·3	58·5
5 Other services	105·5	106·1	104·2	84·2	94·3	98·2	104·3	101·8	85·4	78·6	72·6

have been removed from the productive sector altogether and are now performed within the household. All these factors would contribute to a downward trend in the demand for services.

5 CONSUMPTION OF AND INVESTMENT IN DURABLE GOODS

Purchases of durable goods are essentially additions to capital, a form of investment providing a service, or utility, over a considerable period of time. The usual practice is to regard the purchase of houses as the only form of investment by households. A more consistent procedure would be to reckon all purchases of durables as investment and to include an imputed return, equal to the value of their use, as a part of consumption. While this is accomplished relatively easily for houses, and corresponds to the practice of the tax authorities, for most durable goods the imputation must be much more arbitrary. Nevertheless, it seems worth while attempting to establish orders of magnitude for the values of consumption, investment, and stocks of consumer durables during this period.

In an equilibrium situation the value of consumption would be the same whichever concept was adopted; for the whole of current purchases would then be replacement demand and equal to current consumption. When there is net investment (or disinvestment), however, the two values will diverge.

The consumption of durables in any year can be regarded as the sum of two components, the first a contribution from the initial stock and the second the purchases made during the year. The stock at the end of the year will be equal to the sum of the initial stock and the purchases of the year less the quantity consumed in the year. Net investment is the difference between the initial stock and the end-of-the-year stock or, equally, the difference between purchases and consumption in the year.

In order to obtain actual estimates of these magnitudes—stocks, net investment and consumption—it is necessary to specify the rate at which each commodity is assumed to be used up. For the present purpose it will be assumed that consumption proceeds at a constant proportionate rate: that is, if the annual rate of consumption is some fraction, k, a commodity, whose initial value is q, will have a depreciated value at the end of each successive year of its life of $q(1-k)$, $q(1-k)^2$, $q(1-k)^3$, etc. The further assumption is made that purchases are spread evenly through the year.

Consumption as defined here is equivalent to depreciation calculated by the reducing balance method. Apart from being computationally convenient, there is some further justification for using this formulation in the

present context. It is reasonable to suppose that not only will the residual service of a durable commodity decline continuously with age but the use to be obtained from it in any period will also decrease as it becomes older. It is not possible, for instance, to get the same degree of service from an old car as from a new one.[1]

For the estimates made here, the annual rate of depreciation varies between four-fifths for clothing and one-tenth for the most durable commodities such as books, jewellery, etc. The implications of these values may be more readily grasped, perhaps, if they are expressed in terms of the time taken to use up nine-tenths, say, of the original value of the good. If goods are normally scrapped when they reach this stage of their usefulness, this figure will represent the average length of life. It works out at $1\frac{2}{3}$ years for clothing, 8 years for household durables, 10 years for cars, and rises to over 21 years for the most durable group of commodities dealt with here.

The specific assumptions are as follows:

	Annual depreciation rate	Average life (years)
Clothing	0·80	1·7
Fancy goods, etc.	0·80	1·7
Tyres and tubes	0·57	2·8
Household durables	0·25	8·0
Bicycles	0·33	5·7
Motor-cycles	0·33	5·7
Cars	0·20	10·3
Jewellery, travel goods, etc.	0·14	14·9
Books	0·10	21·8

An estimate of the initial stock in 1900 was required as a starting point for the calculations. It seemed best to assume that purchases had been increasing at a steady rate up to 1900; deviations from this assumed trend would be likely to cancel out, and any error in the initial stock figure has a rapidly diminishing effect on the calculations in subsequent years. For most of the items an average trend of $2\frac{1}{2}$ % a year was assumed;[2] for vehicles, however, trends based on the experience of the first few years after 1900 were used.[3]

---

[1] The fact that no maximum age is specified for a good is of little significance in practice. The application is to aggregates rather than individuals and the contribution to the total stock made by survivors over a reasonable age is negligible. The principle is the same as that adopted for the construction of ordinary life tables. For further details, see [89a] Stone and Rowe, 'The market demand for durable goods', *Econometrica* xxv, no. 3 (July 1957), p. 423.

[2] This represents the average rate of growth of total personal consumption in the preceding decade: see [75] James B. Jefferys and Dorothy Walters, 'National income and expenditure of the United Kingdom, 1870–1952', *Income and Wealth Series V* (1956).

[3] In making these calculations carriages have been omitted as there is too little evidence to provide a reasonable estimate of the value of the stock. Purchases were very small, ceasing altogether in 1915, and it is unlikely that there was any net investment during this period when carriages were being replaced by motor-cars. Even if the whole of the net investment in cars during the years 1900–14 was offset by disinvestment in carriages, the discrepancy involved would not be more than £1–2 m.

One further correction was required to allow for the exclusion of Southern Ireland from 1920 onwards. For this purpose a simple adjustment in proportion to the population change was applied to the calculated end-of-year stock in 1919 to obtain an estimate of the opening stock for 1920 on the revised basis.

It will be noted that in making these calculations it is necessary to assume a value for the rate of depreciation, and that the figure has been kept constant throughout the period. This limitation must be borne in mind when assessing the results. The particular figures chosen are intended to reflect economic rather than merely physical durability; furnishings grow shabby, appliances become less reliable with age. An average rate of obsolescence must also be allowed for, since unfashionable goods, though still serviceable, are often discarded because of their out-of-date appearance.

The results of the calculations are shown in Tables 67–70. In the first of these tables the estimated consumption of semi-durables and durables is shown. The difference between these figures and the purchases given in previous tables represents net investment, which is shown for each group in Table 68. Negative figures in this table indicate disinvestment. The corresponding estimates of average stocks in each period appear in Table 69.

For clothing and other semi-durables net investment represents no more than a few per cent of total purchases. Much the greater part of clothing expenditure is required to maintain the stock, as is necessarily the case for goods with a relatively short life. Correspondingly, the amount of disinvestment during the war periods was also small. There was little net investment in household durables until the early 'twenties, but throughout the inter-war period it accounted for more than 10 % of purchases. This period of accumulation was followed by heavy disinvestment during the war period 1939–45, at a rate equal to more than 60 % of purchases during these years. For each of the three years from 1942 to 1944, in fact, the net disinvestment in household durables was greater than the volume of purchases. Consumption, consequently, fell much less than purchases in these years. In the post-war years, on the other hand, the recovery was slower than might appear from the increase in purchases, since a large part of these purchases was required for rebuilding stocks. The reduction in the purchases of motor vehicles during the war periods was even more marked. In this case, however, consumption could not be maintained by drawing on the stock to the same extent. The shortage of petrol meant that very much less than normal use could be made of cars during these periods. It has been assumed that the years 1915–18 counted as a single year, and the years 1940–5 as two years, of normal depreciation (or consumption). Although consumption of this group fell off more markedly than any other, this was still much less than the fall in purchases, which were effectively nil for the years 1942–5. In the long run much the greater part of all consumer investment was due to the two groups, household durables and motor vehicles.

The consumption of all durables increased by some 60 % in the course of the period, compared with an increase of 45 % for non-durables. The rate of net investment, meanwhile, increased almost sevenfold, while the level of stocks doubled between 1900 and 1955. There was a moderate rise of less than 15 % in the level of stocks in the years up to 1914. During the inter-war period, once the losses of the war years were made good, the rate of accumulation was much more rapid and the level of the stock increased by more than 60 %. The effects of the Second World War extended far into the post-war years and it was not until the end of the period that the volume of total stocks was restored to the pre-war level.

In Table 70 an estimate of total consumption is obtained by deducting net investment in durables from total expenditure. It can be seen that, on the assumptions adoped here, the element of net investment in total expenditure is very small indeed for most years of the period, hardly more than 1 %. More striking, perhaps, is the volume of disinvestment during the years 1939–45, equal to one-fifth of the expenditure on durables. It is worth noting that in the earlier war period consumption was sustained to a very much smaller extent by disinvestment—the dividend of comfort and convenience to be derived from the possession of a stock of durable goods.

In this assessment of consumer stocks no account is taken of the housing position. The size and quality of the stock of dwellings is an important element of the standard of living and investment in this form has always been significant. But most consumers have always bought the service rather than acquired the asset and the usual convention of social accounting—treating the ownership of houses as part of the business sector—probably presents a more meaningful picture in this respect.

6 THE DATA

The long-term comparisons of the preceding sections of this chapter cannot be properly assessed without some knowledge of the data underlying them. A brief account of the sources and methods used to compile the series is given here.

The annual series have been constructed by combining the results of the present study with the corresponding

TABLE 67. ESTIMATED CONSUMPTION OF CONSUMER DURABLE GOODS: UNITED KINGDOM, 1900–55 (£ (1938) M.)

	1900–4	1905–9	1910–14	1915–19	1920–4	1925–9	1930–4	1935–8	1939–45	1946–50	1951–5
Clothing	338·9	331·2	367·3	290·2	351·0	384·0	402·4	430·3	329·0	398·5	447·5
Other semi-durables	27·2	30·7	34·4	37·2	41·4	43·2	47·7	53·8	40·4	41·9	49·2
Household durables	116·4	123·7	128·4	126·9	142·9	186·7	229·5	269·8	194·3	157·2	231·5
Motor-cars and other vehicles	3·9	4·4	5·5	3·4	10·0	20·6	28·0	40·7	17·3	27·2	36·6
Other durables	19·3	21·5	23·6	25·3	26·9	30·4	34·3	40·0	45·1	48·1	54·9
Total	505·7	511·5	559·2	483·0	572·2	664·9	741·9	834·6	626·1	672·9	819·7

TABLE 68. ESTIMATED NET INVESTMENT IN CONSUMER DURABLE GOODS: UNITED KINGDOM, 1900–55 (£ (1938) M.)

	1900–4	1905–9	1910–14	1915–19	1920–4	1925–9	1930–4	1935–8	1939–45	1946–50	1951–5
Clothing	−0·1	2·0	0·0	−0·6	5·7	4·7	0·7	4·5	−13·3	23·1	1·2
Other semi-durables	0·4	0·4	0·7	0·4	0·6	1·0	0·3	1·4	−2·7	2·1	2·1
Household durables	7·1	3·5	6·3	−7·3	34·0	31·3	29·0	19·6	−76·7	55·8	51·1
Motor-cars and other vehicles	0·8	0·8	2·5	0·9	5·6	9·8	5·7	13·7	−10·5	−0·7	23·0
Other durables	2·9	3·1	3·2	1·0	6·8	5·2	6·7	12·1	2·1	12·4	11·9
Total	11·1	9·8	12·7	−5·6	52·7	52·0	42·4	51·3	−101·1	92·7	89·3

TABLE 69. ESTIMATED AVERAGE STOCKS OF CONSUMER DURABLE GOODS: UNITED KINGDOM, 1900–55 (£ (1938) M.)

	1900–4	1905–9	1910–14	1915–19	1920–4	1925–9	1930–4	1935–8	1939–45	1946–50	1951–5
Clothing	209·8	206·4	226·0	186·0	216·6	238·1	250·3	266·0	208·6	243·3	281·2
Other semi-durables	17·5	19·8	22·2	24·0	27·2	29·9	33·5	37·3	28·0	28·0	34·8
Household durables	404·2	429·7	447·5	443·0	495·0	648·9	798·1	932·8	678·3	547·2	807·1
Motor-cars and other vehicles	6·2	11·3	18·5	24·4	39·4	82·8	114·7	164·0	154·3	109·2	149·3
Other durables	130·6	146·0	161·0	171·4	182·1	209·0	238·4	279·2	316·9	350·2	407·6
Total	768·3	813·2	875·2	848·8	960·3	1,208·7	1,435·0	1,679·3	1,386·1	1,277·9	1,680·0

TABLE 70. ESTIMATED TOTAL CONSUMPTION AT CONSTANT (1938) PRICES: UNITED KINGDOM, 1900–55

	1900–4	1905–9	1910–14	1915–19	1920–4	1925–9	1930–4	1935–8	1939–45	1946–50	1951–5
Expenditure on non-durables (£ (1938) m.)	2,736·9	2,781·9	2,856·0	2,648·7	2,734·0	2,976·3	3,189·2	3,490·9	3,260·9	3,775·6	4,017·0
Expenditure on durables	516·8	521·3	571·9	477·4	624·9	716·9	784·3	885·9	525·0	765·6	909·0
Less net investment	−11·1	−9·8	−12·7	5·6	−52·7	−52·0	−42·4	−51·3	101·1	−92·7	−89·3
Total consumption	3,242·6	3,293·4	3,415·2	3,131·7	3,306·2	3,641·2	3,931·1	4,325·5	3,887·0	4,448·5	4,836·7
Consumption per head (£ (1938))	77·3	75·3	75·1	72·5	74·6	80·2	84·9	91·7	86·5	91·2	95·5
Index (1938 = 100·0)	82·6	80·3	80·2	77·4	79·5	85·5	90·5	97·7	92·3	97·3	102·0

estimates for 1900–19[1] and the official figures that have been produced for the years from 1938 onwards.[2] Because of differences of classification and treatment in these sources the definitions adopted for the present purpose are something of a compromise, and a number of adjustments have had to be made to the published data.

For the years 1900–19 the figures relate to Great Britain and Ireland; thereafter Southern Ireland is excluded.

The estimates of total expenditure differ from the concept of consumers' expenditure, as usually defined, by the omission of the adjustment items: income in kind of the Armed Forces and the net balance of travellers' expenditures. The figures are, therefore, more strictly estimates of civilian purchases made in the United Kingdom.

The composition of the main groups is as follows:

(1) *Food:* includes all foods and non-alcoholic beverages. The imputed value of output from backyard poultry, gardens and allotments, is excluded. Food consumed in hotels and restaurants is valued at retail prices.

(2) *Alcoholic drink:* beer, wines, spirits, etc., excluding table waters.

(3) *Tobacco:* all tobacco and tobacco products.

(4) *Rent, rates and water charges:* excludes occupiers' maintenance costs which are regarded as part of gross capital formation and excluded from consumers' expenditure; this treatment is adopted throughout the estimates for 1900–45 and was followed in the official figures until 1952, when these expenses were transferred to consumers' expenditure.[3]

(5) *Fuel and light:* coal, gas, electricity, etc., excluding gas and electricity rentals.

(6) *Clothing:* footwear and other clothing, excluding expenditure on repairs.

(7) *Household durable goods:* furniture and furnishings, radio and electrical goods, hardware, pottery and glassware.

(8) *Transport and communications:* all public and private transport (including purchases of new vehicles and the margin on second-hand sales) and communication services.

(9) *Other goods:* includes other household goods, books, etc., fancy goods, toys and sports goods, drugs and medical appliances.

(10) *Other services:* includes domestic service, entertainments, insurance and other miscellaneous services.

In combining the data from the different sources an effort has been made to remove the more serious inconsistencies of classification and treatment. The discrepancies remaining are likely to be negligible compared with the inevitable errors of estimation. Because of bias in the estimates there are possibilities of larger errors arising

at the points where series from different sources are linked together. In each case, however, the change to a new source occurs at a time when conditions were disturbed and there seemed to be little justification for introducing an arbitrary set of smoothing adjustments. The 'other services' group perhaps shows the most marked discontinuities. While the average level of expenditure on many service items is reasonably well estimated in each period, there is very little information to establish the actual year-to-year variations and the discrepancy would tend to be largest at the extreme points of the series.[4]

It did seem justifiable, however, to adjust the published figures for the period 1939-45 in the light of the latest revisions to the estimates for 1938 and 1946. Although the wartime estimates for commodities subject to rationing and control are likely to have a high degree of reliability, in many cases higher than for later years, the revisions to the 1946 figures strongly suggest that comparable adjustments should be carried through for earlier years as well. It has been assumed that the percentage discrepancy accumulated linearly through the war years, the same correction factors being applied to the figures at current and constant prices.

For the years 1900–38 expenditures at constant prices were calculated by revaluing at 1938 prices as many individual items as possible; there are published figures for 1939–45 compiled in the same way. A different procedure had to be adopted for the years 1946–55. For this period there are published estimates at current and at 1948 prices. The breakdown is much less detailed than that available for the years before 1938 and it is not possible to revalue individual commodities in these years but only the component groups and sub-groups specified. If this is done for as many individual items as possible, the approximation for the main groups will probably be satisfactory. There are two alternative ways of calculating the price links for 1938–48. On the one hand, it is possible to calculate for each item, in 1955 say,

$$\Sigma p_{38} q_{55} \simeq \Sigma p_{48} q_{55} \div (\Sigma p_{48} q_{48} / \Sigma p_{38} q_{48}),$$

where the term in brackets on the right-hand side is the current-weighted (Paasche) form of aggregative price

[1] [87] Prest, *Consumers' Expenditure in the United Kingdom, 1900–1919* (1954).

[2] [58] *Statistical Digest of the War* (1951), and [61] *National Income and Expenditure 1957.*

[3] See [60] *National Income Statistics: Sources and Methods* (1956), pp. 281–2.

[4] The estimates of expenditure on domestic service present perhaps the most serious problem. Although this was the largest single item in the group, before 1948 the only source of information about the number of domestic servants was the Census; even less was known about average earnings. In this connexion see [87] Prest, *Consumers' Expenditure in the United Kingdom, 1900–1919,* p. 118; [69] Chapman, *Wages and Salaries in the United Kingdom, 1920–1938,* pp. 216–17; and [60] *National Income Statistics: Sources and Methods* (1956), pp. 131–2.

index.[1] The gradual abolition of rationing and other causes probably resulted in considerable changes in the quantity pattern between 1948 and 1955, but it seems likely that this would be less marked within the individual groups and would naturally diminish for years closer to 1948.

Alternatively, it would be possible to calculate

$$\Sigma p_{38} q_{55} \simeq \Sigma p_{48} q_{55} \div (\Sigma p_{48} q_{38} / \Sigma p_{38} q_{38}),$$

where the price index takes the base-weighted (Laspeyres) form.[2] Although it might be argued that in these years consumption had tended to return to the pre-war pattern, it is probable that the much wider gap in time would produce a larger discrepancy compared with the first formula.[3]

The component food items presented special problems and required more extensive adjustment of the published data to obtain consistent series. The grouping adopted necessarily follows the classification of the official figures since no further detail is available with respect to these estimates.

The composition of the groups is briefly as follows:

(1) *Bread and cereals:* bread, flour, cakes, biscuits, and miscellaneous cereals and cereal products, including custard and blancmange powders.

(2) *Meat and bacon:* all meat and meat products, bacon and ham, rabbits, game and poultry.

(3) *Fish:* fresh, frozen, cured and canned fish, including shell fish and fish sold by fish fryers.

(4) *Dairy products and eggs:* liquid and condensed milk, cream, cheese, and eggs.

(5) *Oils and fats:* butter, margarine, lard and other edible fats.

(6) *Vegetables:* all fresh, dried, canned and frozen vegetables, pickles and sauces.

(7) *Fruit and nuts:* fresh, canned and frozen fruit, preserved fruits and nuts.

(8) *Sugar, preserves and confectionery:* sugar, syrup and treacle, jam, marmalade and other preserves, chocolate and sugar confectionery.

(9) *Beverages:* tea, coffee and coffee essence, cocoa, soft drinks and table waters.

(10) *Other food:* infant and invalid foods, condiments, ice cream, and other miscellaneous manufactured foods.

The imputed value of output from backyard poultry, and from gardens and allotments, which is not included in the published figures for 1939–55, has been excluded from the series altogether.

In the published estimates for 1900–19, certain manufactured foods (cakes and biscuits, meat products, ham, etc.) are not given separately but are accounted for under their component ingredients, the costs of processing

being included with 'other food'. An attempt has been made to reconstitute these composite foods under their proper headings. This could not be done at all precisely, but it was possible to make simple adjustments of the appropriate order of magnitude. From an estimate of expenditure in 1920 calculated in both ways,[4] the individual items could be identified and a constant proportion of each ingredient and of other costs could be transferred to the new grouping for each year.

The published figures for 1939–55 include an estimate of 'other personal expenditure', representing purchases of food going to caterers, canteens, schools, and institutions, which is valued mainly at wholesale prices. To maintain comparability with the earlier figures, it was necessary to revalue this expenditure at retail prices and to distribute the sum between the separate food groups. Again, it was not possible to make a precise adjustment. On the basis of a detailed analysis for 1938, a first approximation was obtained by assuming a fixed proportion of each category going to caterers in all years. These estimates were then adjusted *pro rata* to coincide with an estimate of the total revalued at retail prices by the addition of a fixed percentage margin. To offset this addition to food expenditure, a corresponding deduction was made from 'other services', which includes all other catering costs.

Estimates of expenditure on food at constant (1938) prices for the period 1900–38 were obtained in the same way as for the main expenditure groups. For the war period 1939–45 there are no published figures of expenditure at constant prices for individual food groups and only the total can be shown. For the years 1946–55 there are figures for individual groups of expenditure at both current and 1948 prices, but no comparable figures at 1948 prices for 1938. To obtain estimates at 1938 prices for these years, therefore, only the first of the alternatives mentioned above was available; in effect, to apply an aggregative price index number with 1948 weights.[5]

Except for the war and immediate post-war years—1915–19 and 1940–50—expenditure per head was calculated by dividing through by the total population. During the war periods little of the expenditure included

[1] Price index numbers in this form for all items of expenditure except food are given in [46] *National Income and Expenditure of the United Kingdom 1946 to 1948*, Cmd 7649 (1949), table 21, pp. 28–9.

[2] [61] *National Income and Expenditure 1957*, table 21, pp. 18–19.

[3] It may be noted that, apart from the difference in (expenditure) weights, the first index is an harmonic mean of the price ratios and would therefore be likely to be lower than the second index which is an arithmetic mean. There is a further difficulty in comparing the two on account of the revision of the data. But comparison with more recent estimates suggested that for most items no major revisions of the price series had been made. The figures from Cmd 7649 have been used, subject only to a few minor adjustments.

[4] [87] Prest, *Consumers' Expenditure in the United Kingdom, 1900–1919*, p. 184.

[5] See [46] Cmd 7649.

TABLE 71. ANNUAL ESTIMATES OF CONSUMERS' EXPENDITURE AT CURRENT PRICES: UNITED KINGDOM, 1900–55 (£ M.)

Year	Food	Alcoholic drink	Tobacco	Rents, etc.	Fuel and light	Clothing	Durable household goods	Transport and communications	Other goods	Other services	Total
1900	531	187	27	177	78	153	58	87	76	252	1,626
1901	543	185	28	184	74	162	58	90	77	260	1,661
1902	551	183	29	191	73	153	58	94	79	259	1,670
1903	568	179	30	196	71	149	56	95	82	263	1,689
1904	572	173	30	201	71	154	59	96	85	269	1,710
1905	578	172	31	204	67	157	58	98	89	275	1,729
1906	588	171	32	208	67	161	58	102	92	280	1,759
1907	598	171	33	211	77	162	64	103	98	287	1,804
1908	603	163	33	213	74	168	64	100	93	292	1,803
1909	616	154	34	221	71	174	61	101	95	294	1,821
1910	628	163	37	221	71	178	61	109	98	300	1,866
1911	648	169	38	222	72	195	64	111	102	305	1,926
1912	679	168	39	225	77	202	67	118	107	313	1,995
1913	693	175	40	230	79	210	76	124	111	320	2,058
1914	667	188	42	234	77	173	75	117	111	322	2,006
1915	834	179	49	237	87	193	82	121	127	330	2,239
1916	947	207	56	237	105	169	81	121	150	330	2,403
1917	1,119	201	65	239	115	212	105	132	176	354	2,718
1918	1,269	232	80	246	134	364	140	154	229	429	3,277
1919	1,518	391	115	264	160	669	211	251	257	589	4,425
1920	1,716	450	120	292	179	795	309	265	317	618	5,061
1921	1,552	409	116	340	172	485	217	247	283	569	4,390
1922	1,297	356	112	353	160	434	198	254	249	494	3,907
1923	1,293	332	109	347	150	409	192	252	227	476	3,787
1924	1,305	337	112	345	162	418	192	267	224	490	3,852
1925	1,339	338	116	349	160	432	200	286	227	506	3,953
1926	1,317	323	117	360	146	417	197	287	234	514	3,912
1927	1,299	320	124	374	168	424	210	289	237	526	3,971
1928	1,317	310	132	382	154	435	217	295	242	540	4,024
1929	1,315	311	136	392	164	439	224	293	241	553	4,068
1930	1,275	301	139	403	164	418	225	288	240	559	4,012
1931	1,204	282	140	410	163	395	218	266	237	557	3,872
1932	1,154	264	139	415	158	364	209	265	225	558	3,751
1933	1,121	258	142	423	159	366	218	273	233	564	3,757
1934	1,148	262	146	432	163	371	237	290	245	575	3,869
1935	1,179	273	153	447	165	388	249	305	252	593	4,004
1936	1,212	283	161	462	177	402	260	319	265	613	4,154
1937	1,276	297	169	475	186	426	277	333	292	631	4,362
1938	1,301	294	176	488	189	438	264	343	311	660	4,464
1939	1,386	313	204	510	200	461	226	315	318	545	4,478
1940	1,440	383	260	519	224	501	218	237	323	546	4,651
1941	1,502	477	317	515	240	460	205	264	326	567	4,873
1942	1,553	563	415	509	242	498	184	279	319	568	5,130
1943	1,487	653	492	511	238	441	151	291	327	577	5,168
1944	1,580	701	509	516	246	510	138	301	344	595	5,440
1945	1,635	732	564	534	267	534	189	363	376	669	5,863
1946	1,876	726	602	548	278	638	334	496	470	849	6,817
1947	2,179	750	689	580	298	736	426	550	527	861	7,596
1948	2,345	826	764	604	324	902	479	536	568	866	8,214
1949	2,557	769	753	620	332	1,013	540	581	605	815	8,585
1950	2,829	759	766	641	353	1,063	617	616	628	824	9,096
1951	3,093	794	800	673	388	1,110	701	675	674	856	9,764
1952	3,397	799	821	706	421	1,083	675	771	705	891	10,269
1953	3,704	814	837	758	447	1,092	744	876	740	911	10,923
1954	3,955	823	855	795	485	1,174	832	959	776	942	11,596
1955	4,258	861	880	837	521	1,268	903	1,106	815	965	12,414

TABLE 72. ANNUAL ESTIMATES OF CONSUMERS' EXPENDITURE AT CONSTANT (1938) PRICES: UNITED KINGDOM, 1900–55 (£ (1938) M.)

Year	Food	Alcoholic drink	Tobacco	Rents, etc.	Fuel and light	Clothing	Durable household goods	Transport and communications	Other goods	Other services	Total
1900	879	615	72	283	132	342	122	104	127	551	3,227
1901	890	610	70	289	132	357	124	107	129	559	3,267
1902	891	601	72	293	137	339	125	109	133	557	3,257
1903	908	581	74	298	135	326	120	109	135	558	3,244
1904	924	567	75	303	136	331	127	108	139	563	3,273
1905	928	558	76	307	129	325	124	110	144	568	3,269
1906	944	554	77	311	128	328	125	113	149	570	3,299
1907	949	556	79	316	138	326	132	115	153	567	3,331
1908	946	529	79	319	135	338	131	115	148	580	3,320
1909	957	486	77	323	135	350	124	117	148	581	3,298
1910	951	484	79	326	138	353	125	124	154	585	3,319
1911	988	502	83	330	142	378	128	127	159	585	3,422
1912	984	500	83	334	128	379	132	132	164	595	3,431
1913	993	519	86	337	140	391	146	141	172	597	3,522
1914	994	508	89	342	138	336	143	133	171	592	3,446
1915	969	490	96	343	147	363	136	135	176	579	3,434
1916	908	435	91	343	146	253	109	134	174	538	3,131
1917	836	301	92	344	142	236	104	111	168	505	2,839
1918	829	287	95	346	127	226	109	127	183	490	2,819
1919	961	428	127	349	136	369	140	179	180	540	3,409
1920	924	419	118	364	141	383	183	183	211	454	3,380
1921	955	363	115	365	122	316	150	169	197	445	3,197
1922	1,001	319	111	368	138	357	175	183	203	455	3,310
1923	1,057	321	109	371	142	361	188	196	205	462	3,412
1924	1,074	336	112	374	151	366	189	211	206	476	3,495
1925	1,084	338	116	378	153	373	199	229	216	489	3,575
1926	1,093	323	118	385	133	374	202	232	210	498	3,568
1927	1,117	321	123	394	164	395	221	242	219	515	3,711
1928	1,140	310	128	402	159	397	229	250	224	530	3,769
1929	1,150	310	133	408	166	405	239	256	232	545	3,844
1930	1,185	300	136	417	165	401	242	257	237	561	3,901
1931	1,229	273	137	423	164	408	246	244	238	572	3,934
1932	1,239	238	134	428	160	392	254	247	237	583	3,912
1933	1,235	250	139	434	163	405	265	261	247	597	3,996
1934	1,267	262	143	442	167	410	285	282	259	608	4,125
1935	1,263	273	150	454	173	425	301	303	273	623	4,238
1936	1,283	283	159	466	181	439	304	322	287	639	4,363
1937	1,296	296	168	478	188	437	290	336	303	650	4,442
1938	1,301	294	176	488	189	438	264	343	311	660	4,464
1939	1,344	299	182	504	199	447	222	314	312	540	4,363
1940	1,177	281	178	508	203	376	169	211	286	495	3,884
1941	1,118	296	196	502	205	280	120	221	248	491	3,677
1942	1,149	277	206	497	199	279	85	239	219	462	3,612
1943	1,111	281	204	498	187	254	72	249	220	440	3,516
1944	1,173	289	205	503	193	284	65	258	228	431	3,629
1945	1,192	316	225	506	197	290	90	305	237	462	3,820
1946	1,332	299	235	511	208	346	166	354	278	557	4,286
1947	1,418	302	206	520	219	389	200	388	300	554	4,496
1948	1,432	287	197	528	224	432	209	375	309	538	4,531
1949	1,501	276	191	533	223	462	233	398	329	486	4,632
1950	1,571	282	193	535	234	479	257	404	333	473	4,761
1951	1,550	290	199	537	247	432	254	414	326	467	4,716
1952	1,543	287	202	541	244	425	239	430	324	470	4,705
1953	1,595	290	206	547	248	435	273	471	347	471	4,883
1954	1,638	294	210	558	260	461	312	500	370	475	5,078
1955	1,658	305	215	569	271	491	335	546	382	476	5,248

TABLE 73. ANNUAL ESTIMATES OF FOOD EXPENDITURE AT CURRENT PRICES: UNITED KINGDOM, 1900–55 (£ M.)

Year	Bread and cereals	Meat and bacon	Fish	Dairy products	Oils and fats	Vege-tables	Fruit and nuts	Sugar, preserves and con-fectionery	Beverages	Other foods	Total
1900	83	167	20	70	45	40	21	50	31	4	531
1901	80	174	19	69	48	40	21	55	33	4	543
1902	87	174	20	70	48	41	23	51	33	4	551
1903	96	176	20	72	48	44	24	51	33	4	568
1904	96	173	19	73	49	44	24	56	34	4	572
1905	97	172	19	75	51	42	25	59	34	4	578
1906	97	176	21	79	54	41	26	56	34	4	588
1907	102	176	20	80	52	41	27	61	35	4	598
1908	101	178	21	80	55	43	27	59	35	4	603
1909	109	183	21	82	52	45	25	60	35	4	616
1910	111	187	22	81	54	41	25	67	36	4	628
1911	105	189	22	86	57	50	29	70	36	4	648
1912	118	197	25	87	58	50	27	75	37	5	679
1913	120	207	26	86	60	50	29	73	37	5	693
1914	107	200	27	87	58	49	29	68	37	5	667
1915	144	248	29	94	75	52	32	111	44	5	834
1916	165	297	32	106	76	63	39	114	49	6	947
1917	220	352	42	124	90	90	34	104	55	8	1,119
1918	203	424	58	145	100	110	48	103	69	9	1,269
1919	218	441	73	189	119	123	103	165	77	10	1,518
1920	253	493	76	234	122	121	107	221	82	7	1,716
1921	230	485	60	212	107	111	88	174	77	8	1,552
1922	185	400	52	166	85	100	82	151	68	8	1,297
1923	179	415	50	168	92	83	84	146	69	7	1,293
1924	188	403	54	164	97	99	85	141	67	7	1,305
1925	193	423	52	171	106	96	91	130	69	8	1,339
1926	194	419	51	170	103	87	89	126	70	8	1,317
1927	195	401	51	170	99	90	91	123	70	9	1,299
1928	186	405	55	177	104	100	88	122	71	9	1,317
1929	182	412	57	177	107	93	95	116	66	10	1,315
1930	180	404	55	176	97	89	88	110	65	11	1,275
1931	159	374	50	165	90	99	86	106	63	12	1,204
1932	162	340	46	163	85	100	84	101	60	13	1,154
1933	162	334	44	157	80	90	84	96	60	14	1,121
1934	164	347	48	165	75	94	82	94	63	16	1,148
1935	172	348	49	167	83	97	85	96	64	18	1,179
1936	179	348	49	180	90	103	78	99	67	19	1,212
1937	202	363	51	186	97	103	80	104	69	21	1,276
1938	191	377	51	200	97	105	79	106	72	23	1,301
1939	222	338	70	207	80	121	88	124	76	60	1,386
1940	254	359	66	203	63	121	85	136	74	79	1,440
1941	298	336	82	243	61	159	37	126	77	83	1,502
1942	293	360	63	256	57	179	63	121	73	88	1,553
1943	271	349	61	249	58	176	52	116	68	87	1,487
1944	275	395	72	254	60	194	57	111	72	90	1,580
1945	281	363	100	271	60	205	67	105	83	100	1,635
1946	325	350	114	321	71	225	120	124	99	127	1,876
1947	375	367	122	322	70	302	213	164	108	136	2,179
1948	402	360	125	394	82	319	232	199	117	115	2,345
1949	464	423	106	444	101	337	224	215	122	121	2,557
1950	493	587	106	472	122	336	227	217	123	146	2,829
1951	539	582	137	487	146	370	264	269	129	170	3,093
1952	568	756	134	550	149	395	227	281	153	184	3,397
1953	580	839	122	599	182	380	277	380	172	173	3,704
1954	558	942	131	589	234	412	315	405	201	168	3,955
1955	558	1,057	142	624	248	460	351	408	238	172	4,258

TABLE 74. ANNUAL ESTIMATES OF FOOD EXPENDITURE AT CONSTANT (1938) PRICES: UNITED KINGDOM, 1900–55 (£ (1938) M.)

Year	Bread and cereals	Meat and bacon	Fish	Dairy products	Oils and fats	Vege-tables	Fruit and nuts	Sugar, preserves and con-fectionery	Beverages	Other foods	Total
1900	131	317	36	121	53	51	42	83	42	3	879
1901	130	322	36	121	55	52	44	84	43	3	890
1902	136	308	41	121	57	58	43	81	43	3	891
1903	144	316	41	124	57	55	45	79	43	4	908
1904	142	318	41	129	59	56	48	85	43	3	924
1905	142	319	40	130	60	61	50	80	43	3	928
1906	145	319	44	134	61	60	49	85	44	3	944
1907	146	317	45	135	60	58	52	88	45	3	949
1908	137	321	45	135	61	58	54	87	45	3	946
1909	141	318	47	137	59	66	51	90	46	2	957
1910	148	310	48	137	61	63	45	90	46	3	951
1911	146	331	48	141	62	64	53	94	46	3	988
1912	157	329	46	139	61	58	49	95	46	4	984
1913	157	327	48	137	65	60	50	99	47	3	993
1914	147	318	56	139	63	62	57	101	48	3	994
1915	146	320	34	128	68	57	56	110	47	3	969
1916	147	312	33	118	58	48	51	93	45	3	908
1917	158	290	31	107	53	43	36	74	42	2	836
1918	163	293	33	97	50	52	24	64	49	4	829
1919	167	312	45	111	58	59	62	85	57	5	961
1920	149	291	49	133	52	71	49	69	58	3	924
1921	143	311	42	139	60	73	54	69	60	4	955
1922	150	320	45	145	64	78	62	75	58	4	1,001
1923	154	354	42	152	69	81	69	73	58	5	1,057
1924	159	356	46	150	69	82	73	76	59	4	1,074
1925	150	354	47	155	72	82	77	82	60	5	1,084
1926	155	350	45	162	74	83	75	83	61	5	1,093
1927	159	361	48	164	74	80	79	84	62	6	1,117
1928	159	371	48	166	77	90	73	86	64	6	1,140
1929	160	361	49	167	79	89	85	88	65	7	1,150
1930	165	368	52	177	82	94	84	88	67	8	1,185
1931	171	390	50	180	87	101	82	91	68	9	1,229
1932	173	391	49	184	88	101	83	91	69	10	1,239
1933	175	380	47	177	95	98	90	93	68	12	1,235
1934	182	372	48	194	98	99	97	95	68	14	1,267
1935	180	375	49	193	98	99	84	100	70	15	1,263
1936	183	375	51	197	98	103	84	104	71	17	1,283
1937	188	375	54	197	98	100	87	106	71	20	1,296
1938	191	377	51	200	97	105	79	106	72	23	1,301
1939	..	..	..	..	..	..	..	..	..	..	1,344
1940	..	..	..	..	..	..	..	..	..	..	1,177
1941	..	..	..	..	..	..	..	..	..	..	1,118
1942	..	..	..	..	..	..	..	..	..	..	1,149
1943	..	..	..	..	..	..	..	..	..	..	1,111
1944	..	..	..	..	..	..	..	..	..	..	1,173
1945	..	..	..	..	..	..	..	..	..	..	1,192
1946	201	291	88	247	61	142	77	76	70	79	1,332
1947	214	279	93	245	62	164	113	94	74	80	1,418
1948	219	261	90	268	72	159	123	92	76	72	1,432
1949	221	274	78	295	84	163	126	106	79	75	1,501
1950	216	352	63	304	89	160	122	103	78	84	1,571
1951	219	297	71	291	85	163	134	119	77	94	1,550
1952	216	326	64	282	78	163	119	117	80	98	1,543
1953	210	348	57	286	79	162	130	150	83	90	1,595
1954	202	366	59	295	83	164	145	154	84	86	1,638
1955	202	375	62	291	87	162	150	152	88	89	1,658

here would represent consumption by those in the Armed Forces. Many were serving abroad and for the rest the greater part of living expenses would be received as income in kind. Accordingly, in these years expenditures are calculated per head of the civilian population only. Even for the immediate post-war years 1946-50, it seems best to exclude those in the services; by 1951 the two series differ by less than 1.%.[1]

Apart from the discrepancies due to inadequate data and inconsistencies of treatment, the series are also subject to all the ambiguities associated with the interpretation of index numbers. It is well known that the ordinary index number, of the type used here, fails to take proper account of quality changes attendant upon technical innovations and the introduction of new products. Nevertheless, it remains useful to the extent that a broad degree of similarity pertains over the greater part of the field of comparison. There are also other inherent ambiguities. For instance, expenditure revalued at 1938 prices has been used here as a measure of the volume of consumption, but a different result would have been obtained if the prices of another year had been chosen instead. In general, the earlier the price set used, the greater would be the proportionate increase in volume over the period as a whole;[2] for the price series, which are obtained as a ratio of value and volume, the increase would be correspondingly reduced. An alternative procedure would be to construct price indices with fixed expenditure weights, and then derive volume estimates as a ratio of value and price. There would be a further large number of variants according to the weights adopted. In the present instance, 1938 has been chosen as the base year for reasons of computational expediency; but it is also a year near enough to the middle of the period to provide a convenient compromise between the more extreme positions. Some additional discrepancy must be incurred for the later years of the period, where it has not been possible to revalue individual commodities at 1938 prices in any detail.

The annual estimates of expenditure at current and constant (1938) prices, which form the basis of all the

TABLE 75. ESTIMATED HOME[a] POPULATION IN THE UNITED KINGDOM, 1900-55 (M.)

Year	Population	Year	Population	Year	Population
1900	41·20	1920	43·74	1940	46·00
1901	41·54	1921	44·02	1941	44·85
1902	41·93	1922	44·33	1942	44·30
1903	42·25	1923	44·55	1943	43·77
1904	42·73	1924	44·92	1944	43·74
1905	42·98	1925	45·06	1945	43·87
1906	43·38	1926	45·23	1946	47·03
1907	43·73	1927	45·39	1947	48·14
1908	44·21	1928	45·58	1948	49·21
1909	44·55	1929	45·67	1949	49·59
1910	44·91	1930	45·87	1950	49·92
1911	45·27	1931	46·07	1951	50·30
1912	45·45	1932	46·34	1952	50·44
1913	45·67	1933	46·52	1953	50·61
1914	46·06	1934	46·67	1954	50·78
1915	43·91	1935	46·87	1955	50·97
1916	43·04	1936	47·08		
1917	42·49	1937	47·29		
1918	42·26	1938	47·49		
1919	44·06	1939	47·76		

[a] Civilian population only in the years 1915-19 and 1940-50.

material presented in the earlier sections of this chapter, are shown in Tables 71-74. The estimates of population used to calculate the per head figures are shown in Table 75.

[1] The sources for the population figures are as follows: for 1900-19, see [82] Prest, Consumers' Expenditure in the United Kingdom, 1900-1919, p. 178; for 1920-38, see Vol. 1 of this study, p. 414; for 1939-55, see the Monthly Digest of Statistics, passim.

[2] Some indication of the magnitudes involved may be obtained by a direct comparison of expenditures in 1900 and 1955, each revalued in terms of the other year's prices. It was not possible to do this in great detail, but the nineteen subgroups—ten food and nine non-food—were treated as individual commodities for this purpose. At 1900 prices the increase in total expenditure between 1900 and 1955 was 51·8%, while at 1955 prices it was only 27·9%.

A LIST OF WORKS CITED

I. OFFICIAL PUBLICATIONS

(A) GOVERNMENT RETURNS, STATISTICS, ETC.

[1] *Accounts relating to Trade and Navigation of the United Kingdom* (Board of Trade), H.C. Paper, monthly.

[2] *Annual Abstract of Statistics* (Central Statistical Office), annual from No. 84, published 1948. For earlier numbers see item [20].

[3] *Annual Report of the Chief Medical Officer of the Board of Education* (Board of Education).

[4] *Annual Report of the Chief Medical Officer of the Ministry of Health* (Ministry of Health).

[5] *Annual Report of the Department of Health for Scotland,* Command Paper.

[6] *Annual Report of the Ministry of Health,* Command Paper.

[7] *Annual Report of the Traffic Commissioners* (Ministry of Transport), from 1931.

[8] *Annual Statement of the Trade of the United Kingdom* (Customs and Excise).

[9] *Assurance Companies Returns* (Board of Trade), annual.

[10] *Local Government Financial Statistics, England and Wales* (Ministry of Health to 1949, later Ministry of Housing and Local Government), annual.

[11] *Persons in receipt of Poor Relief, England and Wales* (Ministry of Health), H.C. Paper, annual.

[12] *Post Office Commercial Accounts* (Post Office), H.C. Paper, annual.

[13] *Racecourse Betting Control Board—Annual Report and Accounts* (Home Office), H.C. Paper, annual from 1929.

[14] *Railway Returns: Returns of the Capital, Traffic, Receipts and Working Expenditure, etc., of the Railway Companies of Great Britain* (Ministry of Transport), annual.

[15] *Report of the Commissioners of H.M. Inland Revenue* (Board of Inland Revenue), Command Paper, annual.

[16] *Report of the Commissioners of H.M. Customs and Excise* (Board of Customs and Excise), Command Paper, annual.

[17] *Report of the Industrial Assurance Commissioner* (Registry of Friendly Societies), H.C. Paper, annual.

[18] *Reports of the Chief Registrar of Friendly Societies, part 4, Trade Unions* (Registry of Friendly Societies), annual.

[19] *Road Vehicles—Great Britain* (Ministry of Transport), monthly.

[20] *Statistical Abstract for the United Kingdom,* Command Paper, annual up to the 83rd number, published 1940. For later numbers in the series see item [2].

[21] *Statistics in regard to Alien Passengers who entered and left the United Kingdom* (Home Office), Command Paper, annual.

[22] *The Ulster Year Book* (Ministry of Finance, Northern Ireland).

[23] *Tramways and Light Railways (Street and Road) and Trolley Vehicle Undertakings* (Ministry of Transport), annual.

(B) CENSUS REPORTS

[24] *Census of England and Wales, 1921.*

[25] *Census of England and Wales, 1931.*

[26] *Report of the 13th Decennial Census of Scotland, 1921.*

[27] *Report of the 14th Decennial Census of Scotland, 1931.*

[28] *Census of Population of Northern Ireland, 1926.*

[29] *Census of Population of Northern Ireland, 1937.*

[30] *Census of Production of the United Kingdom, Final Report, 1924 (Third)* (Board of Trade).

[31] *Census of Production of the United Kingdom, Final Report, 1930 (Fourth)* (Board of Trade).

[32] *Final Report on the Fifth Census of Production and the Import Duties Act Inquiry, 1935* (Board of Trade).

[33] *Report on the Import Duties Act Inquiry (1933)* (Board of Trade).

[34] *Report on the Import Duties Act Inquiry (1934)* (Board of Trade).

[35] *Final Report on the Census of Production for 1948* (Board of (Trade.)

[36] *Census of Distribution and Other Services, 1950* (Board of Trade).

(C) COMMAND PAPERS

[37] *Report of the Committee on the Inland Telegraph Service,* Cmd 3058, 1928.

[38] *Report of the Committee of Enquiry on the Post Office,* Cmd 4149, 1932.

[39] *Interim Report of the Royal Commission on Lotteries and Betting 1932–3,* Cmd 4234, 1933.

[40] *Final Report of the Royal Commission on Lotteries and Betting 1932–3,* Cmd 4341, 1934.

[41] *Eighty-second Report of the Charity Commissioners for England and Wales, for 1934,* Cmd 4857, 1935.

[42] *The British Broadcasting Corporation—Twelfth Annual Report, 1938,* Cmd 5951, 1939.

[43] *Report of the Inter-Departmental Committee on Remuneration of General Practitioners,* Cmd 6810, 1946.

[44] *Report of the Inter-Departmental Committee on the Remuneration of General Dental Practitioners,* Cmd 7402, 1948.

[45] *Report of the Inter-Departmental Committee on the Remuneration of Consultants and Specialists,* Cmd 7420, 1948.

[46] *National Income and Expenditure of the United Kingdom 1946 to 1948,* Cmd 7649, 1949.

[47] *Report of the Royal Commission on Betting, Lotteries and Gaming 1949–51,* Cmd 8190, 1951.

(D) OTHER OFFICIAL PUBLICATIONS

[48] *Report of the Select Committee on Betting Duty,* H.C. Paper 139, 1923.

[49] *Report of the Select Committee on Medicine Stamp Duties,* H.C. Paper 54, 1936–7.

[50] The Monopolies and Restrictive Practices Commission, *Report on the Supply of Electric Lamps*, H.C. Paper 287, 1950–1.

[51] Air Ministry, *The Civil Aviation Statistical and Technical Review*, 1938.

[52] Board of Education, *Report of the Departmental Committee on Private Schools and Others not in receipt of Grants from Public Funds*, 1932.

[53] Board of Trade, *Board of Trade Journal*.

[54] Board of Trade, Committee on Industry and Trade, *Survey of Metal Industries, being part IV of a Survey of Industries*, 1928.

[55] Central Office of Information, *Expenditure on Repairs and Alterations to Domestic Property, on Gardens, Removals and Domestic Service* (by W. F. F. Kemsley and David Ginsburg), The Social Survey, n.s. 704/3, 1950.

[56] Central Office of Information, *Expenditure on hairdressing, cosmetics and toilet necessities* (by W. F. F. Kemsley and David Ginsburg), The Social Survey, n.s. 708/2, 1950.

[57] Central Office of Information, *Holidays and Holiday Expenditure* (by W. F. F. Kemsley and David Ginsburg), The Social Survey, n.s. 709/2, 1949.

[58] Central Statistical Office, *Statistical Digest of the War*, 1951.

[59] Central Statistical Office, *National Income and Expenditure 1955*, 1955.

[60] Central Statistical Office, *National Income Statistics: Sources and Methods*, 1956.

[61] Central Statistical Office, *National Income and Expenditure 1957*, 1957.

[62] Ministry of Labour, *Ministry of Labour Gazette;* especially 'Weekly expenditure of working-class households in the United Kingdom in 1937–38', December 1940, January 1941, February 1941.

[63] Post Office, *Telegraph Census*, by Elsie M. Tostevin and F. W. Fox, no. 14 of the Post Office Green Papers, 1935.

[64] League of Nations, *Balance of Payments 1938*, Economic Intelligence Service, Geneva, 1939.

[64a] United Nations, *A System of National Accounts and Supporting Tables*, Statistical Papers series F, no. 2, New York, 1953.

II. BOOKS AND ARTICLES

[65] Allen, G. C., *British Industries and their Organization*, 2nd ed., London, 1935.

[66] Braithwaite, Constance, *The Voluntary Citizen*, London, 1938.

[67] Browning, H. E. and A. A. Sorrell, 'Cinemas and cinema-going in Great Britain', *J. R. Statist. Soc.* series A, vol. CXVII, 1954, part II, p. 133.

[68] Carr-Saunders, A. M. and P. A. Wilson, *The Professions*, Oxford, 1933.

[69] Chapman, Agatha L., assisted by Rose Knight, *Wages and Salaries in the United Kingdom, 1920–1938*, Studies in the National Income and Expenditure of the United Kingdom no. 5, Cambridge University Press, 1952.

[70] Deane, Marjorie, 'United Kingdom publishing statistics', *J. R. Statist. Soc.* series A, vol. CXIV, 1951, part IV, p. 468.

[71] Glover, K. F., *The Recent Course of Gross Investment in Inland Transport in Great Britain* (unpublished thesis in London University Library).

[72] Hill, A. Bradford, 'The doctor's day and pay', *J. R. Statist. Soc.* series A, vol. CXIV, 1951, part I, p. 1.

[73] Jefferys, James B., assisted by Margaret Maccoll and G. L. Levett, *The Distribution of Consumer Goods*, National Institute of Economic and Social Research, Economic and Social Studies IX, Cambridge University Press, 1950.

[74] Jefferys, James B., *Retail Trading in Britain, 1850–1950*, National Institute of Economic and Social Research, Economic and Social Studies XIII, Cambridge University Press, 1954.

[75] Jefferys, James B. and Dorothy Walters, 'National income and expenditure of the United Kingdom, 1870–1952', in *Income and Wealth Series V*, London, 1956.

[76] Kaldor, Nicholas and Rodney Silverman, *A Statistical Analysis of Advertising Expenditure and of the Revenue of the Press*, National Institute of Economic and Social Research, Economic and Social Studies VIII, Cambridge University Press, 1948.

[77] Kendall, M. G., 'United Kingdom merchant shipping statistics', *J. R. Statist. Soc.* series A, vol. CXI, 1948, part II, p. 143.

[78] Leak, H. and T. Priday 'Migration from and to the United Kingdom', *J. R. Statist. Soc.* vol. XCVI, 1933, part II, p. 215,

[79] Leybourne, G. C. and K. White, *Education and the Birthrate*, London, 1940.

[80] Massey, Philip, 'The expenditure of 1360 British middle-class households in 1938–39', *J. R. Statist. Soc.* vol. CV, 1942, part III, p. 159.

[81] Mess, Henry A., *Voluntary Social Services since 1918*, London, 1947.

[82] Ogilvie, F. W., *The Tourist Movement*, London, 1933.

[83] PEP (Political and Economic Planning), *Report on the British Health Services*, London, 1937.

[84] Peterson, A. W., 'The statistics of gambling', *J. R. Statist. Soc.* series A, vol. CXV, 1952, part II, p. 179.

[85] Prais, S. J., 'Some problems in the measurement of price changes with special reference to the cost of living', *J. R. Statist. Soc.* series A, vol. CXXI, 1958, part III, p. 312.

[86] Prais, S. J. and H. S. Houthakker, *The Analysis of Family Budgets*, Monograph 4 of the University of Cambridge Department of Applied Economics, Cambridge University Press, 1955.

[87] Prest, A. R., assisted by A. A. Adams, *Consumers' Expenditure in the United Kingdom, 1900–1919*, Studies in the National Income and Expenditure of the United Kingdom no. 3, Cambridge University Press, 1954.

[88] Rowson, S., 'A statistical survey of the cinema industry in Great Britain in 1934', *J. R. Statist. Soc.* vol. XCIX, 1936, part I, p. 67.

[89] Silverman, H. A. (ed.), *Studies in Industrial Organisation*, London, 1946.

[89 a] Stone, Richard and D. A. Rowe, 'The market demand for durable goods', *Econometrica*, vol. xxv, no. 3, July 1957, p. 423.

[90] Vaizey, J., *The Costs of Education*, London, 1958.

[91] Wilson, Sir Arnold and Hermann Levy, *Burial Reform and Funeral Costs*, Oxford, 1938.

III. PERIODICAL PUBLICATIONS, YEAR BOOKS AND OTHER SOURCES

[92] *Annual Charities Register and Digest*, London, Charity Organization Society.

[93] Audit Bureau of Circulations, *Advertisers A.B.C.*

[94] London Passenger Transport Board, *Annual Report*.

[95] *The Dentists' Register*, London, Constable.

[96] *The Economist*, London.

[97] *Hospitals Year Book*, Central Bureau of Hospital Information, annual from 1931.

[98] *London Statistics*, London County Council, annual.

[99] *Medical Directory*, London, Churchill, annual.

[100] *Motor Car Index*, Fletcher and Sons, Norwich, 1928 ed.

[101] *The Motor Industry of Great Britain*, Society of Motor Manufacturers and Traders, annual from 1926.

[102] Garcke's *Motor Transport Yearbook*, London.

INDEX

(n., Footnote to text or tables; t., table)